ORCHESTRAL
MUSIC

A HANDBOOK

SECOND EDITION BY
DAVID DANIELS

THE SCARECROW PRESS, INC.
METUCHEN, N.J., & LONDON
1 • 9 • 8 • 2

Library of Congress Cataloging in Publication Data

Daniels, David, 1933-
    Orchestral music.

    1. Orchestral music--Bibliography. I. Title.
ML128.Ò5D3 1981   016.785   81-16678
ISBN 0-8108-1484-6   AACR2

to Jimmie Sue

CONTENTS

FOREWORD

The purpose of this book is to provide in one handy loca-
tion the sorts of information necessary to plan orchestral
programs and organize rehearsals: instrumentation, duration, and source of performance materials. It is prepared
from the viewpoint of the orchestral conductor, but it has
also proven useful to orchestra managers, personnel managers, choral directors, librarians, and students.
It includes orchestral pieces, concertos, choral works
with orchestra, concert arias, and such chamber music as
might be performed with conductor. Operas have been cate-
gorically excluded because of the entirely different set of
problems involved; the reader is referred to Quaintance
Eaton's excellent pair of volumes on *Opera Production* (see
Bibliography). Nor could I include operatic arias in the
present handbook without doubling or tripling its length.
Orchestral excerpts from operas are present, however, as
well as an occasional excerpt in which the voice is optional or incidental (the *Prelude and Liebestod* from *Tristan
und Isolde*, for example).
New features in this second edition include: an increase
of about thirty-five percent in the number of entries;
better intelligibility of individual entries (abandoning
the computer this time around has given me greater flexi-
bility); and a more useful system of appendices, including
a breakdown of orchestral works by size of instrumentation.
As in the first edition, I have only included scores
which I have examined myself. I have corrected a number of
errors found in the first edition, but the enormous amount
of data involved, both new and old, makes it inevitable
that inaccuracies still exist. I will appreciate being in-
formed of them.
Much as I would like to write the complete and definitive
work on this repertoire, this is a manifest impossibility
as long as composers are composing, tastes are changing,
conductors are exploring, and scholars are researching. It
would be a black day for music if such activities were ever
to stop, and so I am happy to announce that this handbook
will be already out of date on the day it appears.

EDITIONS

There are good editions of music and there are bad editions, and both abound in this book. I do from time to time take the liberty of recommending certain versions, but even the non-recommended editions are usually listed. An exception is the case of the Haydn symphonies, where one can either use the Robbins Landon editions with confidence, or play Russian roulette with other versions, most of which are fraught with peril. I could not bring myself to list anything but Robbins Landon. Now let us fervently hope someone with that gentleman's rare combination of scholarship and practicality will tackle Rossini, whose works are in as desperate a situation now as Haydn's ever were.

KEYS OF VOCAL MUSIC

Works for voice and orchestra are often available in more than one key, in order to accomodate different voice ranges. Luck's Music Library in Detroit and Alfred J. Mapleson in Lindenhurst, New York, are the dealers that offer the widest selection of keys for music in the public domain.

PUBLISHERS, AGENTS, IMPORTERS, AND REPRINT HOUSES

Do not expect to make sense of the music trade. It is an intricate network of interrelationships in which symbiosis is more the rule than competition. It changes from year to year, month to month, and even week to week. Like Heraclitus's river, it is never the same the second time one steps into it.

Most of the sources given in this book will remain accurate for awhile, and some will probably endure for a very long time. But don't count on it. Fortunately, publishers are usually very knowledgeable about changes in the trade, and totally helpful in forwarding orders that may have been sent to the wrong firm. A phone call is often a good idea, even to firms who may require a written order; this can speed up the process considerably in a situation where time is important.

It is fashionable in some circles to malign the music reprint houses, of which E.F. Kalmus is the most conspicuous example. However, our entire supply structure for orchestral scores and parts would collapse without them. They keep many works in print that would otherwise disappear from the catalogs, and they are continually producing a stream of obscure delights that are available nowhere else. Moreover, major publishers with a long and distinguished history have been known to order reprints of their own publications from the reprint houses! Symbiosis indeed.

EDWIN A FLEISHER COLLECTION

If all else fails (or even before it fails), turn to the
Fleisher Collection. Originally the private library of an
amateur orchestra in Philadelphia, it is now a major ar-
chive collection of orchestral scores and parts (but no
choral works). The expert staff can answer just about any
question regarding orchestral materials. The Fleisher Collection can also lend scores and parts under certain condi-
tions for a very nominal fee. The full address is given in
Appendix G.

DURATION

The durations given must be considered approximate. Different tempos, observance (or omission) of repeats, and the
use of cuts can lead to a discrepancy of as much as thirty
percent from one performance to another. I have tried to
arrive at a reasonable average duration for each work, suf-
ficiently accurate for general programming, though certain-
ly not for broadcasting or recording purposes. In a few
cases I have been unable to determine the duration.

INSTRUMENTATION FORMULA

The customary formula for woodwinds, brass, percussion
and strings is followed here. The symbols that indicate
the presence of auxiliary instruments (*, +, and =) are
explained in the list of abbreviations, p.xii.

Often I have indicated where more than one auxiliary instrument is required—i.e. where flutes *3 include two or
three piccolos rather than just one. Alas, I did not always gather this information in researching the first edition, and to go back over 2500 works for that purpose was
impossible. The reader is warned: *3 *may* mean two flutes
and one piccolo, or one flute and two piccolos, or three
flutes all doubling on piccolo, or any of several other
permutations. In any case, it can be covered by three
players.

PERCUSSION

Rather than listing specific percussion instruments, I
have given the number of players necessary to cover the
parts, usually in a format such as *tmp+3*, which means that
one timpanist plus three other players are required. Note
that the indication *2tmp* means two timpanists and not two
kettles.

My estimate of the number of percussionists is based on

the possibility of doubling and perhaps cuing one part into another. It is a minimum, though some alert and agile percussion sections might get by with less. Other orchestras may prefer to use more players, particularly if the parts are laid out in such a way that extensive cuing would be needed.

When bass drum and cymbals occur together, I have uniformly counted two players, even in cases where the composer had in mind one player with a cymbal attached to the bass drum. These parts are almost invariably separated in modern orchestras for better tone from the cymbal. Of course, in works by such composers as Mahler and Berg a cymbal attached to the bass drum is occasionally called for as a special effect.

SAMPLE ENTRY

```
Concerto, violin, op.46                                    33'
  +3 *3 =3 3 - 4 2 2 0 - tmp+1 - (opt hp) - str  Marks
```

This hypothetical violin concerto is thirty-three minutes long. It calls for 3 flutes (including alto flute), 3 oboes (including English horn), 3 clarinets (including both bass clarinet and E-flat clarinet), 3 bassoons, 4 horns, 2 trumpets, 2 trombones, no tuba, a timpanist plus one additional percussionist, and the usual string sections. A harp is optional. The score and parts are available from Edward B. Marks Music Corporation.

FLUTES AND RECORDERS

I repent my rather cavalier treatment of recorders in the first edition, and apologize to all recorder players for it.

This time I have tried to be much more clear about what the composer intended, which may or may not be what the particular edition in hand intends. Many twentieth-century editors are not aware that when a baroque composer used the word *flauto* he meant recorder. If he wanted a transverse flute, he called it *traversa* or *flauto traverso* or some such term.

It may be argued that eighteenth-century musicians were fairly casual about instrumental substitutions in general, and that one should therefore feel no qualms about playing recorder music on the flute. On the other hand certain composers—among them Bach and Handel—were very clear about which of the two instruments they wanted. So modern editors who blithely translate *flauto* as *flute* without doing some checking first are doing no one a favor.

vi

OBOE, OBOE D'AMORE, AND OBOE DA CACCIA

Baroque works often call for oboes to double the violin parts, and sometimes these violin parts dip for a few notes below the range of the oboe. I do not consider that this necessarily means that oboes d'amore or da caccia were intended or used. I think the eighteenth-century wind player was accustomed to this and often dealt with it not by using a lower-pitched oboe, but by omitting the passage in question, or transposing it an octave higher, or altering it in some other way—whichever seemed most suitable. When Bach calls for oboe d'amore it seems to be more for reasons of color than of range.

BASSOONS

Eighteenth-century composers and performers assumed that a bassoon (together with cellos and basses) would play the bass line of orchestral works, whether specified or not. Recent editions tend to list the bassoon in such cases, while older editions do not. I have simply followed the work in hand in my listing of instruments, but it should be understood that, whatever the listing, eighteenth-century practice would normally include the bassoon, possibly with the exception of works for string orchestra.

Nineteenth-century French orchestras customarily had four bassoons, although only two real parts were commonly written. Even when four real parts occur, they often persist for only a few bars before returning to the normal two parts. I have attempted to distinguish in these cases between the number of bassoons called for and the number of real parts involved, if different.

TROMBONES

In eighteenth-century choral music it was customary for trombones to double the altos, tenors, and basses of the chorus, and sometimes for a cornetto to double the sopranos. These instruments were often not mentioned in the score at all. It would be possible to add them when they are not indicated, and it would probably be defensible to omit them when they are, since in any case a modern chorus with modern large-bore trombones is not going to sound much like an eighteenth-century chorus (using boy sopranos and male altos) with the lighter brass instruments of the period.

OTHER HISTORIC INSTRUMENTS

Perhaps in another decade we will become as enlightened about the difference between, say, ophicleide and tuba as we now are about flute and recorder. In the meantime, however, I have merely translated ophicleide as tuba, and sarrusophone as contrabassoon.

Even the distinction between cornets and trumpets is hardly meaningful any more—an example of the composer's intended variety being subverted by insidious orchestral routine. I blush to admit that I have become a party to this by indiscriminately lumping together trumpets and cornets in my listings. This is because my practice, here as in woodwinds and percussion, is always to indicate the number of players required. Any conductor who can come up with cornets that really sound like cornets for his players to use has my blessing and my admiration.

ACKNOWLEDGEMENTS

I wish to express my gratitude to many persons and institutions who helped in the long process of preparing this book. Oakland University, having supported the first edition, provided a sabbatical to start work on the second, and a grant to cover some of the expenses. The staff of Oakland's Performing Arts Library has given me every possible assistance, from special loans of restricted materials to birth dates of obscure composers.

William R. Eshelman of Scarecrow Press has been by turns patient, encouraging, and helpful, depending on which attitude was most appropriate for the given moment.

I am especially indebted to Luck's Music Library, where I spent many hours poring over their vast collection of scores and parts, and asking questions of all sorts.

On matters baroque, Lyle Nordstrom of Oakland University has long been my mentor; he was a fountain of information on various problems that came up in this second edition. This is not to suggest that he is responsible for any of the entries; he will in fact be horrified at many of them (the Felix Mottl arrangements of Rameau; the Gustav Holst arrangements of Purcell).

Many colleagues in the orchestral world—conductors and managers alike—have been generous in their approbation for the first edition and their suggestions and corrections for the second. William Wilsen, conductor of the Peoria Symphony, shared some ideas with me that led to the present shape of the appendices; his concepts have been altered enough that he may not recognize them, but nonetheless they were my starting point.

As my deadline approached, and I despaired of working out a list of Jewish composers for Appendix E, Helen Rowin offered to take the problem out of my hands, and in doing so helped preserve my sanity.

I am resigned to the certainty that errors will be discovered in this new edition. I must point out that they can only have occurred during the process of collecting my data; they could hardly have escaped the relentless eye of my proofreader Abigail Daniels, who is also my daughter.

Finally, I wish to reaffirm the thanks expressed in the first edition to Knox College, the Fleisher Collection, Charles J. Gibbs, William Ripperger, James Dixon, Walter S. Collins, and (most of all) my family.

David Daniels
Oakland University
Rochester, Michigan

October 16, 1980

BIBLIOGRAPHY

Altmann, Wilhelm. *Orchester-Literatur-Katalog; Verzeichnis von seit 1850 erschienen Orchester-Werken.* 2. Auflage; 2 vols. Leipzig: F.E.C. Leuckart, 1926-36.

Aronowsky, Salomon. *Performing Times of Orchestral Works.* London: E. Benn, 1959.

ASCAP Symphonic Catalog. 3rd edition. New York: R.R. Bowker, 1977.

BMI Symphonic Catalogue. New York: Broadcast Music, Inc., 1971. *Supplement No. One,* 1978.

Buschkötter, Wilhelm. *Handbuch der Internationalen Konzertliteratur.* Berlin: De Gruyter, 1961.

Conseil International de la Musique. *Musique symphonique, 1880-1954.* Ed. Vladimir Fedorov, Repertoires internationaux de musique contemporaine à l'usage des amateurs et des jeunes, Vol.I, publiés par L'Association Internationale des Bibliothèques Musicales. Frankfurt: C.F. Peters, 1957.

Contemporary Music for Schools. Washington: Music Educators National Conference (Contemporary Music Project), 1966.

Eagon, Angelo. *Catalog of Published Concert Music by American Composers.* Second edition. Metuchen, NJ: Scarecrow Press, 1969.

Eaton, Quaintance. *Opera Production.* 2 vols. Minneapolis: University of Minnesota Press, 1961-74.

The Edwin A. Fleisher Collection of Orchestral Music in the Free Library of Philadelphia; a cumulative catalog, 1929-1977. Boston: G.K. Hall, 1979.

Farish, Margaret K. *Orchestral Music in Print.* Philadelphia: Musicdata, 1979.

Farish, Margaret K. *String Music in Print.* 2nd edition. New York: R.R. Bowker Co., 1973.

Lawrence, Vera Brodsky, ed. *Works for Orchestra and String Instruments*. The CMP Library, vol.2, second edition. Washington: Music Educators National Conference (Contemporary Music Project), 1969.

Mueller, Kate Hevner. *Twenty-Seven Major American Symphony Orchestras; a History and Analysis of their repertoires, Seasons 1842-43 through 1969-70*. Bloomington, IN: Indiana University Press, 1973.

Müller-Reuter, Theodor. *Lexikon der deutschen Konzertliteratur; ein Ratgeber für Dirigenten, Konzertveranstalter, Musikschriftsteller und Musikfreunde*. 2 vols. Leipzig: G.F. Kahnt, 1909-21.

Reddick, William. *The Standard Musical Repertoire, with Accurate Timings*. Garden City, NY: Doubleday, 1947.

Saltonstall, Cecilia D. and Henry. *A New Catalog of Music for Small Orchestra*. Clifton, NJ: European American Music Corporation, 1978.

Seibert, Donald C. *The Hyde Timings; A Collection of Timings Made at Concerts in New York City Between 1894 and 1928*. New York: Juilliard School of Music, 1964.

Stein, Franz A. *Verzeichnis der Orchestermusik von 1700 bis zur Gegenwart*. Bern und München: Francke Verlag, 1963.

Valentin, Erich. *Handbuch der Chormusik*. 2 vols. Regensburg: Gustav Bosse, 1953-58.

ABBREVIATIONS

A	alto voice	Mz	mezzo-soprano voice
afl	alto flute		
asx	alto saxophone	opt	optional
		ob	oboe
B	bass voice	org	organ
Bar	baritone voice		
bcl	bass clarinet	perc	percussion
bsn	bassoon	pf	pianoforte
bsx	baritone saxophone	pic	piccolo
btp	bass trumpet		
		rec	recorder
cbn	contrabassoon		
cel	celeste	S	soprano voice
cl	clarinet	scl	soprano clarinet (i.e.
cnt	continuo		in E-flat or D)
		str	strings
db	double bass	ssx	soprano saxophone
dbl	doubling, or doubles	sx	saxophone
Eh	English horn	T	tenor voice
		tbn	trombone
fl	flute	tmp	timpani
		tp	trumpet
gtr	guitar	tsx	tenor saxophone
harm	harmonium		
hn	horn	va	viola
hp	harp	vc	violoncello
hpsd	harpsichord	vn	violin

---

*   auxiliary instruments: piccolo, English horn, bass clarinet, contrabassoon, respectively

\+   auxiliary instruments: alto flute, E-flat clarinet, respectively

=   both auxiliary instruments: piccolo *and* alto flute, or bass clarinet *and* E-flat clarinet, respectively

/   doubling, or doubles

ALPHABETICAL LISTING

BY COMPOSER

ABEL, KARL FRIEDRICH, 1723-1787

Symphony, op.1, no.5, F major   10'
    0 2 0 0 - 2 0 0 0 - (opt cnt) - str   Vieweg
    (Oboes and horns may be omitted, or may be substi-
    tuted for by flutes and clarinets respectively.)
    Ed. Hilmar Hoeckner.

Symphony, op.1, no.6, G major   10'
    0 2 0 0 - 2 0 0 0 - (opt cnt) - str   Vieweg
    (Oboes and horns may be omitted or may be substi-
    tuted for by flutes and clarinets respectively.)
    Ed. Hilmar Hoeckner.

Symphony, op.7, no.6, E-flat major   12'
    0 0 2 1 - 2 0 0 0 - str   Breitkopf;
    Formerly attributed to Mozart, and   Kalmus; Peters
    still published as Mozart's Symphony no.3
    by both Breitkopf and Kalmus.

ADAM, ADOLPH, 1803-1856

Si j'étais roi (If I were king): Overture   8'
    *3 2 2 2 - 4 2 3 0 - tmp+4 - hp - str   Breitkopf;
                                                   Leduc; Luck

ALBÉNIZ, ISAAC, 1860-1909

Catalonia   7'
    *3 *3 *3 3 - 4 4 3 1 - tmp+4 - 2hp - str   Durand;
                                                      Kalmus

Concerto, piano, no.1, op.78, A minor   24'
    2 2 2 2 - 2 2 3 0 - tmp - str   UME

Iberia (arr. E. F. Arbós)   26'
  *3 *3 =4 *3 - 4 4 3 1 - tsx - tmp+6 -   Eschig
    2hp, cel - str
  Five movements from the piano suite.

Iberia (arr. Carlos Surinach)   43'
  *2 *2 2 2 - 4 2 3 1 - tmp+2 - hp - str   AMP
  Nos.4-5 and 8-12 of the suite, originally for piano.

Navarra (arr. E. F. Arbós)   5'
  *3 *3 *3 3 - 4 3 3 1 - tmp+4 - 2hp - str   Eschig

Rapsodia española   12'
  Solo piano   UME
  *3 *3 2 2 - 4 2 3 1 - tmp+4 - hp, cel - str

   ALBINONI, TOMASO, 1671-1750

Concerto, op.5, no.4, G major   5'
  str, cnt   Ricordi
  Ed. Raffaele Cumar.

Concerto, op.5, no.7, D minor   10'
  str, cnt   Zanibon
  Ed. Ettore Bonelli

Concerto, op.7, no.3, B-flat major   9'
  Solo oboe - str, cnt   Boosey
  Ed. Bernhard Paumgartner.

Concerto, op.9, no.2, D minor   14'
  Solo oboe - str, cnt   Kneusslin; Suvini

Concerto, op.9, no.9, C major   11'
  2ob, str, cnt   Musica Rara; Ricordi

Concerto, op.9, no.10, F major   11'
  Solo violin - str, cnt   Ricordi
  Ed. Remo Giazotto.

   ALFVÉN, HUGO, 1872-1960

Midsommarvaka (Swedish rhapsody no.1)   12'
  *3 *3 =3 3 - 4 2 3 1 - tmp+2 - 2hp - str Hansen; Kalmus

AMRAM, DAVID, 1930-

Autobiography for strings   8'
    str   Peters

Shakespearian concerto   22'
    0 1 0 0 - 2 0 0 0 - str   Peters

Triple concerto   25'
    3 solo quintets: woodwind (fl, ob, cl, bsn,   Peters
    hn), brass (2tp, hn, tbn, tuba), and jazz
    (asx, bsx, pf, db, drums)
    *2 *2 *2 *2 - 2 2 2 0 - tmp+5 - cel - str

ANDERSON, T. J., 1928-

Chamber symphony   14'
    *1 1 1 1 - 1 1 1 0 - 2perc - hp, cel - str   ACA

ANTHEIL, GEORGE, 1900-1959

Symphony no.4 ("1942")   27'
    *3 *3 *3 *3 - 4 3 3 1 - tmp+4 - hp, pf - str   Boosey

Symphony no.5 ("The joyous")   21'
    *3 *3 *3 *3 - 4 3 3 1 - tmp+5 - pf - str   MCA

Symphony no.6 ("After Delacroix")   24'
    *3 *3 *3 *3 - 4 3 3 1 - tmp+4 - pf - str   Weintraub

ARENSKY, ANTON, 1861-1906

Variations on a theme by Tchaikovsky, op.35a   15'
    str   Forberg; Kalmus

ARGENTO, DOMINICK, 1927-

In praise of music; seven songs for orchestra   30'
    =3 *3 *3 *3 - 4 3 3 1 - tmp+3 - hp, pf/cel - str Boosey

ARNE, THOMAS, 1710-1778

Symphony no.1, C major   8'
  0 2 0 1 - 2 0 0 0 - cnt - str   Oxford
  Ed. Richard Platt.

Symphony no.2, F major   9'
  0 2 0 1 - 2 0 0 0 - cnt - str   Oxford
  Ed. Richard Platt.

Symphony no.3, E-flat major   8'
  0 2 0 1 - 2 0 0 0 - tmp - cnt - str   Oxford
  Ed. Richard Platt.

Symphony no.4, C minor   11'
  2 2 0 1 - 2 0 0 0 - cnt - str   Oxford
  Ed. Richard Platt. Flute parts are reconstructed
  by the editor.

ARNOLD, MALCOLM, 1921-

Concerto, 2 violins and string orchestra, op.77   17'
  str   Faber

Four Cornish dances, op.91   10'
  *3 2 2 2 - 4 3 3 1 - tmp+2 - hp - str   Faber

Symphony no.3, op.63   33'
  *3 2 2 2 - 4 3 3 1 - tmp - str   Paterson

Symphony no.6, op.95   26'
  *3 2 2 2 - 4 3 3 1 - tmp+3 - str   Faber

Tam O'Shanter overture, op.51   8'
  *3 2 2 2 - 4 3 3 1 - tmp+2 - str   Paterson

ARRIAGA, JUAN CRISÓSTOMO, 1806-1826

Los esclavos felices: Overture   8'
  2 2 2 2 - 2 0 0 0 - tmp - str   Heugel; Kalmus

Symphony, D minor   25'
  2 2 2 2 - 2 2 0 0 - tmp - str   Kalmus; Luck

ASCHAFFENBURG, WALTER, 1927-

Three dances for orchestra, op.15   12'
  *3 3 =4 *3 - 4 3 3 1 - tmp+6 - hp - str   Presser

AUBER, DANIEL-FRANÇOIS, 1782-1871

Le domino noir: Overture   8'
  *2 2 2 2 - 4 2 3 0 - tmp+3 - str   Ricordi

Fra Diavolo: Overture   8'
  *2 2 2 2 - 4 2 3 0 - tmp+4 - str   Breitkopf; Kalmus

Lestocq: Overture   8'
  *2 2 2 2 - 4 2 1 0 - tmp+3 - str   Luck

Marco Spada: Overture   8'
  *2 2 2 2 - 4 2 3 0 - tmp+3 - str   Luck

Masaniello (La muette de Portici): Overture   8'
  *3 2 2 2 - 4 2 3 1 - tmp+4 - str   Kalmus

AURIC, GEORGES, 1899-

La chambre   18'
  *2 1 2 1 - 2 2 1 1 - tmp+2 - pf - str   Ricordi

Phèdre; suite symphonique   20'
  *3 *3 *3 *3 - 4 4 3 1 - tmp+4 - 2hp, cel - str   Salabert

BABBITT, MILTON, 1916-

Composition for twelve instruments   7'
  1 1 1 1 - 1 1 0 0 - hp, cel - vn, va, vc, db   AMP

BACEWICZ, GRAZYNA, 1913-1969

Contradizione   16'
  *1 1 +1 1 - 1 1 0 0 - 2perc - hp, cel - 2vn, va,   Moeck
  vc, db

BACH, CARL PHILIPP EMANUEL, 1714-1788

Concerto, harpsichord, W.23, D minor   18'
   str, cnt (in addition to solo hpsd)   Breitkopf

Magnificat   52'
   chorus - solos SATB   Eulenburg; Kalmus;
   2 2 0 0 - 2 3 0 0 - tmp - str, cnt   Schirmer, G.

Symphony, W.182, no.1, G major   10'
   str, cnt   Peters; Schott

Symphony, W.182, no.2, B-flat major   11'
   str, cnt   Bärenreiter; Breitkopf; Peters

Symphony, W.182, no.3, C major   12'
   str, cnt   Breitkopf; Kalmus;
                                                            Nagel; Peters

Symphony, W.182, no.4, A major   12'
   str, cnt   Breitkopf; Peters; Schott

Symphony, W.182, no.5, B minor   13'
   str, cnt   Breitkopf; Nagel; Peters

Symphony, W.182, no.6, E major
   str, cnt   Peters

Symphony, W.183, no.1, D major   12'
   2 2 0 2 - 2 2 0 0 - tmp - str   Luck; Peters
   (2nd bsn, both tp, and tmp are optional.)

Symphony, W.183, no.3, F major   11'
   2 2 0 1 - 2 0 0 0 - str, cnt   Luck; Peters

BACH, JOHANN CHRISTIAN, 1735-1782

Concerto, harpsichord, op.7, no.5, E-flat major   17'
   str (without va)   Peters
   Ed. Christian Doebereiner.

Concerto, harpsichord, op.13, no.2, D major   14'
   2 2 0 0 - 2 0 0 0 - str   Peters

Concerto, harpsichord, op.13, no.4, B-flat major   20'
  0 2 0 0 - 2 0 0 0 - str   Peters

Concerto, harpsichord, E-flat major   27'
  str   Eulenburg
  Ed. Ernst Praetorius.

Sinfonia concertante, A major   21'
  Solo violin and violoncello   Eulenburg
  0 2 0 0 - 2 0 0 0 - cnt - str

Sinfonia concertante, E-flat major   25'
  2 solo violins   Eulenburg
  2 1 0 0 - 2 0 0 0 - cnt - str
  Ed. Fritz Stein.

Symphony, op.3, no.1, D major   11'
  0 2 0 0 - 2 0 0 0 - cnt - str   Doblinger; Eulenburg

Symphony, op.3, no.2, C major   8'
  0 2 0 0 - 2 0 0 0 - cnt - str   Doblinger
  Ed. Erik G. S. Smith.

Symphony, op.3, no.4, B-flat major   12'
  0 2 0 0 - 2 0 0 0 - str   Doblinger; Kneusslin

Symphony, op.6, no.1, G major
  0 2 0 0 - 2 0 0 0 - cnt - str   Eulenburg

Symphony, op.6, no.6, G minor   20'
  0 2 0 0 - 2 0 0 0 - cnt - str   Breitkopf
  Ed. Fritz Stein.

Symphony, op.9, no.2, E-flat major   22'
  0 2 0 0 - 2 0 0 0 - cnt - str   Eulenburg
  Ed. Fritz Stein. (The composer indicated that
  oboes may be replaced by flutes, and that horns
  are optional.) J. C. Bach's op.9 was republished
  later as op.21.

Symphony, op.18, no.1, E-flat major   13'
  2 2 0 2 - 2 0 0 0 - (opt cnt) - str   Peters
  For double orchestra.

Symphony, op.18, no.2, B-flat major   12'
  2 2 2 2 - 2 0 0 0 - str   Peters
  Ed. Fritz Stein. Overture to the opera
  "Lucio Silla."

Symphony, op.18, no.3, D major   14'
  2 2 0 1 - 2 0 0 0 - str   Peters

Symphony, op.18, no.4, D major   22'
  2 2 0 1 - 2 2 0 0 - tmp - (opt cnt) - str   Eulenburg
  (Flutes are optional.)
  Ed. Alfred Einstein.

Symphony, op.18, no.5, E major   15'
  2 2 0 1 - 2 0 0 0 - cnt - str   Breitkopf
  Double orchestra. Ed. Fritz Stein.

Symphony, op.18, no.6, D major   15'
  2 2 0 1 - 2 0 0 0 - cnt - str   Breitkopf
  Ed. Fritz Stein.

Symphony, op.21, no.1, B-flat major   15'
  0 2 0 0 - 2 0 0 0 - cnt - str   Breitkopf
  Ed. Fritz Stein.

Symphony, op.21, no.2
  See his: Symphony, op.9, no.2

Symphony, op.21, no.3, B-flat major   8'
  0 2 0 0 - 2 0 0 0 - cnt - str   Augener
  Flutes may be substituted for oboes.
  Ed. Adam Carse.

Symphony, D major   10'
  2 2 *3 2 - 2 2 0 0 - tmp - cnt - str   Breitkopf
  Overture to the opera "Temistocle." The original
  called for "3 clarinette d'amore in D," which the
  editor has adapted for 2cl and bcl. Ed. Fritz Stein.

   BACH, JOHANN LUDWIG, 1677-1741

Denn du wirst meine Seele nicht in der Hölle lassen
  See: Bach, Johann Sebastian, 1685-1750
       Cantata no.15

BACH, JOHANN SEBASTIAN, 1685-1750

Brandenburg concerto no.1, BWV 1046, F major   23'
  solos: 3 oboes, 2 horns, violin   Bärenreiter;
  (originally violino piccolo)   Breitkopf; Kalmus;
  str, bsn, cnt   Peters

Brandenburg concerto no.2, BWV 1047, F major   19'
  solos: recorder, oboe, trumpet, violin   Bärenreiter;
  str, cnt   Breitkopf;
         Kalmus; Peters

Brandenburg concerto no.3, BWV 1048, G major   12'
  3vn, 3va, 3vc, db, cnt   Bärenreiter; Breitkopf;
         Kalmus; Peters

Brandenburg concerto no.4, BWV 1049, G major   20'
  2 solo recorders, solo violin Bärenreiter; Breitkopf;
  str, cnt   Kalmus; Peters

Brandenburg concerto no.5, BWV 1050, D major   24'
  solos: harpsichord, violin, flute   Bärenreiter;
  str (without vnII)   Breitkopf;
         Kalmus; Peters

Brandenburg concerto no.6, BWV 1051, B-flat major   18'
  2va, 2 viole da gamba, vc, db, cnt   Bärenreiter;
         Breitkopf;
         Kalmus; Peters

Cantata no.1: Wie schön leuchtet der Morgenstern   25'
  chorus - solos STB   Breitkopf;
  2ob da caccia - 2hn - str, cnt   Kalmus
  2 solo vn in one movement.

Cantata no.2: Ach Gott, vom Himmel sieh darein   20'
  chorus - solos ATB   Breitkopf
  2ob - str, cnt
  (4 tbn doubling choral parts.)

Cantata no.3: Ach Gott, wie manches Herzeleid (I)   31'
  chorus - solos SATB   Breitkopf
  2ob d'amore - hn, tbn - str, cnt
  (Brass used only to strengthen the cantus firmus.)

Cantata no.4: Christ lag in Todesbanden   24'
  chorus - (optional solos SATB)   Breitkopf;
  str, cnt   Kalmus
  (Cornetto and 3tbn doubling choral parts.)

Cantata no.5: Wo soll ich fliehen hin   24'
  chorus - solos SATB   Breitkopf
  0 2 0 0 - 0 1 0 0 - str, cnt

Cantata no.6: Bleib bei uns, denn es will Abend werden 28'
  chorus - solos SATB   Bärenreiter;
  2ob, ob da caccia - violoncello piccolo - Breitkopf;
    str, cnt   Kalmus

Cantata no.7: Christ unser Herr zum Jordan kam   27'
  chorus - solos ATB   Breitkopf
  2ob d'amore - str, cnt

Cantata no.8: Liebster Gott, wann werd' ich sterben 24'
  chorus - solos SATB   Breitkopf
  fl, 2ob d'amore - hn (used only to strengthen
    the cantus firmus) - str, cnt

Cantata no.9: Es ist das Heil uns kommen her   27'
  chorus - solos SATB   Breitkopf
  fl, ob d'amore - str, cnt

Cantata no.10: Meine Seele erhebt den Herren   24'
  chorus - solos SATB   Breitkopf
  2ob - tp (used only to strengthen the
    cantus firmus) - str, cnt

Cantata no.11: Lobet Gott in seinen Reichen   34'
  chorus - solos SATB   Breitkopf;
  2 2 0 0 - 0 3 0 0 - tmp - str, cnt   Kalmus
  Also known as "Ascension oratorio" or
  "Himmelfahrts-Oratorium."

Cantata no.12: Weinen, Klagen, Sorgen, Zagen   27'
  chorus - solos ATB   Breitkopf;
  0 1 0 1 - 0 1 0 0 - str, cnt   Kalmus

Cantata no.13: Meine Seufzer, meine Tränen   23'
  chorus - solos SATB   Breitkopf
  2rec, ob doubling ob da caccia - str, cnt

Cantata no.14: Wär Gott nicht mit uns diese Zeit   19'
chorus - solos STB   Breitkopf
0 2 0 0 - 1 0 0 0 - str, cnt

Cantata no.15: Denn du wirst meine Seele   15'
solos SATB - chorus in final movement only   Breitkopf
3tp - tmp - str, cnt
Actually composed by Johann Ludwig Bach.

Cantata no.16: Herr Gott, dich loben wir   21'
chorus - solos ATB   Breitkopf
0 *2 0 0 - 1 0 0 0 - str, cnt
One movement calls for oboe da caccia (may be played
by one of the oboists) or violetta (=viol; possible
on viola).

Cantata no.17: Wer Dank opfert, der preiset mich   22'
chorus - solos SATB   Breitkopf;
2ob d'amore - str, cnt   Kalmus

Cantata no.18: Gleichwie der Regen und Schnee   26'
chorus - solos STB   Bärenreiter;
2rec, bsn - 4va, vc (db) - cnt   Breitkopf
An earlier Weimar version (in G minor rather than
A minor) uses no recorders.

Cantata no.19: Es erhub sich ein Streit   22'
chorus - solos STB   Breitkopf;
0 3 0 0 - 0 3 0 0 - tmp - str, cnt   Kalmus
Two of the oboists double on oboe d'amore; one
must double on oboe da caccia. (Possible with only
two oboists, omitting the oboe da caccia.)

Cantata no.20: O Ewigkeit, du Donnerwort (I)   31'
chorus - solos ATB   Breitkopf;
0 3 0 0 - 0 1 0 0 - str, cnt   Mapleson

Cantata no.21: Ich hatte viel Bekümmernis   42'
chorus - solos SATB   Breitkopf;
0 1 0 1 - 0 3 4 0 - tmp - str, cnt   Kalmus
(Trombones only double choral parts.)

Cantata no.22: Jesus nahm zu sich die Zwölfe   20'
chorus - solos ATB   Breitkopf
ob - str, cnt

Cantata no.44: Sie werden euch in den Bann tun (I)   21'
    chorus - solos SATB   Breitkopf
    0 2 0 1 - str, cnt

Cantata no.45: Es ist dir gesagt, Mensch   23'
    chorus - solos ATB   Bärenreiter;
    2 2 0 0 - str, cnt   Breitkopf

Cantata no.46: Schauet doch und sehet   20'
    chorus - solos ATB   Breitkopf;
    2rec, 2ob da caccia - tp - str, cnt   Kalmus

Cantata no.47: Wer sich selbst erhöhet   25'
    chorus - solos SB   Breitkopf
    0 2 0 0 - org - str, cnt

Cantata no.48: Ich elender Mensch   18'
    chorus - solos AT   Breitkopf;
    0 2 0 0 - 0 1 0 0 - str, cnt   Mapleson

Cantata no.49: Ich geh und suche mit Verlangen   29'
    solos SB   Breitkopf
    ob d'amore - violoncello piccolo - org - str

Cantata no.50: Nun ist das Heil und die Kraft   5'
    double chorus   Breitkopf;
    0 3 0 0 - 0 3 0 0 - tmp - str, cnt   Kalmus

Cantata no.51: Jauchzet Gott in allen Landen!   20'
    soprano solo   Breitkopf;
    tp - str, cnt   Kalmus

Cantata no.52: Falsche Welt, dir trau ich nicht   17'
    soprano solo - chorus in final chorale only Breitkopf
    0 3 0 1 - 2 0 0 0 - str, cnt

Cantata no.53: Schlage doch, gewünschte Stunde   10'
    alto solo - bells, str, cnt   Breitkopf;
    Wrongly attributed to Bach; actual composer   Kalmus
    is Georg Melchior Hoffmann.

Cantata no.54: Widerstehe doch der Sünde   15'
    alto solo - str, cnt   Breitkopf;
                                                  Kalmus

Cantata no.55: Ich armer Mensch, ich Sündenknecht   15'
  tenor solo - chorus in final chorale only   Breitkopf
  fl, ob or ob d'amore - str (without va), cnt

Cantata no.56: Ich will den Kreuzstab gerne tragen   22'
  bass solo - chorus in final chorale only   Breitkopf;
  2ob, ob da caccia - str, cnt   Kalmus

Cantata no.57: Selig ist der Mann   31'
  solos SB - chorus in finale chorale only   Breitkopf
  2ob, ob da caccia - str, cnt

Cantata no.58: Ach Gott, wie manches Herzeleid (II)   17'
  solos SB - 2ob, ob da caccia - str, cnt   Breitkopf

Cantata no.59: Wer mich liebet (I)   14'
  solos SB - chorus in choral only   Bärenreiter;
  0 0 0 0 - 0 2 0 0 - tmp - str, cnt   Breitkopf

Cantata no.60: O Ewigkeit, du Donnerwort (II)   23'
  solos ATB - chorus in final chorale only   Breitkopf;
  2ob d'amore - hn (only used to strengthen the   Mapleson
  cantus firmus) - str, cnt

Cantata no.61: Nun komm, der Heiden Heiland (I)   20'
  chorus - solos STB   Bärenreiter;
  0 0 0 1 - str, cnt   Breitkopf; Kalmus

Cantata no.62: Nun komm, der Heiden Heiland (II)   18'
  chorus - solos SATB   Bärenreiter;
  0 2 0 0 - 1 0 0 0 - str, cnt   Breitkopf; Kalmus
  (Horn only used to strengthen the
  cantus firmus.)

Cantata no.63: Christen, ätzet diesen Tag   29'
  chorus - solos SATB   Bärenreiter;
  0 3 0 1 - 0 4 0 0 - tmp - org - str   Breitkopf

Cantata no.64: Sehet welch eine Liebe   27'
  chorus - solos SAB   Breitkopf
  ob d'amore - str, cnt
  (Cornetto and 3tbn doubling choral parts.)

Cantata no.65: Sie werden aus Saba alle kommen   19'
  chorus - solos TB   Breitkopf;
  2rec, 2ob da caccia - 2hn - str, cnt   Kalmus

Cantata no.66: Erfreut euch, ihr Herzen   31'
  chorus - solos ATB   Breitkopf
  0 2 0 1 - 0 1 0 0 - str, cnt
  (Trumpet is optional.)

Cantata no.67: Halt im Gedächtnis Jesum Christ   16'
  chorus - solos ATB   Breitkopf;
  fl, 2ob d'amore - hn - str, cnt   Gray

Cantata no.68: Also hat Gott die Welt geliebt   20'
  chorus - solos SB   Bärenreiter;
  2ob, ob da caccia - violoncello piccolo -   Breitkopf;
    str, cnt   Kalmus
  (Horn strengthens cantus firmus; cornetto
  and 3tbn double choral parts.)

Cantata no.69: Lobe den Herrn, meine Seele (I)   26'
  chorus - solos SATB   Breitkopf
  0 3 0 1 - 0 3 0 0 - tmp - str, cnt
  One oboist must double on oboe d'amore.

Cantata no.70: Wachet! betet! betet! wachet!   28'
  chorus - solos SATB   Breitkopf;
  0 1 0 1 - 0 1 0 0 - str, cnt   Mapleson

Cantata no.71: Gott ist mein König   20'
  chorus - solos SATB   Breitkopf
  2rec 2 0 1 - 0 3 0 0 - tmp - org - str

Cantata no.72: Alles nur nach Gottes Willen   23'
  chorus - solos SAB   Breitkopf
  0 2 0 0 - str, cnt

Cantata no.73: Herr, wie du willt, so schicks mit mir 19'
  chorus - solos STB   Breitkopf
  0 2 0 0 - 1 0 0 0 - str, cnt
  (Organ may substitute for horn.)

Cantata no.74: Wer mich liebet (II)   25'
  chorus - solos SATB   Breitkopf
  2ob, ob da caccia - 3tp - tmp - str, cnt

Cantata no.75: Die Elenden sollen essen   40'
  chorus - solos SATB   Breitkopf
  0 2 0 1 - 0 1 0 0 - str, cnt
  One oboist doubles on oboe d'amore (playable on oboe).

Cantata no.76: Die Himmel erzählen die Ehre Gottes   38'
  chorus - solos SATB   Breitkopf
  0 2 0 0 - 0 1 0 0 - viola da gamba - str, cnt
  One oboist doubles on oboe d'amore.

Cantata no.77: Du sollt Gott, deinen Herren, lieben   16'
  chorus - solos SATB   Breitkopf
  0 2 0 0 - 0 1 0 0 - str, cnt

Cantata no.78: Jesu, der du meine Seele   25'
  chorus - solos SATB   Bärenreiter;
  1 2 0 0 - 1 0 0 0 - str, cnt   Breitkopf;
  (Horn only used to strengthen the   Kalmus
  cantus firmus.)

Cantata no.79: Gott der Herr is Sonn und Schild   18'
  chorus - solos SAB   Breitkopf;
  2 2 0 0 - 2 0 0 0 - tmp - str, cnt   Kalmus

Cantata no.80: Ein feste Burg is unser Gott   30'
  chorus - solos SATB   Breitkopf;
  2ob, ob da caccia - 3tp - tmp - org - str   Kalmus

Cantata no.81: Jesus schläft, was soll ich hoffen?   20'
  solos ATB - chorus in final chorale only   Breitkopf;
  2rec, 2ob d'amore - str, cnt   Kalmus

Cantata no.82: Ich habe genug   22'
  solo bass voice - ob - str, cnt   Breitkopf; Kalmus

Cantata no.83: Erfreute Zeit im neuen Bunde   20'
  solos ATB - chorus in final chorale only   Breitkopf
  0 2 0 0 - 2 0 0 0 - str, cnt

Cantata no.84: Ich bin vergnügt mit meinem Glücke   18'
  soprano solo - chorus in final chorale only   Breitkopf;
  ob - str, cnt   Kalmus

Cantata no.85: Ich bin ein guter Hirt   20'
  solos SATB - chorus in final chorale only   Breitkopf;
  0 2 0 0 - violoncello piccolo - str, cnt   Mapleson;
                                   Ricordi

Cantata no.86: Wahrlich, wahrlich, ich sage euch   19'
  solos SATB - chorus in final chorale only   Breitkopf
  2ob d'amore (playable on ob) - str, cnt

Cantata no.87: Bisher habt ihr nichts gebeten   26'
  solos ATB - chorus in final chorale only   Breitkopf
  3 oboists, 2 of whom double on ob da caccia - str, cnt

Cantata no.88: Siehe, ich will viel Fischer aussenden 21'
  solos SATB - chorus in final chorale only   Breitkopf;
  2ob d'amore, ob da caccia - 2hn - str, cnt   Mapleson

Cantata no.89: Was soll ich aus dir machen, Ephraim?   15'
  solos SAB - chorus in final chorale only   Breitkopf
  0 2 0 0 - 1 0 0 0 - str, cnt

Cantata no.90: Es reisset euch ein schrecklich Ende   15'
  solos ATB - chorus in final chorale only   Breitkopf
  tp - str, cnt

Cantata no.91: Gelobet seist du, Jesu Christ   19'
  chorus - solos SATB   Bärenreiter;
  0 3 0 1 - 2 0 0 0 - tmp - str, cnt   Breitkopf

Cantata no.92: Ich hab in Gottes Herz und Sinn   37'
  chorus - solos SATB   Breitkopf;
  2ob d'amore - str, cnt   Mapleson

Cantata no.93: Wer nur den lieben Gott lässt walten   24'
  chorus - solos SATB   Breitkopf;
  0 2 0 0 - str, cnt   Kalmus

Cantata no.94: Was frag ich nach der Welt   24'
  chorus - solos SATB   Breitkopf
  1 2 0 0 - str, cnt
  One oboist doubles on oboe d'amore.

Cantata no.95: Christus, der ist mein Leben   21'
  chorus - solos STB   Breitkopf;
  0 2 0 0 - 1 0 0 0 - str, cnt   Kalmus
  Both oboists double on oboe d'amore.

Cantata no.96: Herr Christ, der einge Gottessohn   19'
  chorus - solos SATB   Breitkopf
  1 2 0 0 - 1 0 1 0 - str, cnt
  Flutist doubles on sopranino recorder, or this part
  may be played by violino piccolo. (Brass only used
  to strengthen the cantus firmus.)

Cantata no.97: In allen meinen Taten   36'
   chorus - solos SATB   Breitkopf
   0 2 0 1 - str, cnt

Cantata no.98: Was Gott tut, das ist wohlgetan (I)   19'
   chorus - solos SATB   Breitkopf
   2ob, ob da caccia - str, cnt
   (2nd ob and ob da caccia only double inner
   chorus parts.)

Cantata no.99: Was Gott tut, das ist wohlgetan (II)   23'
   chorus - solos SATB   Breitkopf
   fl, ob d'amore - hn (only used to strengthen
     the cantus firmus) - str, cnt

Cantata no.100: Was Gott tut, das ist wohlgetan (III) 28'
   chorus - solos SATB   Breitkopf
   fl, ob d'amore - 2hn - tmp - str, cnt

Cantata no.101: Nimm von uns, Herr, du treuer Gott   30'
   chorus - solos SATB   Breitkopf
   fl, 2ob, ob da caccia - str, cnt
   (Cornetto and 3tbn doubling choral parts.)

Cantata no.102: Herr, deine Augen sehen   25'
   chorus - solos ATB   Breitkopf;
   1 2 0 0 - str, cnt   Kalmus
   Violino piccolo may substitute for flute.

Cantata no.103: Ihr werdet weinen und heulen   19'
   chorus - solos AT   Breitkopf;
   sopranino rec, fl, 2ob d'amore - tp - str, cnt Mapleson
   A solo violin may substitute for the flute.

Cantata no.104: Du Hirte Israel, höre   24'
   chorus - solos TB   Breitkopf;
   2ob, ob da caccia - str, cnt   Kalmus; Ricordi

Cantata no.105: Herr, gehe nicht ins Gericht   27'
   chorus - solos SATB   Breitkopf;
   0 2 0 0 - 1 0 0 0 - str, cnt   Kalmus

Cantata no.106: Gottes Zeit ist die allerbeste Zeit   22'
   chorus - solos SATB   Breitkopf;
   2rec, 2 viole da gamba, cnt   Kalmus

Cantata no.107: Was willst du dich betrüben   23'
  chorus - solos STB   Breitkopf
  2fl, 2ob d'amore - hn (only used to strengthen
    the cantus firmus) - str, cnt

Cantata no.108: Es ist euch gut, dass ich hingehe   20'
  chorus - solos ATB   Breitkopf
  2ob d'amore - str, cnt

Cantata no.109: Ich glaube, lieber Herr   28'
  chorus - solos AT   Breitkopf
  0 2 0 0 - 1 0 0 0 - str, cnt

Cantata no.110: Unser Mund sei voll Lachens   32'
  chorus - solos SATB   Breitkopf
  2 3 0 1 - 0 3 0 0 - tmp - str, cnt
  One oboe doubles on oboe da caccia; one also
  doubles on oboe d'amore.

Cantata no.111: Was mein Gott will   24'
  chorus - solos SATB   Breitkopf
  0 2 0 0 - str, cnt

Cantata no.112: Der Herr ist mein getreuer Hirt   18'
  chorus - solos SATB   Breitkopf;
  2ob d'amore - 2hn - str, cnt   Mapleson

Cantata no.113: Herr Jesu Christ, du höchstes Gut   30'
  chorus - solos SATB   Breitkopf;
  fl, 2ob d'amore - str, cnt   Kalmus

Cantata no.114: Ach, lieben Christen, seid getrost   28'
  chorus - solos SATB   Breitkopf
  1 2 0 0 - 1 0 0 0 - str, cnt
  (Horn used only to strengthen the cantus firmus.)

Cantata no.115: Mache dich, mein Geist, bereit   24'
  chorus - solos SATB   Breitkopf;
  fl, ob d'amore - hn (only used to strengthen   Gray
    the cantus firmus) - violoncello piccolo -
    str, cnt

Cantata no.116: Du Friedefürst, Herr Jesu Christ   21'
  chorus - solos SATB   Breitkopf
  2ob d'amore - hn (only used to strengthen the
    cantus firmus) - str, cnt

Cantata no.117: Sei Lob und Ehr dem höchsten Gut   28'
    chorus - solos ATB   Breitkopf;
    2 2 0 0 - str, cnt   Kalmus
    Both oboists double on oboe d'amore.

Cantata no.118: O Jesu Christ, meins Lebens Licht   7'
    chorus   Breitkopf
    There are two versions of the orchestral accompaniment:
        (1) 2hn, cornetto, 3tbn (without str or cnt)
        (2) 2ob, ob da caccia, bsn - 2hn - str, cnt

Cantata no.119: Preise, Jerusalem, den Herrn   29'
    chorus - solos SATB   Breitkopf
    2rec, 3ob - 4tp - tmp - str, cnt
    Two of the oboists double on oboe da caccia.

Cantata no.120: Gott, man lobet dich in der Stille   28'
    chorus - solos SATB   Breitkopf
    2ob d'amore - 3tp - tmp - str, cnt

Cantata no.121: Christum wir sollen loben schon   24'
    chorus - solos SATB   Breitkopf
    ob d'amore - str, cnt
    (Cornetto and 3tbn doubling choral parts.)

Cantata no.122: Das neugeborne Kindelein   20'
    chorus - solos SATB   Breitkopf
    3rec, 2ob, ob da caccia - str, cnt

Cantata no.123: Liebster Immanuel, Herzog der Frommen 24'
    chorus - solos ATB   Breitkopf
    2fl, 2ob d'amore - str, cnt

Cantata no.124: Meinen Jesum lass ich nicht   19'
    chorus - solos SATB   Breitkopf
    ob d'amore - hn (used only to strengthen the
        cantus firmus) - str, cnt

Cantata no.125: Mit Fried und Freud ich fahr dahin   29'
    chorus - solos ATB   Breitkopf
    1 1 0 0 - 1 0 0 0 - str, cnt
    Oboist doubles on oboe d'amore; horn only used
    to strengthen the cantus firmus.

Cantata no.126: Erhalt uns, Herr, bei deinem Wort   21'
  chorus - solos ATB   Breitkopf
  0 2 0 0 - 0 1 0 0 - str, cnt

Cantata no.127: Herr Jesu Christ, wahr' Mensch   21'
  chorus - solos STB   Breitkopf
  2rec 2 0 0 - 0 1 0 0 - str, cnt

Cantata no.128: Auf Christi Himmelfahrt allein   21'
  chorus - solos ATB   Breitkopf
  2ob (both doubling on oboe d'amore), ob da caccia -
    2hn, tp - str, cnt

Cantata no.129: Gelobet sei der Herr, mein Gott   25'
  chorus - solos SAB   Breitkopf
  1 2 0 0 - 0 3 0 0 - tmp - str, cnt
  One oboist doubles on oboe d'amore.

Cantata no.130: Herr Gott, dich loben alle wir   17'
  chorus - solos SATB   Breitkopf
  1 3 0 0 - 0 3 0 0 - tmp - str, cnt

Cantata no.131: Aus der Tiefe rufe ich, Herr, zu dir   27'
  chorus - solos TB   Breitkopf;
  0 1 0 1 - cnt - str (2va parts; only lvn part)   Kalmus

Cantata no.132: Bereitet die Wege, bereitet die Bahn   21'
  solos SATB - chorus in final chorale only   Bärenreiter;
  0 1 0 1 - str, cnt   Breitkopf

Cantata no.133: Ich freue mich in dir   22'
  chorus - solos SATB   Breitkopf
  2ob d'amore - cornetto (only used to strengthen
    the cantus firmus) - str, cnt

Cantata no.134: Ein Herz, das seinen Jesum   29'
  chorus - solos AT   Bärenreiter;
  0 2 0 0 - str, cnt   Breitkopf

Cantata no.135: Ach Herr, mich armen Sünder   19'
  chorus - solos ATB   Breitkopf
  0 2 0 0 - str, cnt
  (Cornetto and trombone used only to strengthen
  the cantus firmus.)

Cantata no.136: Erforsche mich, Gott   23'
    chorus - solos ATB   Breitkopf
    2ob d'amore (1 doubling on ob) - hn - str, cnt

Cantata no.137: Lobe den Herren   19'
    chorus - solos SATB   Breitkopf;
    0 2 0 0 - 0 3 0 0 - tmp - str, cnt   Kalmus

Cantata no.138: Warum betrübst du dich, mein Herz?   20'
    chorus - solos SATB   Breitkopf
    2ob d'amore - str, cnt

Cantata no.139: Wohl dem, der sich auf seinen Gott   24'
    chorus - solos SATB   Breitkopf
    2ob d'amore - str, cnt

Cantata no.140: Wachet auf, ruft uns die Stimme   33'
    chorus - solos STB   Boosey;
    2ob, ob da caccia, bsn - hn (used only to   Breitkopf;
        strengthen the cantus firmus) -   Kalmus
        violino piccolo - str, cnt

Cantata no.141: Das ist je gewisslich wahr   10'
    chorus - solos ATB   Breitkopf
    0 2 0 0 - str, cnt
    Wrongly attributed to Bach; actual composer is
    G. P. Telemann.

Cantata no.142: Uns ist ein Kind geboren   20'
    chorus - solos ATB   Breitkopf;
    2rec, 2ob - str, cnt   Galaxy; Kalmus
    Actual composer believed to be Johann Kuhnau.

Cantata no.143: Lobe den Herrn, meine Seele (II)   17'
    chorus - solos STB   Breitkopf
    0 0 0 1 - 3 0 0 0 - tmp - str, cnt

Cantata no.144: Nimm, was dein ist, und gehe hin   16'
    chorus - solos SAT   Breitkopf;
    0 2 0 0 - str, cnt   Kalmus
    One oboist doubles on oboe d'amore.

Cantata no.145: Auf, mein Herz, des Herren Tag   20'
    chorus - solos STB   Breitkopf
    fl, 2ob d'amore - tp - str, cnt
    Second movement is actually by Telemann.

Cantata no.146: Wir müssen durch viel Trübsal   40'
  chorus - solos SATB   Breitkopf
  fl, 2ob (both doubling on ob d'amore),
    ob da caccia - org - str

Cantata no.147: Herz und Mund und Tat und Leben   35'
  chorus - solos SATB   Breitkopf;
  0 2 0 1 - 0 1 0 0 - str, cnt   Kalmus
  Both oboists double on oboe da caccia; one also
  doubles on oboe d'amore.

Cantata no.148: Bringet dem Herrn Ehre seines Namens   24'
  chorus - solos AT   Breitkopf
  0 3 0 0 - 0 1 0 0 - str, cnt
  3rd oboe part perhaps intended for oboe da caccia.

Cantata no.149: Man singet mit Freuden   24'
  chorus - solos SATB   Breitkopf;
  0 3 0 1 - 0 3 0 0 - tmp - str, cnt   Gray; Kalmus

Cantata no.150: Nach dir, Herr, verlanget mich   19'
  chorus - solos SATB   Breitkopf
  0 0 0 1 - cnt - str (without va)

Cantata no.151: Süsser Trost, mein Jesus kömmt   19'
  solos SATB - chorus in final chorale only   Breitkopf;
  fl, ob d'amore - str, cnt   Kalmus

Cantata no.152: Tritt auf die Glaubensbahn   20'
  solos SB   Breitkopf
  rec, ob - va d'amore, va da gamba - cnt

Cantata no.153: Schau, lieber Gott, wie meine Feind   18'
  solos ATB - chorus in three chorales only   Breitkopf
  str, cnt

Cantata no.154: Mein liebster Jesus ist verloren   19'
  solos ATB - chorus in two chorales only   Breitkopf
  2ob d'amore - str, cnt

Cantata no.155: Mein Gott, wie lang, ach lange   14'
  solos SATB - chorus in final chorale only   Breitkopf;
  0 0 0 1 - str, cnt   Kalmus

Cantata no.156: Ich steh mit einem Fuss im Grabe   19'
  solos ATB - chorus only in final chorale and   Breitkopf

one soprano cantus firmus
0 1 0 0 - str, cnt

Cantata no.157: Ich lasse dich nicht   23'
   solos TB - chorus in final chorale only   Breitkopf
   fl, ob d'amore - str, cnt

Cantata no.158: Der Friede sei mit dir   14'
   bass solo - chorus only in final chorale   Breitkopf;
     and one soprano cantus firmus   Kalmus
   ob (used only to strengthen the cantus firmus) -
   vn - cnt

Cantata no.159: Sehet, wir gehn hinauf gen Jerusalem   16'
   solos ATB - chorus only in final chorale   Breitkopf;
     and one soprano cantus firmus   Kalmus
   0 1 0 1 - str, cnt

Cantata no.160: Ich weiss, dass mein Erlöser lebt   15'
   tenor solo - vn, bsn, cnt   Breitkopf;
   Wrongly attributed to Bach; actual composer   Kalmus
   is Telemann.

Cantata no.161: Komm, du süsse Todesstunde   22'
   chorus - solos AT   Breitkopf;
   2rec - org - str   Kalmus

Cantata no.162: Ach, ich sehe, jetzt   19'
   solos SATB - chorus in final chorale only   Breitkopf
   0 0 0 1 - 1 0 0 0 - str, cnt

Cantata no.163: Nur jedem das Seine   19'
   solos SATB - chorus in final chorale only   Breitkopf
   ob d'amore - str, cnt

Cantata no.164: Ihr, die ihr euch von Christo nennet   19'
   solos SATB - chorus in final chorale only   Breitkopf
   2 2 0 0 - str, cnt

Cantata no.165: O heilges Geist- und Wasserbad   18'
   solos SATB - chorus in final chorale only   Breitkopf
   0 0 0 1 - str, cnt

Cantata no.166: Wo gehest du hin?   18'
  solos ATB - chorus only in final chorale   Bärenreiter;
    and one soprano cantus firmus   Breitkopf
  0 1 0 0 - str, cnt

Cantata no.167: Ihr Menschen, rühmet Gottes Liebe   19'
  solos SATB - chorus in final chorale only   Breitkopf
  ob doubling on ob d'amore - tp (used only to
    strengthen the cantus firmus) - str, cnt

Cantata no.168: Tue Rechnung! Donnerwort   16'
  solos SATB - chorus in final chorale only   Breitkopf
  2ob d'amore - str, cnt

Cantata no.169: Gott soll allein mein Herze haben   29'
  alto solo - chorus in final chorale only   Breitkopf;
  2ob d'amore, ob da caccia - org - str   Kalmus

Cantata no.170: Vergnügte Ruh, beliebte Seelenlust   22'
  alto solo   Breitkopf
  ob d'amore - org - str
  Flute may be used in one movement.

Cantata no.171: Gott, wie dein Name   21'
  chorus - solos SATB   Breitkopf
  0 2 0 0 - 0 3 0 0 - tmp - str, cnt

Cantata no.172: Erschallet, ihr Lieder (1731 version) 23'
  chorus - solos SATB   Bärenreiter;
  0 0 0 1 - 0 3 0 0 - tmp - org - str   Breitkopf;
  An oboe can substitute for organ in   Kalmus
  one movement.

Cantata no.173: Erhöhtes Fleisch und Blut   19'
  chorus - solos SATB   Breitkopf
  2 0 0 0 - str, cnt

Cantata no.174: Ich liebe den Höchsten   24'
  solos ATB - chorus in final chorale only   Breitkopf
  2ob, ob da caccia, bsn - 2hn - str, cnt

Cantata no.175: Er rufet seinen Schafen mit Namen   19'
  solos ATB - chorus in final chorale only   Breitkopf
  3rec 0 0 0 - 0 2 0 0 - violoncello piccolo -
    str, cnt

Cantata no.176: Es ist ein trotzig und verzagt Ding 14'
 chorus - solos SAB   Bärenreiter;
 2ob, ob da caccia - str, cnt   Breitkopf; Kalmus

Cantata no.177: Ich ruf zu dir, Herr Jesu Christ   32'
 chorus - solos SAT   Breitkopf
 0 2 0 1 - str, cnt
 One oboist doubles on oboe da caccia.

Cantata no.178: Wo Gott, der Herr, nicht bei uns hält 22'
 chorus - solos ATB   Breitkopf;
 0 2 0 0 - 1 0 0 0 - str, cnt   Kalmus
 Both oboists double on oboe d'amore. Horn only
 used to strengthen the cantus firmus.

Cantata no.179: Siehe zu, dass deine Gottesfurcht   17'
 chorus - solos STB   Breitkopf
 0 2 0 0 - str, cnt
 Both oboists double on oboe da caccia.

Cantata no.180: Schmücke dich, o liebe Seele   27'
 chorus - solos SATB   Breitkopf;
 2rec (1 doubling on fl), ob, ob da caccia -   Gray
 violoncello piccolo - str, cnt

Cantata no.181: Leichtgesinnte Flattergeister   15'
 chorus - solos SATB   Breitkopf
 1 1 0 0 - 0 1 0 0 - str, cnt

Cantata no.182: Himmelskönig, sei willkommen   30'
 chorus - solos ATB   Breitkopf;
 rec - str, cnt   Kalmus

Cantata no.183: Sie werden euch in den Bann tun (II) 15'
 solos SATB - chorus in final chorale only   Breitkopf
 2ob d'amore (possible on oboe), 2ob da caccia -
 violoncello piccolo - str, cnt

Cantata no.184: Erwünschtes Freudenlicht   28'
 chorus - solos SAT   Breitkopf
 2 0 0 0 - str, cnt

Cantata no.185: Barmherziges Herze der ewigen Liebe 18'
 solos SATB - chorus in final chorale only   Breitkopf
 0 1 0 1 - str, cnt
 Trumpet may be used in two movements.

Cantata no.186: Ärgre dich, o Seele, nicht   38'
  chorus - solos SATB   Breitkopf;
  2ob, ob da caccia, bsn - str, cnt   Kalmus

Cantata no.187: Es wartet alles auf dich   25'
  chorus - solos SAB   Breitkopf
  0 2 0 0 - str, cnt

Cantata no.188: Ich habe meine Zuversicht   20'
  solos SATB - chorus in final chorale only   Breitkopf
  0 1 0 0 - org - str
  The sinfonia of Cantata no.146 is believed to belong
  with this work also, in which case a 2nd oboe and an
  oboe da caccia are required, and the duration is 29'.

Cantata no.189: Meine Seele rühmt und preist   20'
  solo tenor - rec, ob, vn, cnt   Breitkopf;
  Wrongly attributed to Bach; the actual   Kalmus
  composer is Georg Melchior Hoffmann.

Cantata no.190: Singet dem Herrn ein neues Lied!   17'
  chorus - solos ATB   Breitkopf;
  0 3 0 1 - 0 3 0 0 - tmp - str, cnt   Mapleson
  One oboist doubles on oboe d'amore.
  Portions of the first two movements were lost, and
  have been reconstructed.

Cantata no.191: Gloria in excelsis Deo   19'
  chorus - solos ST   Breitkopf;
  2 2 0 0 - 0 3 0 0 - tmp - str, cnt   Schirmer, G.

Cantata no.192: Nun danket alle Gott   15'
  chorus - solos SB   Breitkopf
  2 2 0 0 - str, cnt
  The tenor part of the chorus is lost, and has
  been reconstructed.

Cantata no.193: Ihr Tore (Pforten) zu Zion   16'
  chorus - solos SA   Breitkopf
  0 2 0 0 - str, cnt
  Certain missing parts have been reconstructed. The
  original orchestra may have included 2 trumpets and
  timpani.

Cantata no.194: Höchsterwünschtes Freudenfest   40'
  chorus - solos STB   Breitkopf
  0 3 0 1 - str, cnt

Cantata no.195: Dem Gerechten muss das Licht   30'
  chorus - solos SB   Breitkopf;
  2 2 0 0 - 2 3 0 0 - tmp - str, cnt   Kalmus
  Both oboists double on oboe d'amore.

Cantata no.196: Der Herr denket an uns   17'
  chorus - solos STB   Breitkopf
  str, cnt

Cantata no.197: Gott ist unsre Zuversicht   40'
  chorus - solos SAB   Breitkopf
  0 2 0 1 - 0 3 0 0 - tmp - str, cnt
  Both oboists double on oboe d'amore.

Cantata no.198: Lass, Fürstin, lass noch einen Strahl   29'
  chorus - solos SATB   Breitkopf;
  2fl, 2ob d'amore - 2va da gamba - 2 lutes -   Mapleson
    org, hpsd - str

Cantata no.199: Mein Herze schwimmt im Blut   26'
  soprano solo   Breitkopf
  0 1 0 1 - str, cnt

Cantata no.200: Bekennen will ich seinen Namen   5'
  alto solo   Peters
  str, cnt
  Only one aria surviving from an otherwise lost
  cantata. Published by Peters in 1935; perhaps
  out of print.

Cantata no.201: Der Streit zwischen Phoebus und Pan   52'
  chorus - solos SATTBB   Breitkopf;
  2 2 0 0 - 0 3 0 0 - tmp - str, cnt   Kalmus
  One oboist doubles on oboe d'amore.

Cantata no.202: Weichet nur, betrübte Schatten   22'
  soprano solo   Breitkopf;
  0 1 0 0 - str, cnt   Kalmus; Peters

Cantata no.203: Amore traditore   15'
  bass solo - hpsd   Breitkopf
  Of doubtful authenticity.

Cantata no.204: Ich bin in mir vergnügt 31'
soprano solo Breitkopf
1 2 0 0 - str, cnt

Cantata no.205: Der zufriedengestellte Äolus 43'
chorus - solos SATB Breitkopf;
2 2 0 0 - 2 3 0 0 - tmp - va d'amore, va da Kalmus
gamba - str, cnt
One oboist doubles on oboe d'amore.

Cantata no.206: Schleicht, spielende Wellen 43'
chorus - solos SATB Breitkopf
3 2 0 0 - 0 3 0 0 - tmp - str, cnt
Both oboists double on oboe d'amore.

Cantata no.207a: Auf, schmetternde Töne 32'
chorus - solos SATB Breitkopf
2fl, 2ob d'amore, ob da caccia - 3tp, tmp -
str, cnt

Cantata no.208: Was mir behagt 38'
solos SSTB Bärenreiter;
2rec, 2ob, ob da caccia, bsn - 2hn - str, cnt Breitkopf

Cantata no.209: Non sa che sia dolore 22'
soprano solo Breitkopf;
1 0 0 0 - str, cnt Mapleson

Cantata no.210: O holder Tag, erwünschte Zeit 35'
soprano solo Breitkopf
fl, ob d'amore - str, cnt

Cantata no.211: Coffee cantata (Schweigt stille) 29'
solos STB - optional chorus (STB) in Breitkopf;
last movement Kalmus; Ricordi
1 0 0 0 - str, cnt

Cantata no.212: Peasant cantata 30'
solos SB Breitkopf;
1 0 0 0 - 1 0 0 0 - str, cnt Kalmus; Peters

Cantata no.213: Hercules auf dem Scheidewege 45'
chorus - solos SATB Breitkopf
0 2 0 0 - 2 0 0 0 - str, cnt
One oboist doubles on oboe d'amore.

Cantata no.214: Tönet, ihr Pauken!   27'
  chorus - solos SATB   Breitkopf
  2 2 0 0 - 0 3 0 0 - tmp - str, cnt
  One oboist doubles on oboe d'amore.

Cantata no.215: Preise dein Glücke, gesegnetes Sachsen
  double chorus - solos STB   37'
  2 2 0 1 - 0 3 0 0 - tmp - str, cnt   Broude, A.
  Both oboists double on oboe d'amore.

Chorale-variations on "Vom Himmel hoch"
  See under: Stravinsky, Igor, 1882-1971

Christmas oratorio (Weihnachtsoratorium), BWV 248   165'
  chorus - solos SATB   Bärenreiter;
  2 4 0 1 - 2 3 0 0 - tmp - str, cnt   Breitkopf;
  Two of the oboists double on oboe d'amore;   Kalmus;
  the other two on oboe da caccia.   Peters
  A series of six cantatas, whose individual
  durations are: (1) 28' (2) 33' (3) 26'
  (4) 27' (5) 26' (6) 25'

Concerto, flute, violin and harpsichord,
  BWV 1044, A minor   22'
  str   Breitkopf; Kalmus; Peters

Concerto, harpsichord, no.1, BWV 1052, D minor   23'
  str   Breitkopf; Kalmus; Peters

Concerto, harpsichord, no.2, BWV 1053, E major   18'
  str   Breitkopf; Kalmus; Peters

Concerto, harpsichord, no.3, BWV 1054, D major   23'
  str   Breitkopf; Kalmus; Peters

Concerto, harpsichord, no.4, BWV 1055, A major   16'
  str   Breitkopf; Kalmus; Peters

Concerto, harpsichord, no.5, BWV 1056, F minor   12'
  str   Breitkopf; Kalmus; Peters

Concerto, harpsichord, no.6, BWV 1057, F major   20'
  2rec - str   Breitkopf;
  An arrangement by the composer of his   Peters
  Brandenburg concerto no.4.

Concerto, harpsichord, no.7, BWV 1058, G minor   15'
  str   Breitkopf; Kalmus; Peters

Concerto, 2 harpsichords, no.1, BWV 1050, C minor   16'
  str   Breitkopf; Kalmus; Peters

Concerto, 2 harpsichords, no.2, BWV 1061, C major   20'
  str   Breitkopf; Kalmus; Peters

Concerto, 2 harpsichords, no.3, BWV 1062, C minor   17'
  str   Breitkopf

Concerto, 3 harpsichords, no.1, BWV 1063, D minor   16'
  str   Breitkopf; Kalmus; Peters

Concerto, 3 harpsichords, no.2, BWV 1064, C major   14'
  str   Breitkopf; Kalmus; Peters

Concerto, 4 harpsichords, BWV 1065, A minor   11'
  str   Breitkopf; Kalmus; Peters

Concerto, violin, no.1, BWV 1041, A minor   15'
  str, cnt   Breitkopf; Kalmus; Peters

Concerto, violin, no.2, BWV 1042, E major   21'
  str, cnt   Breitkopf; Kalmus; Peters

Concerto, 2 violins, BWV 1043, D minor   17'
  str, cnt   Breitkopf; Kalmus; Peters

Concerto, violin and oboe, BWV 1060   16'
  str, cnt   Bärenreiter; Breitkopf
A reconstruction of what is believed to have been
the original version of the concerto no.1 for two
harpsichords (BWV 1060). The Bärenreiter edition
is in C minor; the Breitkopf has been transposed
to D minor.

Easter oratorio (Oster-Oratorium), BWV 249   52'
  chorus - solos SATB   Breitkopf;
  2rec 2 0 1 - 0 3 0 0 - tmp - str, cnt   Kalmus; Schott
One recorder doubles on optional flute; one oboist
doubles on oboe d'amore.

Komm, Gott, Schöpfer, heiliger Geist, BWV 631   5'
  *4 *4 =6 *4 - 4 4 4 1 - tmp+2 - 2hp - str   Universal
  Orchestrated by Arnold Schoenberg.

Komm süsser Tod (arr. Leopold Stokowski)   4'
  3 *3 *1 *2 - 4 3 4 1 - tmp - hp - str   Broude Bros.

Magnificat, BWV 243   30'
  chorus - solos SSATB   Bärenreiter;
  2 2 0 1 - 0 3 0 0 - tmp - str, cnt   Kalmus; Peters
  Both oboists double on oboe d'amore.

Mass, BWV 232, B minor   135'
  chorus - solos SSATB   Bärenreiter;
  2 3 0 2 - 1 3 0 0 - tmp - str, cnt   Breitkopf;
  Two of the oboists double on oboe d'amore.   Kalmus;
                                                      Peters

Mass, BWV 233, F major ("Lutheran mass no.1")   25'
  chorus - solos SAB   Breitkopf;
  0 2 0 2 - 2 0 0 0 - str, cnt   Kalmus; Peters
  One real bassoon part, but designated "fagotti."

Mass, BWV 234, A major ("Lutheran mass no.2")   25'
  chorus - solos SAB   Breitkopf;
  2 0 0 0 - str, cnt   Kalmus; Peters

Mass, BWV 235, G minor ("Lutheran mass no.3")   25'
  chorus - solos ATB   Breitkopf;
  0 2 0 0 - str, cnt   Kalmus; Peters

Mass, BWV 236, G major ("Lutheran mass no.4")   30'
  chorus - solos SATB   Breitkopf; Gray;
  0 2 0 0 - str, cnt   Kalmus; Peters

Musical offering, BWV 1079   60'
  1 *3 0 1 - str, cnt   Kalmus; Peters

Musical offering: Ricercare (arr. Anton Webern)   8'
  1 *2 *2 1 - 1 1 1 0 - tmp - hp - str   Universal

Passacaglia, BWV 582 (arr. Leopold Stokowski)   13'
  =4 *4 *4 *4 - 8 4 4 2 - tmp - str   Broude Bros.
  (May be performed with winds *3 *3 *3 *3 - 4 3 3 1.)

Prelude and fugue, BWV 552, E-flat major ("St. Anne") 16'
*4 *4 =6 *4 - 4 4 4 1 - tmp+2 - hp, cel - str   Universal
Orchestrated by Arnold Schoenberg.

St. John passion (Johannespassion), BWV 245   134'
  chorus - solos SATBB   Breitkopf;
  2 2 0 1 - org, lute - 2va d'amore,   Kalmus;
    va da gamba - str   Peters
  Both oboists double on oboe da caccia; one also
  doubles on oboe d'amore.

St. Matthew passion (Matthäuspassion), BWV 244   200'
  double chorus - solos SATBB -   Bärenreiter;
    semi-chorus of sopranos (boys)   Breitkopf;
  double orchestra: 4 4 0 0 - org -   Kalmus;
    viola da gamba - str   Peters
  All four oboists double on oboe d'amore; two also
  double on oboe da caccia. Two flutists double
  on recorder.

Schmücke dich, o liebe Seele, BWV 654   2'
  *4 *4 =6 *4 - 4 4 4 1 - tmp+2 - hp, cel - str   Universal
  Orchestrated by Arnold Schoenberg.

Sheep may safely graze (from Cantata no.208)   5'
  *3 *3 *3 *3 - 4 3 3 1 - tmp - hp - str   Boosey
  Arr. Lucien Cailliet. (Eh, bcl, cbn, hp are optional.)

Suite no.1, BWV 1066, C major   25'
  0 2 0 1 - str, cnt   Breitkopf; Kalmus; Peters

Suite no.2, BWV 1067, B minor   22'
  solo flute - str, cnt   Breitkopf; Kalmus; Peters

Suite no.3, BWV 1068, D major   22'
  0 2 0 0 - 0 3 0 0 - tmp - str, cnt   Breitkopf;
                                          Kalmus; Peters

Suite no.4, BWV 1069, D major   22'
  0 3 0 1 - 0 3 0 0 - tmp - str, cnt   Breitkopf;
                                          Kalmus; Peters

Toccata and fugue, BWV 565, D minor (arr. Stokowski)   9'
  4 *4 *4 *4 - 6 3 4 1 - tmp - 2hp, cel - str Broude Bros.
  (May be performed with winds 4 *3 *3 *3 - 4 3 3 1.)

BACH, WILHELM FRIEDEMANN, 1710-1784

Ehre sei Gott in der Höhe (Christmas cantata)
  chorus - solos STB   Vieweg
  0 0 0 0 - 2 0 0 0 - str, cnt

Sinfonia, D minor   9'
  2 0 0 0 - str   Eulenburg;
  Ed. Bernhard Päuler.   Kalmus

Sinfonia, F major   13'
  str - cnt   Breitkopf; Luck; Schott

BACON, ERNST, 1898-

The muffin man   4'
  *2 2 2 2 - 4 3 3 1 - tmp+3 - cel - str   Schirmer, G.

BADINGS, HENK, 1907-

Concerto, harp   21'
  2 2 *2 2 - 4 2 2 0 - tmp+2 - cel - str   Donemus

Concerto, piano (1940)   27'
  *2 2 *3 2 - 4 3 3 1 - tmp+3 - cel - str   Donemus
  (Tuba is optional.)

BAKER, DAVID, 1931-

Le chat qui pêche   28'
  soloists: soprano voice and jazz quartet   AMP
    (alto/tenor saxophone; acoustic/electric piano;
    acoustic/electric bass; drums)
  *3 *3 *3 *3 - 4 3 3 1 - tmp+3 - hp - str

BALAKIREV, MILY, 1837-1910

Islamey (arr. Alfredo Casella)   9'
  *4 *3 +3 *4 - 4 4 3 1 - tmp+6 - 2hp - str   MCA; Simrock

Islamey (arr. Sergei Liapounow)   9'
  *4 *2 +3 2 - 4 4 3 1 - tmp+5 - 2hp - str   VAAP

Overture on three Russian folk songs   8'
  2 2 2 2 - 2 2 3 0 - tmp - str   Simrock;
  Optional bass drum and cymbals (2 players).   VAAP

Russia   12'
  3 2 2 2 - 4 2 3 1 - tmp+4 - 2hp - str   Kalmus

Symphony no.1, C major   40'
  *3 *2 3 2 - 4 2 3 1 - tmp+5 - 2hp (doubling   Kalmus
    a single part) - str

Symphony no.2, D minor   33'
  *3 *2 3 2 - 4 2 3 1 - tmp+5 - hp - str   Kalmus

Thamar   20'
  3 *2 3 2 - 4 2 3 1 - tmp+6 - 2hp - str   Breitkopf;
                                                             Kalmus

BAMERT, MATTHIAS, 1942-

Circus parade   12'
  *2 2 *2 2 - 4 2 2 0 - tmp+2 - hp, pf - str   EAM
  Narrator (may be the conductor).

Once upon an orchestra   50'
  *3 *3 *3 *3 - 4 3 3 1 - tmp+3 - hp - str   EAM
  Narrator. May be danced or mimed. Excerpts suitable
  for concert performance without narrator.

BARBER, SAMUEL, 1910-1981

Adagio for strings   8'
  str   Schirmer, G.

Andromache's farewell, op.39   12'
  soprano solo   Schirmer, G.
  *3 *3 *3 2 - 4 3 3 1 - tmp+3 - hp, cel - str

Capricorn concerto   14'
  solo flute, oboe, and trumpet - str   Schirmer, G.

Commando march (orchestra version)   8'
  *3 *3 =4 *3 - 4 3 3 1 - tmp+3 - str   Schirmer, G.
  Originally for band.

Concerto, piano, op.38 26'
  *3 *3 *3 2 - 4 3 3 0 - tmp+2 - hp - str   Schirmer, G.

Concerto, violin, op.14 22'
  2 2 2 2 - 2 2 0 0 - tmp+1 - pf - str   Schirmer, G.

Concerto, violoncello, op.22 20'
  2 *2 *2 2 - 2 3 0 0 - tmp+1 - str   Schirmer, G.

Essay no.1, op.12 8'
  2 2 2 2 - 4 3 3 1 - tmp - pf - str   Schirmer, G.

Essay no.2, op.17 10'
  *3 *3 *2 2 - 4 3 3 1 - tmp+2 - str   Schirmer, G.

Essay no.3, op.47 14'
  *3 *3 =4 *3 - 4 3 3 1 - euphonium -   Schirmer, G.
    2tmp+5 - 2hp, pf - str
  (Euphonium part is cued in other instruments.)

Fadograph of a yestern scene, op.44 7'
  *3 *3 *3 2 - 4 3 3 1 - tmp+1 - cel, pf -   Schirmer, G.
    1 or 2hp - str

Knoxville: summer of 1915, op.24 16'
  soprano solo   Schirmer, G.
  *1 *1 1 1 - 2 1 0 0 - 1perc - hp - str

Medea, op.23 (ballet suite) 23'
  *2 *2 2 2 - 2 2 2 0 - tmp+3 - hp, pf - str Schirmer, G.
  Available for dance performances only; not for
  concert use.

Medea's meditation and dance of vengeance, op.23a 13'
  *3 *3 =4 *3 - 4 3 3 1 - tmp+4 - hp, pf -   Schirmer, G.
    str

Music for a scene from Shelley, op.7 8'
  3 *3 *3 3 - 4 3 3 1 - tmp+1 - hp - str   Schirmer, G.

Die Natali, op.37 16'
  *3 *3 *3 2 - 4 3 3 1 - tmp+4 - hp, cel -   Schirmer, G.
    str

Die Natali, op.37: Silent night   3'
  1 *2 *3 0 - 4 0 3 1 - hp, cel - str   Schirmer, G.
  (Cued to be playable with winds 1 1 2 1 - 2 0 1 0.)

Night flight, op.19a   8'
  *3 *3 =4 2 - 4 3 3 1 - 1perc - pf - str   Schirmer, G.
  An "electric instrument," imitating a signal
  or radio beam, may substitute for the E-flat
  clarinet. This work is a revised version of
  a movement from the 2nd symphony.

Overture to The school for scandal   8'
  *3 *3 *3 2 - 4 3 3 1 - tmp+3 - hp, cel -   Schirmer, G.
    str

Prayers of Kierkegaard, op.30   20'
  chorus - solos ST   Schirmer, G.
  *3 *3 *3 2 - 4 3 3 1 - tmp+4 - hp, pf - str

Souvenirs, op.28   18'
  *2 *2 2 2 - 4 3 3 0 - tmp+3 - hp, cel -   Schirmer, G.
    str

Symphony no.1 in one movement, op.9   19'
  *3 *3 *3 *3 - 4 3 3 1 - tmp+1 - hp - str   Schirmer, G.

Symphony no.2, op.19   27'
  *3 *3 =4 *3 - 4 3 3 1 - tmp+2 - pf - str   Schirmer, G.

Toccata festiva, op.36   14'
  solo organ   Schirmer, G.
  *3 *3 *3 2 - 4 3 3 1 - tmp+4 - str
  Alternate version: solo organ - tp, tmp - str.

Vanessa: Intermezzo   4'
  *3 *3 *3 2 - 4 2 3 1 - tmp+1 - hp - str   Schirmer, G.

Vanessa: Under the willow tree (Country dance)   4'
  *3 *3 *3 2 - 4 2 3 0 - tmp+3 - hp - str   Schirmer, G.
  (Optional mixed chorus)

BARBIROLLI, JOHN, 1899-1970

An Elizabethan suite   12'
  4hn (in last movement only) - str   Oxford
  Arr. by Barbirolli from the following keyboard
  works--Byrd, *The earle of Salisbury's pavane*;
  Anon., *The Irishe ho hoane*; Farnaby, *A toye*;
  Farnaby, *Giles Farnaby's dreame*; Bull, *The
  king's hunt.*

BARLOW, WAYNE, 1912-

Rhapsody for oboe, "The winter's past"   5'
  solo oboe - str   Fischer, C.

BÄRMANN, HEINRICH JOSEPH, 1784-1847

Adagio, clarinet and strings, D-flat major
  See under: Wagner, Richard, 1813-1883

BARTÓK, BÉLA, 1881-1945

Cantata profana   17'
  double chorus - solo tenor and baritone   Boosey
  *3 3 *3 *3 - 4 2 3 1 - tmp+2 - hp - str

Concerto for orchestra   38'
  *3 *3 *3 *3 - 4 3 3 1 - tmp+1 - 2hp - str   Boosey

Concerto, piano, no.1   23'
  *2 *2 *2 2 - 4 2 3 0 - tmp+3 - str   Boosey

Concerto, piano, no.2   25'
  *3 2 2 *3 - 4 3 3 1 - tmp+2 - str   Boosey

Concerto, piano, no.3   23'
  *2 2 2 2 - 4 2 3 1 - tmp+1 - str   Boosey

Concerto, 2 pianos and percussion   25'
  *2 *2 2 *2 - 4 2 3 0 - cel - str   Boosey
  2 or 3 percussion soloists are required. This is
  the orchestral version of the "Sonata for two pianos
  and percussion."

Concerto, viola, op. posth.   21'
  *3 2 2 2 - 3 3 2 1 - tmp+2 - str   Boosey
  Completed by Tibor Serly.

Concerto, violin, no.1 (1907-8), op. posth.   21'
  *2 *3 *2 2 - 4 2 2 1 - tmp+1 - 2hp - str   Boosey

Concerto, violin, no.2 (1938)   32'
  *2 *2 *2 *2 - 4 2 3 0 - tmp+2 - hp, cel - str   Boosey

Dance suite   16'
  *2 *2 *2 *2 - 4 2 2 1 - tmp+3 - hp, cel,   Boosey
    pf (brief passage requires pf 4-hands) - str

Dances of Transylvania   4'
  *2 2 *2 2 - 2 2 2 1 - tmp - hp or pf - str   Boosey

Deux images (Two images), op.10   19'
  *3 *3 *3 *3 - 4 4 3 1 - tmp+1 - 2hp, cel - str   Boosey;
                                      Kalmus

Deux portraits (Two portraits), op.5   12'
  *2 *2 *2 2 - 4 2 2 1 - tmp+4 - 2hp - str   Boosey;
  First movement is for solo violin with   Kalmus
  orchestra accompaniment.

Divertimento (1939)   22'
  str   Boosey

Four orchestral pieces, op.12   25'
  4 *3 =4 *4 - 4 4 4 1 - tmp+2 - 2hp, pf,   Boosey
    cel - str

Hungarian peasant songs   9'
  *2 *2 *2 2 - 2 2 2 1 - tmp - hp - str   Boosey

Hungarian sketches   11'
  *2 2 *2 *2 - 2 2 2 1 - tmp+2 - hp - str   Boosey

Mikrokosmos suite (arr. Tibor Serly)   17'
  *3 *2 *2 *2 - 4 3 3 1 - tmp+4 - hp, cel - str   Boosey

The miraculous mandarin: Suite   20'
  *3 *3 =3 *3 - 4 3 3 1 - tmp+4 - hp, cel,   Boosey
    pf, org - str

Music for strings, percussion and celeste   26'
  tmp+2 - hp, cel, pf - 4vn, 2va, 2vc, 2db   Boosey
  Forces are arranged as a double orchestra.
  Frequently performed with full orchestral strings.

Rhapsody for piano and orchestra, op.1   17'
  *3 2 *2 2 - 4 2 3 0 - tmp+2 - str   Boosey

Rhapsody no.1 for violin and orchestra   11'
  *2 2 *2 2 - 2 2 1 1 - cimbalom (or hp and pf) - Boosey
  str

Rhapsody no.2 for violin and orchestra   12'
  *2 *2 *2 2 - 2 2 1 1 - tmp+1 - hp, pf/cel - str   Boosey

Rumanian folk dances   6'
  *2 0 2 2 - 2 0 0 0 - str   Boosey

Scherzo, op.2   29'
  solo piano   Boosey
  *4 *3 +4 *4 - 4 3 3 1 - tmp+5 - 2hp - str
  One of the four clarinet parts is written for
  "clarinet in A-flat."

Suite no.1 for orchestra   35'
  *4 *3 =4 *4 - 4 3 3 1 - tmp+3 - 2hp - str   Boosey; Kalmus

Suite no.2 for orchestra   25'
  *2 *2 =2 *2 - 3 2 0 0 - tmp+2 - 2hp - str   Boosey

Three village scenes   11'
  female voices (2 or 4 Mz and 2 or 4 A)   Boosey
  *1 *1 +2 1 - 1 1 1 0 - 1perc - hp, pf - string quintet
  One clarinetist doubles on alto saxophone.

The wooden prince: Suite   30'
  *4 *4 *4 *4 - 4 6 3 1 - asx, tsx - tmp+5 -   Boosey
  2hp, cel 4-hands - str
  2pic and 2 Eh are required. There is also a "Little
  concert suite from The wooden prince," 12' in duration.

    BASSETT, LESLIE, 1923-

Echoes from an invisible world   17'
  *3 *3 *3 *3 - 4 4 3 1 - tmp+3 - hp, cel, pf - str   Peters

Variations for orchestra   23'
  *2 *2 *2 *2 - 4 2 3 1 - tmp+2 - hp, cel, pf - str   Peters

    BECKER, JOHN J., 1886-1961

Concerto arabesque   13'
  solo piano   ACA
  1 1 1 *2 - 1 1 0 0 - str

Soundpiece no.1b   12'
  str, pf   ACA

Soundpiece no.2b ("Homage to Haydn")   13'
  str   Presser

Symphony no.3 (Symphonia brevis)   17'
  *3 *3 2 *4 - 4 4 3 1 - tmp+6 - pf - str   Peters

Two pieces for orchestra
  These two works are out of print, but orchestral
  materials are in the Fleisher Collection.

  1. Among the reeds and rushes   3'
     1 1 2 1 - 1 1 0 0 - tmp - hp - str

  2. The mountains   3'
     *3 2 2 1 - 2 2 2 1 - tmp+3 - str

When the willow nods   15'
  1 1 1 1 - 1 1 0 0 - tmp+1 - pf - str
  This work is out of print, but orchestral
  materials are in the Fleisher Collection.

    BEETHOVEN, LUDWIG VAN, 1770-1827

Ah, perfido, op.65   13'
  soprano scene and aria   Breitkopf;
  1 0 2 2 - 2 0 0 0 - str   Kalmus

Cantata on the death of Emperor Joseph II   33'
  chorus - solos SSATB   Breitkopf;
  2 2 2 2 - 2 0 0 0 - str   Kalmus; Schirmer, G.

Christus am Ölberg (Christ on the Mount of Olives)   36'
  chorus - solos STB   Breitkopf;
  2 2 2 2 - 2 2 3 0 - tmp - str   Gray; Kalmus

Concerto, piano, no.1, op.15, C major   34'
  1 2 2 2 - 2 2 0 0 - tmp - str   Breitkopf; Kalmus

Concerto, piano, no.2, op.19, B-flat major   28'
  1 2 0 2 - 2 0 0 0 - str   Breitkopf; Kalmus

Concerto, piano, no.3, op.37, C minor   33'
  2 2 2 2 - 2 2 0 0 - tmp - str   Breitkopf; Kalmus

Concerto, piano, no.4, op.58, G major   33'
  1 2 2 2 - 2 2 0 0 - tmp - str   Breitkopf; Kalmus

Concerto, piano, no.5, op.73, E-flat maj. ("Emperor") 37'
  2 2 2 2 - 2 2 0 0 - tmp - str   Breitkopf; Kalmus

Concerto, piano, no.6, op.61, D major   42'
  The composer has provided a piano version of the solo
  part from his violin concerto, op.61. Use the orchestral parts for the violin concerto.

Concerto, violin, op.61, D major   42'
  1 2 2 2 - 2 2 0 0 - tmp - str   Breitkopf; Kalmus

Concerto, violin, violoncello, piano, op.56,
  C major ("Triple")   35'
  1 2 2 2 - 2 2 0 0 - tmp - str   Breitkopf; Kalmus

Consecration of the house (Die Weihe des Hauses)   12'
  2 2 2 2 - 4 2 3 0 - tmp - str   Breitkopf; Kalmus

Contradances   12'
  1 2 2 2 - 2 0 0 0 - 1perc - str (without va)   Kalmus;
  Twelve dances.   Schott

Coriolan overture, op.62   8'
  2 2 2 2 - 2 2 0 0 - tmp - str   Breitkopf; Kalmus

Egmont (incidental music), op.84   40'
  soprano solo   Kalmus
  *2 2 2 2 - 4 2 0 0 - tmp - str

Egmont: Overture   9'
  *2 2 2 2 - 4 2 0 0 - tmp - str   Breitkopf; Kalmus

Fantasia for piano, chorus and orchestra, op.80   19'
  chorus - solos SSATTB - solo piano   Breitkopf; Gray;
  2 2 2 2 - 2 2 0 0 - tmp - str   Kalmus; Schirmer, G.

Fidelio: Overture   6'
  2 2 2 2 - 4 2 2 0 - tmp - str   Breitkopf; Kalmus

German dances   20'
  *3 2 2 2 - 2 2 0 0 - posthorn or cornet -   Breitkopf;
    tmp+3 - str (without va)   Kalmus
  Twelve dances.

Die Geschöpfe des Prometheus, op.43
  See his: Prometheus, op.43

Grosse Fuge, op.133   16'
  str   Breitkopf
  Edited by Felix Weingartner for string
  orchestra. Originally for string quartet.

Jena symphony
  See under: Witt, Friedrich, 1770-1837

King Stephen: Overture   8'
  2 2 2 *3 - 4 2 0 0 - tmp - str   Breitkopf; Kalmus

Leonore overture no.1   10'
  2 2 2 2 - 4 2 0 0 - tmp - str   Breitkopf; Kalmus

Leonore overture no.2   13'
  2 2 2 2 - 4 2 3 0 - tmp - str   Breitkopf; Kalmus

Leonore overture no.3   14'
  2 2 2 2 - 4 2 3 0 - tmp - str   Breitkopf; Kalmus

Mass, op.86, C major   38'
  chorus - solos SATB   Breitkopf; Gray;
  2 2 2 2 - 2 2 0 0 - tmp - org - str   Kalmus; Peters

Meeresstille und glückliche Fahrt, op.112   10'
  chorus   Breitkopf; Kalmus
  2 2 2 2 - 4 2 0 0 - tmp - str

Missa solemnis, op.123, D major   80'
    chorus - solos SATB   Breitkopf; Kalmus;
    2 2 2 *3 - 4 2 3 0 - tmp - org - str   Peters;
                                          Schirmer, G.

Musik zu einem Ritterballet   13'
    *1 0 2 0 - 2 2 0 0 - tmp - str   Breitkopf; Kalmus

Namensfeier overture, op.115   8'
    2 2 2 2 - 4 2 0 0 - tmp - str   Breitkopf; Kalmus

Prometheus (ballet music), op.43   48'
    2 2 2 2 - 2 2 0 0 - basset horn (may be played   Kalmus
      by one of the clarinets) - tmp - hp - str

Prometheus: Overture   5'
    2 2 2 2 - 2 2 0 0 - tmp - str   Breitkopf; Kalmus

Romance no.1, op.40, G major   8'
    violin solo   Breitkopf;
    1 2 0 2 - 2 0 0 0 - str   Kalmus
    Breitkopf parts are published together
    with Romance no.2.

Romance no.2, op.50, F major   9'
    violin solo   Breitkopf;
    1 2 0 2 - 2 0 0 0 - str   Kalmus
    Breitkopf parts are published together
    with Romance no.1.

Ruins of Athens: Overture   6'
    2 2 2 2 - 4 2 0 0 - tmp - str   Breitkopf; Kalmus

Ruins of Athens: March and chorus (Schmückt die Altäre)
    chorus   Breitkopf;
    *2 2 2 2 - 2 2 3 0 - tmp - str   Kalmus

Ruins of Athens: Turkish march   4'
    *1 2 2 *3 - 2 2 0 0 - 3perc - str   Breitkopf; Kalmus

Septet, op.20, E-flat major   40'
    0 0 1 1 - 1 0 0 0 - vn, va, vc, db   Peters

Symphony no.1, op.21, C major   25'
    2 2 2 2 - 2 2 0 0 - tmp - str   Breitkopf; Kalmus

Symphony no.2, op.36, D major   32'
  2 2 2 2 - 2 2 0 0 - tmp - str   Breitkopf; Kalmus

Symphony no.3, op.55, E-flat major ("Eroica")   48'
  2 2 2 2 - 3 2 0 0 - tmp - str   Breitkopf; Kalmus

Symphony no.4, op.60, B-flat major   34'
  1 2 2 2 - 2 2 0 0 - tmp - str   Breitkopf; Kalmus

Symphony no.5, op.67, C minor   30'
  *3 2 2 *3 - 2 2 3 0 - tmp - str   Breitkopf; Kalmus
  A critical edition of the score is
  available from Norton.

Symphony no.6, op.68, F major ("Pastorale")   40'
  *3 2 2 2 - 2 2 2 0 - tmp - str   Breitkopf; Kalmus

Symphony no.7, op.92, A major   37'
  2 2 2 2 - 2 2 0 0 - tmp - str   Breitkopf; Kalmus

Symphony no.8, op.93, F major   26'
  2 2 2 2 - 2 2 0 0 - tmp - str   Breitkopf; Kalmus

Symphony no.9, op.125, D minor ("Choral")   67'
  chorus - solos SATB   Breitkopf;
  *3 2 2 *3 - 4 2 3 0 - tmp+3 - str   Kalmus

Die Weihe des Hauses
  See his: Consecration of the house

Wellington's victory, op.91   16'
  *3 2 2 2 - 4 6 3 0 - tmp+3 - str   Breitkopf; Kalmus

Zapfenstreich march
  *1 2 2 *3 - 2 2 0 0 - 4perc   Kalmus

   BELLINI, VINCENZO, 1801-1835

Concerto, oboe, E-flat major
  2 2 2 1 - 2 0 0 0 - str   Leuckart

Norma: Overture   6'
  *2 2 2 2 - 4 2 3 1 - tmp+2 - hp - str   Breitkopf;
                                              Kalmus; Lucks;
                                                     Ricordi

Symphony, C minor   10'
  2 2 2 2 - 2 2 3 0 - str   Ricordi
  Ed. Maffeo Zanon.

Symphony, D major   8'
  2 2 2 2 - 2 2 3 0 - tmp - str   Ricordi
  Ed. Maffeo Zanon.

   BENJAMIN, ARTHUR, 1893-1960

Concertino, piano and orchestra   15'
  *2 2 2 2 - 2 2 0 0 - asx - tmp+4 - str   Schott

Two Jamaican pieces   5'
  1 1 2 1 - 2 1 0 0 - asx - tmp+2 - str   Boosey
  (Optional: 2nd cl, asx, tmp.)
    Contents--Jamaican song; Jamaican rhumba.

   BENNETT, RICHARD RODNEY, 1936-

Concerto, guitar and chamber ensemble   20'
  *1 *1 *1 0 - 1 1 0 0 - tmp+1 - cel - vn, va, vc   Universal

Zodiac   17'
  *3 *3 *3 *3 - 4 3 3 1 - tmp+3 - hp, pf/cel - str   Novello

   BENNETT, ROBERT RUSSELL, 1894-

Suite of old American dances   16'
  *2 *2 *3 2 - 4 3 3 1 - tmp+3 - hp - str   Chappell

   BENSON, WARREN, 1924-

Chants and graces   8'
  pic - 4perc - hp - str   Fischer, C.

A Delphic serenade   12'
  *2 2 2 2 - 4 3 3 1 - tmp+3 - hp - str   Fischer, C.

Five brief encounters   7'
  2 0 2 0 - 2 1 1 0 - tmp - str   Fischer, C.

BEREZOWSKY, NICOLAI, 1900-1953

Concerto, harp, op.31   22'
  *3 2 *3 2 - 4 2 3 1 - tmp+2 - str   Elkan-Vogel

BERG, ALBAN, 1885-1935

Altenberg Lieder, op.4   10'
  soprano solo   Universal
  *3 *3 =4 *3 - 4 3 4 1 - tmp+4 - hp, cel, pf, harm - str

Chamber concerto, op.8   37'
  solo violin - solo piano   Universal
  *2 *2 =3 *2 - 2 1 1 0

Concerto, violin   25'
  *2 *2 *4 *3 - 4 2 2 1 - tmp+2 - hp - str   Universal
  3rd clarinet doubles on alto saxophone.

Lulu: Suite   35'
  coloratura soprano solo   Universal
  *3 *3 *4 *3 - 4 3 3 1 - asx - tmp+3 - hp, pf - str

Lulu: Lulu's song   3'
  coloratura soprano solo   Universal
  3 *3 *3 *3 - 4 2 3 1 - asx - 1perc - hp, pf - str

Lyric suite: Three pieces   15'
  str   Universal
  Originally for string quartet.

Three pieces for orchestra, op.6   18'
  *4 *4 =5 *4 - 6 4 4 1 - 2tmp, 5perc - 2hp,   Universal
    cel - str
  Revised 1929.   ⟩

Der Wein; concert aria   15'
  soprano solo   Universal
  *2 *2 *3 *3 - 4 2 2 1 - asx - tmp+2 - hp, pf - str

Wozzeck: Three excerpts   20'
  soprano solo   Universal
  *4 *4 =5 *4 - 4 4 4 1 - tmp+4 - hp, cel - str
  Playable with reduced winds.

BERGSMA, WILLIAM, 1921-

A carol on Twelfth night   8'
  *2 2 2 2 - 4 2 3 1 - tmp+2 - hp - str   Galaxy

Chameleon variations   13'
  *3 2 *3 2 - 4 3 3 1 - tmp+3 - hp, pf - str   Galaxy

BERIO, LUCIANO, 1925-

Allelujah   10'
  *4 2 =4 *3 - 8 5 3 1 - asx, tsx - tmp+7 -   Suvini
  2hp, cel, pf - str

Nones   10'
  *3 2 2 *3 - 4 4 3 1 - asx - tmp+5 - hp, cel,   Suvini
  pf, electric gtr - str

Ritirata notturna di Madrid   10'
  *3 *3 *3 *3 - 4 4 3 1 - tmp+3 - hp - str   Universal
  Available in the United States from AMP.
  "Four original versions of the *Ritirata notturna
  di Madrid* of L. Boccherini, superimposed and
  transcribed for orchestra."

Sinfonia   35'
  eight voices (SSAATTBB)   Universal
  *4 *3 +4 *3 - 4 4 3 1 - asx, tsx - tmp+2 -
    hp, pf, electric org, electric hpsd (Baldwin) - str
  Available in the United States from AMP.

Still   12'
  3 *3 *4 *3 - 4 4 3 1 - asx, tsx - 3perc -   Universal
    hp, pf, electric org - str
  Available in the United States from AMP.

Tempi concertati   16'
  solo flute, violin, 2 pianos (one dbl cel)   Universal
  *1 *2 *3 1 - 1 1 1 0 - 4perc - 2hp - 2va, 2vc, db
  Not to be conducted in performance, though a conductor
  is necessary in rehearsal. Available in the United
  States from AMP.

Variazioni per orchestra da camera   12'
  *2 1 2 2 - 2 2 1 0 - str 8.8.6.4.3   Suvini

BERKELEY, LENNOX, 1903-

Concerto, guitar, op.88   22'
  1 1 1 1 - 2 0 0 0 - str   Chester

Sinfonietta   13'
  2 2 2 2 - 2 0 0 0 - tmp - str   Chester

Symphony no.3 in one movement   14'
  *3 *3 2 *3 - 4 3 3 1 - tmp+2 - hp - str   Chester

Windsor variations, for chamber orchestra   13'
  1 2 0 2 - 2 0 0 0 - str   Chester

BERLIOZ, HECTOR, 1803-1869

Béatrice et Bénédict: Overture   8'
  *2 2 2 2 - 4 3 3 0 - tmp - str   Bote; Breitkopf; Kalmus

Benvenuto Cellini: Overture   11'
  *2 2 *2 4 - 4 6 3 1 - 2tmp, 3perc - str   Breitkopf;
  (4 real bassoon parts in only 3 bars of the   Kalmus
  total piece; otherwise 2 real parts, each doubled.)

Le carnaval romain
  See his: Roman carnival

Cléopâtre   22'
  soprano solo   Broude Bros.;
  *2 2 2 2 - 4 2 3 0 - tmp - str   Luck
  Often listed as *La mort de Cléopâtre.* Sometimes
  the two titles are incorrectly listed as separate works.

Le corsaire   8'
  2 2 2 4 - 4 4 3 1 - tmp - str   Breitkopf;
  (2 real bassoon parts, each doubled.)   Kalmus

La damnation de Faust, op.24   120'
  solos MzTBarB - chorus, opt children's chorus Breitkopf;
  *3 *2 *3 4 - 4 4 3 2 - 2tmp, 3perc -   Kalmus;
    2hp - str   Schirmer, G.

La damnation de Faust: Dance of the sylphs   3'
  *3 0 2 0 - tmp - 2hp - str   Breitkopf; Kalmus

La damnation de Faust: Marche hongroise (Rakoczy march)   5'
  *3 2 2 4 - 4 4 3 1 - tmp+4 - str   Breitkopf;
  (2 real bassoon parts, each doubled.)   Kalmus

La damnation de Faust: Menuet de follets (Will-o-the-wisps)
  *3 2 *3 4 - 4 4 3 0 - 2tmp, 2perc -   5'
  2hp - str   Breitkopf; Kalmus

L'enfance du Christ   93'
  solos S, 2T, Bar, 3B - chorus   Breitkopf; Gray;
  *2 *2 2 2 - 2 4 3 0 - tmp - hp, org (or   Kalmus;
  harm) - str   Schirmer, G.
  (Can be done with solos STBB.)

Les franc-juges   13'
  *2 2 2 *3 - 4 3 3 2 - tmp+1 - str   Kalmus

Harold in Italy, op.16   47'
  solo viola   Breitkopf;
  *2 *2 2 4 - 4 4 3 1 - tmp+3 - hp - str   Kalmus

King Lear   13'
  *2 2 2 2 - 4 2 3 1 - tmp - str   Breitkopf; Kalmus

Lelio, or The return to life, op.14b   53'
  speaker - invisible chorus and solos TTB   Kalmus
  *2 *2 2 2 - 4 4 3 1 - 2tmp, 1perc -
  hp, pf 4-hands - str
  "Continuation and ending of the *Symphonie fantastique*."

La mort de Cléopâtre
  See his: Cléopâtre

Nuits d'été, op.7   30'
  solo voice (Mz or T or Bar, or several   Kalmus;
  different voices alternating)   Mapleson
  2 1 2 2 - 3 0 0 0 - hp - str

Requiem, op.5 (Grande messe des morts)   90'
  chorus - tenor solo   Breitkopf;
  4 *4 4 8 - 12 16 16 6 - 10tmp, 9perc - str   Kalmus
  Number of real parts for winds and percussion,
  exclusive of doublings: 4 *4 2 4 - 6 8 8 3 -
  4tmp, 3perc. G. Schirmer publishes a reduced
  version.

Rêverie et caprice, op.8   11'
  violin solo   Breitkopf;
  *2 2 2 2 - 2 0 0 0 - str   Kalmus

Rob Roy   12'
  *2 *2 2 2 - 4 3 3 0 - tmp - hp - str   Breitkopf; Kalmus

Roman carnival (Le carnaval romain)   8'
  *2 *2 2 4 - 4 4 3 0 - tmp+3 - str   Breitkopf;
  (2 real bassoon parts, each doubled.)   Kalmus

Roméo et Juliette, op.17   95'
  chorus - solos ATB   Breitkopf;
  *3 *2 2 4 - 4 4 3 1 - 2tmp, 4perc - 2hp - str   Kalmus;
                                                            Schirmer, G.

Roméo et Juliette: Love scene   19'
  2 *2 2 4 - 4 0 0 0 - str   Kalmus

Roméo et Juliette: Queen Mab scherzo   8'
  *3 *2 2 4 - 4 0 0 0 - tmp+1 - 2hp - str   Breitkopf;
                                                                 Kalmus

Roméo et Juliette: Romeo alone; Festivities at Capulet's
  *3 2 2 4 - 4 4 3 0 - 2tmp, 6perc -   12'
  2hp - str   Kalmus; Luck

Symphonie fantastique, op.14   52'
  *2 *2 +2 4 - 4 4 3 2 - 4tmp, 2perc -   Bärenreiter;
  2hps - str   Breitkopf;
  A critical edition of the score   Kalmus
  is available from Norton.

Symphonie funèbre et triomphale, op.15   32'
  optional chorus   Bärenreiter;
  *2 2 =4 *3 - 6 6 4 2 - tmp+5 - optional str   Kalmus
  Contrabassoon, bass trombone, timpani are
  also optional. Composer calls for doubling
  and tripling of all parts.

Te deum   55'
  solo tenor - double chorus,   Breitkopf;
    optional children's chorus   Kalmus;
  *4 *4 *4 4 - 4 5 6 2 - tmp+6 - org,   Schirmer, G.
  12hp (doubling 1 real part) - str
  Number of real parts for winds and percussion,

exclusive of doublings: *4 *2 *2 4 -
4 5 3 1 - tmp+3.

Les Troyens: Overture   6'
  2 2 *2 2 - 4 4 3 0 - tmp - str   Kalmus; Luck

Les Troyens: Ballet   12'
  *3 *2 2 2 - 4 4 3 0 - tmp+1 - str   Choudens; Kalmus

Les Troyens: Royal hunt and storm   7'
  *3 2 2 2 - 4 4 3 1 - 2(or3)tmp+1 - str Choudens; Kalmus

Les Troyens: Trojan march   5'
  2 2 2 2 - 4 4 3 1 - tmp+2 - 2hp - str   Breitkopf;
                                           Choudens; Kalmus

Waverley   9'
  *2 2 2 4 - 4 3 3 1 - tmp - str   Kalmus

BERNSTEIN, LEONARD, 1918-

The age of anxiety (Symphony no.2)   30'
  solo piano   Schirmer, G.
  *3 *3 *3 *3 - 4 3 3 1 - tmp+5 - hp, pianino - str

Candide: Overture   5'
  *3 2 =4 *3 - 4 2 3 1 - tmp+4 - hp - str   Schirmer, G.

Chichester psalms   19'
  chorus - solo boy or countertenor   Schirmer, G.
  0 0 0 0 - 0 3 3 0 - tmp+7 - 2hp - str
  (Publisher offers a reduction of the instrumental
  forces for harp, organ, and percussion.)

Facsimile   21'
  *2 2 +2 2 - 4 3 2 1 - tmp+1 - pf - str   Schirmer, G.

Fancy free: Suite   26'
  *2 2 2 2 - 4 3 3 1 - tmp+1 - pf - str   Schirmer, G.

Jeremiah (Symphony no.1)   23'
  solo soprano   Warner
  *3 *3 =3 *3 - 4 3 3 1 - tmp+4 - pf - str

Kaddish (Symphony no.3)   40'
    speaker, soprano solo - mixed chorus,   Schirmer, G.
      boy's chorus
    =4 *3 =4 *3 - 4 4 3 1 - asx - tmp+7 - hp, cel, pf - str
    Revised version 1978.

On the town: Three dance episodes   9'
    *1 1 =3 0 - 3 3 3 0 - tmp+1 - pf - str   Schirmer, G.
    One clarinet doubles on alto saxophone.

On the waterfront: Symphonic suite   23'
    *3 2 =4 *3 - 4 3 3 1 - asx - 2tmp,   Schirmer, G.
      3perc - hp, pf - str

Serenade   33'
    solo violin   Schirmer, G.
    hp - tmp+5 - str

Slava! (A political overture)   5'
    *3 *3 =4 *3 - 4 3 3 1 - ssx - tmp+5 - pf,   Boosey
      electric gtr - pre-recorded tape - str

Songfest   40'
    solo voices: S Mz A T Bar B   Boosey
    *3 *3 =4 *3 - 4 3 3 1 - tmp+6 - hp, pf (doubling
      cel and electric keyboard), fender bass - str

West side story: Overture (arr. M. Peress)   5'
    *2 *2 =2 2 - 4 3 3 1 - tmp+1, dance drums - Schirmer, G.
      hp, pf, opt electric gtr - str

West side story: Symphonic dances   22'
    *3 *3 =4 *3 - 4 3 3 1 - asx - tmp+4 -   Schirmer, G.
      hp, cel, pf - str

    BERWALD, FRANZ, 1796-1868

Estrella de Soria: Overture   8'
    2 2 2 2 - 4 2 3 0 - tmp - str   Gehrmans
    Concert-ending by Moses Pergament.

Symphony, C major ("Sinfonie singulière")   29'
    2 2 2 2 - 4 2 3 0 - tmp - str   Bärenreiter;
    Sometimes listed as Symphony no.5.   Hansen

Symphony, E-flat major   27'
   2 2 2 2 - 4 2 3 0 - tmp - str   Gehrmans;
   Published as Symphony no.3; sometimes   Simrock
   referred to as Symphony no.6.

Symphony, G minor ("Symphonie serieuse")   30'
   2 2 2 2 - 4 2 3 0 - tmp - str   Gehrmans
   Sometimes listed as Symphony no.2.

BIBER, HEINRICH VON, 1644-1704

Battalia   6'
str, cnt   Doblinger; Kerby

BIRTWISTLE, HARRISON, 1934-

Nomos   15'
   amplified solo group: fl, cl, hn, bsn   Universal
   *4 *3 =3 *3 - 4 4 3 1 - tmp+5 - hp, cel -
   10va, 10vc, 8db
   Three of the flutists double on piccolo; two of the
   clarinetists double on E-flat clarinet.

Verses for ensembles   28'
   =1 *1 =2 *1 - 1 2 2 0 - 3perc   Universal

BIZET, GEORGES, 1838-1875

L'Arlésienne: Suite no.1   17'
   2 *2 2 2 - 4 4 3 0 - asx (cued in other   Breitkopf;
     instruments) - tmp+1 - hp (or pf) - str   Choudens;
     Contents--Prelude; Minuet; Adagietto;   Kalmus
   Carillon.

L'Arlésienne: Suite no.2   18'
   *2 *2 2 2 - 4 4 3 0 - asx (cued in other   Breitkopf;
     instruments) - tmp+3 - hp (or pf) - str   Choudens;
     Contents--Pastorale; Intermezzo; Menuet;   Kalmus
   Farandole.

Carmen: Suite no.1   11'
   *2 *2 2 2 - 4 2 3 0 - tmp+3 - hp - str   Breitkopf;
      Contents--Prélude; Aragonaise;   Choudens;
   Intermezzo; Seguedille; Les dragons   Kalmus
   d'Alcala; Les toréadors.

Carmen: Suite no.2   19'
   *2 *2 2 2 - 4 2 3 1 - tmp+4 - hp - str   Breitkopf;
      Contents--Marche des contrabandiers;   Choudens;
   Habanera; Nocturne; La garde montante;   Kalmus
   Danse bohème.

Carmen fantasie, op.25
   See under: Sarasate, Pablo de, 1844-1908

Jolie fille de Perth: Scenes bohémiennes   15'
   *2 *2 2 2 - 4 2 3 0 - tmp+3 - hp - str   Kalmus
      Contents--Prélude; Serenade; Marche;
   Danse bohémienne.

Ouverture   14'
   *2 2 2 2 - 4 2 3 1 - tmp - str   Universal

Patrie   13'
   *2 2 2 2 - 4 4 3 1 - tmp+3 - hp - str   Choudens; Kalmus

Pearlfishers: Overture
   2 2 2 2 - 4 0 0 0 - tmp - str   Kalmus; Luck

Petite suite from "Jeux d'enfants," op.22   10'
   *2 2 2 2 - 4 2 0 0 - tmp+3 - str   Durand; Kalmus;
                                                   Ricordi

Roma   32'
   2 *2 2 2 - 4 2 3 0 - tmp - hp - str   Breitkopf;
                                                Choudens; Kalmus

Symphony no.1, C major   28'
   2 2 2 2 - 4 2 0 0 - tmp - str   Choudens; Kalmus;
                                                   Universal

BLACHER, BORIS, 1903-1975

Orchesterfantasie, op.51   20'
  solo string quartet   Bote
  *3 *3 *3 *3 - 4 3 3 1 - tmp+4 - hp - str

Orchester-Ornament, op.44   14'
  *3 *3 3 3 - 4 3 3 1 - tmp+4 - str   Bote

Orchestra-variations on a theme of Paganini   16'
  *3 *3 *3 *3 - 4 3 3 1 - tmp - str   Bote

BLACKWOOD, EASLEY, 1933-

Symphony no.1, op.3   30'
  *4 *3 =4 *4 - 6 4 3 1 - tmp+3 - cel - str   Elkan-Vogel
  Two of the flutists double on piccolo.

Symphony no.2, op.9   24'
  *3 *3 *3 *3 - 4 4 3 1 - tmp+3 - hp - str   Schirmer, G.

BLISS, ARTHUR, 1891-1975

Introduction and allegro   12'
  *3 *3 *3 *3 - 4 3 3 1 - tmp+2 - hp - str   Boosey

Things to come: Concert suite   17'
  *2 *2 2 2 - 4 3 3 1 - tmp+3 - hp - str   Novello
  Two of the flutists double on piccolo.

BLOCH, AUGUSTYN, 1929-

Enfiando per orchestra   11'
  3 3 3 3 - 4 ·3 3 1 - tmp+3 - org or pf -   Schott
    str 14.12.10.8.6 (possible with 12.8.6.4.2)

BLOCH, ERNEST, 1880-1959

America; an epic rhapsody in three parts   45'
  *3 *3 *3 *3 - 4 3 3 1 - tmp+4 - 2hp, cel - str   Birchard
  Brief unison choral passage at end of the work,
  intended by the composer to be sung by the audience.

Baal Shem; three pictures of Chassidic life   12'
  solo violin   Fischer, C.
  *2 2 2 2 - 4 3 0 0 - tmp+1 - hp, cel - str

Concerto, violin   35'
  *3 *3 *3 *3 - 4 3 3 1 - tmp+2 - hp, cel - str   Boosey

Concerto grosso no.1   23'
  solo piano - str   Birchard

Concerto grosso no.2   19'
  solo string quartet - string orchestra   Schirmer, G.

Concertino   8'
  solo flute - solo viola (or clarinet)   Schirmer, G.
  *3 2 2 2 - 4 3 3 1 - tmp+3 - str
  Winds and percussion play only last 14 bars; they
  may be omitted by using a special ending for strings.

Evocations   17'
  *3 *2 2 2 - 4 2 3 1 - tmp+5 - hp, cel,   Schirmer, G.
    pf - str

Proclamation   6'
  solo trumpet   Broude Bros.
  2 2 2 2 - 4 2 0 0 - tmp+1 - str

Sacred service (Avodath hakodesh)   52'
  baritone solo - chorus   Broude Bros.
  *3 *3 *3 *3 - 4 3 3 1 - tmp+3 - 2hp, cel - str

Schelomo; Hebraic rhapsody   20'
  solo violoncello   Schirmer, G.
  *3 *3 *3 *3 - 4 3 3 1 - tmp+2 - 2hp, cel - str

Symphony for trombone and orchestra   17'
  solo trombone   Broude Bros.
  *3 *3 *3 *3 - 4 3 3 1 - tmp+2 - hp, cel - str

Trois poèmes juifs   24'
  *3 *3 2 *3 - 4 3 3 1 - tmp+4 - hp,   Schirmer, G.
    cel - str

Voice in the wilderness   25'
  violoncello obligato   Schirmer, G.
  *3 *3 *3 *3 - 4 3 3 1 - tmp+4 - 2hp, pf/cel - str

BLOMDAHL, KARL-BIRGER, 1916-1968

Game for eight   25'
  *1 *1 *1 *1 - 1 1 2 0 - tmp+7 - hp, cel, pf -   Schott
  2vn, 2va, 2vc, 2db
  Clarinetist also doubles on alto saxophone.

Sisyphos   20'
  *3 *3 *3 *3 - 4 4 3 1 - tmp+6 - hp, pf - str   Schott

Symphony no.3 ("Facets")   23'
  *3 *3 *3 *3 - 4 4 3 1 - tmp+3 - str   Schott

BOCCHERINI, LUIGI, 1743-1805

Concerto, flute, G.489, D major   20'
  str   Nagel
  Wrongly attributed to Boccherini; actual
  composer is Franz Xaver Pokorný.

Concerto, violin, G.486, D major   24'
  2 2 0 0 - 2 0 0 0 - str   Schott
  Ed. S. Dushkin. Authenticity very doubtful.

Concerto, violoncello, G.474, E-flat major   18'
  0 2 0 0 - 2 0 0 0 - str   Suvini
  Ed. Franco Gallini.

Concerto, violoncello, G.477, C major   15'
  str - (2hn optional)   Schott
  Ed. Walter Lebermann.

Concerto, violoncello, G.482, B-flat major   22'
  2hn - str   Eulenburg
  Ed. Richard Sturzenegger. This is the original
  version of the well-known but unauthentic
  Grützmacher arrangement.

Concerto, violoncello, G.482 (Grützmacher version)   22'
  0 2 0 0 - 2 0 0 0 - str   Breitkopf;
  This frequently-played version of the concerto   Kalmus
  is more Grützmacher than it is Boccherini, and
  heavily romanticized to boot.

Overture, op.43, G.521, D major   5'
  0 2 0 1 - 2 0 0 0 - str   Breitkopf;
  Breitkopf edition calls for 2fl rather   Zanibon
  than 2ob. This work is listed elsewhere
  as Symphony no.19.

Ritirata notturna di Madrid
  See under: Berio, Luciano, 1925-

Sinfonia concertante, G.268, C major   9'
  str   Zanibon
  Ed. Pina Carmirelli. Originally a string quintet,
  op.10, no.4. However, the composer himself
  indicated orchestral performance as possible.

Symphonies
  These works have been published under several
  conflicting numbering systems, as indicated below.

Symphony, G.503, D major (ed. Newell Jenkins)   20'
  1 2 0 0 - 2 0 0 0 - str   Schirmer, G.
  Published by Schirmer as op.16, no.2. Also
  listed elsewhere as op.12, no.1.

Symphony, G.506, D. minor ("Della casa del diavolo") 17'
  0 2 0 0 - 2 0 0 0 - str   Ricordi;
  Listed elsewhere as op.12, no.4, and as   Suvini
  Symphony no.4.

Symphony, G.511, A major (ed. Ettore Bonelli)   15'
  0 2 0 1 - 2 0 0 0 - str   Zanibon
  Published by Zanibon as op.1, no.3. Also listed
  elsewhere as op.35, no.3, and as Symphony no.9.

Symphony, G.512, F major   15'
  (1) 2 0 1 - 2 0 0 0 - str   Ricordi;
  Ricordi version (ed. Guido Guerrini) uses Schirmer, G.
  one flute, and is published as Symphony no.4.
  G. Schirmer version (ed. Newell Jenkins) uses
  no flute, and is published as op.35, no.4. This
  same work is elsewhere identified as Symphony no.10.

Symphony, G.514, B-flat major (ed. Ettore Bonelli) 13'
  0 2 0 1 - 2 0 0 0 - str   Zanibon
  Published by Zanibon as op.1, no.6. Also listed
  elsewhere as op.35, no.6, and as Symphony no.12.

Symphony, G.518, A major   22'
  1 2 0 2 - 2 0 0 0 - str   Ricordi;
  Published by Ricordi as op.37, no.4. Also   Universal
  listed elsewhere as Symphony no.16.

  BOËLLMANN, LÉON, 1862-1897

Symphonic variations, op.23   13'
  solo violoncello   Durand; Fischer, C.;
  2 2 2 2 - 4 2 3 1 - tmp - hp - str   Kalmus

  BOIELDIEU, FRANÇOIS, 1775-1834

Caliph of Bagdad: Overture   8'
  *2 2 2 2 - 2 2 0 0 - tmp+2 - str   Breitkopf;
                                   Heugel; Kalmus

Concerto, harp, C major ("In tre tempi")   22'
  2 2 0 2 - 2 0 0 0 - str   Ricordi

La dame blanche: Overture   9'
  *2 2 2 2 - 2 2 1 0 - tmp - str   Breitkopf;
                                  Kalmus; Luck

  BOISMORTIER, JOSEPH BODIN DE, 1691-1755

Concerto, D major
  solo violoncello, or va da gamba, or bassoon   Ricordi
  str (without va) - cnt
  Ed. Hugo Ruf.

  BORODIN, ALEXANDER, 1833-1887

In the steppes of central Asia   9'
  2 *2 2 2 - 4 2 3 0 - tmp - str   Kalmus; Ricordi; VAAP

Nocturne (arr. Malcolm Sargent)   9'
  str   Boosey
  From the composer's String quartet no.2.

Nocturne (arr. N. Tcherepnin)   9'
  3 2 3 2 - 4 3 3 1 - tmp - hp - str   Universal
  From the composer's String quartet no.2.

Petite suite (arr. Glazunov)   24'
  *3 2 2 2 - 4 2 3 0 - tmp+1 - str   Breitkopf;
  Two of the flutists double on piccolo.   Kalmus; Leduc

Petite suite (arr. Glazunov): Scherzo and Nocturne
  *3 2 2 2 - 4 2 3 0 - tmp - str   Luck

Prince Igor: Overture   10'
  *3 2 2 2 - 4 2 3 1 - tmp - str   Kalmus
  Completed and orchestrated by Glazunov.

Prince Igor: Polovtsian dances   14'
  optional chorus   Fischer, C.;
  *3 *2 2 2 - 4 2 3 1 - tmp+5 - hp - str   Kalmus;
  Nos.8 and 17 from the opera.   Schirmer, G.

Prince Igor: Polovtsian march   5'
  optional chorus   Belaieff
  *3 2 2 2 - 4 2 3 1 - tmp+4 - str -
    optional backstage brass (4 2 0 1) and snare drum
  Orchestrated by Rimsky-Korsakov. This work may be
  out of print, but orchestral materials are in the
  Fleisher Collection.

Symphony no.1, E-flat major   33'
  2 *2 2 2 - 4 2 3 0 - tmp - str   Breitkopf; Kalmus;
                                            Leduc; Universal

Symphony no.2, B minor   28'
  *3 2 2 2 - 4 2 3 1 - tmp+4 -   Breitkopf; Kalmus;
    hp - str   Leduc; Universal

Symphony no.3, A minor   16'
  2 2 2 2 - 4 2 3 0 - tmp - str   Belaieff;
                                            Kalmus; Leduc

        BOULEZ, PIERRE, 1925-

Le marteau sans maître   35'
  alto voice, alto flute, xylorimba,   Universal
    vibraphone, guitar, 1 percussionist

Le soleil des eaux   10'
  chorus - solos STB   Heugel
  *2 *2 *2 2 - 3 2 1 1 - tmp+2 - hp - str 12.10.8.8.6

BOYCE, WILLIAM, 1710-1779

Concerto grosso, B minor   9'
  solos: 2 violins, violoncello   Eulenburg;
  str, cnt   Hinrichsen
  Hinrichsen edition gives title as "Double concerto."

Overture: Ode for his majesty's birthday (1769)   7'
  0 2 0 1 - 2 0 0 0 - str, cnt   Galaxy
  Score only available in the collection *Musica
  Britannica*, v.13, p.1. Parts available from Galaxy.

Overture: Ode for the new year (1758)   4'
  0 2 0 1 - 0 2 0 0 - tmp - str, cnt   Galaxy
  Score only available in the collection *Musica
  Britannica*, v.13, p.103. Parts available from Galaxy.

Overture: Ode for the new year (1772)   4'
  0 2 0 1 - str, cnt   Galaxy
  Score only available in the collection *Musica
  Britannica*, v.13, p.55. Parts available from Galaxy.

Overture: Peleus and Thetis   7'
  0 2 0 1 - str, cnt   Galaxy
  Score only available in the collection *Musica
  Britannica*, v.13, p.131. Parts available from Galaxy.

Symphony no.1, B-flat major   9'
  2 2 0 1 - str   Doblinger; Oxford

Symphony no.2, A major   8'
  0 2 0 1 - str   Doblinger; Oxford

Symphony no.3, C major   9'
  0 2 0 1 - str   Doblinger; Oxford

Symphony no.4, F major   6'
  0 2 0 2 - 2 0 0 0 - str   Doblinger; Oxford

Symphony no.5, D major   10'
  0 2 0 1 - 0 2 0 0 - tmp - str   Doblinger; Oxford

Symphony no.6, F major   8'
  0 2 0 1 - str   Doblinger; Oxford

Symphony no.7, B-flat major   11'
  2 2 0 1 - str   Doblinger; Oxford

Symphony no.8, D minor   11'
  2 2 0 1 - str   Doblinger; Oxford

BRAHMS, JOHANNES, 1833-1897

Academic festival overture, op.80   10'
  *3 2 2 *3 - 4 3 3 1 - tmp+3 - str   Breitkopf; Kalmus

Alto rhapsody, op.53   13'
  alto solo - male chorus   Fischer, C.; Gray;
  2 2 2 2 - 2 0 0 0 - str   Kalmus; Peters

Concerto, piano, no.1, op.15, D minor   44'
  2 2 2 2 - 4 2 0 0 - tmp - str   Breitkopf; Kalmus

Concerto, piano, no.2, op.83, B-flat major   44'
  2 2 2 2 - 4 2 0 0 - tmp - str   Breitkopf; Kalmus

Concerto, violin, op.77, D major   38'
  2 2 2 2 - 4 2 0 0 - tmp - str   Breitkopf; Kalmus

Concerto, violin and violoncello, op.102,
  A minor ("Double")   32'
  2 2 2 2 - 4 2 0 0 - tmp - str   Breitkopf; Kalmus

Ein deutsches Requiem, op.45 (German requiem) 75'
  chorus - soprano and baritone solos   Breitkopf;
  *3 2 2 *3 - 4 2 3 1 - tmp - org - 2 or   Kalmus;
    more hp dbl a single part - str   Peters
  (Contrabassoon and organ are optional.)

Hungarian dances nos.1, 3, 10 (arr. Brahms) 3', 2', 2'
  *3 2 2 2 - 4 2 0 0 - tmp+2 - str   Breitkopf; Kalmus

Hungarian dances nos.2, 7 (arr. Andreas Hallén) 3', 2'
  2 2 2 2 - 4 2 3 0 - tmp+1 - str   Kalmus; Simrock

Hungarian dances nos.5, 6 (arr. A. Parlow) 3', 4'
  *2 2 2 2 - 4 2 3 0 - tmp - str   Luck

Hungarian dances nos.5, 6, 7 (arr. Schmeling)   3', 4', 2'
  *3 2 2 2 - 4 2 3 0 - tmp+3 - str   Breitkopf; Luck

Hungarian dances nos.11-16 (arr. Parlow)   ca. 2' each
  *3 2 2 2 - 4 2 3 0 - tmp - hp - str   Kalmus; Simrock

Hungarian dances nos.17-21 (arr. Dvořák)   ca. 2' each
  *2 2 2 2 - 4 2 3 0 - tmp+3 - str   Kalmus; Simrock
  (Optional harp in no.21.)

Liebeslieder waltzes, op.52 (arr. Friedrich Hermann)   25'
  str   Kalmus; Luck; Simrock

Nänie, op.82   14'
  chorus   Breitkopf;
  2 2 2 2 - 2 0 3 0 - tmp - hp - str   Kalmus;
  (Harp should be doubled if possible.)   Peters

Rinaldo, op.50   45'
  tenor solo - male chorus   Luck;
  *3 2 2 2 - 2 2 3 0 - tmp - str   Simrock

Schicksalslied, op.54 (Song of destiny)   18'
  chorus   Breitkopf;
  2 2 2 2 - 2 2 3 0 - tmp - str   Kalmus; Simrock

Serenade no.1, op.11, D major   40'
  2 2 2 2 - 4 2 0 0 - tmp - str   Breitkopf; Kalmus

Serenade no.2, op.16, A major   32'
  *3 2 2 2 - 2 0 0 0 - str (without vn) Breitkopf; Kalmus

Symphony no.1, op.68, C minor   44'
  2 2 2 *3 - 4 2 3 0 - tmp - str   Breitkopf; Kalmus

Symphony no.2, op.73, D major   42'
  2 2 2 2 - 4 2 3 1 - tmp - str   Breitkopf; Kalmus

Symphony no.3, op.90, F major   36'
  2 2 2 *3 - 4 2 3 0 - tmp - str   Breitkopf; Kalmus

Symphony no.4, op.98, E minor   42'
  *2 2 2 *3 - 4 2 3 0 - tmp+1 - str   Breitkopf; Kalmus

Tragic overture, op.81   13'
  *3 2 2 2 - 4 2 3 1 - tmp - str   Breitkopf; Kalmus

Variations on a theme by Haydn   17'
  *3 2 2 *3 - 4 2 0 0 - tmp+1 - str   Breitkopf;
  A critical edition of the score is available   Kalmus
  from Norton.

   BRANT, HENRY, 1913-

Angels and devils   18'
  solo flute - accompanied by a flute orchestra   MCA
    consisting of 3pic, 5fl, 2afl

Galaxy 2   5'
  *1 0 1 0 - 2 1 1 0 - tmp+1   MCA

Verticals ascending (after the Rodia Towers)   8'
  *2 2 *3 2 - 2 2 1 1 - opt asx - tmp+1 -   MCA
    pf, opt electric org
  One of the clarinetists doubles on alto clarinet.
  Alternate version substitutes violins for organ
  and/or violas and violoncellos for saxophone.
  Instruments divided into two widely separated
  groups, each with its own conductor.

   BRITTEN, BENJAMIN, 1913-1976

Canadian carnival, op.19   14'
  *2 *2 2 2 - 4 3(or2) 3 1 - tmp+2 - hp - str   Boosey

Cantata academica, Carmen Basiliense, op.62   21'
  chorus - solos SATB   Boosey
  *2 2 2 2 - 4 2 3 1 - tmp+4 - 1 or 2hp, pf (dbl
    opt cel) - str

Cantata misericordium, op.69   20'
  chorus - solos TB -   Boosey
  pf, hp, tmp - str - solo string quartet

Concerto, piano, no.1, op.13   33'
  *2 *2 2 2 - 4 2 3 1 - tmp+2 - hp - str   Boosey

Concerto, violin, no.1, op.15   31'
  *3 *2 2 2 - 4 3 3 1 - tmp+2 - hp - str   Boosey

Diversions on a theme, op.21   23'
  solo piano (left hand)   Boosey
  *2 *2 +2 *3 - 4 2 3 1 - asx - tmp+3 - hp - str
  (Saxophone, contrabassoon, and one percussionist
  are optional.)

Gloriana: Symphonic suite   26'
  optional tenor solo   Boosey
  *3 *3 *3 *3 - 4 3 3 1 - tmp+4 - hp - str

Gloriana: Courtly dances   9'
  2 2 2 2 - 4 2 3 1 - tmp+2 - str   Boosey

Les illuminations, op.18   21'
  high voice - str   Boosey

Matinées musicales, op.24 (after Rossini)   13'
  *2 2 2 2 - 2 2 3 0 - tmp+2 - hp(or pf),   Boosey
    cel (or pf) - str

Nocturne, op.60   25'
  solo tenor   Boosey
  1 *1 1 1 - 1 0 0 0 - tmp - hp - str

Paul Bunyan: Overture   5'
  *2 1 *3 1 - 2 2 2 1 - tmp+3 - (opt hp, pf) - str   Faber
  Orchestrated by Colin Matthews.

Peter Grimes: Four sea interludes   15'
  *2 2 +2 *3 - 4 3 3 1 - tmp+3 - hp - str   Boosey

Peter Grimes: Passacaglia   7'
  *2 2 2 *3 - 4 3 3 1 - tmp+3 - hp, cel - str   Boosey

Phaedra, op.93   15'
  mezzo-soprano solo   Faber
  hpsd - tmp, 2perc - str

The prince of the pagodas: Pas de six   12'
  *3 *3 +3 *3 - 4 3 3 1 - tmp+2 - hp, pf - str   Boosey
  Cued so that performance is possible with
  double woodwind.

Saint Nicolas, op.42   50'
   tenor solo, 4 boy sopranos - chorus,   Boosey
     semi-chorus of female voices
   pf 4-hands, org - tmp (+2perc opt) - str

Scottish ballade, op.26   13'
   2 solo pianos   Boosey
   *2 2 2 *3 - 4 2 3 1 - tmp+2 - hp - str
   (Contrabassoon is optional.)

Serenade for tenor, horn, and strings, op.31   24'
   solo tenor - solo horn - str   Boosey

Simple symphony, op.4   16'
   str   Oxford

Sinfonia da requiem, op.20   20'
   =3 *3 =3 *3 - 6 3 3 1 - asx - tmp+4 -   Boosey
     2hp, pf - str
   (The following instruments are optional: afl,
   asx, hn 5 and 6, 2nd hp, 4th perc.)

Sinfonietta, op.1   15'
   1 1 1 1 - 1 0 0 0 - str quintet (or small   Boosey
     str orchestra)

Soirées musicales, op.9 (after Rossini)   11'
   *2 2 2 2 - 4 2 3 0 - tmp+3 - hp(or pf) - str   Boosey
   Playable with the following reduced instrumentation:
     1 1 1 0 - 0 1 1 0 - 2perc - hp(or pf) - str

Spring symphony, op.44   45'
   chorus, boy chorus - solos SAT   Boosey
   =3 *3 *3 *3 - 4 3 3 1 - cow horn - tmp+4 - 2hp - str

Suite on English folk tunes, op.90 ("A time there was...")
   *2 *2 2 2 - 2 2 0 0 - tmp+2 - hp - str   14'
                                     Faber

Symphony for violoncello and orchestra, op.68   33'
   *2 2 *2 *2 - 2 2 1 1 - tmp+2 - str   Boosey

Variations on a theme of Frank Bridge   25'
   str   Boosey

War requiem, op.66   85'
  chorus, boys' choir - solos STB   Boosey
  *4 *4 =4 *4 - 7 4 3 1 - tmp+5 - hp, pf, org - str
  A second conductor is required for the separate
  chamber orchestra, the instrumentation of which
  is included above.

Young person's guide to the orchestra, op.34   18'
  optional speaker   Boosey
  *3 2 2 2 - 4 2 3 1 - tmp+5 - hp - str

   BROWN, EARLE, 1926-

Available forms 1   variable duration
  1 1 =3 1 - 1 1 1 0 - tmp+1 - hp, pf -   AMP
   2vn, va, vc, db

Available forms 2   variable duration
  =4 *3 =4 *3 - 6 3 4 2 - bass tp - tmp+3   AMP
   2hp, pf/cel, gtr - str 16.14.12.10.8
  Two conductors are required.

   BRUBECK, HOWARD, 1916-

Dialogues for jazz combo and orchestra   23'
  *2 *2 2 2 - 4 3 3 1 - tmp+2 - str   Shawnee
  The jazz combo may be varied in instrumentation.
  The length of the solo sections may be varied.

   BRUCH, MAX, 1838-1920

Adagio appassionato, op.57   8'
  solo violin   Fischer, C.;
  2 2 2 2 - 4 2 3 0 - tmp - str   Kalmus; Simrock

Ave Maria, op.61   4'
  solo violoncello   Simrock
  2 2 2 2 - 4 2 3 0 - tmp - str
  This work may be out of print, but orchestral
  materials are in the Fleisher Collection.

Concerto, violin, no.1, op.26, G minor   25'
  2 2 2 2 - 4 2 0 0 - tmp - str   Kalmus; Peters

Concerto, violin, no.2, D minor   25'
  2 2 2 2 - 4 2 3 0 - tmp - str   Fischer, C.; Kalmus

Concerto, violin, no.3, op.58, D minor   34'
  2 2 2 2 - 4 2 3 0 - tmp - str   Kalmus

Kol nidrei, op.47   10'
  solo violoncello   Fischer, C.;
  2 2 2 2 - 4 2 3 0 - tmp - str   Kalmus

Loreley: Prelude   7'
  2 2 2 2 - 4 2 3 0 - tmp - hp - str   Luck
  Adapted by George Dasch.

Scottish fantasy, op.46   30'
  solo violin   Kalmus
  2 2 2 2 - 4 2 3 1 - tmp+2 - hp - str

Serenade, op.75, A minor   37'
  solo violin   Kalmus;
  2 2 2 2 - 4 2 3 0 - tmp - str   Simrock

Swedish dances, op.63, nos.1-7 (Series 1)   12'
  *2 *2 2 2 - 4 2 3 0 - tmp+1 - str   Kalmus; Luck

Swedish dances, op.63, nos.8-15 (Series 2)   11'
  2 *2 2 2 - 4 2 3 1 - tmp+1 - str   Kalmus; Luck

Symphony no.1, op.28, E-flat major   35'
  2 2 2 2 - 4 2 3 0 - tmp - str
  This work is probably out of print, but orchestral
  materials are in the Fleisher Collection.

Symphony no.3, op.51, E major   36'
  2 2 2 2 - 4 3 3 1 - tmp - str   Breitkopf

    BRUCKNER, ANTON, 1824-1896

Helgoland   14'
  male chorus   Bärenreiter;
  2 2 2 2 - 4 3 3 1 - tmp+1 - str   Bruckner Verlag;
                                                        Universal

March in D minor   4'
  2 2 2 2 - 2 2 3 0 - tmp - str   Doblinger;
  Published with his "Three pieces for   Eulenburg
  orchestra," q.v. The Eulenburg version uses
  the collective title "Four orchestral pieces."

Mass, C major (1841)
  chorus   Kalmus
  2hn - org - str

Mass no.1, D minor   43'
  chorus - solos SATB   Bruckner Verlag
  2 2 2 2 - 2 2 3 0 - tmp - str

Mass no.2, E minor   37'
  chorus   Bruckner Verlag
  0 2 2 2 - 4 2 3 0

Mass no.3, F minor ("Great")   60'
  chorus - solos SATB   Bruckner Verlag
  2 2 2 2 - 2 2 3 0 - tmp - str

Missa solemnis, B-flat minor   31'
  chorus - solos SATB   Bruckner Verlag
  0 2 0 2 - 2 2 3 0 - tmp - org - str

Overture, G minor   12'
  *2 2 2 2 - 2 2 3 0 - tmp - str   Universal
  A posthumous work, ed. Jos. V. Wöss.

Psalm 150   9'
  chorus   Bruckner Verlag
  2 2 2 2 - 4 3 3 1 - tmp - str

Requiem, D minor   37'
  chorus - solos SATB   Bruckner Verlag
  0 0 0 0 - 1 0 3 0 - org - str

Symphonies

    *There exist over thirty different versions of the
eleven Bruckner symphonies (nine numbered plus two
early works). This is due to the following factors:*
    *(1) Bruckner made revisions of almost all the
        symphonies.*
    *(2) Well-meaning colleagues (principally Ferdinand
        Löwe, Franz Schalk, and Josef Schalk) tampered*

> *with the scores, in an attempt to make them*
> *more palatable to the public.*
> *(3) After the Bruckner Society had produced its*
> *definitive editions in the 1930's and 40's,*
> *mostly under the editorship of Robert Haas,*
> *Haas was deposed for political reasons, and*
> *his successor, Leopold Nowak, re-edited all*
> *the symphonies himself.*

The best guide through this morass is Deryck Cooke's
pamphlet, The Bruckner problem simplified, *available*
from The Musical Newsletter, 654 Madison Avenue,
Suite 1703, New York, NY 10021.
The following listings give Cooke's recommendations
and mention other more or less reasonable alternatives.
Versions not mentioned below may be considered unac-
ceptable.

Symphony in F minor (Studiensymphonie)   47'
  2 2 2 2 - 4 2 3 0 - tmp - str   Bruckner Verlag
  Ed. Nowak.

Symphony no.0, D minor ("Die Nullte")   43'
  2 2 2 2 - 4 2 3 0 - tmp - str   Bruckner Verlag
  Ed. Nowak.

Symphony no.1, C minor (Linz version, 1866)   48'
  3 2 2 2 - 4 2 3 0 - tmp - str   Bruckner Verlag
  Haas edition and Nowak edition are equally
  acceptable. *Alternative:* Vienna version,
  1891, ed. Haas.

Symphony no.2, C minor (original version, 1872)   65'
  2 2 2 2 - 4 2 3 0 - tmp - str   Bruckner Verlag
  Ed. Haas. *Alternative:* Bruckner-Herbeck
  revision, 1876, ed. Nowak.

Symphony no.3, D minor (first definitive version, 1877)
  2 2 2 2 - 4 3 3 0 - tmp - str   60'
  Ed. Fritz Oeser. *Alternative:*   Bruckner Verlag
  Bruckner-Schalk revision, 1889, ed. Nowak.

Symphony no.4, E-flat major, "Romantic"
  (first definitive version, 1880)   60'
  2 2 2 2 - 4 3 3 1 - tmp - str   Bruckner Verlag
  Ed. Haas. *Alternative:* revised version,
  1886, ed. Nowak; this version has the return

of the opening horn motive at the end of the
work. NB: the title page of this score misleadingly
identifies it as the 1878/80 version; thus in ordering
materials, specify Nowak, 1878/80 (to distinguish it
from the Nowak edition of a preliminary 1874 version).

Symphony no.5, B-flat major (definitive version, 1876) 80'
   2 2 2 2 - 4 3 3 1 - tmp - str   Bruckner Verlag
   Haas edition and Nowak edition are equally
   acceptable.

Symphony no.6, A major (definitive version, 1881)   60'
   2 2 2 2 - 4 3 3 1 - tmp - str   Bruckner Verlag
   Haas edition and Nowak edition are equally
   acceptable.

Symphony no.7, E major (definitive version, 1883)   65'
   2 2 2 2 - 4 3 3 1 - 4 Wagner tubas -   Bruckner Verlag
     tmp - str
   Ed. Haas. (The Nowak edition of this work
   includes a number of tempo modifications
   attributed to conductor Arthur Nikisch.)

Symphony no.8, C minor (1887/90, ed. Haas)   80'
   3 3 3 *3 - 8 3 3 1 - tmp+2 -   Bruckner Verlag
     hp, preferably tripled - str
   Horns 5-8 double on Wagner tubas.
   This edition is based on the revised version of
   1890, but with material restored from the original
   version of 1887. *Alternative:* Bruckner-Schalk
   revision, 1890, without the restored material,
   ed. Nowak.

Symphony no.9, D minor (unfinished, 1896)   60'
   3 3 3 3 - 8 3 3 1 - tmp - str   Bruckner Verlag
   Horns 5-8 double on Wagner tubas.
   Alfred Orel edition and Nowak edition are
   equally acceptable.

Te deum   22'
   chorus - solos SATB   Peters
   2 2 2 2 - 4 3 3 1 - tmp - (opt org) - str

Three pieces for orchestra   9'
   2 2 2 2 - 2 2 1 0 - tmp - str   Doblinger;
   Published with his "March in D minor,"   Eulenburg

q.v. The Eulenburg version uses the collective
title "Four orchestral pieces."

BUSONI, FERRUCCIO, 1866-1924

Concertino, clarinet and chamber orchestra, op.48   9'
  0 2 0 2 - 2 0 0 0 - 1perc - str   Breitkopf

Concerto, piano, op.39   63'
  *4 *3 *3 3 - 4 3 3 1 - tmp+2 - str   Breitkopf;
  (Optional unseen male chorus (48 voices) in   Luck
  final movement.) Two of the flutists double
  on piccolo.

Divertimento, flute and chamber orchestra, op.52   8'
  0 2 2 2 - 2 2 0 0 - tmp+1 - str   Breitkopf

Indianische Fantasie, op.44   28'
  solo piano   Breitkopf
  2 *2 2 2 - 3 2 0 0 - tmp+3 - hp - str

Lustspiel overture, op.38   8'
  *3 2 2 2 - 4 2 0 0 - tmp+2 - str   Breitkopf

Rondo arlecchinesco (Harlekins Reigen), op.46   12'
  tenor voice backstage   Breitkopf
  *2 1 2 2 - 3 2 3 0 - tmp+3 - str

Turandot: Suite, op.41   39'
  *3 *3 *3 *3 - 4 4 3 1 - tmp+4 - hp - str   Breitkopf
  (Optional women's chorus in one movement.)

BUXTEHUDE, DIETRICH, ca.1637-1707

Four chorale preludes (arr. Gordon Binkerd)   20'
  *2 *2 2 2 - 3 3 3 1 - str   AMP
    Contents--Gelobet seist du, Jesu Christ; Puer natus
  in Bethlehem; Nun komm der Heiden Heiland; Wie schön
  leuchtet der Morgenstern.

Magnificat   14'
  chorus   Kalmus;
  str, cnt   Presser

Das neugebor'ne Kindelein
  chorus - str, cnt   Kalmus

CADMAN, CHARLES WAKEFIELD, 1881-1946

American suite   10'
  str   Luck

Oriental rhapsody from Omar Khayyam   9'
  *3 2 2 2 - 4 2 3 1 - tmp+2 - hp - str
  This work is out of print, but orchestral materials
  are in the Fleisher Collection.

CAGE, JOHN, 1912-

Atlas eclipticalis   variable duration
  3 3 3 3 - 5 3 3 3 - 3tmp, 9perc - 3hp -   Peters
    str 12.12.9.9.3
  (The instrumentation given is the maximum, but not
  all instruments need be used. The work may be played
  in whole or part in any ensemble, chamber or orchestral.)

CANNING, THOMAS, 1911-

Fantasy on a hymn by Justin Morgan   10'
  2 solo string quartets and string orchestra Fischer, C.

CARPENTER, JOHN ALDEN, 1876-1951

Adventures in a perambulator   26'
  *3 *3 *3 2 - 4 2 3 1 - tmp+4 - hp, cel,   Schirmer, G.
    pf - str

Sea drift   17'
  2 *2 2 2 - 4 3 3 1 - tmp+2 - hp, cel,   Schirmer, G.
    pf - str

Skyscrapers   28'
  optional chorus   Schirmer, G.
  *3 *3 *3 *3 - 4 4 3 1 - 3sx (covering soprano, alto,
    tenor, baritone) - tmp+5 - pf, cel/pf, banjo - str
  Duration with authorized concert cuts: 15'

CARTER, ELLIOTT, 1908-

Concerto for orchestra 23'
 *3 *3 =3 *3 - 4 3 3 1 - tmp+7 - hp, pf - str AMP

Double concerto, harpsichord and piano 23'
 *1 1 +1 1 - 2 1 1 0 - 4perc - vn, va, vc, db AMP
 Two conductors are recommended.

Holiday overture 10'
 *3 *3 *3 *3 - 4 3 3 1 - tmp+4 - pf - str AMP

The minotaur: Ballet suite 25'
 *2 *2 *2 2 - 4 2 2 0 - tmp+3 - pf - str AMP

Symphony no.1 (1942/54) 27'
 *2 2 +1 2 - 2 2 1 0 - tmp - str AMP

Variations for orchestra 24'
 *2 2 2 2 - 4 2 3 1 - tmp+3 - hp - str AMP

CASELLA, ALFREDO, 1883-1947

Italia, op.11 19'
 *3 *3 =4 *4 - 4 4 3 1 - tmp+6 - 2hp - str Universal

Paganiniana, op.65 19'
 *2 *2 *3 2 - 4 2 1 1 - tmp+2 - str Universal

CASTELNUOVO-TEDESCO, MARIO, 1895-1968

Concerto, guitar, op.99, D major 21'
 1 1 2 1 - 1 0 0 0 - tmp - str 2.2.2.2.1 Schott

CHABRIER, EMMANUEL, 1841-1894

Bourée fantasque (arr. Felix Mottl) 5'
 *3 *3 2 4 - 4 3 3 1 - tmp+4 - 2hp - str Kalmus

España   8'
  *3 2 2 4 - 4 4 3 1 - tmp+4 - 2hp - str   Kalmus

Gwendolyn: Overture   9'
  *3 *3 *3 3 - 4 4 3 1 - tmp+3 - 2hp - str   Kalmus

Habanera   4'
  2 1 2 1 - 2 2 0 0 - tmp+1 - str   Kalmus

Joyeuse marche   4'
  *3 2 2 4 - 4 4 3 1 - tmp+4 - hp - str   Kalmus

Le roi malgré lui: Danse slav   5'
  *2 2 2 2 - 2 2 3 0 - tmp+3 - str   Kalmus

Le roi malgré lui: Fête polonaise   10'
  *2 2 2 2 - 2 2 3 0 - tmp+3 - str   Kalmus

Suite pastorale   18'
  *2 1 2 2 - 2 2 3 0 - tmp+3 - (opt hp) - str   Kalmus

CHADWICK, GEORGE WHITEFIELD, 1854-1931

Melpomene; dramatic overture   12'
  *3 *2 2 2 - 4 2 3 1 - tmp+1 - str   Kalmus

Rip van Winkle: Overture   10'
  *3 2 2 2 - 4 2 3 1 - tmp+1 - str   Fischer, C.

Symphonic sketches   31'
  *3 *2 *3 2 - 4 2 3 0 - tmp+4 - hp - str   Schirmer, G.

Symphony no.2, B-flat major   30'
  2 2 2 2 - 4 2 3 0 - tmp - str
  Score published by Da Capo Press. Parts are
  out of print, but a set is in the Fleisher
  Collection.

Tam O'Shanter   18'
  *3 *3 =4 2 - 4 3 3 1 - tmp+4 - hp - str   Schirmer, G.
  This work may be out of print, but orchestral
  materials are in the Fleisher Collection.

CHAMINADE, CECILE, 1857-1944

Concertino, flute, op.107, D major   8'
  1 2 2 2 - 4 0 3 1 - tmp - hp - str   Boosey;
  Kalmus lists title incorrectly as "Concerto."   Kalmus

CHARPENTIER, GUSTAVE, 1860-1956

Impressions d'Italie   32'
  *3 *3 *3 4 - 4 4 3 1 - asx (dbl opt ssx) -   Heugel;
  tmp+4 - 2hp - str   Kalmus

CHARPENTIER, MARC-ANTOINE, 1634-1704

Te deum   23'
  chorus - solos SSATB   Heugel;
  2 *3 0 1 - 0 1 0 0 - tmp - str, cnt   Universal

CHAUSSON, ERNEST, 1855-1899

Poème de l'amour et de la mer, op.19   22'
  solo voice   Rouart
  2 2 2 2 - 2 2 3 0 - tmp - hp - str
  Available in 2 keys: G for high voice,
  and F for medium voice.

Poème, op.25   16'
  solo violin   AMP; Breitkopf;
  2 2 2 2 - 4 2 3 1 - tmp - hp - str   Kalmus

Symphony, op.20, B-flat major   34'
  *3 *3 *3 3 - 4 4 3 1 - tmp - 2hp - str Kalmus; Salabert

CHÁVEZ, CARLOS, 1899-1978

Concerto, piano   33'
  *3 *3 2 *3 - 4 2 3 1 - tmp+3 - hp, cel -   Schirmer, G.
  str

The daughter of Colchis (La hija de Colquide)   24'
  *3 *3 =4 3 - 4 3 3 1 - tmp+3 - hp - str   Belwin

Resonancias   15'
  *3 *3 *3 *3 - 4 2 3 1 - tmp+3 - str   Belwin

Symphony no.1 (Sinfonia de Antigona)   11'
  =3 *2 =4 3 - 8 3 0 1 - heckelphone -   Schirmer, G.
    tmp+3 - 2hp - str

Symphony no.2 (Sinfonia India)   12'
  *4 3 =4 3 - 4 2 2 0 - tmp+4 - hp - str   Schirmer, G.
  Numerous Indian instruments required for
  percussion section.

Symphony no.3   26'
  *3 *3 =4 *3 - 4 3 3 1 - tmp+3 - hp - str   Boosey

Symphony no.4 (Sinfonia romantica)   21'
  *3 *3 2 *3 - 4 2 3 1 - tmp+3 - str   Boosey

Symphony no.5   18'
  str   Belwin

Toccata for percussion   14'
  6perc   Belwin

Xochipilli   6'
  *2 0 +1 0 - 0 0 1 0 - 6perc   Belwin

CHERUBINI, LUIGI, 1760-1842

Abenceragen: Overture   9'
  2 2 2 2 - 4 2 3 0 - tmp - str   Breitkopf; Kalmus

Ali Baba: Overture   7'
  *2 2 2 2 - 4 4 3 1 - tmp+3 - str   Bärenreiter;
     Breitkopf; Kalmus

Anacreon: Overture   9'
  *2 2 2 2 - 4 2 3 0 - tmp - str   Breitkopf; Kalmus

Démophoon: Overture   10'
  2 2 2 2 - 2 2 3 0 - tmp - str   Suvini
  Ed. Pietro Spada.

Les deux journées: Overture   8'
  2 2 2 2 - 4 0 1 0 - tmp - str   Breitkopf;
  Also known as "Der Wasserträger," or   Kalmus
  "The water carrier."

Faniska: Overture   8'
  2 2 2 2 - 2 2 1 0 - tmp - str   Breitkopf; Ricordi

Medea: Overture   9'
  2 2 2 2 - 4 0 0 0 - tmp - str   Bärenreiter;
                                              Breitkopf; Kalmus

The Portuguese Inn: Overture   8'
  2 2 2 2 - 2 2 1 0 - tmp - str   Breitkopf; Kalmus

Requiem, C minor   44'
  chorus   Breitkopf; Kalmus;
  0 2 2 2 - 2 2 3 0 - tmp - str   Peters; Schirmer, G.

Requiem, D minor   45'
  male chorus   Kalmus; Peters
  *2 2 2 2 - 4 2 3 0 - tmp - str

The water carrier
  See his: Les deux journées

CHOPIN, FRÉDÉRIC, 1810-1849

Chopiniana (piano works orchestrated by Glazunov)
  See under: Glazunov, Alexander, 1865-1936

Concert-allegro (Allegro de concert), op.46   20'
  solo piano   Fischer, C.;
  2 2 2 2 - 4 2 3 0 - tmp - str   Kalmus; PWM
  Arr. J. L. Nicodé.

Concerto, piano, no.1, op.11, E minor   35'
  2 2 2 2 - 4 2 1 0 - tmp - str   Breitkopf; Kalmus; PWM

Concerto, piano, no.2, op.21, F minor   30'
  2 2 2 2 - 2 2 1 0 - tmp - str   Breitkopf; Kalmus; PWM

Fantasy on Polish airs, op.13   15'
  solo piano   Breitkopf;
  2 2 2 2 - 2 2 0 0 - tmp - str   Kalmus; PWM

Grande polonaise, op.22   10'
  solo piano   Breitkopf;
  2 2 2 2 - 2 0 1 0 - tmp - str   Kalmus;
  Preceded by an "Andante spianato" for unaccom- PWM
  panied piano (3'), for a total duration of 13'.

Krakowiak, op.14   14'
  solo piano   Breitkopf;
  2 2 2 2 - 2 2 0 0 - tmp - str   Kalmus; PWM

Mazurka no.7, F-sharp minor (arr. Balakirev)   2'
  str   Kalmus

Polonaise, op.40, no.1 (arr. Glazunov)   4'
  *3 2 2 2 - 4 2 3 0 - tmp+3 - str   Kalmus; Luck

Romanze   8'
  solo violin   Kalmus
  2 0 2 2 - 2 0 0 0 - tmp - str
  Paraphrase by August Wilhelmj of the slow movement
  of Chopin's first piano concerto.

Les sylphides (arr. Glazunov)   20'
  2 2 2 2 - 4 2 0 0 - tmp+3 - hp - str   Kalmus
    Contents--Prelude, op.28 no.7; Nocturne, op.32 no.2;
  Valse, op.70 no.1; Mazurka, op.33 no.2; Mazurka, op.
  67 no.3; Prelude, op.28 no.7 (repeated); Valse, op.64
  no.2; Grande valse brillante, op.18.

Variations on "La ci darem la mano," op.2   14'
  solo piano   Breitkopf;
  2 2 2 2 - 2 0 0 0 - tmp - str   Kalmus; PWM

   CHOU WEN-CHUNG, 1923-

All in the spring wind   8'
  *2 *2 *2 *2 - 2 2 2 1 - tmp+3 - hp, pf/cel - str Peters

And the fallen petals   10'
  *2 *2 *3 2 - 4 2 3 1 - tmp+2 - hp, cel - str   Peters

Landscapes   8'
  *2 *2 0 0 - 2 0 2 0 - tmp+1 - hp - str   Peters

Pien; chamber concerto   14'
  solo piano   Peters
  +2 *1 1 1 - 1 2 2 0 - 4perc

Soliloquy of a bhiksuni   5'
  solo trumpet   Peters
  4hn, 3tbn, tuba - tmp+2

Yü ko   5'
  +1 *1 *1 0 - 0 0 2 0 - 2perc - pf - vn   Peters

   CIMAROSA, DOMENICO, 1749-1801

Concerto (concertante), 2 flutes, G major   18'
  0 2 0 1 - 2 0 0 0 - str   Bote; Southern

Concerto, oboe, C minor   10'
  str   Boosey
  Freely adapted by Arthur Benjamin from piano
  sonatas of Cimarosa.

Il maestro di cappella: Overture   4'
  2 2 0 2 - 2 0 0 0 - tmp - str   Carisch; Ricordi

Il matrimonio segreto: Overture   8'
  2 2 2 2 - 2 2 0 0 - tmp - str   Carisch; Kalmus

Sinfonia, D major   8'
  1 2 0 0 - 2 0 0 0 - str   Zanibon

I traci amanti: Overture   7'
  0 2 0 1 - 2 0 0 0 - str   Zanibon

   CLARKE, JEREMIAH, ca.1673-1707

The prince of Denmark's march
  See: Purcell, Henry, ca.1659-1695
       Trumpet prelude (Trumpet voluntary)

   CLEMENTI, MUZIO, 1752-1832

Symphony no.1, C major   25'
  2 2 2 2 - 2 2 3 0 - tmp - str   Suvini
  Ed. Pietro Spada.

Symphony no.2, D major   35'
   2 2 2 2 - 2 2 3 0 - tmp - str   Suvini
   Ed. Pietro Spada.

Symphony no.3, G major ("Great national symphony")   35'
   2 2 2 2 - 2 2 3 0 - tmp - str   Suvini
   Ed. Pietro Spada.

Symphony no.4, D major   30'
   2 2 2 2 - 2 2 3 0 - tmp - str   Suvini
   Ed. Pietro Spada.

COATES, ERIC, 1886-1957

London suite   13'
   *2 *3 *3 2 - 4 3 3 0 - tmp+4 - hp - str   Chappell; Luck

COLERIDGE-TAYLOR, SAMUEL, 1875-1912

The bamboula (Rhapsodic dance no.1)   8'
   *3 2 2 2 - 4 2 3 1 - tmp+3 - str   Boosey

Christmas overture   5'
   2 1 2 2 - 2 2 3 0 - tmp+2 - hp - str   Boosey; Luck

Danse nègre, op.35, no.4   6'
   *3 2 2 2 - 4 2 3 0 - tmp+3 - str   Luck

Hiawatha: Suite from the ballet music, op.82a   18'
   *2 2 2 2 - 4 2 3 1 - tmp+4 - hp - str   Luck
     Contents--The wooing; The marriage feast; Bird
   scene; Conjuror's dance; The departure; Reunion.

Petite suite de concert, op.77   15'
   *3 2 2 2 - 4 2 3 0 - tmp+3 - str   Boosey
     Contents--Le caprice de Nannette; Demande et
   réponse; Un sonnet d'amour; Le tarantelle frétillante.

The song of Hiawatha, op.30

   1. Hiawatha's wedding feast   31'
     chorus - solo tenor   Gray; Kalmus
     *3 2 2 2 - 4 2 3 1 - tmp+3 - hp - str   Luck

2. The death of Minnehaha   40'
   chorus - solos SB   Gray; Kalmus
   *3 2 2 2 - 4 2 3 1 - tmp+2 - hp - str   Luck

3. Hiawatha's departure   40'
   chorus - solos STB   Gray;
   *3 2 2 2 - 4 2 3 1 - tmp+2 - hp, (opt org) - str   Luck

COLGRASS, MICHAEL, 1932-

As quiet as...   14'
   =3 *3 *3 3 - 4 3 3 1 - tmp+3 - 2hp -   MCA
   pf/cel/hpsd (1 player) - str 12.10.8.8.4

Déjà vu   18'
   solo percussion quartet   Fischer, C.
   =3 0 =3 *3 - 4 3 3 1 - 2hp, pf/cel - str

Rhapsodic fantasy   9'
   solo percussionist   MCA
   =2 1 1 1 - 1 1 1 0 - tmp+3 - hp, cel - str

CONVERSE, FREDERICK SHEPHERD, 1871-1940

The mystic trumpeter   20'
   *3 *3 *3 *3 - 4 3 3 1 - tmp+5 - hp - str   Schirmer, G.

COPLAND, AARON, 1900-

Appalachian spring: Suite (original instrumentation)   23'
   1 0 1 1 - pf - str 2.2.2.2.1   Boosey

Appalachian spring: Suite (full orchestra version)   23'
   *2 2 2 2 - 2 2 2 0 - tmp+2 - hp, pf - str   Boosey

Billy the Kid: Suite   21'
   *3 2 2 2 - 4 3 3 1 - tmp+4 - hp, pf - str   Boosey
   Excerpts for reduced orchestra available separately:
   Prairie night and Celebration dance (5'); Waltz (4').

Concerto, clarinet   18'
   hp, pf - str   Boosey

Concerto, piano   17'
  *3 *3 =4 *3 - 4 3 3 1 - asx - tmp+5 - cel - str   Boosey

Connotations   20'
  *4 *3 =4 *3 - 6 4 4 1 - tmp+5 - pf/cel - str   Boosey

Dance symphony   20'
  *3 *3 =4 *3 - 4 5 3 1 - tmp+4 - 2hp, pf/cel - str   Boosey

Danzón cubano   5'
  *3 *3 *3 *3 - 4 3 3 1 - tmp+5 - pf - str   Boosey

Fanfare for the common man   3'
  brass 4 3 3 1 - tmp+2   Boosey

Inscape   13'
  *3 *3 *3 2 - 4 3 3 1 - tmp+4 - hp, pf/cel - str   Boosey

John Henry   4'
  *2 2 2 2 - 2 2 1 0 - tmp+2 - (opt pf) - str   Boosey
  Possible with woodwinds 1 1 2 1.

Lincoln portrait   14'
  speaker   Boosey
  *2 *3 *3 *3 - 4 3 3 1 - tmp+3 - hp, cel - str
  Both flutists double on piccolo. (Optional
  instruments: Eh, bcl, cbn, 3rd tp, cel.)

Music for the theatre   21'
  *1 *1 +1 1 - 0 2 1 0 - 1perc - pf - str   Boosey
  Minimum number of strings: 2.2.2.2.1

Orchestral variations   13'
  *2 *2 *2 2 - 4 2 3 1 - tmp+3 - hp - str   Boosey

Our town   9'
  3 *3 *3 2 - 3 3 2 1 - 1perc - str   Boosey
  (3rd fl and 2nd ob are optional.)

An outdoor overture   10'
  *3 2 2 2 - 4 2 3 0 - tmp+3 - pf, (opt cel) - str   Boosey

Quiet city   10'
  solo trumpet - solo English horn (or oboe)   Boosey
  str

The red pony   23'
  *2 *2 =4 2 - 4 3 3 1 - tmp+4 - hp, pf/cel - str   Boosey
  (E-flat clarinet and 4th horn are optional.)

Rodeo: Four dance episodes   Boosey

  1. Buckaroo holiday   7'
    *3 *3 *3 2 - 4 3 3 1 - tmp+3 - hp, pf/cel - str
    Two flutists double on piccolo. (Cued to be
    playable without Eh or bcl.)

  2. Corral nocturne   4'
    1 1 2 1 - 2 2 1 0 - hp, cel - str

  3. Saturday night waltz   4'
    1 1 *3 1 - 2 2 1 0 - hp - str
    (Bcl is cued in other instruments.)

  4. Hoe-down   3'
    *3 *3 *3 2 - 4 3 3 1 - tmp+3 - pf - str
    (Playable without Eh or bcl.)

El salón México   11'
  *3 *3 =4 *3 - 4 3 3 1 - tmp+4 - pf - str   Boosey
  (Optional instruments: Eh, scl, bcl, cbn, 3rd tp.)

Statements   18'
  *3 *3 =3 *3 - 4 3 3 1 - tmp+3 - str   Boosey

Symphony for organ and orchestra (1924)   25'
  *3 *3 2 *3 - 4 3 3 1 - tmp+4 - 1 or 2hp,   Boosey
  (opt cel) - str
  A revised version without solo organ was later
  published as Symphony no.1.

Symphony no.1   25'
  *3 *3 *3 *3 - 8 5 3 1 - (opt asx) - tmp+5   Boosey
  2hp, pf/cel - str
  A revision (without organ solo) of his
  Symphony for organ and orchestra.

Symphony no.1: Prelude (arr. for chamber orchestra)   5'
  1 1 1 1 - 1 1 0 0 - hp or pf - str   Boosey
  Arranged by the composer.

Symphony no.2   15'
  =3 *3 *3 *3 - 4 2 0 0 - pf - str   Boosey
  English horn player doubles on optional heckelphone.

Symphony no.3   40'
  *4 *3 *3 *3 - 4 4 3 1 - tmp+5 - 2hp, pf,   Boosey
    cel - str

The tender land: Suite   19'
  *3 *2 *2 2 - 4 3 3 1 - tmp+2 - hp,   Boosey
    (opt pf/cel) - str

Three Latin-American sketches   10'
  *1 1 1 1 - 0 1 0 0 - 1perc - 1 or 2pf - str   Boosey
  Minimum strings 6.4.3.2.1

Variations on a Shaker melody   4'
  *2 2 2 2 - 2 2 2 0 - (opt tmp), 1perc -   Boosey
    (opt hp), pf - str
  Adapted from his "Appalachian spring."

CORELLI, ARCANGELO, 1653-1713

Concerti grossi, op.6   Kalmus;
  2 solo violins, solo violoncello   Peters;
  str, cnt   Ricordi
  Each concerto published separately.

    No.1, D major   12'

    No.2, F major   12'

    No.3, C minor   13'

    No.4, D major   9'

    No.5, B-flat major   11'

    No.6, F major   12'

    No.7, D major   9'

    No.8, G minor ("Christmas concerto") 15'

    No.9, F major   11'

    No.10, C major   14'

    No.11, B-flat major   10'

    No.12, F major   11'

Suite for string orchestra   8'
  str   Luck
  A pastiche, assembled and arranged from various
  individual movements.
    Contents--Sarabanda; Giga; Badinerie.

See also:
    Geminiani, Francesco, 1687-1762
      Concerto grosso no.12 ("La follia," after
        Corelli, op.5, no.12)
      Concerto grosso in C major (after Corelli,
        op.5, no.3)

CORIGLIANO, JOHN, 1938-

Elegy for orchestra   8'
  *2 2 2 2 - 2 1 1 0 - tmp+1 - pf (or hp) -   Schirmer, G.
  str

COUPERIN, FRANÇOIS, 1668-1733

La sultane: Overture and allegro (arr. Milhaud)   7'
  *3 *3 *3 2 - 3 3 3 1 - tmp+1 - hp - str   Elkan-Vogel

COWELL, HENRY, 1897-1965

Ballad   4'
  str   AMP

Carol for orchestra   9'
  2 2 2 2 - 2 2 0 0 - hp (or pf) - str   AMP
  The composer's own version for "western orchestra"
  of his koto concerto.

Fiddler's jig   2'
  solo violin - str   AMP

Hymn and fuguing tune no.2   7'
  str   AMP

Hymn and fuguing tune no.3   7'
  *2 2 2 2 - 4(or 2) 2 2 1 - tmp+2 - str   AMP

Hymn and fuguing tune no.16   6'
  2 2 2 2 - 4(or 2) 3 3 1 - str   Peters

Polyphonica for small orchestra   4'
  1 1 1 1 - 1 1 1 0 - str   AMP

Sinfonietta   15'
  1 1 1 1 - 1 1 1 0 - str 2.2.1.1.1   AMP

Synchrony   15'
  *3 3 +3 *3 - 4 3 3 1 - tmp+4 - str   Peters
  All 3 flutists double on piccolo; 2 of the
  clarinetists double on E-flat clarinet.

   CRESTON, PAUL, 1906-

Dance overture   12'
  *4 *3 *3 *3 - 4 3 3 1 - tmp+3 - str   Templeton

Invocation and dance, op.58   12'
  *4 *3 *3 *3 - 4 3 3 1 - tmp+3 - pf - str   Schirmer, G.
  Possible with winds and percussion: 2 2 2 2 -
  4 2 3 1 - tmp+2.

Symphony no.2, op.35   25'
  *4 *3 *3 *3 - 4 3 3 1 - tmp+4 - pf - str   Schirmer, G.

Symphony no.3, op.48 ("Three mysteries")   28'
  *4 *3 *3 *3 - 4 3 3 1 - tmp - hp - str   Shawnee

Two choric dances, op.17b   12'
  *3 2 2 2 - 4 2 3 1 - tmp+1 - pf - str   Schirmer, G.

   CRUMB, GEORGE, 1929-

Echoes of time and the river   18'
  *3 0 +3 0 - 3 3 3 0 - 6perc - hp, pf, pf/cel,   Belwin
   mandoline - str (minimum 15.15.12.12.9)
  A number of the wind and string players also play
  antique cymbals. Players move in procession from
  place to place, on and off stage, while playing.
  Many other special effects.

Variazioni for large orchestra   25'
  *3 *3 =4 *3 - 4 3 3 1 - tmp+6 - hp, cel,   Peters
    mandoline - str (minimum 14.14.12.12.10)
  Two of the flutists double on piccolo.

    DAHL, INGOLF, 1912-1970

Quodlibet on American folk tunes and folk dances   5'
  3 2 *3 2 - 4 3 3 1 - tmp+2 - pf - str   Peters
  (Bass clarinet, tuba, and piano are optional.)

Variations on a theme by C. P. E. Bach   12'
  str   Broude, A.

    DALLAPICCOLA, LUIGI, 1904-1975

Canti di liberazione   30'
  chorus   Suvini
  *3 *3 =4 *3 - 4 3 3 1 - asx, tsx - tmp+7 -
    2hp, cel - str

Canti di prigionia   25'
  chorus   Carisch
  2hp, 2pf - 8perc

Due pezzi per orchestra   11'
  2 *3 2 *2 - 4 3 2 1 - tmp+4 - 2hp, cel, pf - str   Suvini

Piccola musica notturna   7'
  2 2 2 2 - 2 2 0 0 - tmp+1 - hp, cel - str   Schott
  A version for chamber orchestra also exists:
  1 1 1 0 - hp, cel - vn, va, vc.

Variations for orchestra   15'
  *2 *2 2 2 - 4 2 3 1 - tmp+3 - hp, cel - str   Suvini

    DAVIDOVSKY, MARIO, 1934-

Inflexions   7'
  =2 0 *1 0 - 0 1 1 0 - 4perc - pf/cel -   Marks
    vn, va, vc, db
  Clarinet also doubles on alto saxophone.

DEBUSSY, CLAUDE, 1862-1918

La boîte à joujoux (The toybox)   31'
  2 *3 2 2 - 2 2 0 0 - tmp+4 - hp, cel, pf - str   Durand

Clair de lune (arr. Arthur Luck)   5'
  2 2 2 2 - 4 0 0 0 - hp, cel - str   Luck

La damoiselle élue (The blessed damozel)   20'
  mezzo-soprano solo (or 2 Mz) - female chorus   Durand;
  3 *3 *3 3 - 4 3 3 0 - 2hp - str   Kalmus

Danse (orchestrated by Maurice Ravel)   6'
  2 2 2 2 - 2 2 0 0 - tmp+3 - hp - str   Jobert

Danses sacrée et profane   9'
  solo harp - str   Durand; Kalmus

L'enfant prodigue   45'
  solos STBar - (optional chorus)   Durand
  *3 *3 2 2 - 4 2 3 1 - tmp+2 - 2hp - str   Fischer, C.

Fantasie, piano and orchestra   22'
  3 *3 *3 3 - 4 3 3 0 - tmp+1 - 2hp - str   Jobert

Images

  1. Gigues   7'
     *4 *3 *4 *4 - 4 4 3 0 - ob d'amore - tmp+1 -   Durand
       2hp, cel - str

  2. Ibéria   20'
     *4 *3 3 *4 - 4 3 3 1 - tmp+4 - 2hp, cel - str   Durand

  3. Rondes des printemps   9'
     *3 *3 3 *4 - 4 0 0 0 - tmp+3 - 2hp, cel - str   Durand

L'isle joyeuse (orchestrated by Bernardino Molinari)   7'
  *3 *3 *4 *3 - 4 4 3 1 - tmp+4 - 2hp, cel - str   Durand

Jeux; poème dansé   17'
  *4 *4 *4 *4 - 4 4 3 1 - tmp+3 - 2hp, cel - str   Durand

Marche écossaise sur un thème populaire   7'
  *3 *3 2 2 - 4 2 3 0 - tmp+2 - hp - str   Jobert
  Orchestrated by the composer from a work for
  piano 4-hands.

Le martyre de Saint Sébastien   72'
  chorus - solos SAA   Durand
  *4 *3 *4 *4 - 6 4 3 1 - tmp+1 - 3hp, cel,
    harm - str
  Incidental music to a play by d'Annunzio. Most often
  performed in a format devised by D. E. Inghelbrecht,
  with the approval of Debussy and d'Annunzio, using a
  narrator. The music alone, without narration, lasts
  about an hour.

Le martyre de Saint Sébastien: Fragments symphoniques   20'
  *4 *3 *4 *4 - 6 4 3 1 - tmp+1 - 3hp, cel - str   Durand
    Contents--La cour des lys; Danse extatique et
  Final du premier acte; La passion; Le bon pasteur.

Le martyre de Saint Sébastien: La chambre magique   2'
  *4 *2 *4 *4 - 6 2 3 1 - tmp+1 - 3hp, cel - str   Durand

Le martyre de Saint Sébastien: Two fanfares   3'
  brass 6 4 3 1 - tmp   Elkan-Vogel

La mer   21'
  *3 *3 2 *4 - 4 5 3 1 - tmp+3 - 2hp - str   Durand; Kalmus

Nocturnes   25'
  *3 *3 2 3 - 4 3 3 1 - tmp+2 - 2hp - str   Jobert
  16 women's voices in last movement; if performed
  without this movement, the duration is 14'.
  The Jobert score and parts include important revisions
  made by Debussy only after the initial publication of
  the work. A Kalmus edition is available, but lacks
  these changes.

Petite suite (orchestrated by Henri Busser)   12'
  *2 *2 2 2 - 2 2 0 0 - tmp+3 - hp - str   Durand

Prélude à l'après-midi d'un faune   10'
  3 *3 2 2 - 4 0 0 0 - 1perc - 2hp - str   Jobert;
  A critical edition of the score, including   Kalmus
  the composer's own metronome marks, is
  published by Norton.

Printemps   17'
  *2 *2 2 2 - 4 2 3 0 - tmp+2 - hp,   Durand;
    pf 4-hands - str   Fischer, C.

Rhapsody, alto saxophone and orchestra   10'
  3 *3 2 2 - 4 2 3 1 - tmp+2 - hp - str   Durand;
                                                         Fischer, C.

Rhapsody, clarinet and orchestra   8'
  3 *3 2 3 - 4 2 0 0 - 2perc - 2hp - str   Durand;
                                                         Fischer, C.

Sarabande (orchestrated by Maurice Ravel)   6'
  2 *2 2 2 - 2 1 0 0 - 1 perc - hp - str   Jobert

DELIBES, LÉO, 1836-1891

Coppelia   full concert
  *2 2 2 4 - 4 4 3 1 - tmp+4 - hp - str   Heugel; Kalmus

Coppelia: Suite no.1   24'
  *2 2 2 2 - 4 2 3 0 - tmp+3 - hp - str   Kalmus
    Contents--Slav folk-tune; Festive dance and
  Waltz of the hours; Nocturne; Music of the
  automatons and Waltz; Czardas.

Coppelia: Four petites suites   24'
  The following are sometimes grouped together as
  "Ballet suite no.2." They are published separately.
  Some of the movements also appear in Suite no.1.

  1. Entr'acte and Waltz   4'
    *2 2 2 2 - 2 2 3 1 - tmp - hp - str   Heugel; Kalmus

  2. Prelude and Mazurka   6'
    *2 2 2 2 - 4 4 3 1 - tmp+4 - hp - str   Heugel; Kalmus

  3. Ballade and Thème slave varié   9'
    *2 *2 2 4 - 4 4 3 1 - tmp+3 - str   Heugel; Kalmus

  4. Valse de la poupée and Czardas   5'
    *2 2 2 2 - 4 4 3 1 - tmp+3 - str   Heugel; Kalmus

Le roi s'amuse: Airs de danse dans le style ancien   13'
  2 2 2 2 - 2 2 0 0 - tmp - str   Heugel; Kalmus

Sylvia: Suite   17'
  *2 2 2 2 - 4 4 3 1 - tmp+3 - hp - str   Heugel; Kalmus

DELIUS, FREDERICK, 1862-1934

Appalachia; variations on an old slave song
  with final chorus   34'
  chorus   Boosey;
  *3 *4 =4 *4 - 6 3 3 1 - tmp+3 - 2hp - str   Kalmus

Brigg fair   16'
  3 *3 *4 *4 - 6 3 3 1 - tmp+3 - hp - str   Boosey;
                                          Universal

Dance rhapsody no.1
  *3 *2 *4 *4 - 6 3 3 1 - bass ob (=heckelphone?)   12'
  - tmp+2 - 2hp - str   Universal

Dance rhapsody no.2   8'
  *3 *3 2 2 - 4 2 3 1 - tmp+3 - hp, cel - str   Galaxy

Irmelin: Prelude   4'
  2 *2 *3 2 - 2 0 0 0 - hp - str   Boosey

Sea drift   30'
  chorus - baritone solo   Boosey;
  3 *4 *4 *4 - 6 3 3 1 - tmp+1 - 2hp - str   Kalmus

Sleigh ride   5'
  *3 2 2 2 - 4 4 3 1 - tmp+2 - str   Boosey

Two pieces for small orchestra

  1. On hearing the first cuckoo in spring   4'
    1 1 2 2 - 2 0 0 0 - str   Oxford

  2. Summer night on the river   5'
    2 1 2 2 - 2 0 0 0 - str   Oxford

The walk to the Paradise Garden   8'
  2 *2 2 2 - 4 2 3 0 - tmp - hp - str   Boosey
  Two differing versions are available from the
  publisher: one arr. Sir Thomas Beecham; the
  other ed. Keith Douglas.

DELLO JOIO, NORMAN, 1913-

Arietta   4'
  str   Marks

Five images for orchestra 8'
 *3 2 *3 2 - 4 2 3 1 - tmp+3 - str Marks
 Intended primarily for youth audiences.
   Contents--Cortège; Promenade; Day dreams;
 The ballerina; The dancing sergeant.

Lyric fantasies 17'
 solo viola AMP
 str orchestra or str quintet

Meditations on Ecclesiastes 22'
 str Fischer, C.

The triumph of Saint Joan 27'
 *2 *2 2 2 - 4 2 3 1 - tmp+1 - str Fischer, C.

Variations, chaconne, and finale 21'
 *3 *3 *3 *3 - 4 3 3 1 - tmp+3 - str Fischer, C.

DEL TREDICI, DAVID, 1937-

An Alice symphony 41'
 solo soprano, amplified and with bull horn - Boosey
   folk group: ssx/asx, ssx/asx/tsx, mandoline
   tenor banjo, accordion
 *2 2 +2 *2 - 4 2 2 1 - tmp+5 - str
 Both flutists double on piccolo.
   Contents--Speak roughly/Speak gently; The lobster
 quadrille; 'Tis the voice of the sluggard; Who stole
 the tarts; Dream conclusion.
 *This work may be excerpted in various ways; see
 the following three entries.*

An Alice symphony: Illustrated Alice 17'
 solo soprano, amplified and with bull-horn Boosey
 *2 2 2 *2 - 4 2 2 1 - ssx/asx, ssx/asx/tsx -
   tmp+5 - str
 Both flutes double on piccolo.
   Contents--Speak roughly/Speak gently; Who stole
 the tarts; Dream conclusion.

An Alice symphony: In Wonderland 24'
 solo soprano, amplified - folk group: 2ssx, Boosey
   mandoline, tenor banjo, accordion
 *2 2 +2 *2 - 4 2 2 1 - tmp+4 - str
 Both flutes double on piccolo.
   Contents--The lobster quadrille; 'Tis the voice
 of the sluggard; Dream conclusion.

An Alice symphony: The lobster quadrille   13'
  folk group: 2ssx, mandoline, tenor banjo,   Boosey
    accordion - (opt amplified soprano)
  *2 2 +2 *2 - 4 2 2 1 - 4perc - str
  Both flutes double on piccolo.

Final Alice   70'
  solo soprano, amplified and with bull-horn -   Boosey
    folk group, amplified: 2ssx, mandoline,
    tenor banjo, accordion
  *4 *4 =4 *4 - 6 4 4 1 - tmp+7 - 2hp, cel - str
  The composer indicates a possible cut which reduces the
  duration to 60', and lessens the complexity of the folk
  group amplification.

In memory of a summer day   62'
  solo soprano, amplified   Boosey
  *3 *3 =4 *3 - 4 4 3 1 - tmp+5 - 2hp, cel - str
  String players form an antiphonal whisper-chorus.

Pop-pourri   28'
  solo soprano, amplified - chorus - (opt counter-   Boosey
    tenor or Mz solo)
  rock group: ssx, ssx/tsx, electric gtr, electric
    bass gtr
  *2 *2 *2 *2 - 0 2 2 0 - 3perc - str
  One technician required. Both flutists double on
  piccolo. (Chorus may be omitted by cutting one
  movement.)

Syzygy   26'
  solo group: soprano (amplified), horn, tubular   Boosey
    bells with extended range (2 players)
  =2 *2 *2 *2 - 0 2 0 0 - 2vn, 2va, vc, db

Vintage Alice; fantascene on a mad tea-party   28'
  solo soprano, amplified - folk group: 2ssx,   Boosey
    mandoline, tenor banjo, accordion
  *1 1 +1 1 - 2 1 1 0 - tmp+1 - str
  (May be done with solo strings rather than sections.
  If a large string complement is used, winds may be
  doubled.)

DIAMOND, DAVID, 1915-

Music for Shakespeare's Romeo and Juliet   18'
  *2 *2 *2 2 - 2 2 1 0 - tmp+1 - hp - str   Boosey

Rounds for string orchestra   14'
  str   Elkan-Vogel

The world of Paul Klee   12'
  *3 *3 *3 2 - 4 3 3 0 - tmp+3 - hp, pf/cel - str   Southern

DITTERSDORF, KARL DITTERS VON, 1739-1799

Concerto, double bass, E major   11'
  2 0 0 0 - 2 0 0 0 - str, cnt   Schott
  Ed. Franz Tischer-Zeitz.

Concerto, double bass, E-flat major   17'
  2 2 0 0 - 2 0 0 0 - str   Schott
  Ed. Franz Ortner. (Wind parts may be omitted.)

Concerto, harp, A major (arr. K. H. Pillney)   22'
  0 2 0 0 - 2 0 0 0 - str   Peters

Concerto, harpsichord, B-flat major   14'
  2 0 0 0 - 2 0 0 0 - str (without va)   Kalmus;
  Winds used only in slow movement.   Peters

Sinfonia, C major ("Die vier Weltalter")   13'
  1 2 0 2 - 2 2 0 0 - tmp - str   Doblinger

Sinfonia concertante, double bass and viola   16'
  0 2 0 0 - 2 0 0 0 - str   Hofmeister
  Ed. Wilhelm Altmann.

DOHNÁNYI, ERNST VON, 1877-1960

Concerto, piano, no.1, op.5, E minor   37'
  *3 2 2 *3 - 4 2 3 0 - tmp - str   Doblinger;
  Minimum strings: 12.12.8.8.6   Kalmus

Ruralia hungarica, op.32b   25'
  *3 *3 =3 *3 - 4 3 3 1 - tmp+4 - hp, cel - str   Boosey

Variations on a nursery song, op.25   22'
  solo piano   Simrock
  *3 2 2 *3 - 4 3 3 1 - 2tmp, 2perc - hp - str

DONIZETTI, GAETANO, 1797-1848

Allegro in C major   6'
  str   Peters

Ave Maria   4'
  chorus - soprano solo   Broude, A.;
  str   Peters

Concertino, clarinet, B-flat major   8'
  0 2 0 0 - 2 0 0 0 - str   Eulenburg; Peters

Concertino, English horn, G major   11'
  1 2 0 1 - 2 0 0 0 - str   Peters

Concertino, flute, C major   7'
  0 2 0 1 - 2 0 0 0 - str   Peters
  Orchestrated by Wolfgang Hofmann after the
  composer's sonata for flute and piano.

Concertino, oboe, F major   7'
  2 0 0 1 - 2 0 0 0 - str   Peters
  Orchestrated by Wolfgang Hofmann after the
  composer's sonata for oboe and piano.

Daughter of the regiment: Overture   7'
  *2 2 2 2 - 4 2 3 0 - tmp+2 - str   Breitkopf;
                   Kalmus; Ricordi

Don Pasquale: Overture   6'
  *2 2 2 2 - 4 2 3 0 - tmp+2 - str   Kalmus; Luck; Ricordi

Roberto Devereux: Overture   8'
  *3 2 2 2 - 4 2 3 0 - tmp+2 - str   Ricordi

Sinfonia for winds, G minor   5'
  1 2 2 2 - 2 0 0 0   Broude, A.
  Ed Dou las Townsend.

DRUCKMAN, JACOB, 1928-

Windows   21'
  *3 *3 *3 *3 - 4 3 3 1 - 3perc - hp - pf dbl on   MCA
  electric org (both with amplifier and
  reverberation unit) - str

DUBOIS, THÉODORE, 1837-1924

The seven last words of Christ   46'
  chorus - solos STB   Kalmus
  *2 2 2 2 - 4 2 3 0 - tmp+1 - hp, (opt org) - str

DUKAS, PAUL, 1865-1935

L'apprenti sorcier (The sorcerer's apprentice)   12'
  *3 2 *3 *4 - 4 4 3 0 - tmp+4 - hp - str   Durand; Kalmus

La péri   19'
  *3 *3 *3 3 - 4 3 3 1 - tmp+6 - 2hp, cel - str   Durand

La péri: Fanfare   3'
  brass 4 3 3 1   Durand

Symphony in C major   38'
  *3 2 2 2 - 4 3 3 1 - tmp - str   Salabert

DURUFLÉ, MAURICE, 1902-

Requiem, op.9   38'
  chorus - solos Mz, Bar   Durand
  *3 *3 *3 2 - 4 3 3 1 - tmp+3 - hp, cel, (opt org) - str
  Reduced version of the instrumental accompaniment:
  3tp - tmp - hp, org - str

DUTILLEUX, HENRI, 1916-

Symphony no.2   29'
  *3 *3 *3 *3 - 2 3 3 1 - tmp+3 - hp, cel,   Heugel
  hpsd - str
  Divided into two orchestras, one large and one
  small (12 players).

DVOŘÁK, ANTONÍN, 1841-1904

Amid nature, op.91 (overture)   12'
  2 *3 *3 2 - 4 2 3 1 - tmp+1 - str   Kalmus; Supraphon

Carnival overture, op.92   10'
  *3 *3 2 2 - 4 2 3 1 - tmp+3 - hp - str   Kalmus;
                                                              Supraphon

Concerto, piano, op.33, G minor   35'
  2 2 2 2 - 2 2 0 0 - tmp - str   Kalmus; Peters;
                                                              Supraphon

Concerto, violin, op.53, A minor   32'
  2 2 2 2 - 4 2 0 0 - tmp - str   Kalmus; Supraphon

Concerto, violoncello, op.104, B minor   40'
  *2 2 2 2 - 3 2 3 1 - tmp+1 - str   Kalmus; Supraphon

Concerto, violoncello, (no.2), op.posth., A major   30'
  2 2 2 2 - 4 2 0 0 - tmp - str   Breitkopf

Czech suite, op.39, D major   23'
  2 *3 2 2 - 2 2 0 0 - tmp - str   Kalmus; Supraphon
  (Basset horn may substitute for English horn.)

Fest-Marsch, op.54a   5'
  2 2 2 2 - 4 2 3 1 - tmp+1 - (opt hp) - str   Bote;
                                                                Kalmus;
                                                              Supraphon

Golden spinning wheel, op.109   22'
  *2 *3 2 *3 - 4 2 3 1 - tmp+3 - hp - str   Luck; Supraphon

A hero's song, op.111   23'
  2 2 2 2 - 4 2 3 1 - tmp+3 - str   Luck; Supraphon

Husitská, op.67   14'
  *3 *2 2 2 - 4 2 3 1 - tmp+2 - (opt hp) - str   Kalmus;
                                                                 Luck;
                                                              Supraphon

In nature's realm
  See his: Amid nature, op.91

Legends, op.59: Nos.1-5   5', 4', 5', 7', 5'
  2 2 2 2 - 4 2 0 0 - tmp - hp - str   Kalmus; Simrock

Legends, op.59: Nos.6-10   5', 4', 5', 3', 4'
  2 2 2 2 - 4 0 0 0 - tmp - hp - str   Kalmus; Simrock

Mass, op.86, D major
  chorus - (optional soloists SATB)   Gray; Kalmus;
  0 2 0 2 - 3 2 3 0 - tmp - org - str   Supraphon

Midday witch, op.108   17'
  *3 2 *3 2 - 4 2 3 1 - tmp+3 - str   Luck;
  Also known as "The noonday witch."   Supraphon

Notturno, op.40, B major   7'
  str   Bote; Kalmus

Othello overture, op.93   15'
  *2 *3 2 2 - 4 2 3 1 - tmp+2 - hp - str   Luck; Supraphon

Requiem, op.89   95'
  chorus - solos SATB   Gray; Kalmus;
  *3 *3 *3 *3 - 4 4 3 1 - tmp - hp, org - str   Supraphon

Rhapsody, op.14, A minor   19'
  *3 *3 2 2 - 4 2 3 1 - tmp+3 - hp - str   Fischer, C.;
                        Supraphon

Romance, violin and orchestra, op.11, F minor   8'
  2 2 2 2 - 2 0 0 0 - str   Kalmus; Supraphon

Scherzo capriccioso, op.66   12'
  *3 *3 *3 2 - 4 2 3 1 - tmp+3 - hp - str   Bote; Kalmus;
                        Supraphon

Serenade, op.22, E major   27'
  str   Bote; Kalmus; Supraphon

Serenade, op.44, D minor   26'
  0 2 2 *3 - 3 0 0 0 - vc, db   Luck; Simrock;
  (Contrabassoon is optional.)   Supraphon

Slavonic dances, op.46, nos.1-4   4', 5', 4', 6'
  *2 2 2 2 - 4 2 3 0 - tmp+3 - str   Kalmus; Simrock

Slavonic dances, op.46, nos.5-8   3', 6', 3', 3'
  *2 2 2 2 - 4 2 3 0 - tmp+3 - str   Kalmus; Simrock

Slavonic dances, op.72, nos.1-4 (9-12)   4', 6', 3', 5'
  *2 2 2 2 - 4 2 3 0 - tmp+3 - str   Kalmus; Simrock

Slavonic dances, op.72, nos.5-8 (13-16)   3', 4', 3', 7'
  *2 2 2 2 - 4 2 3 0 - tmp+3 - str   Kalmus; Simrock

Slavonic rhapsody, op.45, no.1, D major   10'
  *3 2 2 2 - 4 2 3 0 - tmp+3 - str   Kalmus; Supraphon

Slavonic rhapsody, op.45, no.2, G minor   13'
   2 2 2 2 - 4 2 3 0 - tmp+3 - hp - str   Kalmus; Supraphon

Slavonic rhapsody, op.45, no.3, A-flat major   14'
  *2 2 2 2 - 4 2 3 0 - tmp+3 - hp - str   Kalmus; Supraphon

Stabat mater, op.58   90'
  chorus - solos SATB   Kalmus;
  2 *2 2 2 - 4 2 3 1 - tmp - org or harm -   Schirmer, G.;
   str   Supraphon

Suite, op.98b, A major   18'
  *3 2 2 *3 - 4 2 3 1 - tmp+3 - str   Simrock; Supraphon

Symphonic variations, op.78   21'
  *2 2 2 2 - 4 2 3 0 - tmp - str   Kalmus; Supraphon

Symphony no.1, op.3, C minor ("Bells of Zlonice")   39'
  *3 *3 2 2 - 4 2 3 0 - tmp - str   Supraphon

Symphony no.2, op.4, B-flat major   45'
  *3 2 2 2 - 4 2 3 0 - tmp - str   Supraphon

Symphony no.3, op.10, E-flat major   35'
  *3 *3 2 2 - 4 2 3 1 - tmp+1 - hp - str   Simrock;
                                                    Supraphon

Symphony no.4, op.13, D minor   38'
  *2 2 2 2 - 4 2 3 0 - tmp+3 - hp - str   Simrock;
                                                    Supraphon

Symphony no.5, op.76, F major   39'
   2 2 *2 2 - 4 2 3 0 - tmp+1 - str   Kalmus;
  Formerly known as Symphony no.3.   Supraphon

Symphony no.6, op.60, D major   40'
  *2 2 2 2 - 4 2 3 1 - tmp - str   Kalmus;
  Formerly known as Symphony no.1.   Supraphon

Symphony no.7, op.70, D minor   37'
  *2 2 2 2 - 4 2 3 0 - tmp - str   Kalmus;
  Formerly known as Symphony no.2.   Supraphon

Symphony no.8, op.88, G major   36'
  *2 *2 2 2 - 4 2 3 1 - tmp - str   Kalmus;
  Formerly known as Symphony no.4.   Supraphon

Symphony no.9, op.95, E minor ("From the New World")   38'
  *2 *3 2 2 - 4 2 3 1 - tmp+1 - str   Kalmus;
  Formerly known as Symphony no.5.   Supraphon

Te deum, op.103   22'
  chorus - solos SB   Gray; Kalmus;
  2 *2 2 2 - 4 2 3 1 - tmp+3 - str   Simrock; Supraphon

Watersprite, op.107   19'
  *3 *3 *2 2 - 4 2 3 2 - tmp+4 - str   Kalmus;
  (2nd tuba is optional.)   Supraphon

Wood dove, op.110   19'
  *2 *3 *3 2 - 4 2 3 1 - tmp+3 - hp - str   Simrock;
                    Supraphon

EFFINGER, CECIL, 1914-

Little symphony no.1, op.31   13'
  *2 1 2 1 - 2 1 0 0 - str   Fischer, C.

EINEM, GOTTFRIED VON, 1918-

Ballade   14'
  *3 2 2 2 - 4 3 3 1 - tmp - str   Schirmer, G.

Capriccio, op.2   8'
  *3 2 2 2 - 4 3 3 1 - tmp - str   Bote

Meditations, op.18   21'
  *2 2 2 2 - 4 2 2 0 - tmp - str   Universal

Wiener Symphonie, op.49   33'
  *3 2 2 2 - 4 3 3 1 - tmp - str   Bote

   ELGAR, EDWARD, 1857-1934

Cockaigne, op.40   13'
  *2 2 2 *3 - 4 4 3(or 5) 1 - tmp+5 -   Boosey;
  (opt org) - str   Kalmus

Concerto, violin, op.61, B minor   46'
  2 2 2 *3 - 4 2 3 1 - tmp - str   Novello
  (Contrabassoon and tuba are optional.)

Concerto, violoncello, op.85, E minor   30'
  2 2 2 2 - 4 2 3 1 - tmp - str   Novello
  (Tuba is optional.)

Dream-children, op.43   6'
  2 2 2 2 - 4 0 0 0 - tmp - hp - str   Luck

The dream of Gerontius, op.38   100'
  solos ATB - chorus, semi-chorus   Gray;
  *3 *3 *3 *3 - 4 3 3 1 - tmp+4 - 1 or 2hp,   Novello
   org - str

Elegy, op.58   5'
  str   Kalmus; Luck; Novello

Enigma variations, op.36   29'
  *2 2 2 *3 - 4 3 3 1 - tmp+3 - (opt org) - str   Gray;
                                    Kalmus; Novello

Falstaff, op.68   30'
  *3 *3 *3 *3 - 4 3 3 1 - tmp+3(or 4) -   Novello
  2hp - str

Introduction and allegro, op.47   14'
  solo string quartet   Gray; Kalmus;
  str   Novello

Pomp and circumstance, military marches, op.39

  No.1, D major   5'
    *4 2 *3 *3 - 4 4 3 1 - tmp+5 - 2hp, org - Boosey;
     str   Kalmus

No.2, A minor   3'
  *3 2 *3 *3 - 4 4 3 1 - tmp+5 - str   Boosey; Kalmus

No.3, C minor   5'
  *3 *3 *3 *4 - 4 4 3 1 - tmp+5 - str   Boosey

No.4, G major   4'
  *3 *3 *3 *3 - 4 3 3 1 - tmp+3 - hp - str   Boosey

No.5, C major   5'
  *3 *3 *3 *3 - 4 3 3 1 - tmp+4 - str   Boosey

Salut d'amour   4'
  1 2 2 2 - 2 0 0 0 - str   Kalmus

Sea pictures   14'
  alto solo   Boosey
  2 2 2 2 - 4 2 3 1 - tmp+2 - hp, org - str

Serenade, op.20, E minor   12'
  str   Breitkopf; Kalmus

Symphony no.1, op.55, A-flat major   51'
  *3 *3 *3 *3 - 4 3 3 1 - tmp+3 - 2hp - str   Novello

Symphony no.2, op.63, E-flat major   52'
  *3 *3 =4 *3 - 4 3 3 1 - tmp+4 - 2hp - str   Novello

    ENESCO, GEORGES, 1881-1955

Rumanian rhapsody no.1, op.11, A major   11'
  *3 *3 2 2 - 4 4 3 1 - tmp+3 - 2hp - str   Kalmus; Peer

Rumanian rhapsody no.2, op.11, D major   11'
  3 *3 2 2 - 4 2 3 0 - tmp+1 - 2hp - str   Kalmus

    ERB, DONALD, 1927-

Concerto for solo percussionist and orchestra   10'
  *3 2 *3 *3 - 4 3 3 1 - tmp - hp, pf/cel - str   Merion

Symphony of overtures   16'
  *3 2 *3 *3 - 4 3 3 1 - tmp+3 - hp, pf - str   Galaxy
    Contents--The blacks; Endgame; The maids;
  Rhinoceros.

ETLER, ALVIN, 1913-1973

Elegy for small orchestra   5'
  1 1 2 2 - 2 0 0 0 - str   AMP

FALLA, MANUEL DE, 1876-1946

El amor brujo: Ballet suite   20'
  alto solo   Chester
  *2 *1 2 1 - 2 2 0 0 - tmp - pf - str
  (English horn is optional.)

El amor brujo: Ritual fire dance   5'
  *2 1 2 1 - 2 2 0 0 - tmp - pf - str   Chester

Concerto, harpsichord, D major   14'
  1 1 1 0 - vn, vc   Eschig

Nights in the gardens of Spain   25'
  solo piano   Eschig
  *3 *3 2 2 - 4 2 3 1 - tmp+2 - hp, cel - str

Three-cornered hat (El sombrero de tres picos)   30'
  *3 *3 2 2 - 4 3 3 1 - tmp+5 - hp, pf, cel - str   Chester

Three-cornered hat: Scenes and dances from
  Part I (Suite no.1)   11'
  *2 *2 2 2 - 2 2 0 0 - tmp+1 - hp, pf - str   Chester
    Contents--Introduction - Afternoon; Dance of
  the miller's wife (Fandango); The corregidor;
  The grapes.

Three-cornered hat: Three dances (Suite no.2)   12'
  *3 *3 2 2 - 4 3 3 1 - tmp+5 - hp, pf/cel - str   Chester
    Contents--The neighbors; Miller's dance;
  Final dance.

La vida breve: Interlude and dance   8'
  *3 *3 *3 2 - 4 2 3 1 - tmp+4 - 2hp, cel - str   Eschig

FASCH, JOHANN FRIEDRICH, 1688-1758

Concerto, trumpet, D major   13'
  0 2 0 0 - str, cnt   Sikorski

FAURÉ, GABRIEL, 1845-1924

Ballade, piano and orchestra, op.19   15'
  2 2 2 2 - 2 0 0 0 - str   Hamelle; Kalmus

Dolly, op.56 (orchestrated by Henri Rabaud)   17'
  *2 2 2 2 - 4 2 3 0 - tmp+3 - hp - str   Kalmus

Elegy, violoncello and orchestra, op.24   8'
  2 2 2 2 - 4 0 0 0 - str   Fischer, C.; Kalmus

Fantasy, flute and chamber orchestra   6'
  0 2 2 2 - 2 0 0 0 - str   Hamelle
  (Clarinets are optional.)

Fantasy, piano and orchestra, op.111   18'
  2 2 2 2 - 4 1 0 0 - tmp - hp - str   Durand; Kalmus

Masques et bergamasques, op.112   14'
  2 2 2 2 - 2 2 0 0 - tmp - hp - str   Durand

Pavane, op.50   7'
  (optional chorus)   Hamelle;
  2 2 2 2 - 2 0 0 0 - str   Kalmus

Pelléas et Mélisande, op.80: Suite   17'
  2 2 2 2 - 4 2 0 0 - tmp - hp - str   Hamelle; Kalmus

Pénélope: Prelude   7'
  2 *3 *3 2 - 4 2 3 1 - tmp - str   Heugel

Requiem, op.48   43'
  chorus - solo soprano and baritone   Hamelle; Kalmus;
  2 0 2 2 - 4 2 3 0 - tmp - hp, org - str   Schirmer, G.

Shylock, op.57: Nocturne   5'
  str   Luck

FELDMAN, MORTON, 1926-

Atlantis   8'
  *3 0 *2 *2 - 1 1 1 1 - 2perc - hp, pf - vc, db   Peters
  Graph notation.
  Alternate version: 1 0 *1 0 - 1 1 1 0 - 2perc -
  hp, pf - vc

Intersection no.1 for orchestra   13'
  woodwinds, brass, strings (the precise number   Peters
    of players being indeterminate)
  Graph notation.

Marginal intersection   6'
  "Large orchestra," unspecified except that   Peters
  it includes piano, xylophone, vibraphone, amplified
  guitar, 2 oscillators, recording of riveting, and
  6 percussionists, together with the usual woodwinds,
  brass, and strings. Graph notation.

...Out of "Last pieces"   9'
  2 *3 *3 2 - 4 2 3 0 - bass tp - 8perc - hp,   Peters
    pf/cel, amplified gtr - str (without vn or va)
  Graph notation.

Structures for orchestra   10'
  +3 *3 *3 2 - 4 3 3 1 - 2perc - hp, cel - str   Peters
  Conventional notation.

   FINE, IRVING, 1914-1962

Diversions for orchestra   8'
  2 *2 2 2 - 4 3 3 1 - (opt 2asx, tsx,   Broude Bros.
    bsx) - tmp+2 - pf or cel - str
  (English horn is optional.)

Serious song; a lament for string orchestra   10'
  str   Broude Bros.

Symphony (1962)   24'
  *3 *3 *3 *3 - 4 3 3 1 - tmp+4 - hp, pf/cel - str   Belwin

   FINNEY, ROSS LEE, 1906-

Landscapes remembered   14'
  =1 0 1 0 - 0 1 1 0 - 1perc - hp, pf - 2vn, va,   Peters
    vc, db (Strings may be increased to 4.4.4.2.2)

FLOTOW, FRIEDRICH VON, 1812-1883

Alessandro Stradella: Overture   7'
   2 2 2 2 - 4 2 3 0 - tmp+1 - str   Luck

Martha: Overture   9'
   *2 2 2 2 - 4 2 3 1 - tmp+3 - str   Breitkopf; Kalmus

FLOYD, CARLISLE, 1926-

In celebration   10'
   2 *2 2 2 - 4 2 2 1 - tmp+2 - hp, cel - str   Belwin

FOOTE, ARTHUR, 1853-1937

Air and gavotte
   2fl - str   Kalmus; Luck

Irish folk song   4'
   str   Luck

Suite, op.63, E major   15'
   str
   This work is out of print, but orchestral
   materials are in the Fleisher Collection.

FOSS, LUKAS, 1922-

Baroque variations   25'
   *3 *2 3 1 - 3 3 1 1 - (opt recorder) -   Fischer, C.
     tmp+3 - cel, electric pf, electric gtr,
     electric org, hpsd - str
   (3rd clarinetist doubles on soprano saxophone *or*
   E-flat clarinet.)

Geod   29'
   +2 *1 *3 3 - 4 2 3 0 - 4perc - hp, pf,   Fischer, C.
     org - str 12.12.8.8.8 (with substitutions
     possible)
   1 principal conductor and 4 sub-conductors. If possible, 4 microphones, 4 loudspeakers, and mixer. Also
   "11 or 12 instruments, several of these folk instruments

of the country of performance." Aleatoric procedures.

Song of songs   27'
    soprano (or mezzo-soprano) solo   Fischer, C.
    *3 *3 *3 *3 - 4(or 2) 3 2 0 - tmp+2 - hp - str

Time cycle   22'
    solo soprano   Fischer, C.
    *2 0 *2 0 - 2 2 1 0 - tmp+2 - hp, cel/pf - str
    Chamber version by the composer: soprano - cl -
    1perc - pf/cel - vc

FRACKENPOHL, ARTHUR, 1924-

Short overture   4'
    1 1 2 2 - 2 2 2 1 - tmp+3 - str   Boosey

FRANÇAIX, JEAN, 1912-

Concertino, piano   10'
    2 2 2 2 - 2 2 2 0 - str   Schott

Sei preludi (Six preludes)   15'
    str 3.3.2.2.1   Schott
    One movement features solo vc, another solo db.

FRANCK, CÉSAR, 1822-1890

Le chasseur maudit (The accursed huntsman)   14'
    *3 2 2 4 - 4 4 3 1 - tmp+3 - str   Kalmus; Presser;
                                                                      Ricordi

Les djinns   13'
    solo piano   Kalmus
    2 2 2 4 - 4 2 3 1 - tmp - str

Eight short pieces, nos.1-4   10'
    1 1 1 1 - 1 1 0 0 - tmp - str   Kalmus

Eight short pieces, nos.5-8   9'
    *1 *1 1 1 - 1 1 0 0 - tmp - str   Kalmus

Les Éolides   11'
  2 2 2 2 - 4 2 0 0 - tmp+1 - hp - str   Kalmus

Psalm 150   5'
  chorus   Breitkopf; Kalmus;
  2 2 2 2 - 4 2 3 0 - tmp+1 - hp, org - str   Peters;
                                                    Ricordi

Psyché

  1. Sommeil de Psyché   8'
     2 *3 *3 4 - 4 4 3 1 - tmp - str   Kalmus

  2. Psyché enlevée par les Zéphirs   3'
     2 *3 *3 4 - 4 4 0 0 - tmp - 2hp - str   Kalmus

  3. Les jardins d'Eros   4'
     *3 *3 *3 4 - 4 4 3 1 - tmp - str   Kalmus

  4. Psyché et Eros   6'
     2 *3 *3 4 - 4 4 3 1 - tmp - str   Kalmus

Rédemption   75'
  chorus - solo soprano   Heugel;
  2 2 2 2 - 4 2 3 1 - tmp+1 - str   Kalmus

Rédemption: Morceau symphonique   13'
  2 2 2 2 - 4 2 3 1 - tmp - str   Heugel; Kalmus; Ricordi

Symphonic variations   15'
  solo piano   Kalmus
  2 2 2 2 - 4 2 0 0 - tmp - str

Symphony in D minor   37'
  2 *3 *3 2 - 4 4 3 1 - tmp - hp - str   Boosey; Kalmus

        FREDERICK II ("THE GREAT"), 1712-1786

Concerto, flute, no.3, C major   14'
  str, cnt   Vieweg
  Ed. Gustav Lenzewski.

Concerto, flute, no.4, D major   15'
  str, cnt   Vieweg
  Ed. Gustav Lenzewski.

Symphony no.1, G major
  str, cnt   Vieweg
  Ed. Gustav Lenzewski.

Symphony no.2, G major
  str, cnt   Vieweg
  Ed. Gustav Lenzewski

  FUX, JOHANN JOSEPH, 1660-1741

Overture, C major   12'
  str - (opt cnt)   Doblinger
  Ed. Paul Angerer.

  GABRIELI, GIOVANNI, 1551-1612

Canzona   6'
  double string orchestra   Zanibon
  Ed. Franco Michele Napolitano.

Canzona noni toni, a 12, for three brass choirs   6'
  brass 0 6 6 3 or 3 6 3 3 (tubas may be omitted) Peters
  Ed. Robert Austin Boudreau.

Sonata pian' e forte   7'
  brass 1 2 4 1 - baritone horn   King
  Possible with brass 4 1 3 0, or a variety of other
  combinations. One of the parts originally intended
  for viola.

Sonata pian' e forte (ed. Fritz Stein)   7'
  brass 2 2 4 1 (possible to omit tuba)   Peters

  GADE, NIELS, 1817-1890

Nachklänge von Ossian, op.1   14'
  *2 2 2 2 - 4 2 2 1 - tmp - hp - str   Breitkopf
  (Contrabassoon may substitute for tuba.)

Symphony no.1, op.5, C minor   25'
  *3 2 2 2 - 4 2 3 1 - tmp - str   Mapleson
  (Contrabassoon may substitute for tuba.)

GALUPPI, BALDASSARE, 1706-1785

Concerto, flute, D major
  str, cnt
  Ed. Felix Schroeder.
                      13'
                   Breitkopf

Concerto, flute, G major
  str, cnt
  Ed. Johannes Brinckmann.
                   Peters

Concerto, 2 flutes, E minor
  str, cnt
  Ed. Felix Schroeder.
                      21'
                   Peters

Concerto, harpsichord, F major
  str
  Ed. Edoardo Farina.
                      14'
                  Zanibon

Concerto a quattro, no.1, G minor
  str, cnt
  Ed. Horst Heussner.
                       9'
                 Doblinger

Concerto a quattro, no.2, G major
  str, cnt
  Ed. Horst Heussner.
                       4'
                 Doblinger

Sinfonia, D major
  2hn - str
  Ed. Ettore Bonelli.
                       7'
                  Zanibon

Sinfonia, F major ("Della serenata")
  2hn - str
  Ed. Ettore Bonelli.
                       7'
                  Zanibon

GEMINIANI, FRANCESCO, 1687-1762

Concerto grosso, op.2, no.2, C minor
  str
                       9'
           Galaxy; Luck

Concerto grosso, op.2, no.3, D minor
  str, cnt
  Ed. Walter Upmeyer.
                     Vieweg

Concerti grossi, op.3
 solo concertino: 2vn, va, vc
 str (without va), cnt

 No.1, D major   14'
                Kalmus; Peters

 No.2, G minor   16'
          Kalmus; Peters; Schirmer, G.

 No.3, E minor   12'
                Kalmus; Peters

 No.4, D minor   13'
                Kalmus; Peters

 No.5, B-flat major   9'
                Kalmus; Peters

 No.6, E minor   10'
                Kalmus; Peters

Concerto grosso, op.7, no.1, D major   9'
 solo concertino: 2vn, va, vc   Bärenreiter;
 str, cnt   Nagel

Concerto grosso no.12, D minor ("La follia")   12'
 solo concertino: 2vn, va, vc   Ricordi;
 str (without va), cnt   Schott
 After Corelli, op.5, no.12.

Concerto grosso, C major   11'
 solo concertino: 2vn, vc   Nagel
 str, cnt
 After Corelli, op.5, no.3. Ed. Hugo Ruf.

  GERHARD, ROBERTO, 1896-1970

Concerto for orchestra   21'
 *3 *3 *3 *3 - 4 4 3 1 - 2tmp, 3perc - hp -   Oxford
  str 16.14.12.10.8
 All three flutists play piccolo.

Epithalamion   17'
 *4 *4 *4 *4 - 4 4 3 1 - 2tmp, 6perc - hp, pf -   Oxford
  str 16.14.12.10.8
 Two of the flutists play piccolo.

GERMAN, EDWARD, 1862-1936

Three dances from "Henry VIII"   8'
  2 2 2 2 - 2 2 3 0 - tmp+2 - str   Gray; Kalmus; Novello

GERSHWIN, GEORGE, 1898-1937

American in Paris   16'
  *3 *3 *3 2 - 4 3 3 1 - asx, tsx, bsx -   Luck;
    tmp+4 - cel - str   Warner

Concerto, piano, F major   31'
  *3 *3 *3 2 - 4 3 3 1 - tmp+3 - str   Luck; Warner

"I got rhythm" variations   9'
  solo piano   Warner
  *2 *2 *4 2 - 4 3 3 1 - (opt 2asx, tsx, bsx) -
    tmp+3 - str

Porgy and Bess: Symphonic picture   24'
  *3 *3 *3 2 - 4 3 3 1 - 2asx, tsx - tmp+3 -   Chappell
    2hp, banjo - str
  Symphonic version by Robert Russell Bennett.

Rhapsody in blue   15'
  solo piano   Luck;
  2 2 *3 2 - 4 3 3 1 - 2asx, tsx - tmp+3 -   Warner
    banjo - str

Second rhapsody for piano and orchestra   13'
  solo piano   Luck:
  *3 *3 *3 2 - 4 3 3 1 - tmp+4 - hp - str   Warner

GIANNINI, VITTORIO, 1903-1966

Symphony no.2   22'
  *3 2 2 2 - 4 3 3 1 - tmp+1 - str   Chappell

GILBERT, HENRY F., 1868-1928

Dance in the Place Congo   20'
  *3 2 *3 *3 - 4 3 3 1 - tmp+4 - hp - str   Gray

GILLIS, DON, 1912-1978

Short overture to an unwritten opera   4'
  2 2 *3 2 - 3 3 3 1 - tmp+2 - hp - str   Boosey

GINASTERA, ALBERTO, 1916-

Concerto, harp, op.25   23'
  *2 2 2 2 - 2 2 0 0 - tmp+4 - cel - str   Boosey

Concerto, piano, no.1, op.28   25'
  *3 *3 =4 *3 - 4 3 3 1 - tmp+6 - hp, cel - str   Barry

Estancia: Ballet suite   12'
  *2 2 2 2 - 4 2 0 0 - tmp+7 - pf - str   Barry

Pampeana no.3   17'
  *3 *2 2 2 - 4 3 3 1 - tmp+2 - hp, pf/cel - str   Barry

Panambí: Suite   12'
  *4 *4 =4 *4 - 4 4 3 1 - tmp+7 - 2hp, cel,   Barry
  pf - str

Variaciones concertantes   21'
  *2 1 2 1 - 2 1 1 0 - tmp - hp - str   Boosey

GLANVILLE-HICKS, PEGGY, 1912-

Gymnopédie no.1   4'
  ob - hp - str   AMP

GLAZUNOV, ALEXANDER, 1865-1936

Chant du ménestrel, op.71   3'
  solo violoncello   Belaieff;
  *3 2 2 2 - 2 0 0 0 - str   Kalmus

Chopiniana   14'
  *3 2 2 2 - 4 2 3 0 - tmp+4 - str   Belaieff;
  Chopin piano works orchestrated by Glazunov.   Kalmus
    Contents--Polonaise, op.40, no.1; Nocturne, op.15,
  no.1; Mazurka, op.50, no.3; Tarentelle, op.43.

Concerto, alto saxophone, op.109   13'
  str   Leduc

Concerto, violin, op.82, A minor   21'
  *3 2 2 2 - 4 2 3 0 - tmp+3 - hp - str   Belaieff; Kalmus

Scènes de ballet, op.52   30'
  *3 *2 3 2 - 4 3 3 1 - tmp+4 - hp - str Belaieff; Kalmus

The seasons: Autumn   10'
  *3 *2 2 2 - 4 2 3 1 - tmp+5 - hp, cel - str   Belaieff;
                                                   Kalmus

The seasons: Winter   10'
  *3 2 2 2 - 4 2 3 1 - tmp+1 - hp, cel - str   Belaieff;
                                                   Kalmus

Stenka Razine, op.13   16'
  *3 2 2 2 - 4 2 3 1 - tmp+3 - hp - str   Belaieff; Kalmus

Symphony no.4, op.48   32'
  *3 *2 3 2 - 4 2 3 1 - tmp - str   Belaieff; Kalmus

Valse de concert no.1, op.47, D major   11'
  *3 *2 3 2 - 4 2 3 0 - tmp+5 - hp - str   Belaieff;
                                                   Kalmus

Valse de concert no.2, op.51, F major   10'
  *3 2 2 2 - 4 2 3 0 - tmp+3 - hp - str   Belaieff; Kalmus

   GLIÈRE, REINHOLD, 1875-1956

Concerto, coloratura soprano and orchestra, op.82   14'
  2 2 2 2 - 3 0 0 0 - tmp - hp - str   Kalmus;
                                                Schirmer, G.

Concerto, harp, op.74, E-flat major   25'
  2 2 2 2 - 3 0 0 0 - tmp+1 - str   VAAP

Concerto, horn, op.91, B-flat major   26'
  3 2 2 2 - 3 2 3 1 - tmp+4 - hp - str   VAAP

The red poppy: Suite   20'
  *3 *3 =3 *3 - 4 3 3 1 - tmp+7 - 2hp, cel - str   VAAP

The red poppy: Russian sailors' dance   7'
  3 *3 *3 *3 - 4 3 3 1 - tmp+5 - str   Kalmus; VAAP

Symphony no.3 ("Ilya Murometz")   71'
  *4 *4 *4 *4 - 8 4 4 1 - tmp+4 - 2hp, cel - str   Kalmus;
                                                 VAAP

GLINKA, MIKHAIL, 1804-1857

Jota aragonesa (Capriccio brillante)   9'
  2 2 2 2 - 4 2 3 1 - tmp+3 - hp - str   Kalmus; Universal

Kamarinskaya   7'
  2 2 2 2 - 2 2 1 0 - tmp - str   Belaieff; Kalmus

A life for the Tsar: Overture   10'
  2 2 2 2 - 4 2 3 0 - tmp - str   Kalmus

Russlan and Ludmilla: Overture   5'
  2 2 2 *3 - 4 2 3 0 - tmp - str   Belaieff; Kalmus;
                                                 Universal

Summer night in Madrid (Spanish overture no.2)   10'
  2 2 2 2 - 4 2 1 0 - tmp+5 - str   Kalmus; Schirmer, G.

Valse fantaisie   6'
  2 2 2 2 - 2 2 1 0 - tmp+1 - str   Kalmus; Schirmer, G.;
                                                 Universal

GLUCK, CHRISTOPH WILLIBALD, 1714-1787

Alceste: Overture   10'
  2 2 2 *3 - 2 0 3 0 - str   Breitkopf; Kalmus
  (Contrabassoon is optional.)
  Concert-ending by Felix Weingartner. Bärenreiter
  publishes a version for 2 2 0 2 - 2 0 3 0 - str,
  presumably with the original ending.

Ballet suite no.1 (arr. Felix Mottl)   16'
  *3 *2 2 2 - 4 2 0 0 - tmp+2 - str   Kalmus; Peters
  Freely adapted from ballet music of various Gluck operas.

Ballet suite no.2 (arr. Felix Mottl)   15'
  *2 2 2 2 - 2 2 3 0 - tmp+2 - str   Kalmus; Peters
  Freely adapted from ballet music of various Gluck operas.

Concerto, flute, G major   15'
  2hn - str   Kalmus; Peters

Don Juan: Four movements   28'
  2 2 0 2 - 2 0 1 0 - str   Kalmus

Iphigenie in Aulis: Overture   10'
  2 2 2 2 - 4 3 0 0 - tmp - str   Breitkopf;
  Concert-ending by Richard Wagner.   Kalmus
  Bärenreiter publishes a version calling for
  2 2 0 2 - 2 2 0 0 - str, presumably with the
  original ending.

Orfeo ed Euridice: Dance of the blessed spirits   6'
  2 *1 0 0 - 2 0 0 0 - str   Kalmus
  Arr. Felix Mottl.

Orfeo ed Euridice: Dance of the furies   5'
  0 2 0 1 - 2 0 0 0 - str   Kalmus; Luck

Orfeo ed Euridice: Overture   5'
  0 2 0 1 - 2 2 0 0 - tmp - str   Kalmus; Luck

Overture, D major   5'
  str, cnt   Kalmus; Luck

Sinfonia, F major   13'
  2hn - str   Kalmus; Luck

Sinfonia, G major
  str, cnt   Kalmus

     GOŁĄBEK, JAKUB, ca.1739-1789

Symphony in C major   14'
  2 2 0 0 - 2 0 0 0 - str   PWM
  Probably originally for 2tp rather than 2hn;
  manuscript indicates "clarini."

Symphony in D major (I)   14'
  0 2 0 1 - 2 0 0 0 - str   PWM

Symphony in D major (II)   18'
  0 2 0 0 - 2 0 0 0 - str   PWM

GOLDMARK, KARL, 1830-1915

Concerto, violin, op.28, A minor   33'
  2 2 2 2 - 4 2 3 0 - tmp - str   Kalmus; Luck

Rustic wedding symphony, op.26   45'
  2 2 2 2 - 4 2 3 0 - tmp+3 - str   Kalmus; Schott

Sakuntala: Overture   19'
  2 *3 2 2 - 4 2 3 1 - tmp - hp - str   Kalmus

GOOSENS, EUGENE, 1893-1962

Concerto in one movement for oboe and orchestra, op.45 11'
  *2 0 *2 1 - 2 1 0 0 - 2perc - hp, cel - str   Leduc

GOSSEC, FRANÇOIS JOSEPH, 1734-1829

Christmas suite (Première suite de noëls, 1766)   10'
  chorus   Vieweg
  0 2 0 0 - 2 0 0 0 - str, cnt
  (Horns are optional; flutes may substitute for oboes.)

Symphony op.6, no.6
  str   Breitkopf
  Ed. Fritz Zobeley.

GOTTSCHALK, LOUIS MOREAU, 1829-1869

Grande tarantelle, piano and orchestra   8'
  2 2 2 2 - 2 2 0 0 - tmp+2 - str   Boosey
  Reconstructed and orchestrated by Hershy Kay.

Night in the tropics   19'
  *3 2 +5 2 - 4 3 2 1 - bsx, baritone horn -   Boosey
    tmp+5 - str
  Reconstructed by Gaylen Hatton.

Symphony no.2--Romantique (Montivideo)   16'
  *3 2 2 2 - 2 2 2 1 - tmp - str   Belwin

  GOULD, MORTON, 1913-

American symphonette no.2   9'
  1 1 1 1 - 2 3 3 0 - 2asx, tsx, bsx -   Belwin;
    tmp+2 - hp, pf, gtr - str   Luck
  (Percussion can be handled by a single player
  using a dance drum set.)

Fall River legend: Ballet suite (1961 version)   20'
  *2 2 2 2 - 4 2 3 0 - tmp+3 - pf - str   Chappell

Latin-American symphonette   18'
  *3 2 *4 2 - 4 3 3 1 - (opt 4sx: 2alto, tenor,   Mills
    baritone, all dbl on cl) - tmp+4 - hp,
    (opt pf, opt gtr) - str

Spirituals for orchestra   18'
  *2 2 *3 2 - 4 3 3 1 - tmp+4 - hp, (opt pf) - str   Belwin
  (Piccolo is optional.)

  GOUNOD, CHARLES, 1818-1893

Faust: Ballet music   17'
  *2 2 *3 2 - 4 4 3 1 - tmp+3 - hp - str   Kalmus

Funeral march of a marionette   6'
  *2 2 2 2 - 2 2 3 1 - tmp+3 - str   Bote; Kalmus; Luck

Little symphony for wind instruments   18'
  1 2 2 2 - 2 0 0 0   Kalmus; Luck

Messe solennelle ("St. Cecilia")   41'
  chorus - solos STB   Gray; Kalmus;
  *3 2 2 4 - 4 4 3 0 - tmp+2 - 6hp (playing   Leduc
    a single part), org - str

Symphony no.1, D major   25'
  2 2 2 2 - 2 2 0 0 - tmp - str   Kalmus

GRANADOS, ENRIQUE, 1867-1916

Dante, op.21   15'
  alto solo   Schirmer, G.
  3 *3 *3 *4 - 4 3 4 1 - 4 Wagner tubas -
  tmp+1 - 2hp (preferably doubled) - str

Goyescas: Intermezzo (from the opera)   4'
  3 *2 2 3 - 4 1 3 0 - tmp+2 - 2hp - str   Schirmer, G.

Tres danzas españolas   13'
  *3 *2 *3 2 - 4 2 3 1 - tmp+3 - hp - str   UME
  Orchestrated by J. Lamote de Grignon.

GRANDJANY, MARCEL, 1891-1975

Aria in classic style   4'
  solo harp - str   AMP

GRAUN, JOHANN GOTTLIEB, 1703-1771

Concerto, violin and viola, C minor   23'
  str, cnt   Breitkopf; Kalmus

Sinfonia, F major, M.95
  2 0 0 0 - 2 0 0 0 - str   Kalmus
  Ed. H. T. David.

GRAUPNER, CHRISTOPH, 1683-1760

Concerto, bassoon, G major
  str, cnt   Luck

Concerto, oboe, F major
  str, cnt   Kalmus

GRÉTRY, ANDRÉ, 1741-1813

Concerto, flute, C major   14'
  2hn - str   Kalmus; Peters

Zémire et Azor: Ballet suite   14'
  *2 2 2 2 - 2 0 0 0 - 2perc - str   Boosey
  Ed. and arr. by Sir Thomas Beecham.

GRIEG, EDVARD, 1843-1907

Concerto, piano, op.16, A minor   29'
  2 2 2 2 - 4 2 3 0 - tmp - str   Kalmus; Peters

Erotik, op.43, no.5 (arr. Max Spicker)   3'
  str - (opt hp)   Kalmus; Luck

Holberg suite, op.40   20'
  str   Kalmus; Peters

Landsighting, op.31   7'
  male chorus - solo baritone   Peters
  2 2 2 2 - 4 2 3 1 - tmp - (opt org) - str

Lyric pieces, op.68   6'
  0 1 0 0 - 1 0 0 0 - str   Luck;
  Piano works arranged by the composer.   Peters
  Contents--Evening in the mountains (op.68,
  no.4); At the cradle (op.68, no.5).

Lyric suite, op.54   19'
  *3 2 2 2 - 4 2 3 1 - tmp+2 - hp - str   Kalmus; Peters

Norwegian dances, op.35   17'
  *3 2 2 2 - 4 2 3 1 - tmp+2 - hp - str   Kalmus; Peters

Peer Gynt: Prelude (Im Hochzeitshof)
  *3 2 2 2 - 4 2 3 0 - tmp - hp - str   Kalmus

Peer Gynt: Suite no.1   15'
  *3 2 2 2 - 4 2 3 1 - tmp+2 - str   Kalmus;
  Contents--Morning; Ase's death; Anitra's   Peters
  dance; In the hall of the mountain king.

Peer Gynt: Suite no.2   16'
  *3 2 2 2 - 4 2 3 1 - tmp+4 - hp - str   Kalmus;
  Contents--Ingrid's lament; Arabian dance;   Peters
  Peer Gynt's homeward journey; Solveig's song.

Sigurd Jorsalfar, op.56: Three orchestral pieces   14'
  *2 2 2 2 - 4 3 3 1 - tmp+3 - hp - str   Kalmus;
    Contents--Prelude; Intermezzo; Triumphal   Peters
  march.

Symphonic dances, op.64   31'
  *3 2 2 2 - 4 2 3 1 - tmp - hp - str Fischer, C.; Kalmus

Two elegiac melodies, op.34   10'
  str   Kalmus;
    Contents--Heartwounds; Last spring.   Peters

Two melodies, op.53   5'
  str   Kalmus; Luck;
    Contents--Norwegian; The first meeting.   Peters

Two Norwegian airs, op.63   9'
  str   Kalmus;
    Contents--Popular song; Cow keeper's tune and   Luck
  Country dance.

    GRIFFES, CHARLES TOMLINSON, 1884-1920

Bacchanale   5'
  *3 *3 *3 *4 - 4 3 3 1 - tmp+2 - 2hp,   Schirmer, G.
  cel - str

Clouds   5'
  3 3 *3 3 - 4 0 0 0 - 1perc - 2hp, cel -   Schirmer, G.
  str

The pleasure dome of Kubla Khan   13'
  *3 *3 *3 3 - 4 3 3 1 - tmp+2 - 2hp,   Schirmer, G.
  cel, pf - str

Poem for flute and orchestra   9'
  2hn - 2perc - hp - str   Schirmer, G.

The white peacock   6'
  *2 2 2 2 - 2 2 2 0 - tmp - 2hp, cel -   Schirmer, G.
  str

GROFÉ, FERDE, 1892-1972

Grand Canyon suite   31'
  *3 *3 *3 *3 - 4 3 3 1 - tmp+3 - hp, pf/cel -   Luck;
    str   Robbins

GRUENBERG, LOUIS, 1884-1964

Concerto, violin, op.47   37'
  *3 *3 *3 *3 - 4 3 3 1 - harmonica - tmp+3 -
    hp, pf/cel - str
  This work is out of print, but orchestral materials
  are in the Fleisher Collection.

GUTCHE, GENE, 1907-

Holofernes overture, op.27, no.1   9'
  =3 *3 *3 *3 - 4 4 3 1 - asx - tmp+8 - str   Highgate
  (Optional instruments: afl, asx, 3rd and 4th tp.
  May be performed with 3 percussionists.)

Symphony no.5   22'
  str   Highgate

HALFFTER, ERNESTO, 1905-

La muerte de Carmen: Habanera   9'
  *3 *3 *3 3 - 4 3 3 1 - tmp+6 - 2hp - str   Eschig

HAMILTON, IAIN, 1922-

Circus   17'
  2 solo trumpets   Presser
  2 2 2 2 - 4 0 3 1 - tmp+1 - hp, pf, amplified gtr - str

Voyage, for horn and chamber orchestra   18'
  *1 1 +1 0 - 0 2 1 0 - 1perc - pf - str or   Presser
    str quintet
  Some aleatoric procedures.

HANDEL, GEORGE FRIDERIC, 1685-1759

Alceste: Instrumental pieces
0 2 0 1 - 0 1 0 0 - str, cnt   Kalmus
Ed. H. T. David.
   Contents--Overture; Symphony; Grand entrée.

Alcina: Overture   5'
   (opt 2ob) - str, cnt   Hofmeister;
   Published as "Festival music (overture and   Kalmus
   dances from 'Alcina') for string orchestra."

Alexander's feast   85'
   chorus - solos STB   Bärenreiter;
   2rec 2 0 3 - 2 2 0 0 - tmp - str, cnt   Kalmus

Alexander's feast: Overture   5'
   2ob - str, cnt   Kalmus; Luck

L'allegro, il penseroso ed il moderato   full concert
   chorus - solos SATB   Bärenreiter;
   2rec 2 0 2 - 2 2 0 0 - carillon - tmp -   Kalmus
     str, cnt

Belshazzar   150'
   chorus - solos S, 2A, 2T, 2B   Bärenreiter;
   0 2 0 0 - 0 2 0 0 - tmp - str, cnt   Peters

Brockes' passion
   See his: Passion nach Barthold Heinrich Brockes

The choice of Hercules   55'
   chorus - solos SSAT   Bärenreiter;
   2 2 0 1 - 2 2 0 0 - str, cnt   Novello

Concerto, harp, op.4, no.6, B-flat major   12'
   2rec - str, cnt   Bärenreiter; Breitkopf;
   Solo part for harp or organ   Peters; Schott

Concerto, oboe, no.1, B-flat major   6'
   str, cnt   Breitkopf
   Also known as Concerto grosso no.8.

Concerto, oboe, no.2, B-flat major   9'
   str (without va), cnt   Breitkopf
   Also known as Concerto grosso no.9.

Concerto, oboe, no.3, G minor   8'
  str, cnt   Breitkopf
  Also known as Concerto grosso no.10.

Concerto, oboe, E-flat major   10'
  str, cnt   Peters
  Ed. Fritz Stein, with added embellishments.

Concerto, organ, op.4, no.1, G minor   15'
  0 2 0 1 - str, cnt   Bärenreiter;
  (Bassoon is optional.)   Breitkopf; Schott

Concerto, organ, op.4, no.2, B-flat major   12'
  0 2 0 1 - str, cnt   Bärenreiter;
  (Bassoon is optional.)   Breitkopf, Schott

Concerto, organ, op.4, no.3, G minor   13'
  solo violin, solo violoncello, in   Bärenreiter;
    addition to solo organ   Breitkopf;
  0 2 0 1 - str, cnt   Schott
  (Bassoon is optional.)

Concerto, organ, op.4, no.4, F major   15'
  0 2 0 1 - str, cnt   Bärenreiter;
  (Bassoon is optional.)   Breitkopf; Schott

Concerto, organ, op.4, no.5, F major   10'
  0 2 0 1 - str, cnt   Bärenreiter;
  (Bassoon is optional.)   Breitkopf; Schott

Concerto, organ, op.4, no.6, B-flat major   12'
  2rec - str, cnt   Bärenreiter; Breitkopf;
  Solo part for organ or harp.   Peters; Schott

Concerto, organ, op.7, no.1, B-flat major   18'
  0 2 0 1 - str, cnt   Breitkopf; Schott

Concerto, organ, op.7, no.2, A major   18'
  0 2 0 1 - str, cnt   Breitkopf; Schott

Concerto, organ, op.7, no.3, B-flat major   10'
  0 2 0 1 - str, cnt   Breitkopf; Schott

Concerto, organ, op.7, no.4, D minor   16'
  0 2 0 1 - str, cnt   Breitkopf; Schott

Concerto, organ, op.7, no.5, G minor   14'
  0 2 0 1 - str, cnt   Breitkopf; Schott

Concerto, organ, op.7, no.6, B-flat major   13'
  0 2 0 1 - str, cnt   Breitkopf; Schott

Concerto, viola, B minor   12'
  2 0 0 2 - str   Eschig
  An assortment of movements from various works of
  Handel, compiled and arranged as a viola concerto
  by Henri Casadesus.

Concerto a due cori, no.1, B-flat major   12'
  0 4 0 2 - str, cnt   Breitkopf;
  Breitkopf title is Concerto grosso no.27.   Kalmus

Concerto a due cori, no.2, F major   10'
  0 4 0 2 - 4 0 0 0 - str (without cnt)   Breitkopf;
  Some authorities believe this and the   Kalmus
  Concerto a due cori no.3 are actually a single
  work. Breitkopf title is Concerto grosso no.28.

Concerto a due cori, no.3, F major   14'
  0 4 0 2 - 4 0 0 0 - str (without cnt)   Breitkopf;
  Some authorities believe this and the   Kalmus
  Concerto a due cori no.2 are actually a single
  work. Breitkopf title is Concerto grosso no.29.

Concerto grosso, no.7, C major ("Alexanderfest")   13'
  solo concertino: 2 violins, violoncello   Breitkopf;
  0 2 0 0 - str, 2cnt   Kalmus

Concerto grosso, nos.8-10
  See his: Concerto, oboe, nos.1-3

Concerto grosso, op.3, no.1, B-flat major   11'
  2 2 0 2 - str, 2cnt   Bärenreiter;
                                Breitkopf; Kalmus; Peters

Concerto grosso, op.3, no.2, B-flat major   12'
  solo concertino: 2 violins, violoncello   Bärenreiter;
  0 2 0 1 - str, 2cnt   Breitkopf; Kalmus; Peters

Concerto grosso, op.3, no.3, G major   9'
  solo concertino: violin, flute (or oboe)   Bärenreiter;
  str, 2cnt   Breitkopf; Kalmus; Peters

Concerto grosso, op.3, no.4, F major   12'
  0 2 0 1 - str, cnt   Bärenreiter;
                      Breitkopf; Kalmus; Peters

Concerto grosso, op.3, no.5, D minor   9'
  0 2 0 0 - str, cnt   Bärenreiter;
                      Breitkopf; Kalmus; Peters

Concerto grosso, op.3, no.6, D major   9'
  0 2 0 1 - org - str   Bärenreiter;
                      Breitkopf; Kalmus; Peters

Concerti grossi, op.6   Bärenreiter;
  solo concertino: 2 violins, violoncello   Breitkopf;
  str, 2cnt   Kalmus;
  Each concerto published separately.   Peters
  Bärenreiter edition includes 2ob and bsn in
  nos.1, 2, 5, 6.

    No.1, G major   13'

    No.2, F major   14'

    No.3, E minor   13'

    No.4, A minor   13'

    No.5, D major   17'

    No.6, G minor   20'

    No.7, B-flat major   16'
      Concertino merely doubles ripieno
      in this work.

    No.8, C minor   16'

    No.9, F major   16'

    No.10, D minor   18'

    No.11, A major   18'

    No.12, B minor   15'

Dettingen Te deum   40'
  chorus - solo bass   Peters
  0 2 0 1 - 0 3 0 0 - tmp - org, hpsd - str

Dixit dominus (Psalm 109)   30'
  chorus - solos SSATB   Bärenreiter;
  str, cnt   Kalmus

The faithful shepherd (Il pastor fido): Suite   25'
  2 2 2 2 - 4 2 0 0 - tmp+1 - str   Boosey
  Arr. Sir Thomas Beecham.

Israel in Egypt   100'
  double chorus - solos SSATBB   Bärenreiter;
  0 2 0 2 - 0 2 3 0 - tmp - org, hpsd - str   Kalmus;
  Bärenreiter edition includes 2 flutes.   Peters

Joshua   105'
  chorus - solos SSATB   Kalmus;
  2 2 0 1 - 2 3 0 0 - tmp - str, cnt   Peters

Jubilate for the Peace of Utrecht   15'
  chorus - solos AAB   Kalmus
  0 2 0 0 - 0 2 0 0 - str, cnt

Judas Maccabaeus   100'
  chorus - solos SSATBB   Kalmus;
  2 2 0 2 - 2 3 0 0 - tmp - org, hpsd - str   Peters

Judas Maccabaeus: Overture
  0 2 0 1 - str, cnt   Kalmus; Luck

Messiah   120'
  chorus - soloists SATB   Bärenreiter;
  0 2 0 2 - 0 2 0 0 - tmp - org, cnt - str   Novello;
  Novello edition (ed. Watkins Shaw) offers   Peters
  the largest number of variant movements.

Messiah (orchestrated by W. A. Mozart)   120'
  chorus - solos SATB   Peters
  2 2 2 2 - 2 2 3 0 - tmp - org - str

Messiah (orchestrated by Ebenezer Prout)   120'
  chorus - solos SATB   Schirmer, G.
  2 2 2 2 - 2 2 3 0 - tmp - pf, org - str

Occasional oratorio: Overture   10'
  0 2 0 0 - 0 3 0 0 - tmp - str, cnt   Kalmus

Ode for St. Cecilia's Day   55'
  chorus - solos ST   Bärenreiter
  1 2 0 1 - 0 2 0 0 - tmp - lute - str, cnt

Orlando: Overture
0 2 0 0 - str, cnt   Kalmus

Overture, D major (Arr. Franz Wüllner)   8'
2 3 2 *3 - 4 3 0 0 - tmp - str   Luck

Passion nach Barthold Heinrich Brockes   full concert
chorus - solos 6S, 4A, 3T, 5B (possible,   Bärenreiter
by combining roles, with solos SATTBB)
0 2 0 2 - str, cnt

Prelude and fugue, D minor   6'
*3 *3 *3 2 - 4 3 3 1 - tmp - pf - str   Belwin
Freely transcribed by Hans Kindler from op.3, no.5.

Psalm 89: My song shall be alway   30'
chorus - solos STB   Peters
0 1 0 1 - str (without va), cnt

Psalm 96: O sing unto the Lord   20'
chorus - solos ST   Peters
0 1 0 1 - str (without va), cnt

Rodrigo: Overture   15'
0 2 0 1 - str, cnt   Kalmus; Peters

Royal fireworks music   18'
0 3 0 *3 - 3 3 0 0 - tmp - str, cnt   Bärenreiter;
Breitkopf; Peters

Royal fireworks music (arr. Hamilton Harty)   11'
0 2 0 2 - 4 3 0 0 - tmp+1 - str   Chappell

Samson   85'
chorus - solos SATBB   Bärenreiter;
2 2 0 2 - 2 2 0 0 - tmp - str, cnt   Kalmus; Peters

Samson: Overture   6'
0 2 0 0 - 2 0 0 0 - str, cnt   Bärenreiter; Kalmus

Saul   full concert
chorus - solos 2S, A, 5T, 4B   Bärenreiter
2rec 2 0 2 - 0 2 3 0 - carillon - tmp -
hp, org - str, cnt

Saul: Overture   14'
  0 2 0 1 - org - str, cnt   Bärenreiter; Kalmus

Solomon   100'
  chorus - solos 4S, A, T, B   Bärenreiter;
  2 2 0 2 - 2 2 0 0 - tmp - str, cnt   Breitkopf; Gray

Solomon: Overture   12'
  0 2 0 0 - str, cnt   Kalmus

Solomon: Entrance of the Queen of Sheba   3'
  0 2 0 0 - str, cnt   Kalmus; Luck

Theodora: Overture   12'
  0 2 0 0 - str, cnt   Kalmus

Water music   50'
  1 2 0 1 - 2 2 0 0 - str, cnt   Breitkopf;
  Flute doubles flageolet or sopranino recorder.   Peters
  This version is based on the old collected
  edition of Handel's works. More recent scholarship
  suggests that the division into three separate suites
  (as in the following entries) is preferable.

Water music: Suite no.1, F major   30'
  0 2 0 1 - 2 0 0 0 - str, cnt   Bärenreiter; Eulenburg

Water music: Suite no.2, D major   11'
  0 2 0 1 - 2 2 0 0 - str, cnt   Bärenreiter; Eulenburg

Water music: Suite no.3, G major   10'
  1 2 0 1 - str, cnt   Bärenreiter;
  Flute doubles on flageolet or sopranino   Eulenburg
  recorder.

Water music suite (arr. Hamilton Harty)   16'
  *2 2 2 2 - 4 2 0 0 - tmp - str   Chappell

Xerxes: Largo (arr. Arthur Luck)   5'
  2 2 2 2 - 4 3 3 1 - hp - str   Luck

Zadok the priest (Coronation anthem no.1)   6'
  chorus - solos SSAATBB   Kalmus;
  0 2 0 2 - 0 3 0 0 - tmp - str, cnt   Schirmer, G.

HANSON, HOWARD, 1896-1981

Cherubic hymn   12'
  chorus   Fischer, C.
  *3 2 2 2 - 4 3 3 1 - tmp+1 - pf - str

Merrymount: Suite   16'
  *3 *3 *3 *3 - 4 3 3 1 - tmp+6 - 2hp - str   Warner

Serenade, op.35   6'
  solo flute   Fischer, C.
  hp - str

Symphony no.2 ("Romantic")   25'
  *3 *3 2 *3 - 4 3 3 1 - tmp+2 - hp - str   Fischer, C.

Symphony no.3   36'
  *3 *3 *3 *3 - 4 3 3 1 - tmp - str   Fischer, C.

Symphony no.4, op.34 ("Requiem")   22'
  *3 2 *2 *2 - 4 3 3 1 - tmp+2 - str   Fischer, C.

Symphony no.5 (Sinfonia sacra)   13'
  *3 2 2 2 - 4 3 3 1 - tmp+2 - hp - str   Fischer, C.

HARRIS, ROY, 1898-1979

Elegy for orchestra   6'
  *3 *3 2 *3 - 4 3 3 1 - tmp+1 - hp, cel - str   AMP

Horn of plenty   10'
  *3 *3 *3 3 - 4 4 3 1 - baritone horn - tmp+3 - str   AMP

Ode to consonance   10'
  *2 *2 *3 2 - 2 3 2 1 - baritone horn - tmp+1 -   AMP
    hp - str

Symphony no.3   18'
  *3 *3 *3 2 - 4 3 3 2 - tmp+2 - str   Schirmer, G.

Symphony no.5   26'
  *3 *3 *3 3 - 4 3 3 1 - tmp+6 - hp, pf - str   Belwin
  (Additional optional instruments: tenor saxophone,
  baritone tuba, E-flat clarinet. The composer
  specifies from 4 to 8 horns.)

Symphony no.7   19'
  *4 *4 *4 *4 - 6 4 3 1 - baritone horn - tmp+3 -   AMP
    hp, pf - str
  (5th and 6th horns and 4th trumpet are optional.)

Symphony no.9   25'
  *4 *4 *4 *4 - 6 4 4 1 - baritone horn - tmp+3 -   AMP
    hp, pf - str

When Johnny comes marching home   8'
  *3 *3 *3 3 - 4 3 3 1 - euphonium -   Schirmer, G.
    2tmp, 2perc - str

HARSÁNYI, TIBOR, 1898-1954

L'histoire du petite tailleur (The story of   30'
    the little tailor)   25' without narration
    narrator   Eschig
  *1 0 1 1 - 0 1 0 0 - 1perc - pf - vn, vc
  Composed for marionettes, after a tale of Grimm.

HARTMANN, KARL AMADEUS, 1905-1963

Symphony no.6   27'
  *3 *3 *3 *3 - 4 4 3 1 - tmp+8 - hp, cel,   Schott
    pf 4-hands, mandoline - str

HAYDN, FRANZ JOSEPH, 1732-1809

Concertino, harpsichord, Hob.XIV:11, C major   10'
    str   Doblinger
  Ed. H. C. Robbins Landon.

Concerto, flute, Hob.VIIf:D1, D major   20'
    str - (opt cnt)   Leuckart
  Ed. Alexander Kowatscheff. Authenticity doubtful.

Concerto, 2 flutes, Hob.VIIh:1, C major   16'
    2hn - str   Doblinger
  Originally for 2 lire organizzate. Ed. H. C.
  Robbins Landon.

Concerto, flute and oboe, Hob.VIIh:2, G major   14'
  2hn - str   Doblinger
  Originally for 2 lire organizzate. Ed. H. C.
  Robbins Landon.

Concerto, flute and oboe, Hob.VIIh:3, G major   15'
  2hn - str   Doblinger
  Originally for 2 lire organizzate. Ed. H. C.
  Robbins Landon.

Concerto, flute and oboe, Hob.VIIh:4, F major   14'
  2hn - str   Doblinger
  Originally for 2 lire organizzate. Ed. H. C.
  Robbins Landon.

Concerto, flute and oboe, Hob.VIIh:5, F major   13'
  2hn - str   Doblinger
  Originally for 2 lire organizzate. Ed. H. C.
  Robbins Landon.

Concerto, harpsichord, Hob.XVIII:4, G major   15'
  0 2 0 0 - 2 0 0 0 - str   Nagel;
  (Winds are optional.) Ed. Bruno Hinze-Reinhold. Peters

Concerto, harpsichord, Hob.XVIII:7, F major   12'
  str (va optional)   KaWe
  Ed. Klaas Weelink.

Concerto, harpsichord, Hob.XVIII:11, D major   20'
  0 2 0 0 - 2 0 0 0 - str   Breitkopf; Peters

Concerto, harpsichord, Hob.XVIII:F1, F major   12'
  2fl - str   Vieweg
  Ed. Gustav Lenzewski. Probably incorrectly
  attributed to Haydn.

Concerto, horn, no.1, Hob.VIId:3, D major   14'
  2ob - str, cnt   Boosey; Bote; Kalmus

Concerto, horn, no.2, Hob.VIId:4, D major   15'
  str   Boosey; Breitkopf

Concerto, oboe, Hob.VIIg:C1, C major   23'
  0 2 0 0 - 2 2 0 0 - tmp - str   Breitkopf;
  Authenticity doubtful.   Oxford; Peters

Concerto, organ, Hob.XVIII:1, C major   19'
  2ob - str   Breitkopf
  Ed. Michael Schneider.

Concerto, organ, no.2, Hob.XVIII:8, C major   13'
  str - (opt 2tp, opt tmp)   Doblinger
  Ed. H. C. Robbins Landon.

Concerto, organ, F major   14'
  2hn - str   Breitkopf
  Ed. Belsky and Sramek. First published in
  1962, and not listed in Hoboken.

Concerto, trumpet, Hob.VIIe:1, E-flat major   14'
  2 2 0 2 - 2 2 0 0 - tmp - str   Boosey; Breitkopf;
                                 Fischer, C.; Kalmus

Concerto, violin, no.1, Hob.VIIa:1, C major   24'
  str, cnt   Breitkopf; Eulenburg

Concerto, violin, no.2, Hob.VIIa:4, G major   20'
  str, cnt   Breitkopf; Doblinger

Concerto, violin, no.3, Hob.VIIa:B2, B-flat major   27'
  str, cnt   Breitkopf
  Of very doubtful authenticity.

Concerto, violoncello, Hob.VIIb:2, D major   26'
  0 2 0 0 - 2 0 0 0 - str   Peters; Schott

Concerto, violoncello, Hob.VIIb:2, D major
  (arr. F. A. Gevaert)   26'
  2 2 2 2 - 2 0 0 0 - str   Breitkopf

Concerto, violoncello, Hob.VIIb:5, C major   17'
  2 2 2 2 - 2 0 0 0 - str   Kalmus
  Completed by David Popper after a sketch by Haydn.

The creation (Die Schöpfung)   105'
  chorus - solos SSTBB (or STB)   Breitkopf; Kalmus;
  3 2 2 *3 - 2 2 3 0 - tmp - hpsd - str   Peters;
                                  Schirmer, G.

Divertimento no.9, Hob.II:21, E-flat major
  2hn - str   Möseler
  Also exists as a string quartet (Hob.III:9).

Die Jahreszeiten
    See his: The seasons

Kindersymphonie
    See his: Toy symphony

March for the Royal Society of Musicians   4'
    2 0 2 2 - 2 2 0 0 - tmp - str   Doblinger
    The second (orchestral) version of the "March for
    the Prince of Wales." Ed. H. C. Robbins Landon.

Masses

    The Haydn masses have acquired such a multitude of
    titles, subtitles, and nicknames over the years, that
    these are listed below, together with the Hoboken
    number under which the complete entry appears.

Caecilienmesse	Hob.XXII: 5
Coronation mass	XXII:11
Creation mass	XXII:13
Grosse Orgelsolo Messe	XXII: 4
Harmoniemesse	XXII:14
Heiligmesse	XXII:10
L'impérial	XXII:11
Jugendmesse	XXII: 1
Kleine Orgelmesse	XXII: 7
Little organ mass	XXII: 7
Lord Nelson mass	XXII:11
Mariazeller Messe	XXII: 8
Mass in time of war	XXII: 9
Missa brevis	XXII: 1
Missa brevis alla capella	XXII: 3
Missa brevis Sancti Johannis de Deo	XXII: 7
Missa cellensis	XXII: 5, or 8
Missa in angustiis	XXII:11
Missa in honorem beatissimae virginis Mariae	XXII: 4
Missa in tempore belli	XXII: 9
Missa Sanctae Caeciliae	XXII: 5
Missa Sancti Bernardi von Offida	XXII:10
Missa Sancti Josephi	XXII: 6
Missa Sancti Nicolai	XXII: 6
Nelsonmesse	XXII:11
Nicolaimesse	XXII: 6
Orgel-Solo-Messe	XXII: 4

Paukenmesse   Hob.XXII: 9
Rorati coeli desuper   XXII: 3
Saint Cecilia   XXII: 5
Schöpfungsmesse   XXII:13
Theresienmesse   XXII:12

Mass, Hob.XXII:1, F major ("Missa brevis")   13'
  chorus - 2 solo sopranos   Doblinger
  str - org
  Ed. Richard Moder. Also known as "Jugendmesse."
  Additional instrumental parts were supplied later,
  supposedly at Haydn's suggestion: 1 0 2 2 - 0 2 0 0 - tmp.

Mass, Hob.XXII:2
  This work is for chorus a cappella, and thus
  outside the scope of this book.

Mass, Hob.XXII:3, G major ("Rorate coeli desuper")   10'
  chorus - org - str   Universal
  Ed. H. C. Robbins Landon. Also known as "Missa
  brevis alla capella."

Mass, Hob.XXII:4, E-flat major ("Grosse Orgelsolomesse")
  chorus - solos SATB   41'
  2Eh, bsn - 2hn - org - str   Doblinger
  Ed. Alois Strassl. Also known as "Missa in honorem
  beatissimae virginis Mariae."

Mass, Hob.XXII:5, C major ("St. Cecilia mass")   70'
  chorus - solos SATB   Universal
  0 2 0 2 - 0 2 0 0 - tmp - org - str
  In the Benedictus, the composer may have added
  2 horns later. Both this work and Hob.XXII:8 are
  also known as "Missa cellensis."

Mass, Hob.XXII:6, G major ("Missa Sancti Nicolai")   26'
  chorus - solos SATB   Faber;
  0 2 0 1 - 0 2 0 0 - org - str   Kalmus
  Faber edition is by H. C. Robbins Landon. Also
  sometimes referred to as "Missa St. Josephi."

Mass, Hob.XXII:7, B-flat major ("Kleine Orgelmesse") 20'
  chorus - soprano solo   Bärenreiter
  str - org
  Ed. H. C. Robbins Landon. Also known as "Missa brevis
  Sancti Johannis de Deo."

Mass,Hob.XXII:8, C major ("Mariazeller Messe")   40'
  chorus - solos SATB   Bärenreiter;
  0 2 0 1 - 0 2 0 0 - tmp - org - str   Kalmus
  Both this work and Hob.XXII:5 are also known
  as "Missa cellensis."

Mass, Hob.XXII:9, C major ("Missa in tempore belli"
  or "Mass in time of war")   45'
  chorus - solos SATB   Bärenreiter;
  0 2 2 2 - 2 2 0 0 - tmp - org - str   Kalmus;
  Also known as "Paukenmesse."   Schirmer, G.

Mass, Hob.XXII:10, B-flat major ("Heiligmesse")   45'
  chorus - solos SATB (or SSATBB)   Bärenreiter;
  0 2 2 2 - 0 2 0 0 - tmp - org - str   Peters
  Clarinets are used only in the Incarnatus
  and Vitam. Peters edition treats them as an
  alternative to the oboes (i.e. 2ob *or* 2cl).

Mass, Hob.XXII:11, D minor ("Lord Nelson mass")   45'
  chorus - solos SATB
  original instrumentation (Schott):
    3tp - tmp - org - str
  later instrumentation, with winds added supposedly
    at Haydn's suggestion (Breitkopf, Peters):
    1 2 0 2 - 0 3 0 0 - tmp - org - str
  the same, but with the optional clarinets and horns
    suggested at the same time (Bärenreiter):
    1 2 2 1 - 2 3 0 0 - tmp - org - str
  Also known as: "Missa in angustiis," "Nelsonmesse,"
  "L'impérial," and "Coronation mass."

Mass, Hob.XXII:12, B-flat major ("Theresienmesse")   43'
  chorus - solos SATB   Bärenreiter;
  0 0 2 1 - 0 2 0 0 - tmp - org - str   Gray
  (An authentic copy has additional parts for 2ob
  and 2hn, though these are not as yet available
  in any modern edition.)

Mass, Hob.XXII:13, B-flat major ("Schöpfungsmesse")   46'
  chorus - solos SATB (or SSATTB)   Kalmus
  0 2 2 2 - 2 2 0 0 - tmp - org - str

Mass, Hob.XXII:14, B-flat major ("Harmoniemesse")   40'
  chorus - solos SATB (or SSATTB)   Bärenreiter; Kalmus;
  1 2 2 2 - 2 2 0 0 - tmp - org - str   Peters; Schirmer, G.

Die Schöpfung
  See his: The creation

The seasons (Die Jahreszeiten)   120'
  chorus - solos STB   Breitkopf; Gray;
  *2 2 2 *3 - 4 3 3 0 - tmp+2 - pf - str   Kalmus; Peters

Seven last words of Christ (choral version)   60'
  chorus - solos SATB   Bärenreiter; Breitkopf;
  2 2 2 *3 - 2 2 2 0 - tmp - str   Kalmus; Peters

Seven last words of Christ (orchestral version)   62'
  2 2 0 2 - 4 2 0 0 - tmp - str   Bärenreiter

Sinfonia Berchtolsgadensis
  See his: Toy symphony

Sinfonia concertante, op.84, Hob.I:105, B-flat major   23'
  solos: oboe, bassoon, violin, violoncello   Breitkopf
  1 2 0 2 - 2 2 0 0 - tmp - str

Stabat mater, Hob.XXbis   80'
  chorus - solos SATB   Faber;
  2Eh, bsn - org - str   Kalmus
  Faber edition by H. C. Robbins Landon.

Symphonies

    *Although there are many editions of the various
  Haydn symphonies, most fail to meet modern standards
  of scholarship. The editions cited here (those of
  the Haydn-Mozart Presse, edited by H. C. Robbins
  Landon) are by far the best.*

    *Entries for the individual symphonies are preceded
  by a reference list of popular titles.*

                Alleluja   Symphony no.30
                La chasse   73
                The clock   101
                Il distratto   60
                Drum roll   103
                Farewell   45
                Feuersymphonie   59
                Hornsignal   31
                L'imperiale   53
                Lamentatione   26
                Laudon   69

```
      London           Symphony no.104
      Maria Theresia            48
      Le matin                   6
      Mercury                   43
      Le midi                    7
      Military                 100
      The miracle               96
      L'ours                    82
      Oxford                    92
      La passione               49
      Paukenschlag              94
      Paukenwirbel             103
      The philosopher           22
      La poule                  83
      La reine                  85
      La Roxelane               63
      Der Schulmeister          55
      Le soir                    8
      Surprise                  94
      Tempora mutantur          64
      Toy symphony     listed by title
      Trauer-Symphonie          44
```

Symphony "A," Hob.I:107, B-flat major   10'
  0 2 0 1 - 2 0 0 0 - str, cnt   Doblinger

Symphony "B," Hob.I:108, B-flat major   15'
  0 2 0 1 - 2 0 0 0 - str, cnt   Doblinger

Symphony no.1, D major   11'
  0 2 0 1 - 2 0 0 0 - str, cnt   Doblinger

Symphony no.2, C major   10'
  0 2 0 1 - 2 0 0 0 - str, cnt   Doblinger

Symphony no.3, G major   16'
  0 2 0 1 - 2 0 0 0 - str, cnt   Doblinger

Symphony no.4, D major   15'
  0 2 0 1 - 2 0 0 0 - str, cnt   Doblinger

Symphony no.5, A major   14'
  0 2 0 1 - 2 0 0 0 - str, cnt   Doblinger

Symphony no.6, D major ("Le matin")   21'
  1 2 0 1 - 2 0 0 0 - str, cnt   Doblinger

Symphony no.7, C major ("Le midi")   24'
2 2 0 1 - 2 0 0 0 - str, cnt   Doblinger

Symphony no.8, G major ("Le soir")   21'
1 2 0 1 - 2 0 0 0 - str, cnt   Doblinger

Symphony no.9, C major   13'
2 2 0 1 - 2 0 0 0 - str, cnt   Doblinger

Symphony no.10, D major   14'
0 2 0 1 - 2 0 0 0 - str, cnt   Doblinger

Symphony no.11, E-flat major   14'
0 2 0 1 - 2 0 0 0 - str, cnt   Doblinger

Symphony no.12, E major   12'
0 2 0 1 - 2 0 0 0 - str, cnt   Doblinger

Symphony no.13, D major   20'
1 2 0 1 - 4 0 0 0 - tmp - str, cnt   Doblinger

Symphony no.14, A major   16'
0 2 0 1 - 2 0 0 0 - str, cnt   Doblinger

Symphony no.15, D major   22'
0 2 0 1 - 2 0 0 0 - str, cnt   Doblinger

Symphony no.16, B-flat major   13'
0 2 0 1 - 2 0 0 0 - str, cnt   Doblinger

Symphony no.17, F major   14'
0 2 0 1 - 2 0 0 0 - str, cnt   Doblinger

Symphony no.18, G major   15'
0 2 0 1 - 2 0 0 0 - str, cnt   Doblinger

Symphony no.19, D major   12'
0 2 0 1 - 2 0 0 0 - str, cnt   Doblinger

Symphony no.20, C major   20'
0 2 0 1 - 2 2 0 0 - tmp - str, cnt   Doblinger

Symphony no.21, A major   22'
0 2 0 1 - 2 0 0 0 - str, cnt   Doblinger

Symphony no.22, E-flat major ("The philosopher")   23'
  2Eh, bsn - 2hn - str, cnt   Doblinger

Symphony no.23, G major   20'
  0 2 0 1 - 2 0 0 0 - str, cnt   Doblinger

Symphony no.24, D major   21'
  1 2 0 1 - 2 0 0 0 - str, cnt   Doblinger

Symphony no.25, C major   14'
  0 2 0 1 - 2 0 0 0 - str, cnt   Doblinger

Symphony no.26, D minor ("Lamentatione")   21'
  0 2 0 1 - 2 0 0 0 - str, cnt   Doblinger

Symphony no.27, G major   14'
  0 2 0 1 - 2 0 0 0 - str, cnt   Doblinger

Symphony no.28, A major   16'
  0 2 0 1 - 2 0 0 0 - str, cnt   Doblinger

Symphony no.29, E major   17'
  0 2 0 1 - 2 0 0 0 - str, cnt   Doblinger

Symphony no.30, C major ("Alleluja")   12'
  1 2 0 1 - 2 0 0 0 - str, cnt   Doblinger

Symphony no.31, D major ("Hornsignal")   28'
  1 2 0 1 - 4 0 0 0 - str, cnt   Doblinger

Symphony no.32, C major   20'
  0 2 0 1 - 2 2 0 0 - tmp - str, cnt   Doblinger

Symphony no.33, C major   21'
  0 2 0 1 - 2 2 0 0 - tmp - str, cnt   Doblinger

Symphony no.34, D minor   18'
  0 2 0 1 - 2 0 0 0 - str, cnt   Doblinger

Symphony no.35, B-flat major   17'
  0 2 0 1 - 2 0 0 0 - str, cnt   Doblinger

Symphony no.36, E-flat major   18'
  0 2 0 1 - 2 0 0 0 - str, cnt   Doblinger

Symphony no.37, C major   15'
   0 2 0 1 - 2 0 0 0 - str, cnt   Doblinger
   (An alternative version substitutes 2 trumpets
   and timpani for the horns.)

Symphony no.38, C major   22'
   0 2 0 1 - 2 2 0 0 - tmp - str, cnt   Doblinger

Symphony no.39, G minor   21'
   0 2 0 1 - 4 0 0 0 - str, cnt   Doblinger

Symphony no.40, F major   17'
   0 2 0 1 - 2 0 0 0 - str, cnt   Doblinger

Symphony no.41, C major   24'
   1 2 0 1 - 2 2 0 0 - tmp - str   Doblinger

Symphony no.42, D major   22'
   0 2 0 2 - 2 0 0 0 - str   Doblinger

Symphony no.43, E-flat major ("Mercury")   23'
   0 2 0 1 - 2 0 0 0 - str   Doblinger

Symphony no.44, E minor ("Trauer-Symphonie") 24'
   0 2 0 1 - 2 0 0 0 - str   Doblinger

Symphony no.45, F-sharp minor ("Farewell")   25'
   0 2 0 1 - 2 0 0 0 - str   Doblinger

Symphony no.46, B major   22'
   0 2 0 1 - 2 0 0 0 - str   Doblinger

Symphony no.47, G major   24'
   0 2 0 1 - 2 0 0 0 - str   Doblinger

Symphony no.48, C major ("Maria Theresia")   23'
   0 2 0 1 - 2 2 0 0 - tmp - str   Doblinger

Symphony no.49, F minor ("La passione")   21'
   0 2 0 1 - 2 0 0 0 - str, cnt   Doblinger

Symphony no.50, C major   22'
   0 2 0 1 - 2 2 0 0 - tmp - str   Universal

Symphony no.51, B-flat major   23'
   0 2 0 1 - 2 0 0 0 - str   Universal

Symphony no.52, C minor   23'
 0 2 0 1 - 2 0 0 0 - str   Universal

Symphony no.53, D major ("L'imperiale")   24'
 1 2 0 1 - 2 0 0 0 - tmp - str   Universal
(Alternate finales, one of which calls for
2 bassoons.)

Symphony no.54, G major   34'
 2 2 0 2 - 2 2 0 0 - tmp - str   Universal

Symphony no.55, E-flat major ("Der Schulmeister")   21'
 0 2 0 2 - 2 0 0 0 - str   Universal

Symphony no.56, C major   28'
 0 2 0 1 - 2 2 0 0 - tmp - str   Universal

Symphony no.57, D major   24'
 0 2 0 1 - 2 0 0 0 - tmp - str   Universal

Symphony no.58, F major   22'
 0 2 0 1 - 2 0 0 0 - str, cnt   Universal

Symphony no.59, A major ("Feuersymphonie")   22'
 0 2 0 1 - 2 0 0 0 - str, cnt   Universal

Symphony no.60, C major ("Il distratto")   28'
 0 2 0 1 - 2 2 0 0 - tmp - str   Universal

Symphony no.61, D major   26'
 1 2 0 2 - 2 0 0 0 - tmp - str   Universal

Symphony no.62, D major   22'
 1 2 0 2 - 2 0 0 0 - str   Universal

Symphony no.63, C major ("La Roxelane")   22'
 1 2 0 1 - 2 0 0 0 - str   Universal

Symphony no.64, A major ("Tempora mutantur")   20'
 0 2 0 1 - 2 0 0 0 - str   Universal

Symphony no.65, A major   23'
 0 2 0 1 - 2 0 0 0 - str   Universal

Symphony no.66, B-flat major   21'
 0 2 0 2 - 2 0 0 0 - str   Universal

Symphony no.67, F major   25'
  0 2 0 2 - 2 0 0 0 - str   Universal

Symphony no.68, B-flat major   23'
  0 2 0 2 - 2 0 0 0 - str   Universal

Symphony no.69, C major ("Laudon")   22'
  0 2 0 2 - 2 2 0 0 - tmp - str   Universal

Symphony no.70, D major   22'
  1 2 0 1 - 2 2 0 0 - tmp - str   Universal

Symphony no.71, B-flat major   21'
  1 2 0 1 - 2 0 0 0 - str   Universal

Symphony no.72, D major   26'
  1 2 0 1 - 4 0 0 0 - tmp - str, cnt   Universal

Symphony no.73, D major ("La chasse")   21'
  1 2 0 2 - 2 2 0 0 - tmp - str   Universal

Symphony no.74, E-flat major   21'
  1 2 0 2 - 2 0 0 0 - str   Universal

Symphony no.75, D major   24'
  1 2 0 1 - 2 2 0 0 - tmp - str   Universal

Symphony no.76, E-flat major   23'
  1 2 0 2 - 2 0 0 0 - str   Universal

Symphony no.77, B-flat major   23'
  1 2 0 2 - 2 0 0 0 - str   Universal

Symphony no.78, C minor   22'
  1 2 0 2 - 2 0 0 0 - str   Universal

Symphony no.79, F major   21'
  1 2 0 2 - 2 0 0 0 - str   Universal

Symphony no.80, D minor   20'
  1 2 0 2 - 2 0 0 0 - str   Universal

Symphony no.81, G major   21'
  1 2 0 2 - 2 0 0 0 - str   Universal

Symphony no.82, C major ("L'ours")   23'
  1 2 0 2 - 2 2 0 0 - tmp - str   Universal
  (Trumpets are optional.)

Symphony no.83, G minor ("La poule")   22'
  1 2 0 2 - 2 0 0 0 - str   Universal

Symphony no.84, E-flat major   25'
  1 2 0 2 - 2 0 0 0 - str   Universal

Symphony no.85, B-flat major ("La reine")   21'
  1 2 0 2 - 2 0 0 0 - str   Universal

Symphony no.86, D major   26'
  1 2 0 2 - 2 2 0 0 - tmp - str   Universal

Symphony no.87, A major   21'
  1 2 0 2 - 2 0 0 0 - str   Universal

Symphony no.88, G major   25'
  1 2 0 2 - 2 2 0 0 - tmp - str   Universal

Symphony no.89, F major   23'
  1 2 0 2 - 2 0 0 0 - str   Universal

Symphony no.90, C major   24'
  1 2 0 2 - 2 2 0 0 - tmp - str   Universal

Symphony no.91, E-flat major   24'
  1 2 0 2 - 2 0 0 0 - str   Universal

Symphony no.92, G major ("Oxford")   25'
  1 2 0 2 - 2 2 0 0 - tmp - str   Universal

Symphony no.93, D major   26'
  2 2 0 2 - 2 2 0 0 - tmp - str   Universal

Symphony no.94, G major ("Surprise")   24'
  2 2 0 2 - 2 2 0 0 - tmp - str   Universal

Symphony no.95, C minor   25'
  1 2 0 2 - 2 2 0 0 - tmp - str   Universal

Symphony no.96, D major ("The miracle")   25'
  2 2 0 2 - 2 2 0 0 - tmp - str   Universal

Symphony no.97, C major   26'
  2 2 0 2 - 2 2 0 0 - tmp - str   Universal

Symphony no.98, B-flat major   30'
  1 2 0 2 - 2 2 0 0 - tmp - str   Universal
  Brief harpsichord solo in 4th movement.

Symphony no.99, E-flat major   29'
  2 2 2 2 - 2 2 0 0 - tmp - str   Universal

Symphony no.100, G major ("Military")   28'
  2 2 2 2 - 2 2 0 0 - tmp+3 - str   Universal

Symphony no.101, D major ("The clock")   28'
  2 2 2 2 - 2 2 0 0 - tmp - str   Universal

Symphony no.102, B-flat major   26'
  2 2 0 2 - 2 2 0 0 - tmp - str   Universal

Symphony no.103, E-flat major ("Drum roll")   30'
  2 2 2 2 - 2 2 0 0 - tmp - str   Universal

Symphony no.104, D major ("London")   29'
  2 2 2 2 - 2 2 0 0 - tmp - str   Universal

Te deum for the Empress Maria Therese, Hob.XXIIIc:2   12'
  chorus   Doblinger
  1 2 0 2 - 2 3 3 0 - tmp - org - str
  (Trombones only double chorus parts.)
  Ed. H. C. Robbins Landon

Toy symphony, Hob.II:47, C major   12'
  str (without va) - 5 players for toys   Breitkopf;
    (trumpet, drum, cuckoo, nightingale,   Kalmus
    rattle, triangle, quail)
  Though commonly attributed to Haydn, the actual
  composer is believed to be Leopold Mozart.

HAYDN, MICHAEL, 1737-1806

Andromeda ed Perseo, P.25: Overture   5'
  0 2 0 2 - 2 2 0 0 - tmp - str   Bärenreiter; Doblinger

Concertino, horn, D major   12'
  0 2 0 1 - 2 0 0 0 - str, cnt   Universal
  Ed. Charles H. Sherman.

Concerto, violin, A major   18'
  0 2 0 1 - 2 0 0 0 - str   Doblinger
  Ed. Charles H. Sherman.

Missa pro defunctis   45'
  chorus - solos SATB   Universal
  0 0 0 1 - 0 4 3 0 - tmp - org - str
  Ed. Charles H. Sherman.

Missa Sancti Hieronymi   45'
  chorus   Universal
  0 4 0 2 - 0 0 3 0 - org - double basses
  Ed. Charles H. Sherman.

Pastorello, P.91 ("Christmas music, Salzburg, 1766")   10'
  4tp - tmp - str, cnt   Peters
  (3rd and 4th tp parts may be played on tbn.)

Symphony, P.8, G major   5'
  str   Doblinger
  Ed. Charles H. Sherman.

Symphony, P.21, D major (1785)   19'
  1 2 0 2 - 2 0 0 0 - str   Doblinger
  Ed. Pál Gombás.

Symphony, P.26, E-flat major (1788)   8'
  0 2 0 2 - 2 0 0 0 - str   Doblinger
  Ed. Antal Várhelyi.

Symphony, P.29, D major (1788)   8'
  1 2 0 2 - 2 0 0 0 - str   Doblinger
  Ed. Lászlo Kalmár.

Symphony, P.33, A major   15'
  0 2 0 2 - 2 0 0 0 - str   Doblinger
  Ed. Charles H. Sherman.

Symphony, P.37, G major
  See: Mozart, Wolfgang Amadeus, 1756-1791
       Symphony no.37

Symphony, P.42, D major   18'
  0 2 0 1 - 2 0 0 0 - str   Doblinger
  Ed. H. C. Robbins Landon.

Veni, sancte spiritus
  chorus   Peters
  0 2 0 0 - 2 0 3 0 - org - str (without va)
  (Trombones are optional.) Ed. Harry Graf.

   HENZE, HANS WERNER, 1926-

Compases para preguntas ensimismadas (Music for
  viola and 22 players)   26'
  =1 *1 *1 1 - 1 0 0 0 - recorder - tmp+1 -   Schott
    hp, pf/cel, amplified hpsd - 6vn, no va, 4vc, db

Ode an den Westwind   22'
  violoncello solo   Schott
  *2 *2 *2 *2 - 2 2 1 1 - tmp+8 - hp, pf, cel -
    str: 20vn, 12va, no vc, 8 db

Symphony no.5   18'
  =4 *4 0 0 - 4 4 4 0 - tmp - 2hp, 2pf - str   Schott
  Two of the oboists double on English horn.

   HERBERT, VICTOR, 1859-1924

Concerto, violoncello, no.2, op.30   23'
  2 2 2 2 - 4 2 3 0 - tmp - str   Luck

Serenade, op.12   22'
  str   Luck

   HÉROLD, LOUIS JOSEPH F., 1791-1833

Zampa: Overture   8'
  *2 2 2 2 - 4 2 3 1 - tmp+3 - str   Kalmus; Luck; Ricordi

   HESELTINE, PHILIP, 1894-1930
    See the pseudonym: Warlock, Peter, 1894-1930

HINDEMITH, PAUL, 1895-1963

Concert music for strings and brass, op.50   18'
  brass 4 4 3 1 - str   Schott

Concert music for viola and
  large chamber orchestra, op.48   20'
  *2 *2 *2 *3 - 3 2 1 1 - 4vc, 4db   Schott

Concerto, horn (1949)   15'
  *1 2 2 2 - tmp - str   Schott

Concerto for orchestra, op.38   17'
  *2 2 =3 *3 - 3 2 2 1 - tmp+5 - str   Schott

Concerto, organ (1962)   25'
  *2 2 2 *3 - 2 2 3 1 - tmp+2 - cel - str   Schott

Concerto, piano, op.36, no.1 (Kammermusik no.2)   20'
  1 1 *2 1 - 1 1 1 0 - vn, va, vc, db   Schott

Concerto, viola, op.36, no.4 (Kammermusik no.5)   17'
  *1 1 =3 *3 - 1 2 2 1 - 4vc, 4db   Schott

Concerto, violin (1939)   26'
  *2 2 *3 2 - 4 2 3 1 - tmp+3 - str   Schott

Concerto for woodwinds, harp, and orchestra (1949)   15'
  solos: flute, oboe, clarinet, bassoon, harp   Schott
  brass 2 2 1 0 - str

Cupid and Psyche: Overture   6'
  *2 2 2 2 - 2 2 2 0 - tmp+1 - str   Schott

Die Harmonie der Welt: Symphony   34'
  *2 2 *3 *3 - 4 2 3 1 - tmp+5 - str   Schott

Mathis der Maler: Symphony   26'
  *2 2 2 2 - 4 2 3 1 - tmp+3 - str   Schott

Neues vom Tage: Overture   8'
  *2 *2 =3 *3 - 1 2 2 1 - asx - 3perc - str   Schott

Nobilissima visione   23'
  *2 2 2 2 - 4 2 3 1 - tmp+4 - str   Schott

Philharmonic concerto   20'
  *3 *3 *3 *3 - 4 3 3 1 - tmp+3 - str   Schott

Pittsburgh symphony   26'
  *2 *3 *3 *3 - 4 2 3 1 - tmp+4 - str   Schott

Der Schwanendreher   25'
  solo viola   Schott
  *2 1 2 2 - 3 1 1 0 - tmp - hp - str (without vn or va)

Sinfonietta in E   21'
  *2 2 2 2 - 3 1 2 1 - tmp+1 - cel - str   Schott

Spielmusik, op.43, no.1   7'
  2 2 0 0 - str   Schott

Suite of French dances   8'
  *2 *2 0 1 - 0 1 0 0 - lute - str (3va, 2vc;   Schott
    or 2vn, va, 2vc; *or* string orchestra)
  (Winds are optional.) After 16th century dances.

Symphonia serena   28'
  *3 *3 *3 *3 - 4 2 2 1 - tmp+4 - cel - str Schott

Symphonic metamorphoses of themes by Weber 18'
  *3 *3 *3 *3 - 4 2 3 1 - tmp+4 - str   Schott

Symphony in E-flat   34'
  *3 *3 *3 *3 - 4 3 3 1 - tmp+4 - str   Schott

Theme and variations ("The four temperaments") 28'
  solo piano - str   Schott

Trauermusik (Music of mourning)   6'
  solo viola (or violin or violoncello)   Schott
  str

Tuttifäntchen: Suite for small orchestra   20'
  *1 1 1 1 - 1 1 0 0 - tmp+1 - str   Schott
  The work from which the suite is drawn is
  a Christmas fairy tale in three scenes.

HOAG, CHARLES KELSO, 1931-

An after-intermission overture for youth orchestra   3'
   2 2 2 2 - 4 3 3 1 - tmp+1 - pf - str   Schirmer, G.

HOFER, ANDREAS, 1629-1684

Te deum   9'
   double chorus   Universal
   2 cornetti (or 2ob or 2cl), bsn, (opt cbn) -
     4tp, 3tbn, bass tp (or bsn) - tmp - str, cnt
   Forces are divided into 3 orchestras and 2 choruses.
   Ed. Charles H. Sherman.

HOFFMANN, GEORG MELCHIOR, 18th century

Meine Seele rühmt und preist
   See: Bach, Johann Sebastian, 1685-1750
       Cantata no.189

Schlage doch, gewünschte Stunde
   See: Bach, Johann Sebastian, 1685-1750
       Cantata no.53

HOLLINGSWORTH, STANLEY, 1924-

Concerto, piano   14'
   *2 2 2 2 - 2 1 0 0 - tmp+2 - str   Belwin

Stabat mater   12'
   chorus   Schirmer, G.
   2 2 2 2 - 2 2 1 0 - tmp - hp, pf - str

HOLST, GUSTAV, 1874-1934

Brook green suite   11'
   1 1 1 0 - str   Curwen
   (Woodwinds are optional.)

Capriccio   6'
   *1 *2 *2 2 - 2 3 2 1 - 2perc - hp, cel, pf - str   Faber
   Ed. Imogen Holst

Christmas day   7'
  chorus - solos SATB   Novello
  *2 2 2 2 - 2 2 2 0 - tmp+1 - pf or org - str
  (Optional instruments: piccolo, trombones,
  one percussionist.)

Egdon Heath, op.47   15'
  2 *3 2 *3 - 4 3 3 1 - str   Novello
  (Optional instruments: 2nd ob, cbn, 3rd and 4th hn,
  3rd tp, tuba.)

First choral symphony, op.41   52'
  chorus - solo soprano   Novello
  *3 *3 *3 *3 - 4 3 3 1 - tmp+2 - hp, cel, org - str
  Minimum instrumentation (should be used if the chorus
  is small): *2 *2 2 2 - 2 2 3 0 - tmp - hp - str

The perfect fool: Ballet music   13'
  *3 *3 *3 *3 - 4 4 3 1 - tmp+3 - hp, cel - str   Gray
  (Playable with: *3 *2 2 2 - 4 2 3 1 - tmp+3 - hp - str.)

The planets   53'
  hidden female chorus in one movement   Schirmer, G.
  =4 *4 *4 *4 - 6 4 3 1 - tenor tuba - 2tmp, 4perc -
    2hp, cel, org - str
  3rd ob doubles on bass ob; 2 flutists double on pic.
  Cued to make performance possible with the following
  minimum instrumentation:
    *3 *3 *3 2 - 4 3 3 1 - 2tmp, 4perc - 2hp, cel - str

Saint Paul's suite   12'
  str   Curwen

A Somerset rhapsody   10'
  *2 2 2 2 - 4 2 3 1 - tmp+3 - str   Boosey
  One of the oboists should use oboe d'amore if possible.

HONEGGER, ARTHUR, 1892-1955

Chant de joie   7'
  *3 *3 *3 *3 - 4 3 3 1 - 2perc - hp, cel - str   Salabert

Concertino, piano and orchestra   13'
  *2 *2 *2 2 - 2 2 1 0 - str   Salabert

Le dit des jeux du monde   50'
  *1 0 0 0 - 0 1 0 0 - tmp+3 - str   Salabert

Jeanne d'Arc au bûcher   80'
  chorus, children's chorus - solos SSSATB -   Salabert
    4 spoken roles (1 female, 3 male)
  *2 2 =3 *4 - 0 4 4 0 - 3asx - tmp+2 - 2pf, cel,
    ondes martenot - str

Mouvement symphonique no.3   10'
  *3 *3 2 *3 - 4 3 3 1 - asx - 2perc - str   Salabert

Pacific 231 (Mouvement symphonique no.1)   7'
  *3 *3 *3 *3 - 4 3 3 1 - 4perc - str   Salabert

Pastorale d'été   7'
  1 1 1 1 - 1 0 0 0 - str   Salabert

Prélude pour "La tempête" de Shakespeare   8'
  *2 *2 *2 *2 - 4 2 3 1 - 4perc - str   Salabert

Le roi David (King David)   67'
  chorus - solos SAT - speaker   Schirmer, E.
  *2 *2 *2 *2 - 4 2 3 1 - tmp+3 - hp, cel, org - str

Rugby (Mouvement symphonique no.2)   8'
  *3 *3 *3 *3 - 4 3 3 1 - str   Salabert

Symphony no.1   22'
  *3 *3 *3 *3 - 4 3 3 1 - 1perc - str   Salabert

Symphony no.2   25'
  str - (opt tp)   Salabert

Symphony no.3 ("Symphonie liturgique")   30'
  *3 *3 *3 *3 - 4 3 3 1 - tmp+4 - pf - str   Salabert

Symphony no.4 ("Deliciae Basilienses")   32'
  2 1 2 1 - 2 1 0 0 - 2perc - pf - str   Salabert

Symphony no.5 ("Di tre re")   27'
  *3 *3 *3 3 - 4 3 3 1 - (opt tmp) - str   Salabert

HOVHANESS, ALAN, 1911-

Magnificat, op.157   33'
  chorus - solos STB   Peters
  0 2 0 0 - 2 2 1 0 - 2perc - hp - str

Mysterious mountain (Symphony no.2)   16'
  3 *3 *3 *3 - 5 3 3 1 - tmp - hp, cel - str   AMP

Overture, op.76, no.1   5'
  solo trombone - str   Peters

Psalm and fugue, op.40a   11'
  str   Peters

Symphony no.15 ("Silver pilgrimage")   20'
  2 *2 2 2 - 4 3 3 1 - tmp+2 - hp - str   Peters

Variations and fugue   13'
  3 *3 2 2 - 4 3 3 1 - tmp+1 - hp - str   Peters

HUMMEL, JOHANN NEPOMUK, 1778-1837

Concerto, trumpet, E major (original key)   19'
  1 2 2 2 - 2 0 0 0 - tmp - str   Universal
  Ed. Edward Tarr. For the same work in the more
  commonly used key of E-flat major, see below.

Concerto, trumpet, E-flat major (transposed version)   19'
  1 2 2 2 - 2 0 0 0 - tmp - str   Kalmus;
  A version without clarinets is published by   King
  Billaudot; a version without clarinets or
  timpani is published by EMT.

HUMPERDINCK, ENGELBERT, 1854-1921

Dornröschen (Sleeping beauty): Suite   22'
  2 2 2 2 - 4 2 3 1 - tmp+1 - hp - str
  This work is out of print, but orchestral materials
  are in the Fleisher Collection.

Handel and Gretel: Prelude   8'
  *3 2 2 2 - 4 2 3 1 - tmp+2 - str   Kalmus; Schott

Hansel and Gretel: Knusperwalzer (Crackle-waltz)   5'
    *2 2 2 2 - 4 2 3 0 - tmp+2 - str   Kalmus
    Arr. Hans Steiner. (Trombones and 3rd and 4th
    horns are optional.)

Hansel and Gretel: Three excerpts   12'
    *3 *2 2 2 - 4 2 3 1 - tmp+1 - hp - str   Kalmus;
        Contents--Sandman's song; Evening prayer;   Luck;
    Dream-pantomime.   Schott

Hansel and Gretel: Witch's ride (Hexenritt)   4'
    *3 2 2 2 - 4 2 3 1 - tmp+4 - str   Kalmus

Königskinder: Prelude ("The king's son")   8'
    *2 2 *3 *3 - 4 3 3 1 - tmp+1 - str

Königskinder: Introduction to Act II   4'
    *3 2 2 *3 - 4 2 3 1 - tmp+1 - str   Luck; Mapleson

Königskinder: Introduction to Act III   9'
    *3 *3 *3 *3 - 4 3 3 1 - tmp - hp - str   Luck; Mapleson

Eine Trauung in der Bastille   10'
    2 *2 2 2 - 4 3 3 1 - tmp+2 - hp, (opt org
        or harm) - str
    Introduction and interlude from the opera "Die
    Heirat wider Willen." This work is out of print,
    but orchestral materials are in the Fleisher Collection.

    HUSA, KAREL, 1921-

Apotheosis of this earth   26'
    chorus   AMP
    *4 *4 *4 *3 - 4 4 4 1 - tmp+4 - str

Fantasies for orchestra   20'
    *2 1 1 0 - 0 3 0 0 - 2perc - pf -   Schott
        str ("symphonic or chamber")

Music for Prague 1968 (orchestral version)   19'
    *3 *3 *3 *3 - 4 4 3 1 - tmp+4 - hp, pf - str   AMP
    Originally for concert band.

Symphony no.1   28'
    *3 *3 *3 *3 - 4 3 3 1 - tmp+3 - pf, 1 or 2hp - str   Schott

Two sonnets by Michelangelo   16'
  *3 *3 2 2 - 4 3 3 1 - asx - tmp+2 - hp - str   AMP

    IBERT, JACQUES, 1890-1962

Bacchanale   10'
  *3 *3 *3 *4 - 4 3 3 1 - tmp+5 - hp - str   Leduc

Le chevalier errant   27'
  *3 *3 *3 *4 - 6 4 3 1 - asx - tmp+5 - 2hp,   Leduc
  cel, gtr - str

Concertino da camera, alto saxophone and orchestra   12'
  1 1 1 1 - 1 1 0 0 - str quintet or small   Leduc
  str complement.

Concerto, flute   18'
  2 2 2 2 - 2 1 0 0 - tmp - str   Leduc

Divertissement   15'
  *1 0 1 *1 - 1 1 1 0 - 1perc - pf/cel -   Durand
  3vn, 2va, 2vc, db

Escales   17'
  *3 *3 2 3 - 4 3 3 1 - tmp+7 - 2hp, cel - str   Leduc

Hommage à Mozart   5'
  2 2 2 2 - 2 2 0 0 - 2tmp - str   Leduc

Louisville concerto   12'
  *2 2 2 2 - 4 2 3 1 - tmp+3 - hp - str   Leduc

    INDY, VINCENT D', 1851-1931

Istar; variations symphoniques, op.42   17'
  *3 *3 *3 3 - 4 3 3 1 - tmp+2 - 2hp - str   Durand; Kalmus

Symphony on a French mountain air, op.25   26'
  solo piano   Hamelle
  *3 *2 *3 3 - 4 4 3 1 - tmp+3 - hp - str

IPPOLITOV-IVANOV, MIKHAIL, 1859-1935

Caucasian sketches   20'
  *3 *2 2 2 - 4 4 3 0 - tmp+5 - hp - str   Kalmus; VAAP
    Contents--In the mountain pass; In the village;
In the mosque; Procession of the Sardar.

Turkish fragments, op.62   14'
  *3 *3 2 2 - 3 2 3 1 - tmp+5 - hp - str   Kalmus;
    Contents--The caravan; During a rest;   VAAP
In the night; At the festival.

ISHII, MAKI, 1936-

Kyō-Sō   22'
  *3 3 *3 *3 - 6 4 3 1 - tmp+5 - hp, cel - str   Moeck

IVES, CHARLES, 1874-1954

  The Charles Ives Society since 1973 has been sup-
porting the preparation along scholarly-critical lines
of performing editions of Ives' music. These should
be sought out as they become available, since the
previous editions have many errors.

Calcium light night
  See his: The gong on the hook and ladder

Chromâtimelôdtune   6'
  0 1 1 1 - 1 1 1 1 - 2perc - pf - 3vn, va, vc, db   MJQ
  Reconstructed and completed by Gunther Schuller.

Country band march, for theater orchestra   4'
  *1 0 1 0 - 0 1 2 0 - asx - 3perc - pf -   Merion
  str (without va)
  Ed. James Sinclair (Ives Society).

General William Booth enters into heaven   5'
  medium voice (or chorus)   Merion
  1 1 1 1 - 1 1 1 0 - 1perc - pf - str
  Orchestrated by John J. Becker in collaboration
  with the composer.

The gong on the hook and ladder   3'
  1 0 1 1 - 0 2 1 0 - tmp+2 - pf, (opt gong) - str   Peer
  Alternative titles: "Firemen's parade on Main Street,"
  "Calcium light," or "Calcium light night." New ed. by
  James Sinclair (Ives Society).

Holidays symphony
  The movements may be played separately.

  1. Washington's Birthday   9'
     *1 0 0 0 - 1 0 0 0 - 3 Jew's harps (or 2cl) - str   AMP
    (Optional: bells or pf, extra hr or tbn.)

  2. Decoration Day   10'
     *3 *3 +3 2 - 4 2 3 1 - tmp+5 - str   Peer
    (An ossia is provided for the E-flat clarinet.)

  3. The Fourth of July   7'
     *3 2 2 *3 - 4 4 3 1 - tmp+6 - pf - str   AMP

  4. Thanksgiving and/or Forefathers' Day   15'
    chorus   Peer
    *3 2 2 *3 - 4 3 3 1 - tmp+5 - pf, cel - str

Hymn (Largo cantabile)   3'
  str   Peer

Lincoln the great commoner   4'
  chorus   Kalmus;
  2 2 2 2 - 0 2 2 1 - tmp+1 - pf - str   Presser

Symphony no.1, D minor   45'
  2 *3 2 *3 - 4 2 3 1 - tmp - str   Peer
  (Contrabassoon is optional.)

Symphony no.2   35'
  *3 2 2 *3 - 4 2 3 1 - tmp+2 - str   Peer
  New ed. by M. Goldstein in progress (Ives Society).

Symphony no.3 ("The camp meeting")   18'
  1 1 1 1 - 2 0 1 0 - (opt distant bells) - str   AMP
  New ed. by K. Singleton in progress (Ives Society).

Symphony no.4   30'
  chorus   AMP
  *3 2 3 3 - 4 6 4 1 - tmp+9 - 2hp, cel, 2pf 6-hands,
   org - str
  (The following additional instruments are optional:
  1 saxophonist doubling on alto, tenor and baritone;
  theremin; quarter-tone piano. Use of an assistant
  conductor is also optional.) New ed. by W. Brooks
  in progress (Ives Society).

Symphony no.4: Fugue   8'
  1 0 1 0 - 1 0 0 0 - tmp - (opt org) - str   AMP
  (Trombone may substitute for horn.)

Three harvest home chorales   8'
  chorus   Mercury
  brass 0 4 3 1 - org - db
  New ed. by P. Echols in progress (Ives Society).

Three places in New England (chamber orchestra version)
  *2 *2 1 1 - 4 4 3 1 - tmp+2 - pf, (opt org,   18'
    opt cel) - str   Mercury
  This version was actually intended for:
  1 *2 1 1 - 2 2 1 0 - tmp - pf - 7vn, 2va, 2vc, db.
  The extra instruments were probably considered
  optional. Published 1935.

Three places in New England (large orchestra version) 18'
  *3 *2 2 *3 - 4 2 3 1 - tmp+4 - 1 or 2hp,   Merion
    pf/cel, (opt org) - str
  Full orchestration restored and edited by
  James B. Sinclair (Ives Society).

Tone roads no.1   -   8'
  1 0 1 1 - str   Peer
  New ed. by R. Swift and J. Kirkpatrick in
  progress (Ives Society).

Tone roads no.3   9'
  1 0 1 0 - 0 1 1 0 - 1perc - pf - str   Peer
  New ed. by R. Swift in progress (Ives Society).

The unanswered question   6'
  4fl - tp (or Eh or ob or cl) - backstage str   Peer
    quartet or str orchestra
  (Oboe may substitute for 3rd flute; clarinet may
  substitute for 4th flute.) New ed. by N. Zahler
  in progress (Ives Society).

Variations on "America"   8'
  *3 2 2 2 - 4 3 3 1 - tmp+3 - str   Merion
  Orchestrated by William Schuman; originally for organ.

    JACOB, GORDON, 1895-

The barber of Seville goes to the devil; comedy overture
  *2 1 2 1 - 2 2 2 0 - tmp+2 - hp (or pf) - str   4'
                                              Oxford

Fantasia on the Alleluia hymn   8'
  2 2 2 2 - 4 2 3 1 - tmp+2 - str   Galaxy
  (3rd and 4th horns are optional.)

JANÁČEK, LEOŠ, 1854-1928

Adagio 6'
  *2 *2 2 2 - 2 2 2 0 - tmp - str   Universal

Glagolitic mass (M'sa glagolskaja) 45'
  chorus - solos SATB   Universal
  *4 *3 *3 *3 - 4 4 3 1 - tmp+2 - 2hp, cel, org - str

Idyla 21'
  str   Supraphon

Jealousy 6'
  *2 *3 *3 2 - 4 2 3 1 - tmp - hp - str   Universal

Lachian dances 20'
  *2 *3 *3 2 - 4 2 3 0 - tmp+1 - hp, org - str   Supraphon
  (Eh, bcl, org are optional.)

Sinfonietta 25'
  *4 *2 =3 2 - 4 12 4 1 - 2 bass tp,   Universal
    2 tenor tubas - tmp+1 - hp - str
  Two reduced versions are available from the publisher:
  one by the composer, and one by Joseph Keilberth.

Sokal fanfare (1st movement of the Sinfonietta) 4'
  9tp, 2 tenor tubas (B-flat), 2 bass tp, tmp   Universal
  (Baritone horns or trombones may substitute
  for the tenor tubas; trombones may substitute
  for the bass trumpets.)

Taras Bulba 24'
  *3 *3 +2 *3 - 4 3 3 1 - tmp+2 - hp, org - str   Supraphon

JÄRNEFELT, ARMAS, 1869-1958

Praeludium 3'
  1 1 2 1 - 2 2 0 0 - tmp+2 - str   Breitkopf; Kalmus; Luck

JOACHIM, JOSEPH, 1831-1907

Concerto, violin, D minor, op.11 ("Hungarian") 34'
  2 2 2 2 - 4 2 0 0 - tmp - str   Breitkopf; Kalmus

JOLIVET, ANDRÉ, 1905-1974

Symphony no.1   25'
  *3 *3 *3 3 - 4 4 3 1 - tmp - hp - str   Heugel

JONES, SAMUEL, 1935-

Let us now praise famous men   16'
  *3 *3 *3 *3 - 4 3 3 1 - tmp+3 - hp - str -   Fischer, C.
    offstage fl choir: 3fl and afl, preferably
    doubled or tripled at the conductor's discretion
  (May be performed without the offstage flute choir
  by using flutes =4 in the orchestra.)

KABALEVSKY, DMITRI, 1904-

Colas Breugnon: Overture   5'
  *3 3 3 *3 - 4 3 3 1 - tmp+5 - hp - str   Kalmus; VAAP

Colas Breugnon: Suite   20'
  *3 *3 3 *3 - 4 3 3 1 - tmp+5 - hp - str   Kalmus; VAAP

The comedians, op.26   16'
  *1 *1 2 1 - 2 2 1 1 - tmp+4 - pf - str   Kalmus; VAAP

The comedians: Galop   2'
  1 1 2 1 - 2 2 1 1 - tmp+3 - pf - str   Kalmus

Concerto, piano, no.3, op.50, D major ("Youth")   18'
  2 2 2 2 - 2 2 2 0 - tmp+3 - str   Kalmus; VAAP

Concerto, violin, op.48   16'
  1 1 2 1 - 2 1 1 0 - tmp+4 - str   Kalmus; VAAP

Concerto, violoncello, no.1, op.49, G minor   17'
  1 1 2 1 - 2 1 1 0 - tmp+2 - str   VAAP

Symphony no.1, op.18   25'
  *3 *3 *3 *3 - 4 3 3 1 - tmp+4 - str   Kalmus; VAAP

Symphony no.2, op.19   26'
  *3 *3 *3 *3 - 4 3 3 1 - tmp+4 - str   Kalmus; VAAP

Symphony no.3, op.22 ("Requiem")   20'
  chorus   VAAP
  *3 *3 *3 *3 - 4 3 3 1 - tmp+4 - pf - str

  KALINNIKOV, VASSILI, 1866-1901

Chanson triste
  str   Luck

Symphony no.1, G minor   35'
  *3 *3 2 2 - 4 2 3 1 - tmp+1 - hp - str   Kalmus;
                                              Universal; VAAP

Symphony no.2, A major   45'
  *3 *2 2 2 - 4 2 3 1 - tmp - hp - str   Universal; Kalmus

  KARŁOWICZ, MIECZYSŁAW, 1876-1909

Lithuanian rhapsody, op.11   19'
  *3 *3 *3 2 - 4 2 3 0 - tmp+2 - str   PWM

Odwieczne pieśni (Eternal songs), op.10   22'
  *3 *3 *3 *3 - 4 3 3 1 - tmp+2 - str   PWM

Stanisław i Anna Oświecimowie, op.12   22'
  *4 *4 =4 *4 - 6 3 3 1 - tmp+3 - 2hp - str   PWM

  KAY, ULYSSES, 1917-

Fantasy variations   15'
  *2 2 2 2 - 4 3 3 1 - tmp+4 - str   MCA

Scherzi musicali for chamber orchestra   17'
  1 1 1 1 - 1 0 0 0 - str   MCA

Serenade for orchestra   18'
  *2 2 2 2 - 4 2 3 1 - tmp - str   AMP

Theater set for orchestra   15'
  *3 *3 *3 2 - 4 3 3 1 - tmp+3 - hp - str   MCA

Umbrian scene   15'
  2 2 2 2 - 4 3 3 1 - tmp+4 - hp - str   MCA

KENNAN, KENT, 1913-

Night soliloquy   4'
    solo flute - pf, str   Fischer, C.

KHACHATURIAN, ARAM, 1903-1978

Concerto, piano   33'
    *2 2 *3 2 - 4 2 3 1 - tmp+2 - flexatone - str   Kalmus;
                                                                 VAAP

Concerto, violin   33'
    *3 *3 2 2 - 4 3 3 1 - tmp+3 - hp - str   VAAP

Concerto-rhapsody, violin and orchestra   23'
    *3 2 2 2 - 4 2 0 0 - tmp+3 - hp - str   VAAP

Concerto-rhapsody, violoncello and orchestra   23'
    2 2 2 2 - 4 2 0 0 - tmp+4 - hp - str   VAAP

Gayane
    *Although this ballet has been excerpted in various
    ways, the following three suites are the only ones
    authorized by the composer. The "Three pieces"
    (wrongly published as Suite no.1) and the "Sabre
    dance" are available separately.*

Gayane: Suite no.1   36'
    *3 *3 *3 2 - 4 3 3 1 - tmp+4 - hp, cel - str   Kalmus;
    One of the clarinetists doubles on alto saxophone. VAAP
        Contents--Introduction; Dance of the young
    maidens; Ayshe's awakening and dance; Mountaineers'
    dance; Lullaby, Gayane and Guiko; Gayane's adagio;
    Lesginka.

Gayane: Suite no.2   30'
    *3 *3 *3 2 - 4 3 3 1 - tmp+4 - hp, pf - str   Kalmus;
        Contents--Dance of welcome; Lyric duet;   VAAP
    Russian dance; Noune's variation; Dance of an
    old man and carpet weavers; Armen's variation;
    Fire.

Gayane: Suite no.3   26'
   *3 *3 *3 2 - 4 3 3 1 - asx - tmp+4 - hp, pf - str Kalmus;
      Contents--Cotton picking; Dance of the young   VAAP
   Kurds; Introduction and dance of the old men;
   The carpet weavers; Sabre dance; Hopak.

Gayane: Sabre dance   2'
   *3 *3 *3 2 - 4 3 3 1 - asx - tmp+3 - hp,   Kalmus;
      pf - str   VAAP

Gayane: Three pieces   9'
   *3 *3 *3 2 - 4 3 3 1 - asx - tmp+3 - hp,   Kalmus;
      cel/pf - str   VAAP
      Contents--Sabre dance; Lullaby; Dance of
   the young rose maidens.
   Originally published as "Suite no.1."

Masquerade: Suite   15'
   *2 2 2 2 - 4 2 3 1 - tmp+3 - str   Kalmus; VAAP

Spartacus: Suite no.1   24'
   *3 *3 *3 2 - 4 4 3 1 - tmp+5 - hp, cel,   Kalmus;
      pf - str   VAAP
      Contents--Introduction and dance of nymphs;
   Introduction, Adagio of Aegina and Harmocius;
   Variation of Aegina and Bacchanalia; Scene and
   dance with crotalums; Dance of Gaditanae and
   Victory of Spartacus.

Spartacus: Suite no.2   20'
   *3 *3 *3 2 - 4 3 3 1 - tmp+4 - hp, pf - str   Kalmus
      Contents--Adagio of Spartacus and Phrygia;
   Entrance of Merchants, Dance of a Roman courtesan,
   General dance; Entrance of Spartacus, Quarrel,
   Treachery of Harmodius; The dance of the pirates.

Spartacus: Suite no.3   15'
   *3 *3 *3 2 - 4 3 3 1 - tmp+5 - hp, pf - str   Kalmus
      Contents--Market; Dance of a Greek slave;
   Dance of an Egyptian girl; Dance of Phrygia and the
   Parting scene; Sword dance of young Thracians.

Symphony no.2   50'
   *3 *3 =4 2 - 4 3 3 1 - tmp+4 - hp, pf - str   VAAP

KHRENNIKOV, TIKHON, 1913-

Concerto, violin   18'
  *3 2 *3 *3 - 4 3 0 0 - tmp+4 - hp, pf/cel -   Kalmus;
  str   VAAP

Symphony no.1, op.4   22'
  *3 2 2 2 - 4 2 3 1 - tmp+4 - cel - str   Kalmus; VAAP

KIRCHNER, LEON, 1919-

Music for orchestra   13'
  *3 *3 *3 *3 - 4 3 3 1 - tmp+5 - pf/cel - str   AMP

Toccata   14'
  0 1 1 1 - 1 1 1 0 - 4perc - cel - str   AMP

KIRK, THERON, 1919-

An orchestra primer   13'
  narrator   Oxford
  *2 2 2 2 - 4 3 3 1 - tmp+2 - str
  Possible with winds *1 1 2 1 - 3 2 1 0.

KODÁLY, ZOLTÁN, 1882-1967

Concerto for orchestra   19'
  *3 2 2 2 - 4 3 3 1 - tmp+1 - hp - str   Boosey

Galanta dances   15'
  2 2 2 2 - 4 2 0 0 - tmp+2 - str   Universal

Háry János: Suite   24'
  *3 2 +2 2 - 4 6 3 1 - tmp+6 - cel, pf,   Universal
    cimbalom (or hpsd)- str
  One clarinetist doubles on alto saxophone.

Háry János: Intermezzo   5'
  3 2 2 2 - 4 3 0 0 - tmp+4 - cimbalom or pf -   Universal
    str
  (3rd flute and 3rd trumpet are optional.)

Marosszek dances   12'
  *2 2 2 *2 - 4 2 0 0 - tmp+3 - str   Universal

Missa brevis   32'
  chorus   Boosey
  *3 2 2 2 - 4 3 3 1 - tmp - (opt org) - str

Psalmus hungaricus   23'
  chorus - solo tenor - (opt boy choir)   Universal
  3 2 2 2 - 4 3 3 0 - tmp+1 - hp, (opt org) - str

Summer evening   20'
  1 *2 2 2 - 2 0 0 0 - str   Universal

Symphony   30'
  *3 2 2 2 - 4 3 3 1 - tmp+1 - str   Boosey

Te deum   21'
  chorus - solos SATB   Universal
  2 2 2 2 - 4 3 3 1 - tmp - (opt org) - str

Theater overture   12'
  *3 2 2 2 - 4 3 3 1 - tmp+4 - pf - str   Universal
  Also known as the "Overture for Háry János."

Variations on a Hungarian folksong ("The peacock")   25'
  *3 *2 2 2 - 4 3 3 0 - tmp+1 - hp - str   Boosey

        KOECHLIN, CHARLES, 1867-1950

Les bandar-log, op.176   15'
  *4 *3 =4 *3 - 4 4 4 1 - ssx, tsx, bugle in   Eschig
    B-flat - tmp+9 - 2hp, cel, pf - str
  Two of the flutists double on piccolo.

        KORNGOLD, ERICH WOLFGANG, 1897-1957

Schauspiel-Ouvertüre, op.4   16'
  *3 2 *3 *3 - 4 3 3 1 - tmp+3 - hp - str   Schott

Symphonic serenade, op.39   27'
  str 16.16.12.12.8   Schott

Theme and variations, op.42   7'
  2 1 2 1 - 2 2 2 0 - tmp+2 - pf, (opt hp) - str   Belwin
  May be performed with winds 2 0 2 0 - 0 2 2 0 .

  KOUSSEVITZKY, SERGE, 1874-1951

Concerto, double bass, op.3, F-sharp minor   20'
  2 2 2 2 - 4 0 0 0 - tmp - hp - str   Boosey

Concerto, double bass, op.3, F-sharp minor (orchestrated
  by Wolfgang Meyer-Tormin)   20'
  2 2 *3 2 - 3 2 0 0 - tmp - str   Forberg

  KRAFT, WILLIAM, 1923-

Configurations; concerto for 4 percussionists
  and jazz orchestra   16'
  4 percussion soloists   MCA
  3 woodwind players with extensive doublings:
    1. pic/fl/cl/asx; 2. fl/afl/cl/tsx; 3. cl/bcl/bsx -
    brass 2 3 3 1 - pf, electric gtr, db

Contextures: Riots--decade '60   17'
  *4 *4 =4 *4 - 4 4 4 1 - tmp+6 - hp, pf/cel - str -   MCA
    offstage jazz quartet including ssx and (from the
    orchestra) tp, db, drums
  4th clarinet also doubles on alto saxophone.

  KŘENEK, ERNST, 1900-

Eleven transparencies for orchestra   20'
  *2 2 2 2 - 4 2 2 1 - tmp+2 - hp - str   Schott; Universal

Sinfonietta ("The Brazilian")   15'
  str   Universal

Symphonic elegy   12'
  str   Elkan-Vogel

Symphony "Pallas Athena"   21'
  *2 2 *2 2 - 4 2 2 0 - tmp+3 - hp, cel/pf - str   Schott;
                                                 Universal

KUBIK, GAIL, 1914-

Divertimento I for thirteen players   16'
  *1 *1 *1 1 - 1 1 1 0 - tmp - pf/hpsd - vn, va, vc, db MCA

Gerald McBoing Boing   9'
  solo percussion - narrator   Southern
  1 1 1 1 - 1 1 0 0 - pf - va, vc

Symphony concertante   25'
  solos: trumpet, viola, piano   Colombo
  *2 2 *2 *2 - 2 1 1 0 - 1perc - str

KUHLAU, FRIEDRICH, 1786-1832

Concertino, 2 horns, F minor
  2 2 2 2 - 2 2 1 0 - tmp - str   Hofmeister; Musica Rara

Concerto, piano, op.7, C major   30'
  1 2 2 2 - 2 2 0 0 - tmp - str   Samfundet

William Shakespeare: Overture, op.74   11'
  *2 2 2 2 - 4 2 1 0 - tmp+2 - str   Dania

KUHNAU, JOHANN, 1660-1722

Uns ist ein Kind geboren
  See: Bach, Johann Sebastian, 1685-1750
          Cantata no.142

KURKA, ROBERT, 1921-1957

The good soldier Schweik: Suite   20'
  *2 *2 *2 *2 - 3 2 1 0 - tmp+1   Weintraub
  (Double bass may substitute for contrabassoon.)

LADERMAN, EZRA, 1924-

Concerto for orchestra   22'
  *3 *3 *3 *3 - 4 3 3 1 - tmp+5 - hp, cel - str   Oxford

Magic prison   25'
    2 narrators (one male, one female)   Oxford
    2 2 *3 2 - 4 3 3 0 - tmp+2 - hp, cel, org - str
    Text selected by Archibald MacLeish from the poems and
    letters of Emily Dickinson and the recollections of
    T. W. Higginson.

    LALANDE, MICHEL-RICHARD DE, 1657-1726

Christmas symphony (Symphonie de Noël)
    2 0 0 1 - str, cnt   Vieweg
    (Fl parts may be played by ob, or both fl and
    ob may be used.) Ed. Felix Schroeder.

    LALO, EDOUARD, 1823-1892

Concerto, piano   23'
    2 2 2 2 - 4 4 3 0 - tmp - str   Heugel; Kalmus

Concerto, violin, op.20, F minor   30'
    *3 2 2 2 - 2 2 3 0 - tmp+1 - str   Durand; Kalmus

Concerto, violoncello, D minor   24'
    2 2 2 2 - 4 2 3 0 - tmp - str   Bote; Kalmus

Namouna: Ballet suite no.1   23'
    2 2 2 4 - 4 4 3 1 - tmp+3 - 2hp - str   Kalmus

Namouna: Ballet suite no.2   14'
    *2 *2 2 4 - 4 4 3 1 - tmp+3 - 2hp - str   Kalmus
    Both oboists double on English horn.

Rapsodie norvégienne   10'
    *3 2 2 2 - 4 4 3 1 - tmp+2 - hp - str   Bote;
    Also known as "Rapsodie pour orchestre."   Kalmus

Le roi d'Ys: Overture   11'
    2 2 2 4 - 4 4 3 1 - tmp+2 - str   Heugel;
    (2 real bassoon parts, each doubled.)   Kalmus

Symphonie espagnole, op.21   29'
    solo violin   Breitkopf;
    *3 2 2 2 - 4 2 3 0 - tmp+2 - hp - str   Durand; Kalmus

LA MONTAINE, JOHN, 1920-

Birds of paradise, op.34   13'
  solo piano   Fischer, C.
  *3 *3 2 2 - 4 3 3 1 - tmp+3 - hp - str

Concerto, piano, op.9   25'
  *3 *3 *3 *3 - 4 3 3 0 - tmp+2 - str   Galaxy

Songs of the rose of Sharon   15'
  solo soprano   Broude Bros.
  2 2 2 *3 - 4 2 3 1 - tmp - hp - str
  (Tuba and timpani are optional.)

A summer's day   5'
  1 1 1 0 - 1 1 0 0 - tmp - hp - str   Schirmer, G.

LANNER, JOSEPH, 1801-1843

Die Werber Walzer, op.103   7'
  *2 1 +2 1 - 2 2 1 0 - tmp+1 - str   Luck

LECLAIR, JEAN MARIE, 1697-1764

Concerto, violin, op.7, no.4, F major
  str, cnt   Schirmer, E.
  Ed. Claude Crussard.

Concerto, violin, op.7, no.5, A minor   14'
  str, cnt   Nagel
  Ed. Hugo Ruf.

Sonata, D major (transcribed for string orchestra)
  str   Kalmus

LEES, BENJAMIN, 1924-

Concerto, violin   21'
  *3 *3 *3 *3 - 4 3 3 1 - tmp+2 - str   Boosey

Symphony no.2   21'
  *2 *2 2 2 - 4 3 3 1 - tmp+3 - hp - str Boosey

The trumpet of the swan   17'
  narrator   Boosey
  *2 *2 2 2 - 4 3 3 1 - tmp+4 - str

LEHÁR, FRANZ, 1870-1948

The merry widow: Overture   9'
  *3 *3 *3 *3 - 4 2 3 1 - tmp+4 - hp, cel - str   Glocken

LEO, LEONARDO, 1694-1744

Concerto, violoncello, D major   14'
  str (without va), cnt   Eulenburg
  Ed. Felix Schroeder.

Santa Elena al Calvario: Sinfonia   5'
  0 2 0 0 - 2 0 0 0 - str, cnt   Eulenburg
  Ed. Richard Engländer.

LEONCAVALLO, RUGGERO, 1858-1919

I pagliacci: Intermezzo   4'
  *3 *2 *3 3 - 4 2 3 1 - tmp - 2hp (doubling   Kalmus
  a single part) - str

LIADOV, ANATOL, 1855-1914

Baba-Yaga, op.56   4'
  *3 *3 *3 *3 - 4 2 3 1 - tmp+3 - str   Belaieff; Kalmus

Eight Russian folk songs, op.58   15'
  *3 *3 2 2 - 4 2 0 0 - tmp+2 - str   Belaieff; Kalmus

The enchanted lake, op.62   6'
  3 2 3 2 - 4 0 0 0 - tmp+1 - hp, cel - str   Belaieff;
                        Kalmus

Kikimora, op.63   7'
  *3 *3 *3 2 - 4 2 0 0 - tmp+1 - cel - str   Belaieff;
                        Kalmus

LIGETI, GYÖRGY, 1923-

Apparitions   9'
  *3 0 +3 *3 - 6 4 3 1 - 4perc - hp, cel,   Universal
  pf, hpsd - str

Atmosphères   9'
  *4 4 +4 *4 - 6 4 4 1 - pf (2 players, if   Universal
  possible percussionists) - str 14.14.10.10.8

Ramifications   9'
  str orchestra or 12 solo strings   Schott
  Two groups, tuned a quarter-tone apart.

Requiem   27'
  2 mixed choruses - solos S, Mz   Peters
  *3 *3 =3 *3 - 4 3 2 1 - bass tp, contrabass tbn -
  3perc - hp, hpsd - str 12.12.10.8.6
  3rd clarinet doubles on contrabass clarinet; 2 of
  the flutists double on piccolo.

LISZT, FRANZ, 1811-1886

Battle of the Huns (Hunnenschlacht; Symphonic
  poem no.11)   16'
  *3 2 2 2 - 4 3 3 1 - tmp+1 - org - str   Breitkopf;
                                                   Kalmus

Ce qu'on entend sur la montagne (Symphonic poem no.1) 38'
  *3 2 *3 2 - 4 3 3 1 - tmp+3 - hp - str   Breitkopf;
                                                   Kalmus

Christus   165'
  chorus - solos SATB   Kalmus;
  *3 *3 2 2 - 4 3 3 1 - tmp+2 - hp, harm, org - str Peters
    In three parts: I. Christmas oratorio (60');
  II. After Epiphany (50'); III. Passion and
  resurrection (55').

Concerto, piano, no.1, E-flat major   19'
  *3 2 2 2 - 2 2 3 0 - tmp+2 - str   Breitkopf; Kalmus

Concerto, piano, no.2, A major   20'
  *3 2 2 2 - 2 2 3 1 - tmp+1 - str   Breitkopf; Kalmus

Concerto pathétique   14'
  solo piano   Breitkopf;
  *3 2 2 2 - 2 2 3 0 - tmp+2 - hp - str   Kalmus
  Originally for 2 pianos; arranged for solo piano
  with orchestral accompaniment by Eduard Reuss.

Dante symphony   46'
  chorus of women's or boys' voices   Breitkopf;
  *3 *3 *3 2 - 4 2 3 1 - 2tmp, 3perc -   Kalmus
    2hp, harm - str

Episodes from Lenau's Faust
  See separate entries: Mephisto waltz no.1
                    Nocturnal procession

A Faust symphony   72'
  male chorus - tenor solo   Breitkopf;
  *3 2 2 2 - 4 3 3 1 - tmp+2 - hp, org - str Kalmus
  (An alternative ending without organ or voices
  is 7' shorter.)

Festklänge (Symphonic poem no.7)   18'
  2 2 2 2 - 4 3 3 1 - tmp+2 - str   Breitkopf

From the cradle to the grave
  See his: Von der Wiege bis zum Grabe

Funeral triumph of Tasso (Symphonic poem no.2a) 11'
  *3 2 2 2 - 4 2 3 1 - tmp+1 - str   Breitkopf
  Epilogue to "Tasso, lament and triumph"
  (see below).

Hamlet (Symphonic poem no.10)   10'
  *3 2 2 2 - 4 2 3 1 - tmp - str   Breitkopf

Héroïde funèbre (Symphonic poem no.8)   20'
  *3 *3 2 2 - 4 2 3 1 - tmp+5 - str Breitkopf; Kalmus

Huldigungs-Marsch   6'
  *3 2 2 2 - 4 2 3 1 - tmp+1 - str   Bote; Kalmus

Hungaria (Symphonic poem no.9)   22'
  *3 *3 2 2 - 4 3 3 1 - tmp+4 - str   Breitkopf

Hungarian fantasy, piano and orchestra   15'
  *3 2 2 2 - 2 2 3 0 - tmp+3 - str Kalmus; Peters

Hungarian march (Rákóczi march)   6'
   *3 2 2 2 - 4 2 3 1 - tmp+3 - str   Broude, A.

Hungarian rhapsodies

   *Of the nineteen Hungarian rhapsodies for solo piano,
   six were orchestrated by the composer in collaboration
   with Franz Doppler, and were renumbered in the process.
   Some were also transposed into other keys for the
   orchestral versions. Later orchestrators did not
   always follow Liszt's numbering or choice of keys (as
   in the case of the well-known Müller-Berghaus version
   of No.2).*

Hungarian rhapsody no.1, F minor (piano version no.14) 11'
   *3 2 2 3 - 4 3 3 1 - tmp+2 - 2hp (in unison) -   Kalmus
   str
   Orchestrated by the composer and Franz Doppler.

Hungarian rhapsody no.2, C minor (piano version no.2) 11'
   *2 2 2 2 - 4 2 3 0 - tmp+4 - hp - str   Kalmus
   Orchestrated by Karl Müller-Berghaus. For Liszt's
   own orchestral version of this rhapsody, see the
   following listing.

Hungarian rhapsody no.2, D minor (piano version no.2) 11'
   *3 2 +3 2 - 4 2 3 1 - tmp+2 - str   Mapleson
   Orchestrated by the composer and Franz Doppler.
   Originally published as no.4 of the orchestral series;
   renumbered in the reprinting.

Hungarian rhapsody no.3, D major (piano version no.6)   7'
   *3 2 2 2 - 4 2 3 1 - tmp+3 - hp, cimbalom - str   Kalmus
   Orchestrated by the composer and Franz Doppler.

Hungarian rhapsody no.4, D minor (piano version no.12) 11'
   *3 2 2 2 - 4 2 3 1 - tmp+3 - hp - str   Kalmus
   Orchestrated by the composer and Franz Doppler.
   Originally published as no.2 of the orchestral series;
   renumbered in the reprinting.

Hungarian rhapsody no.5, E minor (piano version no.5)   8'
   2 2 2 2 - 4 0 3 0 - tmp - hp - str   Kalmus
   Orchestrated by the composer and Franz Doppler.

Hungarian rhapsody no.6, D major ("Pesther Carneval;"
  piano version no.9)   10'
  *3 2 2 2 - 4 2 3 1 - tmp+3 - hp - str   Kalmus
  Orchestrated by the composer and Franz Doppler.

Die Idéale (Symphonic poem no.12)   30'
  2 2 2 2 - 4 2 3 1 - tmp+1 - str   Breitkopf; Luck

Malediction   13'
  solo piano - str   Breitkopf; Kalmus

Mazeppa (Symphonic poem no.6)   17'
  *3 *3 =3 3 - 4 3 3 1 - tmp+3 - str   Breitkopf; Kalmus

Mephisto waltz no.1 (Der Tanz in der Dorfschenke)   11'
  *3 2 2 2 - 4 2 3 1 - tmp+2 - hp - str   Breitkopf;
  One of two "Episodes from Lenau's Faust."   Kalmus

Mephisto waltz no.2
  *3 2 2 2 - 4 2 3 1 - tmp+2 - hp - str   out of print

Nocturnal procession (Der nächtliche Zug)   15'
  3 *3 2 2 - 4 2 3 1 - tmp+1 - hp - str
  (Playable without English horn.)
  One of two "Episodes from Lenau's Faust." This work
  is out of print, but orchestral materials are in
  the Fleisher Collection.

Orpheus (Symphonic poem no.4)   13'
  *3 *3 2 2 - 4 2 3 1 - tmp - 2hp - str   Breitkopf; Kalmus

Les préludes (Symphonic poem no.3)   16'
  *3 2 2 2 - 4 2 3 1 - tmp+3 - hp - str   Breitkopf; Kalmus

Prometheus (Symphonic poem no.5)   12'
  *3 *3 2 2 - 4 2 3 1 - tmp - str   Breitkopf; Kalmus

Rhapsodie espagnole, piano and orchestra   14'
  *3 2 2 2 - 4 2 3 1 - tmp+2 - str   Kalmus
  Originally for piano; arranged as a concert piece
  for piano and orchestra by Ferruccio Busoni.

Tasso, lament and triumph (Symphonic poem no.2)   19'
  *3 2 *3 2 - 4 4 3 1 - tmp+4 - hp - str   Breitkopf;
                                                    Kalmus

Totentanz, piano and orchestra   16'
  *3 2 2 2 - 2 2 3 1 - tmp+3 - str   Breitkopf; Kalmus

Von der Wiege bis zum Grabe (From the cradle to
  the grave; Symphonic poem no.13)   14'
  *3 *2 2 2 - 4 2 3 1 - tmp+1 - (opt hp) - str   Bote;
                                                       Schirmer, G.

Wanderer fantasy
  See under: Schubert, Franz, 1797-1828

    LITOLFF, HENRY CHARLES, 1818-1891

Concerto symphonique no.4, op.102, D minor   25'
  solo piano   Kalmus
  *2 2 2 2 - 4 2 3 0 - tmp+1 - str

Robespierre: Overture   10'
  *2 2 2 2 - 4 2 3 0 - tmp+3 - str   Kalmus; Peters

    LOCATELLI, PIETRO, 1695-1764

Concerto grosso, op.1, no.6, C minor
  str, cnt   Vieweg
  Ed. Arthur Egidi.

Concerto grosso, op.1, no.8, F minor   20'
  solos: 2 violins, 2 violas, violoncello   Kahnt
  str, cnt
  Ed. Arnold Schering.

Concerto grosso, op.1, no.9, D major   12'
  2 solo violins, solo violoncello   Zanibon
  str
  Ed. Ettore Bonelli.

Concerto grosso, op.7, no.6, E-flat major ("Il
  pianto d'Arianna")   22'
  solos: 2 violins, viola, violoncello   Ricordi
  str
  Ed. Remo Giazotto.

Concerto grosso, op.7, no.12, F major   12'
  4 solo violins   Peters
  str, cnt
  Ed. Newell Jenkins.

Trauer-Symphonie   15'
  str, cnt   Kahnt

  LOEFFLER, CHARLES MARTIN, 1861-1935

A pagan poem   22'
  *3 *3 *3 2 - 4 6 3 1 - tmp+1 - hp, pf - str   Schirmer, G.

  LOMBARDO, MARIO, 1931-

Drakestail; a symphonic fairy tale for children   18'
  narrator   Chappell
  *3 *3 *3 2 - 4 3 3 1 - tmp+3 - hp, cel - str

  LORTZING, ALBERT, 1801-1851

Zar und Zimmermann: Overture   7'
  *2 2 2 2 - 4 2 3 0 - tmp+2 - str   Breitkopf;
  (Playable with winds 1 0 2 0 - 2 2 1 0.)   Kalmus

  LUENING, OTTO, 1900-

Prelude to a hymn tune by William Billings   10'
  1 1 1 1 - 1 0 0 0 - pf - str   Peters

Rhapsodic variations (composed with Vladimir Ussachevsky)
  *2 2 2 2 - 4 2 3 0 - tmp+1 - electronic tape -   17'
  str   Peters

Synthesis   9'
  *2 2 2 2 - 2 2 3 0 - 3perc - pf, electronic   Peters
  tape - str

LUIGINI, ALEXANDRE, 1850-1906

Ballet égyptien   20'
  *3 2 2 2 - 4 2 3 1 - tmp+4 - 2hp - str   Kalmus

LULLY, JEAN BAPTISTE, 1632-1687

Ballet music
  str (without va)   Vieweg
  Ed. Arthur Egidi.

Ballet suite (arr. Felix Mottl)   15'
  2 2 2 2 - 4 2 0 0 - tmp - str   Kalmus;
  Taken from ballet music of five Lully operas.   Peters

Roland: Suite
  1 2 0 1 - 2 2 0 0 - tmp - str   Kalmus
  Arr. William Lynen.

Le triomphe de l'amour: Ballet suite   20'
  str   Doblinger
  Ed. Paul Angerer.

LUTOSŁAWSKI, WITOLD, 1913-

Concerto for orchestra   29'
  *3 *3 *3 *3 - 4 4 4 1 - tmp+5 - 2hp,   Chester;
    cel, pf - str   PWM

Little suite (Mala suita)   11'
  *2 2 2 2 - 4 3 3 1 - tmp+1 - str   Chester; PWM

Postludium   4'
  *3 3 *3 *3 - 4 3 3 1 - tmp+2 - hp, cel, pf - str   Chester
  No.1 of the "Three Postludes."

Three postludes for orchestra   17'
  *3 3 *3 *3 - 4 3 3 1 - tmp+3 - 2hp,   Chester;
    cel, pf - str   PWM

Venetian games   13'
  *2 1 *3 1 - 1 1 1 0 - tmp+3 - hp,   Moeck;
    cel/pf 4-hands - 4vn, 3va, 3vc, 2db   PWM

MacDOWELL, EDWARD, 1861-1908

Concerto, piano, no.1, op.15, A minor   29'
  2 2 2 2 - 4 2 0 0 - tmp - str   Breitkopf; Kalmus

Concerto, piano, no.2, op.23, D minor   25'
  2 2 2 2 - 4 2 3 0 - tmp - str   Breitkopf; Kalmus

Suite no.1, op. 42   19'
  *3 2 2 2 - 4 2 3 1 - tmp+2 - str   Kalmus

Suite no.2, op.48 ("Indian")   30'
  *3 2 2 2 - 4 2 4 1 - tmp+2 - str   Breitkopf; Kalmus

MADERNA, BRUNO, 1920-1973

Aura   20'
  *4 *4 =5 *3 - 4 5 4 0 - tmp+13 - 2hp, cel -   Ricordi
  str 12.12.12.10.8
  4 flutists double on piccolo; 2 clarinetists double
  on bass clarinet.

Serenata no.2   16'
  *1 0 *2 0 - 1 1 0 0 - vibraphone/xylophone,   Suvini
  pf/glockenspiel, hp - vn, va, db

MAHLER, GUSTAV, 1860-1911

    *To resolve the many textual problems in Mahler,
    the new collected edition (begun in 1960 and still
    in progress) should be consulted.*

Blumine
  See his: Symphony no.1: "Blumine" movement

Kindertotenlieder   24'
  solo voice (medium)   Kalmus;
  *3 *3 *3 *3 - 4 0 0 0 - tmp+1 - hp, cel -   Peters;
  str   Universal

Das klagende Lied   40'
  chorus - solos SAT   Universal
  *6 *5 =7 *3 - 8 6 3 1 - 2tmp, 5perc - 2hp - str
  (The above instrumentation includes backstage winds
  and percussion: *3 2 +4 0 - 4 2 0 0 - tmp+2.)

Das Lied von der Erde   63'
  alto (or baritone) and tenor solos   Universal
  *4 *3 =4 *3 - 4 3 3 1 - tmp+3 - 2hp, cel,
    mandoline - str

Lieder aus "Des Knaben Wunderhorn"   43'
  solo voice   Universal
  *3 *3 +3 3 - 4 2 1 1 - tmp+4 - hp - str
  Songs are available individually, each with a choice
  of high or low key (the original keys are in italics
  in the list below). Instrumentation varies from song
  to song, within the aggregate given above.

    1. Der Schildwache Nachtlied (C major,
       B-flat major) 6'
    2. Verlorne Müh' (*A major*, G major) 3'
    3. Trost im Unglück (*A major*, G major) 3'
    4. Wer hat dies Liedlein erdacht? (*F major*,
       E-flat major) 3'
    5. Das irdische Leben (*E-flat minor*, D minor) 4'
    6. Des Antonius von Padua Fischpredigt (D minor,
       C minor) 4'
    7. Rheinlegendchen (*A major*, G major) 4'
    8. Lied des verfolgten im Turm (*D minor*, C minor) 5'
    9. Wo die schönen Trompeten blasen (*D minor*,
       C minor) 7'
   10. Lob des hohen Verstandes (*D major*, C major) 4'

  Other songs from "Des Knaben Wunderhorn" appear as
  movements of Symphonies nos.2, 3, and 4, and are also
  available separately, though only in the original keys.

Lieder eines fahrenden Gesellen (Songs of a wayfarer) 14'
  solo voice (medium)   Kalmus;
  *3 *2 *3 2 - 4 2 3 0 - tmp+2 - hp - str   Weinberger

Sieben Lieder aus letzter Zeit (Seven last songs)   30'
  solo voice   Universal
  *2 *3 *3 *3 - 4 3 3 1 - tmp+3 - hp, pf/cel - str
  One oboist doubles on oboe d'amore.
  Songs are available individually, each with a choice
  of high, medium, or low key (the original keys are
  in italics in the list below). Instrumentation varies
  from song to song, within the aggregate given above.

    1. Revelge (*D minor*, C minor, B-flat minor) 7'
    2. Der Tamboursg'sell (E minor, *D minor*, C minor) 5'

3. Blicke mir nicht in die Lieder (A-flat major,
   F major, E-flat major) 2'
4. Ich atmet' einen Linden Duft (F major, *D major*,
   C major) 2'
5. Ich bin der Welt abhanden gekommen (*F major*,
   E-flat major, D-flat major) 5'
6. Um Mitternacht (*F major*, E-flat major,
   D-flat major) 6'
7. Liebst du um Schönheit? (E-flat major, *C major*,
   B-flat major) 3'

Symphony no.1, D major   52'
 *4 *4 =4 *3 - 7 4 3 1 - 2tmp, 3perc - hp - str   Universal
A 5th trumpet and 4th trombone should be
used in the last movement to strengthen
the horns if necessary. (A reduced version is
available from Universal.)

Symphony no.1: "Blumine" movement   8'
 2 2 2 2 - 4 1 0 0 - tmp - hp - str   Presser
In its original form, the symphony included this
piece as the second of five movements. The five-
movement version was performed under Mahler's
direction in 1889 and 1894, but this movement was
deleted in the published version of 1899.

Symphony no.2, C minor ("Resurrection")   80'
 chorus - solos SA   Universal
 *4 *4 =5 *4 - 10 8 4 1 - 2tmp, 4perc -
   2hp, org - str
(A reduced version is available from the publisher.)

Symphony no.3, D minor   68'
 alto solo - women's chorus, boys' chorus   Universal
 *4 *4 =5 *4 - 8 4 4 1 - 2tmp, 5perc - 2hp - str
One of the trumpets doubles on posthorn in B-flat.

Symphony no.4, G major   55'
 soprano solo   Universal
 *4 *3 =3 *3 - 4 3 0 0 - tmp+4 - hp - str

Symphony no.5, C-sharp minor   70'
 *4 *3 =3 *3 - 6 4 3 1 - tmp+4 - hp - str   Peters
Ed. Erwin Ratz. The earlier Peters edition,
not by Ratz, should not be used.

Symphony no.5, C-sharp minor: Adagietto   10'
    str, hp   Peters

Symphony no.6, A minor   72'
    *5 *5 =5 *5 - 8 6 4 1 - tmp+5 - 2hp, cel - str   Kahnt
    Ed. Erwin Ratz.

Symphony no.7, E minor   80'
    *5 *4 =5 *4 - 4 3 3 1 - tenorhorn - tmp+5 -   Bote
      2hp, gtr, mandoline - str

Symphony no.8, E-flat major ("Symphony of   85'
    a thousand")   Universal
    double chorus, boys' chorus - solos SSSAATBB
    *6 *5 =6 *5 - 8 8 7 1 - tmp+3 - 2hp, cel, pf,
      org, harm, mandoline - str
    (A reduced version is available from the publisher.)

Symphony no.9, D major   75'
    *5 *4 =5 *4 - 4 3 3 1 - tmp+3 - 1 or 2hp   Universal
      (2nd hp merely doubles certain passages) - str
    Ed. Erwin Ratz.

Symphony no.10, F-sharp major   70'
    *3 *3 =3 *3 - 4 4 4 1 - 2tmp, 3perc - hp - str   Faber
    Unfinished at the composer's death. This performing
    version by Deryck Cooke. Score is published by
    Faber; parts are available from AMP.

Symphony no.10, F-sharp major: Movements I and III   25'
    *3 3 3 3 - 4 4 3 1 - tmp+1 - hp - str   AMP
    Ed. Otto A Jokl, after a performing version by
    Ernst Křenek.

    MALIPIERO, GIAN FRANCESCO, 1882-1973

Concerto, violoncello   14'
    *3 2 2 2 - 4 0 0 0 - 2perc - str   Suvini

Sinfonia per Antigenida   20'
    *3 *3 2 2 - 4 2 3 1 - 3perc - hp, cel - str   Ricordi

MANFREDINI, FRANCESCO, ca.1680-1748

Christmas symphony, op.2, no.12, D major (Sinfonia
  pastorale per il santissimo natale")
  str, cnt   Vieweg
  Ed. Felix Schroeder.

Concerto grosso, op.3, no.9, D major   11'
  solo concertino: 2 violins, violoncello   Zanibon
  str
  Ed. Ettore Bonelli.

Concerto grosso, op.3, no.10, G minor   12'
  solo concertino: 2 violins   Peters
  str, cnt
  Ed. Bernhard Paumgartner.

Concerto grosso, op.3, no.12, C major ("Christmas
  concerto")   10'
  solo concertino: 2 violins   Eulenburg;
  str, cnt   Kahnt; Schott

MARCELLO, ALESSANDRO, ca.1684-ca.1750

Concerto, oboe, C minor
  See under: Marcello, Benedetto, 1686-1739

MARCELLO, BENEDETTO, 1686-1739

Concerto, oboe, C minor   10'
  str   Zanibon
  Ed. Ettore Bonelli. Actually by Alessandro Marcello.

Concerti grossi, op.1
  str, cnt - most of these works have soloistic   Zanibon
    parts for 2 violins and 1 violoncello; occasionally
    brief solo passages occur for viola, a 3rd violin,
    or even double bass
  Ed. Ettore Bonelli.

    No.1, D major   10'

    No.2, E minor   12'

    No.3, E major   10'

No.4, F major	15'
No.5, B minor	13'
No.6, B-flat major	10'
No.7, F minor	10'
No.8, F major	9'
No.9, A major	10'
No.10, C major	12'

Introduction, aria, and presto, A minor   9'
  str   Zanibon
  Ed. Ettore Bonelli.

MARTIN, FRANK, 1890-1974

Ballade, saxophone and orchestra   13'
  solo alto saxophone   Universal
  str - pf - tmp+1

Concerto, 7 winds   22'
  solos: fl, ob, cl, bsn, hn, tp, tbn   Universal
  str - tmp+3

Etudes for string orchestra   20'
  str   Universal

The four elements (Les quatre éléments)   20'
  *3 *3 =3 *3 - 4 3 3 1 - asx - tmp+4 - 2hp,   Universal
    cel, pf - str

Passacaille   11'
  str   Universal

Petite symphonie concertante   22'
  hp, pf, hpsd - 2 string orchestras   Universal

MARTINO, DONALD, 1931-

Concerto, piano   27'
  *3 *2 *3 *3 - 4 2 3 1 - tmp+4 - hp,   Ione
    cel/orchestral pf - str 14.12.10.10.8 minimum
  Bcl doubles on contrabass cl; tuba doubles on

euphonium; 2 flutists double on piccolo.

Mosaic for grand orchestra   16'
  =4 *4 *4 *4 - 4 4 4 1 - tmp+5 - 2hp,   Dantalian
    cel/electric org, electric gtr -
    str 16.14.10.10.9
  Two of the flutists double on piccolo; one clarinetist
  doubles on contrabass clarinet in B-flat.

Paradiso choruses   29'
  chorus (including opt children's voices) -   Dantalian
    solos 3S, 4Mz, 3T, 2Bar
  *3 *3 *3 *4 - 4 4 4 1 - tmp+4 - hp, pf (preferably
    electric), org - pre-recorded tape - str
  Two of the flutists double on piccolo.

Ritorno   15'
  2 *3 *3 2 - 4 3 3 1 - tmp+3 - hp, cel/pf -   Dantalian
    str

  MARTINU, BOHUSLAV, 1890-1959

Comedy on the bridge: Little suite   6'
  *1 1 1 1 - 2 1 1 0 - 3perc - pf - str   Boosey

Concerto, oboe   17'
  2 0 2 1 - 2 1 0 0 - pf - str   Eschig

Concerto, violin   27'
  2 2 2 2 - 4 3 3 1 - tmp+2 - str   Boosey

Estampes   20'
  *2 *2 2 2 - 4 2 3 0 - tmp+2 - hp, pf - str   Southern

Fantasia concertante, piano and orchestra   20'
  *3 2 2 2 - 4 2 3 0 - tmp+3 - str   Universal

The frescos of Piero della Francesca   21'
  *4 *3 3 3 - 4 3 3 1 - tmp+3 - hp - str   Universal

Sinfonia concertante for 2 orchestras   16'
  1st orchestra: 0 3 0 1 - 2 0 0 0 - str   Schott
  2nd orchestra: *2 0 2 1 - 2 2 3 1 - tmp+2 - str

Symphony no.1   35'
  *3 *3 3 *3 - 4 3 3 1 - tmp+3 - hp, pf - str   Boosey

Symphony no.2   24'
  *3 3 3 2 - 4 3 3 1 - tmp+3 - hp, pf - str   Boosey

Symphony no.3   30'
  *3 *3 3 2 - 4 3 3 1 - tmp+3 - hp, pf - str   Boosey

Symphony no.4   32'
  *4 *4 3 2 - 4 3 3 1 - tmp+3 - pf - str   Boosey

Symphony no.5   27'
  *3 3 3 3 - 4 3 3 1 - tmp+3 - pf - str   Boosey

Symphony no.6 (Fantaisies symphoniques)   25'
  *4 3 3 3 - 4 3 3 1 - tmp+4 - str   Boosey

Toccata e due canzoni   18'
  *1 2 1 1 - 0 1 0 0 - tmp - pf - str   Boosey

      MARTIRANO, SALVATORE, 1927-

Contrasto   9'
  *3 *3 *3 *3 - 4 3 3 1 - tmp+3 - hp, cel - str   Schott

      MASCAGNI, PIETRO, 1863-1945

L'amico Fritz: Intermezzo   4'
  *3 2 2 2 - 4 2 3 1 - tmp+1 - hp - str   Luck; Sonzogno

Cavalleria rusticana: Intermezzo   3'
  2 2 0 0 - (opt hp), org - str   Kalmus;
  (Organ may be replaced by 2cl, 2bsn, 1hn.)   Sonzogno

Cavalleria rusticana: Prelude and Siciliana
  *3 2 2 2 - 4 2 3 1 - tmp+2 - (opt hp) - str   Kalmus;
                                                      Luck

      MASSENET, JULES, 1842-1912

Le Cid: Ballet music   16'
  *2 *2 2 2 - 4 4 3 1 - tmp+3 - 2hp - str   Heugel; Kalmus

Concerto, piano   28'
  *3 2 2 2 - 4 2 3 0 - tmp+3 - cel - str   Heugel

Hérodiade: Prelude to Act III   2'
  0 1 2 2 - 4 0 0 1 - tmp - hp - str   Heugel

Phèdre: Overture   9'
  *3 2 2 2 - 4 4 3 1 - tmp - str   Heugel; Kalmus

Scènes alsaciennes   21'
  *2 2 2 2 - 4 4 3 1 - tmp+3 - str   Heugel; Kalmus

Scènes pittoresques   16'
  *2 2 2 2 - 4 4 3 0 - tmp+4 - str   Heugel; Kalmus

Suite no.1, op.13   22'
  *3 2 2 2 - 4 4 3 1 - tmp+3 - 2hp - str   Durand

MAXWELL DAVIES, PETER, 1934-

Second fantasia on John Taverner's In nomine   40'
  =2 *2 *2 *2 - 4 4 2 2 - tmp+4 - hp - str   Boosey

The shepherd's calendar   21'
  chorus - treble soloist (or soprano, or a group   Boosey
    of trebles and/or sopranos, doubled by a flute,
    if necessary)
  1 1 5 1 - 0 1 1 0 - 6rec - 11perc - handbells -
    str quartet

Stone litany; runes from a house of the dead   20'
  solo mezzo-soprano   Boosey
  *2 0 =2 *2 - 2 2 2 1 - tmp+5 - hp, cel - str

Symphony   58'
  =3 *3 *3 *3 - 4 3 3 0 - tmp+4 - hp, cel - str   Boosey
  Two of the flutists play piccolo.

McBRIDE, ROBERT, 1911-

Pumpkin-eater's little fugue   4'
  *2 2 2 2 - 4 2 3 1 - tmp+2 - str   AMP
  (Optional: 2nd oboe, 2nd bassoon, 3rd trombone.)

MENDELSSOHN, FELIX, 1809-1847

Athalia: Overture   10'
 2 2 2 2 - 2 2 3 0 - tmp - hp - str   Breitkopf; Kalmus

Athalia: War march of the priests   5'
 2 2 2 2 - 2 2 3 1 - tmp - str   Kalmus; Luck

Calm sea and prosperous voyage (Meeresstille und
 glückliche Fahrt)   12'
 *3 2 2 *3 - 2 3 0 1 - tmp - str   Breitkopf; Kalmus

Capriccio brillant, op.22, B minor   12'
 solo piano   Breitkopf;
 2 2 2 2 - 2 2 0 0 - tmp - str   Kalmus

Concerto, piano, no.1, op.25, G minor   22'
 2 2 2 2 - 2 2 0 0 - tmp - str   Breitkopf; Kalmus

Concerto, piano, no.2, op.40, D minor   25'
 2 2 2 2 - 2 2 0 0 - tmp - str   Breitkopf; Kalmus

Concerto, 2 pianos, E major   30'
 1 2 2 2 - 2 2 0 0 - tmp - str   Broude, A.

Concerto, violin, op.64, E minor   26'
 2 2 2 2 - 2 2 0 0 - tmp - str Breitkopf; Kalmus; Peters

Concerto, violin, (posth.), D minor (1822)   23'
 str   Peters
 Discovered and edited by Yehudi Menuhin.

Elijah (Elias), op.70   133'
 chorus - solos SSATB (or more)   Breitkopf; Kalmus;
 2 2 2 2 - 4 2 3 1 - tmp - org - str   Peters;
                                             Schirmer, G.

Die erste Walpurgisnacht, op.60   45'
 chorus - solos ATBB   Breitkopf; Kalmus;
 *3 2 2 2 - 2 2 3 0 - tmp+2 - str   Peters; Schirmer, G.

The Hebrides (Fingal's cave), op.26   10'
 2 2 2 2 - 2 2 0 0 - tmp - str   Breitkopf; Kalmus

Heimkehr aus der Fremde (Son and stranger), op.89   7'
 2 2 2 2 - 2 2 0 0 - str   Breitkopf; Kalmus

Die Hochzeit des Camacho (Camacho's wedding): Overture 6'
    2 2 2 2 - 4 2 3 0 - tmp - str   Breitkopf; Kalmus

Lobgesang, op.52   65'
    chorus - solos SST   Breitkopf; Gray;
    2 2 2 2 - 4 2 3 0 - tmp - org - str   Kalmus;
                                               Schirmer, G.

Märchen von der schönen Melusine (Fair Melusina)   10'
    2 2 2 2 - 2 2 0 0 - tmp - str   Breitkopf; Kalmus

Meeresstille und glückliche Fahrt
    See his: Calm sea and prosperous voyage

Midsummernight's dream, op.21
    women's chorus - 2 solo sopranos   Fischer, C.;
    2 2 2 2 - 2 3 3 1 - tmp+2 - str   Gray; Kalmus

Midsummernight's dream: Overture   12'
    2 2 2 2 - 2 2 0 1 - tmp - str   Breitkopf; Kalmus

Midsummernight's dream: Four pieces

    1. Scherzo   5'
        2 2 2 2 - 2 2 0 0 - tmp - str   Breitkopf; Kalmus

    2. Intermezzo   4'
        2 2 2 2 - 2 0 0 0 - str   Breitkopf; Kalmus

    3. Nocturne   6'
        2 2 2 2 - 2 0 0 0 - str   Breitkopf; Kalmus

    4. Wedding march   5'
        2 2 2 2 - 2 3 3 1 - tmp+1 - str   Breitkopf; Kalmus

Octet, strings, op.20, E-flat major   32'
    4vn, 2va, 2vc   Kalmus

Overture for winds, op.24, C major   10'
    *2 2 +4 *3 - 4 2 3 1 - 2 basset horns - 4perc   Kalmus
    An arrangement of this work for contemporary band
    by Felix Greissle is published by G. Schirmer.

Psalm 42, op.42 (As the hart pants)   27'
    chorus - solo soprano - solo male quartet (TTBB) Gray;
    2 2 2 2 - 4 2 3 0 - tmp - str   Kalmus;
    (4 horns playing 2 real parts.)   Schirmer, G.

Rondo brillant, op.29   10'
  solo piano   Breitkopf;
  2 2 2 2 - 2 2 0 0 - tmp - str   Fischer, C.

Ruy Blas, op.95: Overture   7'
  2 2 2 2 - 4 2 3 0 - tmp - str   Breitkopf; Kalmus

St. Paul (Paulus), op.36   130'
  chorus - solos SATBB   Breitkopf; Gray;
  2 2 2 *3 - 4 2 3 1 - tmp - org - str   Kalmus; Peters

St. Paul: Overture   7'
  2 2 2 2 - 2 2 3 1 - tmp - org - str   Breitkopf; Kalmus

Sinfonia no.8, D major   30'
  str   Deutscher
  A wind version of this work, calling for
  2 2 2 2 - 2 2 0 0, is available from the publisher.

Sinfonia no.9, C major ("Swiss")   30'
  str   Deutscher; Luck

Sinfonia no.11, F minor   35'
  str orchestra - 3perc in one brief passage   Deutscher

Symphony no.1, op.1, C minor   34'
  2 2 2 2 - 2 2 0 0 - tmp - str Breitkopf; Kalmus; Peters

Symphony no.2 (from the "Lobgesang," op.52)   22'
  2 2 2 2 - 4 2 3 0 - tmp - str   Breitkopf
  The three movements of this symphony are the
  opening instrumental sections of the symphony-cantata
  "Lobgesang," op.52. Breitkopf also offers an edition
  "with final chorus in the version shortened by Mendelssohn." This requires chorus and solos SST in
  addition to the above instrumentation. Total
  duration: 37'

Symphony no.3, op.56, A minor ("Scotch")   37'
  2 2 2 2 - 4 2 0 0 - tmp - str   Breitkopf; Kalmus

Symphony no.4, op.90, A major ("Italian")   27'
  2 2 2 2 - 2 2 0 0 - tmp - str   Breitkopf; Kalmus

Symphony no.5, op.107, D major ("Reformation")   27'
  2 2 2 *3 - 2 2 3 1 - tmp - str   Breitkopf; Kalmus

Trumpet overture, op.101   8'
  2 2 2 2 - 2 2 3 0 - tmp - str   Kalmus

MENNIN, PETER, 1923-

Canto   8'
  *3 *3 *3 2 - 4 3 3 1 - tmp+3 - str   Fischer, C.

The Christmas story   24'
  chorus - solos ST   Fischer, C.
  brass 0 2 2 0 - tmp - str

Concertato (Moby Dick)   11'
  *3 *3 *3 2 - 4 3 3 1 - tmp+3 - str   Fischer, C.

Symphony no.6   25'
  *3 *3 *3 2 - 4 2 3 1 - tmp+3 - str   Fischer, C.

Symphony no.7 ("Variation symphony")   26'
  *3 *3 *3 *3 - 4 3 3 1 - tmp+3 - str   Fischer, C.

MENOTTI, GIAN CARLO, 1911-

Concerto, piano   28'
  *3 2 +2 2 - 4 3 3 1 - tmp+4 - str   Ricordi

Sebastian: Suite   20'
  *1 *1 *2 1 - 2 2 2 0 - tmp+2 - hp, pf - str   Colombo

MESSIAEN, OLIVIER, 1908-

L'ascension   30'
  3 *3 *3 3 - 4 3 3 1 - tmp+2 - str   Leduc

Chronochromie   30'
  *4 *3 =4 3 - 4 4 3 1 - 6perc - str   Leduc

Couleurs de la cité céleste   18'
  solo piano   Leduc
  0 0 3 0 - 2 4 4 0 - 6perc

Les offrandes oubliées   11'
  3 *3 *3 3 - 4 3 3 1 - tmp+3 - str   Durand

Oiseaux exotiques   14'
  solo piano   Universal
  *2 1 =4 1 - 2 1 0 0 - 7perc

Trois petites liturgies de la présence divine   31'
  solo piano, solo ondes martenot - women's chorus   Durand
  str - cel - 4perc

Turangalîla-symphonie   75'
  solo piano, solo ondes martenot   Durand
  *3 *3 *3 3 - 4 5 3 1 - 7perc - cel - str

    MEYERBEER, GIACOMO, 1791-1864

Fackeltanz no.1 (Torch dance no.1)   6'
  *2 2 2 2 - 4 2 3 1 - tmp+3 - str   Bote; Kalmus

Les Huguenots: Overture   7'
  *3 *3 2 2 - 4 4 3 1 - tmp+1 - str   Fischer, C.; Kalmus

Le prophète: Ballet music
  *3 2 2 4 - 4 4 3 1 - tmp+3 - str   Kalmus

Le prophète: Coronation march   4'
  *3 2 2 4 - 4 4 3 1 - tmp+3 - str   Breitkopf; Kalmus

    MIARI, GIANGIACOMO, 1929-

Concerto, double bass   12'
  str   Zanibon

    MIASKOVSKY, NIKOLAI, 1881-1950

Sinfonietta, op.32, no.2   20'
  str   Kalmus; VAAP

Symphony no.21, op.51, F-sharp minor   19'
  *3 *3 *3 *3 - 4 3 3 1 - tmp - str   VAAP

Symphony no.22, op.54   35'
  *3 *3 *3 *3 - 4 3 3 1 - tmp+3 - str   VAAP

MILHAUD, DARIUS, 1892-1974

Aubade 18'
 2 2 2 2 - 2 2 2 0 - tmp+3 - hp, cel - str Heugel

Le boeuf sur le toit 15'
 *2 1 2 1 - 2 2 1 0 - 2perc - str Eschig

Le carnaval d'Aix; fantasy for piano and orchestra 19'
 *2 1 2 1 - 2 2 1 1 - tmp+3 - str Heugel

Le carnaval de Londres 30'
 *1 1 1 1 - 0 1 1 0 - asx - 2perc - hp - str Salabert

Les Choëphores 34'
 chorus - solos SSA Heugel
 *3 *3 *3 4 - 4 3 3 1 - tmp+14 - hp, cel - str
 Three of the movements are scored for speaking
 chorus and percussion only.

Concertino de printemps, violin and orchestra 9'
 1 1 1 1 - 1 1 0 0 - tmp+1 - str Salabert

Concertino d'hiver, trombone and strings 18'
 str AMP

Concerto, percussion and small orchestra 7'
 1 percussion soloist, using a large number Universal
  of percussion instruments
 *2 0 2 0 - 0 1 1 0 - str

Concerto, piano, no.1 12'
 *2 2 =3 2 - 2 3 2 1 - tmp+2 - hp - str Salabert

Concerto, piano, no.3 19'
 *2 2 2 2 - 2 2 2 1 - tmp+2 - str AMP

Concerto, violin, no.2 22'
 *2 *3 *3 2 - 2 2 2 1 - tmp+1 - str AMP

Concerto, violoncello, no.1 15'
 *2 2 2 2 - 2 2 2 1 - tmp+2 - hp - str Salabert

Concerto, violoncello, no.2 20'
 *2 2 2 2 - 2 2 2 1 - tmp+2 - hp - str AMP

Cortège funèbre   14'
  *2 1 2 1 - 0 2 2 1 - 2perc - hp - str   AMP
  (Clarinets may be replaced by 2 alto saxophones.)

La création du monde   16'
  2 1 2 1 - 1 2 1 0 - asx - tmp+1 - pf - 2vn,   Eschig
    vc, db

Les funérailles de Phocion   8'
  *3 2 *3 *3 - 4 3 3 1 - tmp+3 - str   Heugel

Murder of a great chief of state   4'
  2 2 2 2 - 4 3 3 1 - tmp - str   Eschig

Ouverture méditerranéene   5'
  2 2 2 2 - 4 2 2 0 - tmp+3 - str   Heugel

Overture philharmonique   9'
  *2 *2 *3 *3 - 4 3 3 1 - tmp+3 - hp - str   EMT

Saudades do Brazil   40'
  *2 *2 2 2 - 2 2 2 0 - tmp - str   Eschig

Suite concertante, piano and orchestra   18'
  2 2 2 2 - 2 2 2 1 - tmp+3 - hp, cel - str   Enoch

Suite française   16'
  *2 2 2 2 - 2 2 2 0 - tmp+2 - str   MCA
  Orchestrated by the composer from a work for
  concert band.

Suite provençale   16'
  *2 *3 +2 2 - 4 3 3 1 - tmp+3 - str   Salabert

Suite symphonique no.2 (from "Protée")   22'
  *3 *3 *3 4 - 4 3 3 1 - tmp+1 - hp, cel - str   Durand

Symphonies for small orchestra

  1. Le printemps   4'
    *2 1 1 0 - hp - str quartet   Universal

  2. Pastorale   4'
    1 *1 0 1 - vn, va, vc, db   Universal

  3. Sérénade   3'
    1 0 1 1 - vn, va, vc, db   Universal

4. Dixtuor à cordes   6'
  4vn, 2va, 2vc, 2db   Universal

5. Dixtuor d'instruments à vent   6'
  *2 *2 *2 2 - 2 0 0 0   Universal

6. Sinfonie   6'
  solo voices (or chorus) SATB - ob - vc   Universal

Symphony no.1   27'
  *3 *3 *3 *3 - 4 3 3 1 - tmp+3 - hp - str   Heugel

Symphony no.2   27'
  *3 *3 *3 *3 - 4 3 3 1 - tmp+3 - hp, cel - str   Heugel
  One clarinetist doubles on alto saxophone.

Symphony no.3   32'
  chorus   Heugel
  *3 *3 =4 *3 - 4 3 3 1 - tmp+4 - hp - str

Symphony no.10   22'
  *3 *3 *3 *3 - 4 3 3 1 - tmp+4 - hp - str   Heugel

Symphony no.11 ("Romantique")   22'
  *3 *3 *3 *3 - 4 3 3 1 - tmp+2 - hp - str   Heugel

Symphony no.12 ("Rurale")   17'
  *2 2 *3 2 - 2 2 3 1 - tmp+5 - hp - str   Heugel

MONIUSZKO, STANISŁAW, 1819-1872

The countess (Hrabina): Overture   8'
  *2 2 2 2 - 4 2 3 1 - tmp+4 - str   PWM

Halka: Mazur   4'
  *2 2 2 2 - 4 2 3 1 - tmp+4 - str   PWM

MONN, GEORG MATTHIAS, 1717-1750

Concerto, harpsichord (1746)
  See: Schoenberg, Arnold, 1874-1951
      Concerto, violoncello

MONTEVERDI, CLAUDIO, 1567-1643

Combattimento di Tancredi e Clorinda   22'
  solos SAT   Chester;
  str, cnt   Oxford
  Chester edition by G. F. Malipiero; Oxford
  edition by Denis Stevens.

Laudate dominum (Psalm 117)   4'
  chorus - solos SSTTB   Eulenburg
  (opt 4tbn) - str (without va), cnt
  Ed. Denis Arnold.

Orfeo: Overture   5'
  *2 2 0 0 - 0 2 3 0 - 2hp (or lute and   Luck
    chittarone), org - str

Orfeo: Sinfonie e ritornelli   9'
  str   Ricordi
  Arr. G. F. Malipiero.

Orfeo: Toccata and ritornelli   4'
  *3 2 *3 2 - 4 3 4 0 - 1perc - hp - str   Schirmer, G.
  Two of the flutists double on piccolo.
  (4th trombone is optional.) Arr. Maurice Peress.

Vespro della beata vergine (ed. Jürgen Jürgens, 1977)
  double chorus - solos SSATTBB   full concert
  2rec/fl, 3cornetti (or tp's and ob's),   Universal
    2bsn - 4tbn - org, hpsd, chitarrone/lute,
    hp - str
  A "practical Urtext" edition.

Vespro della beata vergine (ed. Walter Goehr, 1956)
  chorus - solos SSATTBB   full concert
  *2 0 0 *2 - 0 0 3 0 - (opt 2rec),   Universal
    3cornetti, va da gamba - org, positiv org,
    hpsd - str

MOSSOLOV, ALEXANDER, 1900-

Iron foundry, op.19   3'
  *3 *3 *3 *3 - 4 3 3 1 - tmp+5 - str   VAAP

MOUSSORGSKY, MODESTE, 1839-1881
  See: Mussorgsky, Modest, 1839-1881

MOZART, LEOPOLD, 1719-1787

Concerto, trumpet, D major   9'
  2hn - str, cnt   Kneusslin; Schott

Toy symphony
  See under: Haydn, Franz Joseph, 1732-1809

MOZART, WOLFGANG AMADEUS, 1756-1791

A questo seno--Or che il cielo, K.374   6'
  soprano recitative and rondo   Breitkopf
  0 2 0 0 - 2 0 0 0 - str

The abduction from the seraglio, K.384: Overture   6'
  *1 2 2 2 - 2 2 0 0 - tmp+3 - str   Breitkopf;
  With concert-ending by Johann André.   Kalmus

Adagio, violin and orchestra, K.261, E major   5'
  2 0 0 0 - 2 0 0 0 - str   Breitkopf

Adagio and fugue, K.546, C minor   9'
  str   Breitkopf

Ah, lo previdi--Ah, t'invola--Deh, non varcar, K.272   12'
  soprano recitative, aria, and cavatina   Breitkopf
  0 2 0 0 - 2 0 0 0 - str

Ah se in ciel, benigne stelle, K.538   7'
  soprano aria   Breitkopf;
  0 2 0 2 - 2 0 0 0 - str   Broude Bros.

Alcandro, lo confesso--Non so d'onde viene, K.294   8'
  soprano recitative and aria   Breitkopf;
  2 0 2 2 - 2 0 0 0 - str   Kalmus

Alcandro, lo confesso--Non so d'onde viene, K.512
  bass recitative and aria   Breitkopf
  1 2 0 2 - 2 0 0 0 - str

Alma dei creatoris, K.272a (277)   10'
  chorus - solos SAT   Kalmus;
  0 0 0 1 - 0 0 3 0 - org - str   Peters

Alma grande e nobil core, K.578   3'
  soprano aria   Breitkopf;
  0 2 0 2 - 0 2 0 0 - str   Kalmus

Andante, flute and orchestra, K.285e (315), C major   4'
  0 2 0 0 - 2 0 0 0 - str   Breitkopf; Kalmus

Apollo and Hyacinth, K.38: Prelude   3'
  0 2 0 0 - 2 0 0 0 - str   Bärenreiter; Kalmus; Luck

Ave verum corpus, K.618   6'
  chorus - org - str   Bärenreiter; Breitkopf; Kalmus

Un baccio di mano, K.541
  bass arietta   Breitkopf;
  1 2 0 2 - 2 0 0 0 - str   Kalmus

Basta, vincesti--Ah non lasciarmi, K.295a (486a)   3'
  soprano recitative and aria   Breitkopf
  2 0 0 2 - 2 0 0 0 - str

Bastien and Bastienne, K.46b (50): Overture   2'
  0 2 0 0 - 2 0 0 0 - str   Breitkopf; Kalmus

Bella mia fiamma--Resta, oh cara, K.528   5'
  soprano recitative and aria   Breitkopf;
  1 2 0 2 - 2 0 0 0 - str   Kalmus

Benedictus sit deus, K.66a (117)   9'
  chorus - soprano solo   Kalmus
  2 0 0 0 - 2 2 0 0 - tmp - org - str

Cassation no.1, K.63, G major   15'
  0 2 0 0 - 2 0 0 0 - str   Breitkopf; Kalmus

Cassation no.2, K.63a (99), B-flat major   14'
  0 2 0 0 - 2 0 0 0 - str   Breitkopf; Kalmus

Ch'io mi scordi di te--Non temer, K.505   11'
  soprano scene and rondo   Breitkopf;
  0 0 2 2 - 2 0 0 0 - pf - str   Kalmus

Chi sa, chi sa, qual sia, K.582
  soprano aria   Breitkopf;
  0 0 2 2 - 2 0 0 0 - str   Kalmus

Clarice cara mia sposa, K.256
  tenor aria   Kalmus;
  0 2 0 0 - 2 0 0 0 - str   Luck

La clemenza di Tito, K.621: Overture   5'
  2 2 2 2 - 2 2 0 0 - tmp - str   Breitkopf; Kalmus

Con ossequio, con rispetto, K.210   3'
  tenor aria   Breitkopf
  0 2 0 0 - 2 0 0 0 - str

Concerto, bassoon, K.186e (191), B-flat major   19'
  0 2 0 0 - 2 0 0 0 - str   Breitkopf; Kalmus

Concerto, bassoon, no.2, K.Anh.C 14.03, B-flat major 17'
  0 2 0 0 - 2 2 0 0 - tmp - str   Peters
  Ed. Max Seiffert. Probably spurious.

Concerto, clarinet, K.622, A major   28'
  2 0 0 2 - 2 0 0 0 - str   Breitkopf; Kalmus

Concerto, flute, no.1, K.285c (313), G major   24'
  0 2 0 0 - 2 0 0 0 - str   Breitkopf; Kalmus

Concerto, flute, no.2, K.285d (314), D major   16'
  0 2 0 0 - 2 0 0 0 - str   Breitkopf; Kalmus

Concerto, flute and harp, K.297c (299), C major   27'
  0 2 0 0 - 2 0 0 0 - str   Breitkopf; Kalmus

Concerto, horn, no.1, K.386b (412), D major   8'
  0 2 0 2 - str   Breitkopf; Kalmus

Concerto, horn, no.2, K.417, E-flat major   14'
  0 2 0 0 - 2 0 0 0 - str   Breitkopf; Kalmus

Concerto, horn, no.3, K.447, E-flat major   14'
  0 0 2 2 - str   Breitkopf; Kalmus

Concerto, horn, no.4, K.495, E-flat major   15'
  0 2 0 0 - 2 0 0 0 - str   Breitkopf; Kalmus

Concerto, oboe, K.285d (314), C major   16'
  0 2 0 0 - 2 0 0 0 - str   Boosey
  Ed. Bernhard Paumgartner. Believed to be the
  original version of the flute concerto K.285d (314).

Concertos, piano, nos.1-4
  These pieces are Mozart's arrangements of works
  by other composers.

Concerto, piano, no.5, K.175, D major   20'
  0 2 0 0 - 2 2 0 0 - tmp - str   Breitkopf; Kalmus

Concerto, piano, no.6, K.238, B-flat major   21'
  2 2 0 0 - 2 0 0 0 - str   Breitkopf; Kalmus

Concerto, 3 pianos, no.7, K.242, F major   23'
  0 2 0 0 - 2 0 0 0 - str   Breitkopf; Kalmus
  (A version by the composer for 2 pianos is
  also available.)

Concerto, piano, no.8, K.246, C major   23'
  0 2 0 0 - 2 0 0 0 - str   Breitkopf; Kalmus

Concerto, piano, no.9, K.271, E-flat major   32'
  0 2 0 0 - 2 0 0 0 - str   Breitkopf; Kalmus

Concerto, 2 pianos, no.10, K.316a (365), E-flat major   24'
  0 2 0 2 - 2 0 0 0 - str   Breitkopf; Kalmus

Concerto, piano, no.11, K.387a (413), F major   23'
  0 2 0 2 - 2 0 0 0 - str   Breitkopf; Kalmus; Peters

Concerto, piano, no.12, K.385p (414), A major   26'
  0 2 0 0 - 2 0 0 0 - str   Breitkopf; Kalmus; Peters

Concerto, piano, no.13, K.387b (415), C major   23'
  0 2 0 2 - 2 2 0 0 - tmp - str   Breitkopf;
                                            Kalmus; Peters

Concerto, piano, no.14, K.449, E-flat major   24'
  0 2 0 0 - 2 0 0 0 - str   Breitkopf; Kalmus; Peters

Concerto, piano, no.15, K.450, B-flat major   23'
  1 2 0 2 - 2 0 0 0 - str   Breitkopf; Kalmus

Concerto, piano, no.16, K.451, D major   22'
1 2 0 2 - 2 2 0 0 - tmp - str   Breitkopf; Kalmus

Concerto, piano, no.17, K.453, G major   30'
1 2 0 2 - 2 0 0 0 - str   Breitkopf; Kalmus

Concerto, piano, no.18, K.456, B-flat major   29'
1 2 0 2 - 2 0 0 0 - str   Breitkopf; Kalmus

Concerto, piano, no.19, K.459, F major   24'
1 2 0 2 - 2 0 0 0 - str   Breitkopf; Kalmus

Concerto, piano, no.20, K.466, D minor   30'
1 2 0 2 - 2 2 0 0 - tmp - str   Breitkopf; Kalmus

Concerto, piano, no.21, K.467, C major   29'
1 2 0 2 - 2 2 0 0 - tmp - str   Breitkopf; Kalmus

Concerto, piano, no.22, K.482, E-flat major   34'
1 0 2 2 - 2 2 0 0 - tmp - str   Breitkopf; Kalmus

Concerto, piano, no.23, K.488, A major   25'
1 0 2 2 - 2 0 0 0 - str   Bärenreiter;
     Breitkopf; Kalmus

Concerto, piano, no.24, K.491, C minor   30'
1 2 2 2 - 2 2 0 0 - tmp - str   Bärenreiter;
     Breitkopf; Kalmus

Concerto, piano, no.25, K.503, C major   31'
1 2 0 2 - 2 2 0 0 - tmp - str   Bärenreiter;
     Breitkopf; Kalmus

Concerto, piano, no.26, K.537, D major ("Coronation") 32'
1 2 0 2 - 2 2 0 0 - tmp - str   Breitkopf; Kalmus

Concerto, piano, no.27, K.595, B-flat major   30'
1 2 0 2 - 2 0 0 0 - str   Breitkopf; Kalmus

Concerto, 2 pianos, K.242, F major
   See note to no.7 in the series of piano concertos above.

Concerto, 2 pianos, K.316a (365), E-flat major
   Listed as no.10 in the series of piano concertos above.

Concerto, 3 pianos, K.242, F major
Listed as no.7 in the series of piano concertos above.

Concerto, violin, no.1, K.207, B-flat major   20'
  0 2 0 0 - 2 0 0 0 - str   Breitkopf; Kalmus

Concerto, violin, no.2, K.211, D major   23'
  0 2 0 0 - 2 0 0 0 - str   Breitkopf; Kalmus

Concerto, violin, no.3, K.216, G major   26'
  2 2 0 0 - 2 0 0 0 - str   Breitkopf; Kalmus; Schott

Concerto, violin, no.4, K.218, D major   26'
  0 2 0 0 - 2 0 0 0 - str   Breitkopf; Kalmus

Concerto, violin, no.5, K.219, A major   30'
  0 2 0 0 - 2 0 0 0 - str   Bärenreiter;
        Breitkopf; Kalmus

Concerto, violin, no.6, K.268, E-flat major   24'
  1 2 0 2 - 2 0 0 0 - str   Breitkopf; Kalmus
  Authenticity doubtful.

Concerto, violin, no.7, K.271i (271a), D major   27'
  0 2 0 0 - 2 0 0 0 - str   Breitkopf

Concertone, 2 violins and orchestra, K.186e (190),
  C major   24'
  0 2 0 0 - 2 2 0 0 - str   Breitkopf; Kalmus

Concert-rondo, horn and orchestra, K.371, E-flat major   5'
  0 2 0 0 - 2 0 0 0 - str   Breitkopf;
  Completed by Waldemar Spiess.   Universal

Concert-rondo, piano and orchestra, K.382, D major   8'
  1 2 0 0 - 2 2 0 0 - tmp - str   Breitkopf;
  Sometimes listed as piano concerto no.28.   Kalmus

Contradances, K.271c (267)   7'
  1 2 0 1 - 2 0 0 0 - str (without va)   Breitkopf
  4 dances.

Così dunque--Aspri rimorsi atroci, K.421a (432)   5'
  bass recitative and aria   Breitkopf;
  2 2 0 2 - 2 0 0 0 - str   Kalmus

Così fan tutte, K.588: Overture   5'
    2 2 2 2 - 2 2 0 0 - tmp - str   Breitkopf; Kalmus

Dite almeno in che mancai, K.479
    solo quartet: soprano, tenor, 2 basses   Breitkopf
    0 2 2 2 - 2 0 0 0 - str

Divertimento, K.113, E-flat major   18'
    2ob, 2Eh, 2cl, 2bsn - 2hn - str   Breitkopf;
    (Alternative version: 0 0 2 0 - 2 0 0 0 - str)   Kalmus

Divertimento, K.131, D major   26'
    1 1 0 1 - 4 0 0 0 - str   Breitkopf; Kalmus

Divertimenti, K.125a, b, c (136, 137, 138)   13', 9', 9'
    str   Kalmus; Peters

Divertimento, K.167a (205), D major   17'
    0 0 0 1 - 2 0 0 0 - str (without vnII) Breitkopf; Kalmus

Divertimento, K.247, F major   28'
    2hn - str   Breitkopf; Kalmus

Divertimento, K.251, D major   21'
    0 1 0 0 - 2 0 0 0 - str   Breitkopf; Kalmus

Divertimento, K.271h (287), B-flat major   47'
    2hn - str   Breitkopf; Kalmus

Divertimento, K.320b (334), D major   43'
    2hn - str   Breitkopf; Kalmus

Dixit et magnificat, K.186g (193)   12'
    chorus - solos STB   Schirmer, G.
    0 0 0 1 - 0 2 3 0 - tmp - org - str

Don Giovanni, K.527: Overture   7'
    2 2 2 2 - 2 2 0 0 - tmp - str   Breitkopf;
    Concert-ending by Johann André.   Kalmus

Don Giovanni, K.527: Overture (arr. Busoni)   6'
    2 2 2 2 - 2 2 3 0 - tmp - str   Mapleson
    Concert-ending by Busoni, using material from
    Act I and from the closing scene of the opera.

Die Entführung aus dem Serail
See his: The abduction from the seraglio

Ergo interest--Quaere superna, K.73a (143)   6'
  soprano recitative and aria   Breitkopf
  str - org

Exsultate jubilate, K.158a (165)   16'
  soprano solo   Breitkopf;
  0 2 0 0 - 2 0 0 0 - org - str   Kalmus

La finta giardiniera, K.196: Overture   3'
  0 2 0 0 - 2 0 0 0 - str   Breitkopf; Kalmus

Gloria from the Twelfth mass, K.Anh.C 1.04
  chorus   Kalmus; Luck;
  0 2 0 2 - 2 2 0 0 - tmp - str   Schirmer, G.
  Spurious.

Idomeneo, K.366: Overture   5'
  2 2 2 2 - 2 2 0 0 - tmp - str   Breitkopf;
  Available either in the original version, or   Kalmus
  with a concert-ending by Carl Reinecke.

The impresario, K.486: Overture   5'
  2 2 2 2 - 2 2 0 0 - tmp - str   Breitkopf; Kalmus

Inter natos mulierum, K.74f (72)   6'
  chorus - org - str   Breitkopf

Io ti lascio, K.621a
  bass aria - str   Kalmus; Luck

Eine kleine Nachtmusik (Serenade, K.525)   15'
  str   Bärenreiter; Breitkopf; Kalmus; Peters

Kyrie, K.368a (341)   6'
  chorus   Bärenreiter;
  2 2 2 2 - 4 2 0 0 - tmp - org - str   Luck

Litaniae de venerabili altaris sacramento,
  K.125, B-flat major   35'
  chorus - solos SATB   Bärenreiter;
  2 2 0 0 - 2 2 0 0 - org - str   Gray;
                                                 Kalmus

Litaniae de venerabili altaris sacramento,
  K.243, E-flat major   39'
  chorus - solos SATB   Breitkopf;
  2 2 0 2 - 2 0 3 0 - org - str   Kalmus

Litaniae lauretanae, K.74e (109), B-flat major
  chorus - solos SATB   Kalmus
  org - str

Litaniae lauretanae, K.186d (195), D major   30'
  chorus - solos SATB   Breitkopf;
  0 2 0 0 - 2 0 0 0 - org - str   Kalmus

Lucio Silla, K.135: Overture   9'
  0 2 0 0 - 2 2 0 0 - tmp - str   Breitkopf; Kalmus

Ma che vi fece--Sperai vicino il lido, K.368   9'
  soprano recitative and aria   Breitkopf
  2 0 0 2 - 2 0 0 0 - str

The magic flute, K.620: Overture   7'
  2 2 2 2 - 2 2 3 0 - tmp - str   Breitkopf; Kalmus

Mandina amabile, K.480
  trio for soprano, tenor, and bass   Breitkopf;
  2 2 2 2 - 2 0 0 0 - str   Kalmus

The marriage of Figaro, K.492: Overture   4'
  2 2 2 2 - 2 2 0 0 - tmp - str   Breitkopf; Kalmus

Masonic funeral music (Mauerische Trauermusik),
  K.479a (477)   6'
  0 2 1 *1 - 2 0 0 0 - basset horn - str   Bärenreiter;
  (Two additional basset horns may be   Breitkopf;
  substituted for the two horns.)   Kalmus

Mass
  See also: Missa brevis

Mass, K.167, C major ("Trinity")
  chorus   Breitkopf;
  0 2 0 0 - 0 2 2 0 - tmp - org - str (without va) Kalmus
  Trombone parts were originally very low trumpet
  parts.

Mass, K.246a (262), C major ("Longa")
  chorus - solos SATB
  0 2 0 0 - 2 2 0 0 - org - str (without va)

Mass, K.257, C major ("Credo-Messe")   30'
  chorus - solos SATB   Breitkopf
  0 2 0 0 - 0 2 3 0 - tmp - org - str (without va)

Mass, K.258, C major ("Spaur-Messe")
  chorus - solos SATB   Kalmus
  0 0 0 0 - 0 2 0 0 - tmp - org - str (without va)

Mass, K.317, C major ("Coronation")   30'
  chorus - solos SATB   Breitkopf;
  0 2 0 1 - 2 2 3 0 - tmp - org - str (without va) Kalmus

Mass, K.337, C major ("Missa solemnis")
  chorus - solos SATB   Kalmus
  0 2 0 2 - 0 2 3 0 - tmp - org - str (without va)

Mass, K.417a (427), C minor ("The great")   60'
  chorus - solos SSTB   Peters
  1 2 0 2 - 2 2 3 0 - tmp - org - str
  Ed. H. C. Robbins Landon. The older edition by
  Alois Schmitt has been superceded.

Mentre ti lascio, o figlia, K.513   8'
  bass aria   Breitkopf;
  1 0 2 2 - 2 0 0 0 - str   Kalmus

Mia speranza--Ah, non sai, K.416   8'
  soprano scene and rondo   Breitkopf;
  0 2 0 2 - 2 0 0 0 - str   Kalmus

Misera, dove son--Ah, non son io che parlo, K.369   7'
  soprano recitative and aria   Breitkopf
  2 0 0 0 - 2 0 0 0 - str

Misericordias domini, K.205a (222)
  chorus - org - str   Kalmus

Misero, o sogno--Aura, che intorno spiri, K.425b (431) 10'
  tenor recitative and aria   Breitkopf;
  2 0 0 2 - 2 0 0 0 - str   Kalmus

Missa brevis, K.186f (192), F major   25'
  chorus - solos SATB   Breitkopf; Kalmus;
  org - str (without va)   Schirmer, G.

Missa brevis, K.186h (194), D major   22'
  chorus - solos SATB   Breitkopf;
  org - str (without va)   Kalmus

Missa brevis, K.196b (220), C major ("Spatzenmesse") 20'
  chorus - solos SATB   Breitkopf;
  2tp - tmp - org - str (without va)   Kalmus

Missa brevis, K.259, C major ("Orgelsolo")   14'
  chorus - solos SATB   Breitkopf;
  2tp - tmp - org - str (without va)   Kalmus

Missa brevis, K.272b (275), B-flat major   20'
  chorus - solos SATB   Breitkopf;
  org - str (without va)   Kalmus

Mitridate, K.74a (87): Overture   5'
  2 2 0 0 - 2 0 0 0 - str   Breitkopf

A musical joke (Ein musikalischer Spass), K.522 22'
  2hn - str   Breitkopf; Peters

Nehmt meinen Dank, K.383   4'
  soprano solo   Breitkopf;
  1 1 0 1 - str   Kalmus; Luck

No, no, che non sei capace, K.419   4'
  soprano aria   Breitkopf;
  0 2 0 0 - 2 2 0 0 - tmp - str   Kalmus

Le nozze di Figaro
  See his: The marriage of Figaro

Nun liebes Weibchen, ziehst mit mir, K.592a (625)
  duet for soprano and bass   Kalmus
  1 2 0 2 - 2 0 0 0 - str

Ombra felice--Io ti lascio, K.255   8'
  alto recitative and aria   Breitkopf;
  0 2 0 0 - 2 0 0 0 - str   Kneusslin

Overture, K.Anh.C 11.05 (311a), B-flat major ("Paris")　10'
　2 2 2 2 - 2 2 0 0 - tmp - str　　　　　　　　　　Peters
　Authenticity doubtful.

Per pietà, non ricercate, K.420　　　　　　　　　　　　6'
　tenor aria　　　　　　　　　　　　　　　　　Breitkopf;
　0 0 2 2 - 2 0 0 0 - str　　　　　　　　　　　　Kalmus

Per questa bella mano, K.612　　　　　　　　　　　　8'
　bass aria - with obligato double bass　　　Breitkopf;
　1 2 0 2 - 2 0 0 0 - str　　　　　　　　　　Doblinger

Les petits riens, K.299b (Anh.10)　　　　　　　　　16'
　2 2 2 2 - 2 2 0 0 - tmp - str　　　　Breitkopf; Kalmus

Popoli di Tessagua--Io non chiedo, K.300b (316)　　11'
　soprano recitative and aria　　　　　　　　Breitkopf
　0 1 0 1 - 2 0 0 0 - str

Il re pastore, K.208: Overture　　　　　　　　　　　4'
　0 2 0 0 - 2 2 0 0 - str　　　　　　　Breitkopf; Kalmus

Regina coeli, K.74d (108), C major
　chorus - soprano solo
　2 2 0 0 - 2 2 0 0 - tmp - org - str

Regina coeli, K.127, B-flat major
　chorus - soprano solo
　2 2 0 0 - 2 0 0 0 - org - str

Regina coeli, K.321b (276), C major
　chorus - solos SATB　　　　　　　　　　　Breitkopf;
　0 2 0 0 - 0 2 0 0 - tmp - org ⌐ str (without va)　Kalmus

Requiem, K.626 (completed by Franz Süssmayr)　　　55'
　chorus - solos SATB　　　　　　　　　　Bärenreiter;
　0 0 0 2 - 0 2 3 0 - 2 basset horns - tmp - str　　Breitkopf;
　(Basset horns may be replaced by clarinets.)　　Kalmus;
　This version has been superceded by the following.　Peters

Requiem, K.626 (instrumentation by Franz Beyer)　　55'
　chorus - solos SATB　　　　　　　　　　　Eulenburg
　0 0 0 2 - 0 2 3 0 - 2 basset horns - tmp - str
　Recommended in place of the Süssmayr version. This
　is much more than a mere re-orchestration. Voice parts
　are unchanged, but the rest of the texture is much
　improved.

Rivolgete a lui lo sguardo, K.584　　　　　　　　　5'
　bass aria　　　　　　　　　　　　　　　　　Breitkopf;
　0 2 0 2 - 0 2 0 0 - tmp - str　　　　　　　　Mapleson

Rondo, violin and orchestra, K.261a (269), B-flat major   8'
0 2 0 0 - 2 0 0 0 - str   Breitkopf

Rondo, violin and orchestra, K.373, C major   4'
0 2 0 0 - 2 0 0 0 - str   Breitkopf; Kalmus

Sancta Maria, K.273   4'
chorus   Bärenreiter;
org - str   Kalmus

Scande coeli limina, K.34
chorus - soprano solo
0 0 0 0 - 0 2 0 0 - tmp - org - str (without va)

Der Schauspieldirektor
See his: The impresario

Se al labbro mio non credi, K.295
tenor aria   Breitkopf
2 2 0 2 - 2 0 0 0 - str

Serenade no.1, K.62a (100), D major   24'
2 2 0 0 - 2 2 0 0 - str   Breitkopf; Kalmus

Serenade no.2, K.250a (101), F major   7'
1 2 0 1 - 2 0 0 0 - str (without va)   Breitkopf;
Four contradances.   Kalmus

Serenade no.3, K.167a (185), D major   25'
2 2 0 0 - 2 2 0 0 - str   Breitkopf; Kalmus

Serenade no.4, K.189b (203), D major   38'
2 2 0 1 - 2 2 0 0 - str   Breitkopf; Kalmus

Serenade no.5, K.213a (204), D major   27'
2 2 0 1 - 2 2 0 0 - str   Breitkopf; Kalmus

Serenade no.6, K.239, D major ("Serenata notturna")   11'
solo string quartet   Breitkopf;
str - tmp   Kalmus

Serenade no.7, K.248b (250), D major ("Haffner")   53'
2 2 0 2 - 2 2 0 0 - str   Breitkopf; Kalmus

Serenade no.8, K.269a (286), D major ("Notturno")   16'
4 orchestras, each consisting of 2hn and str   Breitkopf

Serenade no.9, K.320, D major ("Posthorn")   36'
2 2 0 2 - 2 2 0 0 - tmp - str   Breitkopf;
                                  Kalmus

Serenade no.10, K.370a (361), B-flat major   40'
0 2 2 *3 - 4 0 0 0 - 2 basset horns   Breitkopf;
(Double bass may substitute for contrabassoon.) Kalmus

Serenade no.11, K.375, E-flat major   24'
0 2 2 2 - 2hn   Breitkopf;
An earlier version without oboes exists also.   Kalmus

Serenade no.12, K.384a (388), C minor   18'
0 2 2 2 - 2hn   Kalmus

Serenade, K.525, G major
See his: Eine kleine Nachtmusik

Si mostra la sorte, K.209   6'
tenor aria   Breitkopf
2 0 0 0 - 2 0 0 0 - str

Sinfonia concertante, K.Anh.C 14.01 (297b),
E-flat major   30'
solos: oboe, clarinet, horn, bassoon   Breitkopf;
0 2 0 0 - 2 0 0 0 - str   Kalmus
The authenticity of this work is in question;
possibly it is an arrangement by another hand
of a lost Mozart composition for flute, oboe,
horn, and bassoon.

Sinfonia concertante, K.320d (364), E-flat major   30'
solo violin, solo viola   Breitkopf;
0 2 0 0 - 2 0 0 0 - str   Kalmus

Sonatas, organ and orchestra   Bärenreiter;
solo organ   Mercury
str (without va), except as indicated below.
Available separately.

    No.1, K.41h (67), E-flat major   2'

    No.2, K.41i (68), B-flat major   4'

    No.3, K.41k (69), D major   3'

    No.4, K.124a (144), D major   4'

    No.5, K.124b (145), F major   3'

No.6, K.212, B-flat major   4'

No.7, K.241a (224), F major   5'

No.8, K.241b (225), A major   5'

No.9, K.244, F major   4'

No.10, K.245, D major   5'

No.11, K.271d (274), G major   5'

No.12, K.271e (278), C major   4'
   0 2 0 0 - 0 2 0 0 - tmp - str (without va)

No.13, K.317c (328), C major   4'

No.14, K.317a (329), C major   4'
   0 2 0 0 - 2 2 0 0 - tmp - str (without va)

No.15, K.336d (336), C major   3'

No.16, K.241, G major   3'

No.17, K.263, C major   5'
   2tp - str (without va)

Symphony, K.141a, D major   9'
   2 2 0 0 - 2 2 0 0 - tmp - str   Bärenreiter
The first two movements are the overture to
"Il sogno di Scipione."

Symphony, K.196/121, D major   10'
   0 2 0 0 - 2 0 0 0 - str   Bärenreiter

Symphony no.1, K.16, E-flat major   11'
   0 2 0 0 - 2 0 0 0 - str   Breitkopf; Kalmus

Symphony no.2, K.Anh.C 11.02 (17), B-flat major   12'
   0 2 0 0 - 2 0 0 0 - str   Breitkopf
Authenticity doubtful.

Symphony no.3, K.Anh.A 51 (18), E-flat major   12'
   0 0 2 1 - 2 0 0 0 - str   Breitkopf; Kalmus
Though published under Mozart's name, this is
actually Symphony op.7, no.6, by Karl Friedrich Abel.

Symphony no.4, K.19, D major   8'
   0 2 0 0 - 2 0 0 0 - str   Breitkopf; Kalmus

Symphony no.5, K.22, B-flat major   9'
  0 2 0 0 - 2 0 0 0 - str   Breitkopf; Kalmus

Symphony no.6, K.43, F major   13'
  0 2 0 0 - 2 0 0 0 - str   Breitkopf; Kalmus

Symphony no.7, K.45, D major   10'
  0 2 0 0 - 2 2 0 0 - tmp - str   Kalmus

Symphony no.8, K.48, D major   14'
  0 2 0 0 - 2 2 0 0 - tmp - str   Kalmus

Symphony no.9, K.73, C major   12'
  0 2 0 0 - 2 2 0 0 - tmp - str   Breitkopf; Kalmus

Symphony no.10, K.74, G major   9'
  0 2 0 0 - 2 0 0 0 - str   Breitkopf; Kalmus

Symphony no.11, K.73q (84), D major   11'
  0 2 0 0 - 2 0 0 0 - str   Breitkopf; Kalmus

Symphony no.12, K.75b (110), G major   13'
  0 2 0 0 - 2 0 0 0 - str   Breitkopf; Kalmus

Symphony no.13, K.112, F major   17'
  0 2 0 0 - 2 0 0 0 - str   Breitkopf; Kalmus

Symphony no.14, K.114, A major   14'
  2 2 0 0 - 2 0 0 0 - str   Breitkopf; Kalmus

Symphony no.15, K.124, G major   14'
  0 2 0 0 - 2 0 0 0 - str   Breitkopf; Kalmus

Symphony no.16, K.128, C major   13'
  0 2 0 0 - 2 0 0 0 - str   Bärenreiter; Breitkopf; Kalmus

Symphony no.17, K.129, G major   12'
  0 2 0 0 - 2 0 0 0 - str   Bärenreiter; Breitkopf; Kalmus

Symphony no.18, K.130, F major   13'
  2 0 0 0 - 4 0 0 0 - str   Bärenreiter; Breitkopf; Kalmus

Symphony no.19, K.132, E-flat major   14'
  0 2 0 0 - 4 0 0 0 - str   Bärenreiter; Breitkopf; Kalmus

Symphony no.20, K.133, D major   16'
1 2 0 0 - 2 2 0 0 - str   Bärenreiter;
Breitkopf; Kalmus

Symphony no.21, K.134, A major   17'
2 0 0 0 - 2 0 0 0 - str   Bärenreiter;
Breitkopf; Kalmus

Symphony no.22, K.162, C major   10'
0 2 0 0 - 2 2 0 0 - str   Bärenreiter;
Breitkopf; Kalmus

Symphony no.23, K.162b (181), D major   10'
0 2 0 0 - 2 2 0 0 - str   Bärenreiter;
Breitkopf; Kalmus

Symphony no.24, K.173da (182), B-flat major   9'
2 2 0 0 - 2 0 0 0 - str   Bärenreiter;
Breitkopf; Kalmus

Symphony no.25, K.173db (183), G minor   20'
0 2 0 2 - 4 0 0 0 - str   Bärenreiter;
Breitkopf; Kalmus

Symphony no.26, K.161a (184), E-flat major   11'
2 2 0 2 - 2 2 0 0 - str   Bärenreiter;
Breitkopf; Kalmus

Symphony no.27, K.161b (199), G major   12'
2 0 0 0 - 2 0 0 0 - str   Bärenreiter; Breitkopf

Symphony no.28, K.189k (200), C major   17'
0 2 0 0 - 2 2 0 0 - str   Bärenreiter;
Breitkopf; Kalmus

Symphony no.29, K.186a (201), A major   24'
0 2 0 0 - 2 0 0 0 - str   Bärenreiter; Breitkopf;
Kalmus; Peters

Symphony no.30, K.186b (202), D major   17'
0 2 0 0 - 2 2 0 0 - str   Bärenreiter;
Breitkopf; Kalmus

Symphony no.31, K.300a (297), D major ("Paris")   18'
2 2 2 2 - 2 2 0 0 - tmp - str   Bärenreiter;
Breitkopf; Kalmus

Symphony no.32, K.318, G major   9'
  2 2 0 2 - 4 2 0 0 - tmp - str   Breitkopf; Kalmus

Symphony no.33, K.319, B-flat major   22'
  0 2 0 2 - 2 0 0 0 - str   Breitkopf; Kalmus

Symphony no.34, K.338, C major   19'
  0 2 0 2 - 2 2 0 0 - tmp - str   Breitkopf; Kalmus
    This work lacks a minuet, though some authorities
  believe the minuet K.383f (409) was written for this
  purpose. The following edition includes that minuet:
    2 2 0 2 - 2 2 0 0 - tmp - str   Alkor (25')

Symphony no.35, K.385, D major ("Haffner")   19'
  2 2 2 2 - 2 2 0 0 - tmp - str   Breitkopf; Kalmus

Symphony no.36, K.425, C major ("Linz")   26'
  0 2 0 2 - 2 2 0 0 - tmp - str   Bärenreiter;
                                         Breitkopf; Kalmus

Symphony no.37, K.425a (444), G major   15'
  1 2 0 0 - 2 0 0 0 - str   Breitkopf;
  Only the adagio introduction is by   Doblinger;
  Mozart; the remainder of this symphony   Kalmus
  is by Michael Haydn.

Symphony no.38, K.504, D major ("Prague")   26'
  2 2 0 2 - 2 2 0 0 - tmp - str   Bärenreiter;
                        Breitkopf; Kalmus; Peters

Symphony no.39, K.543, E-flat major   27'
  1 0 2 2 - 2 2 0 0 - tmp - str   Bärenreiter;
                        Breitkopf; Kalmus; Peters

Symphony no.40, K.550, G minor   26'
  1 2 2 2 - 2 0 0 0 - str   Bärenreiter;
  An earlier version of this work, without   Breitkopf;
  the clarinets, is also available from   Kalmus;
  Bärenreiter.   Peters

Symphony no.41, K.551, C major ("Jupiter")   29'
  1 2 0 2 - 2 2 0 0 - tmp - str   Bärenreiter;
                        Breitkopf; Kalmus; Peters

Te deum laudamus, K.66b (141)   7'
  chorus   Breitkopf;
  0 0 0 1 - 0 4 0 0 - tmp - org - str (without va) Kalmus

Titus
  See his: La clemenza di Tito

Turkish march from Piano sonata in A major,
  K.300i (331) (arr. Prosper Pascal)   4'
  *3 2 2 2 - 2 2 0 0 - 3perc - str   Luck

Vado, ma dove, o dei, K.583
  soprano aria   Breitkopf;
  0 0 2 2 - 2 0 0 0 - str   Kalmus

Veni sancte spiritus, K.47
  chorus - solos SATB   Kalmus
  0 2 0 0 - 2 2 0 0 - tmp - org - str

Venite populi, K.248a (260)
  double chorus   Broude, A.
  0 0 0 1 - 0 0 3 0 - org - str

Vesperae solennes de confessor, K.339   26'
  chorus - solos SATB   Breitkopf;
  0 0 0 1 - 0 2 3 0 - tmp - org - str (without va) Kalmus

Vesperae solennes de dominica, K.321   26'
  chorus - solos SATB   Breitkopf;
  0 0 0 1 - 0 2 3 0 - tmp - org - str (without va) Kalmus

Voi avete un cor fedele, K.217   6'
  soprano aria   Breitkopf
  0 2 0 0 - 2 0 0 0 - str

Vorrei spiegarvi, oh dio, K.418   6'
  soprano aria   Breitkopf;
  0 2 0 2 - 2 0 0 0 - str   Kalmus

Die Zauberflöte
  See his: The magic flute

MUSGRAVE, THEA, 1928-

Concerto for orchestra   20'
  *3 *3 *3 *3 - 4 3 3 1 - tmp+3 - hp - str   Chester

Night music, for chamber orchestra   18'
  *1 2 0 1 - 2 0 0 0 - str (minimum 6.4.3.2.1;   Chester
    maximum 10.8.6.4.3)

MUSSORGSKY, MODEST, 1839-1881

   Edward R. Reilly's The music of Mussorgsky; a guide
   to the editions *(available from The Musical Newsletter,*
   654 Madison Avenue, Suite 1703, New York NY 10021)
   is very helpful in distinguishing the composer's own
   versions from the many arrangements inflicted upon
   them by Rimsky-Korsakov and others. However, it does
   not deal with the availability of orchestral parts.

Boris Godunov: Polonaise   6'
  *3 *3 3 3 - 4 4 3 1 - tmp+4 - str   Breitkopf;
  Arr. Rimsky-Korsakov.   Kalmus

The fair at Sorochinsk: Introduction   5'
  *3 *3 2 2 - 4 2 3 1 - tmp+2 - str   Breitkopf;
  Arr. Liadov.   Kalmus

The fair at Sorochinsk: Gopak   3'
  *3 2 2 2 - 4 2 3 1 - tmp+2 - str   Breitkopf;
  Arr. Liadov.   Kalmus

Intermezzo in the classic style   7'
  2 2 2 2 - 4 2 3 1 - tmp+1 - str   Universal;
  Arr. Rimsky-Korsakov.   VAAP

Khovantchina: Introduction   5'
  2 2 2 2 - 4 0 0 0 - tmp+1 - hp - str   Breitkopf;
  Arr. Rimsky-Korsakov.   Kalmus; Universal

Khovantchina: Dance of the Persian maidens   6'
  *3 *2 2 2 - 4 2 3 1 - tmp+4 - hp - str   Breitkopf;
  Arr. Rimsky-Korsakov.   Kalmus; VAAP

Khovantchina: Entr'acte   4'
  3 2 2 2 - 4 2 3 1 - tmp - str   Luck
  Arr. Rimsky-Korsakov.

Mlada: Festive march   6'
  *3 2 2 2 - 4 4 3 1 - tmp+4 - str   Luck;
  Arr. Rimsky-Korsakov.   Universal; VAAP

Night on Bald Mountain   12'
  *3 2 2 2 - 4 2 3 1 - tmp+3 - hp - str   Kalmus;
  Arr. Rimsky-Korsakov.   Universal; VAAP

Pictures at an exhibition (arr. Goehr)   25'
  *2 *2 *2 2 - 4 2 3 0 - tmp+3 - hp, pf, org - str Boosey
  2nd clarinet doubles on alto saxophone.
  (Cross-cued for smaller combinations.)

Pictures at an exhibition (arr. Ravel)   30'
  *3 *3 *3 *3 - 4 3 3 1 - asx - tmp+5 - 2hp,   Boosey
  cel - str

Pictures at an exhibition (arr. Touschmaloff)   20'
  *3 *3 *3 2 - 4 2 3 1 - tmp+5 - hp, pf - str   Kalmus
  Instrumentation by M. Touschmaloff with
  collaboration by Rimsky-Korsakov.

Scherzo, B-flat major   5'
  2 2 2 2 - 2 2 3 0 - tmp - str   Kalmus;
  Arr. Rimsky-Korsakov.   Universal; VAAP

Songs and dances of death   21'
  solo voice (medium)   VAAP
  *2 2 *2 *2 - 4 2 3 1 - tmp+2 - hp - str
  Orchestrated by Shostakovich.

  NELHYBEL, VACLAV, 1919-

Music for orchestra   8'
  *4 2 *3 2 - 4 3 3 1 - tmp+4 - str   Colombo

  NICOLAI, OTTO, 1810-1849

The merry wives of Windsor: Overture   8'
  2 2 2 2 - 4 2 3 0 - tmp+2 - str Bote; Breitkopf; Kalmus

  NIELSEN, CARL, 1865-1931

Concerto, clarinet, op.57   24'
  0 0 0 2 - 2 0 0 0 - 1perc - str   Samfundet

Concerto, flute (1926)   20'
  0 2 2 2 - 2 0 1 0 - tmp - str   Samfundet

Concerto, violin, op.33   35'
  *2 2 2 2 - 4 2 3 0 - tmp - str   Hansen

Helios overture, op.17   12'
  *3 2 2 2 - 4 3 3 1 - tmp - str   Hansen; Kalmus

Little suite, op.1   15'
  str   Hansen; Kalmus

Maskarade: Overture   5'
  *3 2 2 2 - 4 3 3 1 - tmp+2 - str   Hansen

Saul and David: Prelude to Act II   6'
  3 2 2 2 - 4 3 3 1 - tmp - str   Hansen

Symphony no.1, op.7   34'
  *3 2 2 2 - 4 2 3 0 - tmp - str   Hansen

Symphony no.2, op.16 ("The four temperaments")   30'
  3 2 2 2 - 4 3 3 1 - tmp - str   Hansen; Kalmus

Symphony no.3, op.27 ("Sinfonia espansiva")   36'
  soprano and baritone solo (textless)   Hansen;
  *3 *3 3 *3 - 4 3 3 1 - tmp - str   Kahnt
  (A clarinet and trombone may substitute for
  the voices.)

Symphony no.4, op.29 ("The inextinguishable")   36'
  *3 3 3 *3 - 4 3 3 1 - 2tmp - str   Hansen

Symphony no.5, op.50   37'
  *3 2 2 *2 - 4 3 3 1 - tmp+3 - cel - str   Hansen
  (Contrabassoon doubling is optional.)

Symphony no.6 ("Sinfonia semplice")   32'
  *2 2 2 2 - 4 2 3 1 - tmp+3 - str   Hansen; Samfundet

       NONO, LUIGI, 1924-

Canti di vita e d'amore   18'
  soprano and tenor solos   Schott
  3 3 3 3 - 4 4 4 0 - tmp+5 - str 8.8.8.6.6

Il canto sospeso   28'
  chorus - solos SAT   Schott
  *4 2 *3 2 - 6 5 4 0 - 3tmp, 3perc - 2hp, cel - str

      NOSKOWSKI, SIGISMUND, 1846-1909

The steppe   18'
  *3 2 2 2 - 4 2 3 1 - tmp+1 - hp - str   PWM

      OFFENBACH, JACQUES, 1819-1880

La belle Hélène: Overture   8'
  *2 2 2 2 - 4 2 3 0 - tmp+4 - hp - str   Kalmus; Luck

Orpheus in the underworld: Overture (arr. Binder)   10'
  *2 2 2 2 - 4 2 3 1 - tmp+3 - hp - str   Kalmus

Tales of Hoffmann: Intermezzo and Barcarolle   6'
  2 2 2 2 - 4 2 3 0 - tmp+3 - hp - str   Bote;
    Contents--Prelude; Entr'acte to Act II;   Kalmus;
  Intermezzo from the end of Act IV (includes   Luck
  an orchestral reprise of the Barcarolle).

      ORFF, CARL, 1895-

Carmina burana   62'
  large chorus, small chorus, boys' chorus -   Schott
    solos STB, short solos TTBBB
  *3 *3 =3 *3 - 4 3 3 1 - tmp+6 - cel, 2pf - str

Trionfo di Afrodite   45'
  chorus - solos SSTTB   Schott
  *3 *3 +3 *3 - 6 3 3 2 - tmp+9 - 2hp, 3pf, 3gtr - str

      PACHELBEL, JOHANN, 1653-1706

Canon   5'
  str, (opt cnt)   Schott
  Originally for 3 solo violins and continuo.
  Arr. Helmut May.

PADEREWSKI, IGNACE JAN, 1860-1941

Concerto, piano, A minor, op.17   34'
 *3 *2 2 2 - 4 2 3 0 - tmp - str   Bote; Kalmus

Symphony   58'
 *3 *3 *3 *3 - 4 4 3 1 - 3 contrabass   Heugel
   sarrusophones - tmp+2 - hp, org - str

PAGANINI, NICCOLÒ, 1782-1840

Concerto, violin, no.1, op.6, D major   30'
 2 2 2 *2 - 2 2 3 0 - tmp - str   Breitkopf;
 Originally in E-flat, with the soloist tuned   Kalmus
 a half-step sharp; now normally performed in D.

Concerto, violin, no.1, op.6, D major (arr.
 August Wilhelmj)   20'
 2 2 2 2 - 4 2 1 0 - tmp - str   Kalmus;
 A condensation of the first movement   Luck
 of the concerto.

Concerto, violin, no.2, op.7, B minor ("La clochette") 25'
 1 2 2 1 - 2 2 3 0 - str   Fischer, C.; Kalmus

Moto perpetuo, op.11
     *The following are only a few of the many versions
   and arrangements of this popular work, some with
   violin solo and some without. The work was originally
   composed for solo violin and orchestra.*

Moto perpetuo, op.11   4'
   solo violin   Luck
 2 2 2 2 - 2 0 3 1 - str

Moto perpetuo, op.11 (arr. Bernardino Molinari)   4'
 2 2 2 2 - 2 0 3 1 - str   Ricordi
 First violins play solo part in unison.

Moto perpetuo, op.11 (arr. Wilhelm Jerger)   4'
   solo violin   Universal
 *2 2 2 2 - 2 0 0 0 - 1perc - str

PAINE, JOHN KNOWLES, 1839-1906

Oedipus tyrannus: Prelude   8'
  2 2 2 2 - 4 2 3 0 - tmp - str   Kalmus

Symphony no.1, op.23, C minor
  2 2 2 2 - 4 2 3 0 - tmp - str   AMP

PAISIELLO, GIOVANNI, 1740-1816

Nina, o La pazza per amore: Overture   5'
  0 2 2 2 - 2 0 0 0 - str   Carisch
  Ed. Giuseppe Piccioli.

La scuffiara: Overture   6'
  2 2 0 2 - 2 2 0 0 - str   Carisch
  Ed. Giuseppe Piccioli.

Sinfonia funebre   10'
  2 2 2 2 - 2 2 0 0 - tmp - str   Carisch
  Ed. Giuseppe Piccioli.

Sinfonia in tre tempi, D major   6'
  0 2 0 0 - 2 0 0 0 - str   Carisch
  Ed. Giuseppe Piccioli.

PARKER, HORATIO, 1863-1919

Hora novissima   61'
  chorus - solos SATB   Gray; Kalmus;
  2 2 2 2 - 4 2 3 1 - tmp+2 - hp, org - str   Luck

PARTOS, ÖDÖN, 1907-

Yiskor (In memoriam)   9'
  solo viola - str   Broude, A.

PENDERECKI, KRZYSZTOF, 1933-

Anaklasis   9'
  tmp+5 - hp, cel, pf - str 10.10.8.8.6   Moeck; PWM

De natura sonoris (no.1)   8'
  *4 *4 *3 *4 - 6 4 3 1 - 2asx - tmp+5 -   Moeck;
    pf, harm - str   PWM
  Two of the flutists play piccolo.

De natura sonoris no.2   12'
  brass 4 0 4 1 - tmp+6 - pf, harm -   PWM
    str 12.12.8.8.6   Schott

Emanations   8'
  2 str orchestras (minimum 10.10.8.6.5;   Moeck;
    maximum 20.20.16.16.12)   PWM
  One orchestra tuned a half-step higher than
  the other.

Flourescences   14'
  *4 4 4 4 - 6 4 3 2 - tmp+5 - pf -   Moeck;
    str 12.12.8.8.6   PWM

Passion according to St. Luke   80'
  chorus, boys' chorus - solos SBB - reciter   Moeck;
  =4 0 *1 *4 - 6 4 4 1 - 2asx - tmp+6 - hp, pf,   PWM
    org, harm - str 12.12.10.10.8

Sonata, violoncello and orchestra   10'
  0 0 0 *4 - 6 0 3 1 - 4perc - pf - str   Belwin; PWM

To the victims of Hiroshima; threnody   9'
  str 12.12.10.10.8   Belwin; PWM

        PERGOLESI, GIOVANNI BATTISTA, 1710-1736

Concertino, E-flat major   7'
  str   Ricordi
  Ed. Renato Fasano.

Concerto, flute, G major   13'
  str (without va), cnt   Boosey;
  Authenticity doubtful.   Sikorski

Concerto, violin, B-flat major   18'
  0 2 0 1 - 2 0 0 0 - str   Carisch
  Ed. Adriano Lualdi.

Magnificat
  chorus - solos SATB   Kalmus
  str, cnt
  Ed. Clayton Westermann.

Stabat mater   41'
  soprano and alto solos   Kalmus;
  str, cnt   Ricordi;
  Although sometimes performed with treble chorus, Schott
  the work is intended for soloists, not chorus.

    PERSICHETTI, VINCENT, 1915-

Night dances, op.114   19'
  *3 *3 *3 2 - 4 3 3 1 - tmp+3 - str   Elkan-Vogel

Symphony, op.61   18'
  str   Elkan-Vogel

    PFITZNER, HANS, 1869-1949

Palestrina: Three preludes   20'
  *4 *3 =4 *4 - 6 4 4 1 - tmp+2 - hp - str   Schott

    PHILLIPS, BURRILL, 1907-

Selections from McGuffey's reader   17'
  *3 2 2 2 - 4 3 3 1 - tmp+3 - hp, cel - str   Fischer, C.

    PIERNE, GABRIEL, 1863-1937

March of the lead soldiers, op.14, no.6   4'
  1 0 1 0 - 0 1 0 0 - 1perc - pf - str   Kalmus; Leduc

    PINKHAM, DANIEL, 1923-

Catacoustical measures   5'
  *4 *3 *4 *4 - 4 4 4 1 - tmp+3 - hp, cel, pf - str Peters

Signs of the zodiac   21'
  (optional speaker)   Peters
  *3 *3 *3 2 - 4 3 3 1 - tmp+2 - hp, pf/cel - str

Symphony no.1   17'
  *3 *3 *3 *3 - 4 3 3 1 - tmp+2 - hp, cel/pf - str   Peters

Symphony no.2   16'
  *3 *3 *3 2 - 4 3 3 1 - tmp+5 - hp, pf - str   Peters

    PISTON, WALTER, 1894-1976

Concertino, piano and chamber orchestra   14'
  *2 2 2 2 - 2 0 0 0 - str   AMP

Concerto for orchestra   14'
  3 *3 *3 *3 - 4 3 3 1 - tmp+5 - pf - str   AMP

Concerto, viola   23'
  *3 *3 *3 *3 - 4 2 3 1 - tmp+4 - hp - str   AMP

Divertimento for nine instruments   8'
  1 1 1 1 - 2vn, va, vc, db   AMP

The incredible flutist: Suite   17'
  *3 *3 *3 *3 - 4 3 3 1 - tmp+4 - pf - str   AMP

Lincoln Center festival overture   12'
  *3 *3 *3 *3 - 4 3 3 1 - tmp+4 - 2hp - str   AMP

Serenata   14'
  2 2 2 2 - 4 2 0 0 - tmp - hp - str   AMP

Sinfonietta   17'
  2 2 2 2 - 2 0 0 0 - str   Boosey

Symphony no.1   27'
  *3 *3 *3 *3 - 4 3 3 1 - tmp - str   Schirmer, G.

Symphony no.2   26'
  *3 *3 *3 *3 - 4 3 3 1 - tmp+4 - str   AMP

Symphony no.3   31'
  *3 *3 *3 *3 - 4 3 3 1 - tmp+4 - 2hp - str   Boosey

Symphony no.4   23'
  *3 *3 *3 *3 - 4 3 3 1 - tmp+5 - 2hp - str   AMP

Symphony no.5   23'
  *3 *3 *3 *3 - 4 3 3 1 - tmp+3 - 2hp - str   AMP

Symphony no.6   25'
  *3 *3 *3 *3 - 4 3 3 1 - tmp+4 - 2hp - str   AMP

Symphony no.7   19'
  *3 *3 *3 *3 - 4 3 3 1 - tmp+5 - 2hp - str   AMP

Symphony no.8   20'
  *3 *3 *3 *3 - 4 3 3 1 - tmp+4 - 2hp - str   AMP

Three New England sketches   17'
  *3 *3 *3 *3 - 4 3 3 1 - tmp+4 - 2hp - str   AMP

Toccata   9'
  *3 *3 *3 *3 - 4 3 3 1 - tmp+5 - str   Boosey

     POKORNÝ, FRANZ XAVER, 1729-1794

Concerto, flute, D major
  See: Boccherini, Luigi, 1743-1805
          Concerto, flute, G.489, D major

     PONCE, MANUEL, 1882-1948

Concierto del sur, guitar and orchestra   23'
  1 1 1 1 - tmp+1 - str   Peer

     PONCHIELLI, AMILCARE, 1834-1886

La Gioconda: Dance of the hours   9'
  *3 2 2 2 - 4 4 3 1 - tmp+3 - 2hp - str   Kalmus; Ricordi

     POPPER, DAVID, 1843-1913

Hungarian rhapsody, op.68   8'
  solo violoncello   Hofmeister;
  2 2 2 2 - 4 2 3 0 - tmp - str   Kalmus; Luck

Tarantelle, op.33   5'
  solo violoncello   Kalmus;
  2 2 2 2 - 2 0 0 0 - (opt tmp), 2perc - str   Luck
  Orchestrated by Paul Gilson.

    PORTER, QUINCY, 1897-1966

Symphony no.2   25'
  *3 *2 2 2 - 4 2 3 1 - tmp+1 - str   Peters

    POULENC, FRANCIS, 1899-1963

Aubade, piano and 18 instruments   21'
  2 *2 2 2 - 2 1 0 0 - tmp - 2va, 2vc, 2db   Rouart

Les biches: Suite   16'
  *3 *3 *3 *3 - 4 3 3 1 - tmp+2 - hp, cel - str   Heugel

Concerto, organ, G minor   17'
  str - tmp   Salabert

Concerto, piano   21'
  *2 *2 2 2 - 4 2 3 1 - tmp - str   Salabert

Concerto, 2 pianos, D minor   20'
  *2 *2 2 2 - 2 2 2 1 - 1perc - str 8.8.4.4.4   Rouart

Concerto champêtre, harpsichord (or piano)   24'
  *2 *2 2 2 - 4 2 1 1 - tmp+2 - str 8.8.4.4.4   Rouart
  Both flutists play piccolo.

Deux marches et un interlude   6'
  1 1 1 1 - 0 1 0 0 - str   Rouart

Gloria   28'
  chorus - solo soprano   Salabert
  *3 *3 *3 *3 - 4 3 3 1 - tmp - hp - str

Secheresses   18'
  chorus   Durand
  *2 *2 2 2 - 4 2 3 1 - tmp+1 - hp, cel - str

Sinfonietta   28'
  2 2 2 2 - 2 2 0 0 - tmp - hp - str   Chester

Stabat mater   35'
  chorus - soprano solo   Salabert
  *3 *3 *3 3 - 4 2 3 1 - tmp - 2hp - str

The story of Babar, the little elephant   22'
  narrator   Chester
  *2 *2 *2 *2 - 2 2 1 1 - tmp - hp - str

Suite française   12'
  0 2 0 2 - 0 2 3 0 - 1perc - hpsd   Durand
  After Claude Gervaise (16th century).

    PREVIN, ANDRÉ, 1929-

Overture to a comedy   9'
  *3 2 *3 2 - 4 3 3 1 - tmp+3 - hp - str   MCA

    PROKOFIEV, SERGE, 1891-1953

Ala and Lolly, op.20
  See his: Scythian suite

Alexander Nevsky, op.78   39'
  chorus - mezzo-soprano solo   Kalmus;
  *3 *3 *3 *3 - 4 3 3 1 - tsx - tmp+7 -   VAAP
    hp (doubled if possible) - str

Andante, from String quartet, op.50   9'
  str   Boosey

Buffoon (Chout), op.21: Symphonic suite   35'
  *3 *3 *3 3 - 4 3 3 1 - tmp+6 - 2hp, pf - str   Boosey

Cinderella: Suite no.1   29'
  *3 *3 *3 *3 - 4 3 3 1 - tmp+6 - hp, pf - str   Kalmus;
                                                       VAAP

Cinderella: Suite no.3   27'
  *3 *3 *3 *3 - 4 3 3 1 - tmp+4 - hp, pf - str   Kalmus;
                                                       VAAP

Classical symphony, op.25 (Symphony no.1)   15'
  2 2 2 2 - 2 2 0 0 - tmp - str   Boosey; Kalmus; VAAP

Concerto, piano, no.1, op.10, D-flat major   16'
  *3 2 2 *3 - 4 2 3 1 - tmp+1 - str   Kalmus; VAAP

Concerto, piano, no.3, op.26, C major   27'
  *2 2 2 2 - 4 2 3 0 - tmp+1 - str   Boosey; Kalmus; VAAP

Concerto, piano (left hand), no.4, op.53   24'
  2 2 2 2 - 2 1 1 0 - 1perc - str   VAAP

Concerto, piano, no.5, op.55   23'
  *2 2 2 2 - 2 2 2 1 - tmp+2 - str   Boosey; Kalmus

Concerto, violin, no.1, op.19, D major   23'
  *2 2 2 2 - 4 2 0 1 - tmp+2 - hp - str   Boosey;
                      Kalmus; VAAP

Concerto, violin, no.2, op.63, G minor   26'
  2 2 2 2 - 2 2 0 0 - 1perc - str   Boosey; Kalmus; VAAP

Lieutenant Kijé, op.60: Suite   20'
  *3 2 2 2 - 4 2 3 1 - tsx, (opt cornet) -   Boosey;
    3perc - hp, pf/cel - str   Kalmus
  (Optional baritone voice; saxophone is optional
  if voice is used.)

Love of the three oranges: Symphonic suite   20'
  *3 *3 *3 *3 - 4 3 3 1 - tmp+5 - 2hp - str   Boosey;
                      Kalmus

Love of the three oranges: March and scherzo   6'
  *3 *3 *3 *3 - 4 3 3 1 - tmp+5 - 2hp - str   Boosey;
                      Kalmus

Overture, op.42   8'
  1 1 2 1 - 0 2 1 0 - tmp - 2hp, cel, 2pf -   Boosey
    vc, 2db

Le pas d'acier, op.41 (The age of steel)   35'
  *3 *3 =4 *3 - 4 4 3 1 - tmp+4 - pf - str   Boosey

Le pas d'acier: Suite, op.41b   14'
  *3 *3 =4 *3 - 4 4 3 1 - tmp+4 - pf - str   Boosey

Peter and the wolf   25'
  narrator   Boosey;
  1 1 1 1 - 3 1 1 0 - tmp+1 - str   Kalmus; VAAP

Romeo and Juliet: Suite no.1   27'
  *3 *3 *3 *3 - 4 3 3 1 - tsx - tmp+5 - hp, pf - str   Kalmus;
    Contents--Folk dance; Scene; Madrigal;   VAAP
  Minuet; Masks; Romeo and Juliet; The death
  of Tybalt.

Romeo and Juliet: Suite no.2   28'
  *3 *3 *3 *3 - 4 3 3 1 - tsx - tmp+3 - hp,   Kalmus;
    pf/cel, (opt va d'amore) - str   VAAP
    Contents--The Montagues and the Capulets;
  Juliet--the young girl; Friar Laurence; Dance;
  Romeo and Juliet before parting; Dance of the maids
  from the Antilles; Romeo at Juliet's grave.

Romeo and Juliet: Suite no.3   20'
  *3 *3 *3 *3 - 4 3 3 1 - tmp+2 - hp, cel, pf -   Kalmus;
  str   VAAP
    Contents--Romeo at the fountain; Morning dance;
  Juliet; Nurse; Morning serenade; Juliet's death.

Scythian suite (Ala and Lolly), op.20   21'
  =4 *4 =4 *4 - 8 5 4 1 - tmp+9 - 2hp, cel,   Boosey
    pf - str
  (5th trumpet is optional.)

Sinfonia concertante, op.125   36'
  solo violoncello   Boosey
  *2 2 2 2 - 4 3 3 1 - tmp+2 - cel - str
  (3rd trumpet is optional.)

Sinfonietta, op.5/48   25'
  2 2 2 2 - 4 2 0 0 - str   Boosey

A summer day (children's suite), op.65   11'
  2 2 2 2 - 2 2 0 0 - tmp+2 - str   Boosey; Kalmus; VAAP

Symphony no.1, op.25
  See his: Classical symphony, op.25

Symphony no.2, op.40   35'
  *3 *3 *3 *3 - 4 3 3 1 - tmp+2 - pf - str   Boosey

Symphony no.3, op.44   33'
  *3 *3 *3 *3 - 4 3 3 1 - tmp+2 - 2hp - str   Boosey

Symphony no.4, op.47/112   39'
  *3 *3 =4 *3 - 4 3 3 1 - tmp+3 - hp, pf - str   Boosey;
                                                                 VAAP

Symphony no.5, op.100   43'
  *3 *3 =4 *3 - 4 3 3 1 - tmp+4 - hp, pf - str   Kalmus;
                                                                 VAAP

Symphony no.6, op.111   44'
  *3 *3 =4 *3 - 4 3 3 1 - tmp+4 - hp, cel,   Kalmus;
    pf - str   VAAP

Symphony no.7, op.131   32'
  *3 *3 *3 2 - 4 3 3 1 - tmp+3 - hp, pf - str   Kalmus;
                                                                 VAAP

War and peace: Overture   8'
  *3 *3 *3 *3 - 4 3 3 1 - tmp+1 - hp - str   Kalmus

          PUCCINI, GIACOMO, 1858-1924

Capriccio sinfonico   16'
  *3 2 2 2 - 4 2 3 1 - tmp+2 - hp - str   Elkan-Vogel

I crisantemi (The chrysanthemums)   6'
  str   Luck;
  Originally for string quartet.   Ricordi

Edgar: Preludio   8'
  *3 *3 *3 2 - 4 4 3 1 - tmp+2 - hp - str   Elkan-Vogel

Preludio sinfonico   12'
  *3 *2 2 2 - 4 2 3 1 - tmp+2 - hp - str   Elkan-Vogel
  Ed. Pietro Spada.

          PURCELL, HENRY, ca.1659-1695

Abdelazar: Suite   13'
  str, cnt   Mercury
  Ed. Edvard Fendler.

Canon on a ground bass (arr. Wallingford Riegger)   4'
  str   AMP

Chacony in G minor   7'
   str - (opt hpsd)   Boosey
   Ed. Benjamin Britten.

Dido and Aeneas: Suite   11'
   str, cnt   Oxford
   Ed. E. J. Dent.
   Perhaps out of print, but orchestral materials
   are in the Fleisher Collection.

The double dealer: Suite
   str, cnt   Mercury
   Ed. Paul Stassevich.

The fairy queen: Suite no.1   6'
   str   Eulenburg
   Ed. William Reed.

The fairy queen: Suite no.2   9'
   str   Eulenburg
   Ed. William Reed.

The Gordian knot untied: Suite no.1   11'
   2 2 2 1 - 2 2 0 0 - tmp - str   Novello
   (Winds and timpani, added by Gustav Holst,
   are optional.)

The Gordian knot untied: Suite no.2   7'
   2 2 2 1 - 2 2 0 0 - tmp - str   Novello
   (Winds and timpani, added by Gustav Holst,
   are optional.)

The married beau: Suite   12'
   2 2 2 1 - 2 2 0 0 - tmp - str   Novello
   Arr. Gustav Holst.

Ode for St. Cecilia's Day   57'
   chorus - solos SAATBB   Schott
   2 2 0 0 - 0 2 0 0 - tmp - str
   Ed. Tippett and Bergmann.

The rival sisters: Overture   7'
   str, cnt   Mercury
   Ed. Paul Stassevitch.

Sonata for trumpet and strings   6'
  str   Musica Rara
  Ed. Alan Lumsden.

Te deum and Jubilate   19'
  chorus - solos SSAATB   Eulenburg
  2tp - str, cnt
  Ed. Denis Arnold.

Trumpet overture, from "The Indian Queen"
  tp - tmp - str   Oxford
  Arr. Lionel Salter.

Trumpet prelude (Trumpet voluntary)   3'
  *3 2 2 2 - 4 3 3 1 - tmp+1 - hp - str   Luck
  Orchestrated by Arthur Luck. Neither the title of
this work nor its attribution to Purcell is correct.
Actually it is "The Prince of Denmark's march," by
Jeremiah Clarke.

The virtuous wife: Suite   10'
  2 2 2 1 - 2 2 0 0 - tmp - str   Novello
  Arr. Gustav Holst.

    QUANTZ, JOHANN JOACHIM, 1697-1773

Concerto, flute, C major
  str, cnt   Peters
  Ed. Hanns-Dieter Sonntag.

Concerto, flute, C minor
  str, cnt   Pegasus
  Ed. Dieter Sonntag.

Concerto, flute, D major
  str, cnt   Möseler
  Ed. Hanns-Dieter Sonntag.

Concerto, flute, D major ("Pour Potsdam")   16'
  str, cnt   Bärenreiter; Kalmus

Concerto, flute, G major   16'
  str, cnt   Eulenburg
  Ed. Felix Schroeder.

RABAUD, HENRI, 1873-1949

La procession nocturne, op.6   16'
  3 2 2 2 - 4 2 3 1 - tmp - hp - str   Durand; Kalmus

RACHMANINOFF, SERGEI, 1873-1943

The bells, op.35   35'
  chorus - solos STB   Boosey
  *4 *4 *4 *4 - 6 3 3 1 - tmp+5 - hp, cel,
    pianino, (opt org) - str

Capriccio bohémien, op.12   20'
  *3 2 2 2 - 4 2 3 1 - tmp+5 - hp - str   Boosey; Kalmus

Concerto, piano, no.1, op.1, F-sharp minor   26'
  2 2 2 2 - 4 2 3 0 - tmp - str   Boosey; Foley; Kalmus

Concerto, piano, no.2, op.18, C minor   34'
  2 2 2 2 - 4 2 3 1 - tmp+2 - str   Boosey; Foley; Kalmus

Concerto, piano, no.3, op.30, D minor   39'
  2 2 2 2 - 4 2 3 1 - tmp+2 - str   Boosey; Foley; Kalmus

Concerto, piano, no.4, op.40, G minor   28'
  *3 *3 2 2 - 4 2 3 1 - tmp+5 - str   Foley

Rhapsody on a theme of Paganini, op.43   22'
  solo piano   Foley
  *3 *3 2 2 - 4 2 3 1 - tmp+4 - hp - str

The rock; fantasy, op.7   18'
  *3 2 2 2 - 4 2 3 1 - tmp+2 - hp - str   Foley; Forberg;
                                            Kalmus; VAAP

Symphonic dances, op.45   33'
  *3 *3 *3 *3 - 4 3 3 1 - asx - tmp+5 -   Foley
    hp, pf - str

Symphony no.1, op.13, D minor   40'
  *3 2 2 2 - 4 3 3 1 - tmp+5 - str   Breitkopf; VAAP

Symphony no.2, op.27, E minor   46'
  *3 *3 *3 2 - 4 3 3 1 - tmp+3 - str   Boosey; Foley;
                                                 Kalmus

Symphony no.3, op.44, A minor   39'
  *3 *3 *3 *3 - 4 3 3 1 - tmp+5 - hp, cel - str   Foley

Three Russian songs, op.41   14'
  chorus of altos and basses   Foley
  *3 *3 *3 *3 - 4 3 3 1 - tmp+4 - hp, pf - str

Die Toteninsel (Isle of the dead), op.29   20'
  *3 *3 *3 *3 - 6 3 3 1 - tmp+2 - hp - str   Boosey;
                            Foley; Kalmus

Vocalise   6'
  2 *3 2 2 - 2 0 0 0 - str   Boosey;
  16-20 violins playing solo line, accompanied Foley
  by the remainder of the orchestra.

RAMEAU, JEAN PHILIPPE, 1683-1764

Ballet suite (arr. Felix Mottl)   12'
  *2 *2 2 2 - 2 2 0 0 - tmp+2 - str   Kalmus;
    Contents--Menuett (Platée); Musette (Fêtes Peters
  d'Hébé); Tambourin (Fêtes d'Hébé).

Dardanus: Suite   11'
  2 2 0 2 - str   Mercury
  Ed. Paul Henry Lang.

Les fêtes d'Hébé: Divertissement   20'
  *2 2 0 1 - 2 1 0 0 - tmp - str   EMT
  Arr. Fernand Oubradous.

Les Paladins: Suite no.2
  *2 2 0 2 - 2 0 0 0 - str, cnt   Oiseau Lyre
  Ed. Roger Desormière.

Platée: Suite des danses   8'
  *2 2 0 1 - str   EMT
  Arr. Fernand Oubradous.

Suite for string orchestra   15'
  str   Boosey
  Arr. from six harpsichord pieces by R. Temple-Savage.

RAVEL, MAURICE, 1875-1937

Alborada del gracioso   9'
  *3 *3 2 *3 - 4 2 3 1 - tmp+6 - 2hp - str   Eschig

Bolero   13'
  *3 *3 =3 *3 - 4 4 3 1 - ssx, tsx - tmp+4 -   Durand
  hp, cel - str
One oboist doubles on oboe d'amore. Score actually
calls for sopranino saxophone also, but the passage
in question is normally played on soprano saxophone.

Concerto, piano, G major   22'
  *2 *2 +2 2 - 2 1 1 0 - tmp+3 - hp - str   Durand

Concerto, piano (left hand), D major   19'
  *3 *3 =4 *3 - 4 3 3 1 - tmp+4 - hp - str   Durand

Daphnis et Chloé   50'
  chorus   Durand
  =4 *3 =4 *4 - 4 4 3 1 - tmp+8 - 2hp, cel - str
(The chorus may be dispensed with by playing the cues
in the orchestral parts; these cues are not indicated
in the score.)

Daphnis et Chloé: Suite no.1   12'
  (optional chorus)   Durand
  =4 *3 =4 *4 - 4 4 3 1 - tmp+6 - 2hp, cel - str
    Contents--Nocturne; Interlude; Danse guerrière.

Daphnis et Chloé: Suite no.2   17'
  (optional chorus)   Durand
  =4 *3 =4 *4 - 4 4 3 1 - tmp+8 - 2hp, cel - str
    Contents--Lever du jour; Pantomime; Danse générale.

Introduction and allegro   11'
  solo harp   Kalmus
  fl, cl - str quartet

Ma mère l'Oye (Mother Goose): 5 pièces enfantines   16'
  *2 *2 2 *2 - 2 0 0 0 - tmp+3 - hp, cel - str   Durand
    Contents--Pavane de la Belle au bois dormant;
  Petit Poucet; Laideronnette, impératrice des
  pagodes; Les entretiens de la Belle et de la Bête;
  Le jardin féerique.

Ma mère l'Oye (Mother Goose): Prélude et Danse du rouet 6'
  *2 *2 2 2 - 2 0 0 0 - tmp+2 - hp, cel - str   Durand

Menuet antique   9'
  *3 *3 *3 *3 - 4 3 3 1 - tmp - hp - str   Enoch

Pavane pour une infante défunte   6'
  2 1 2 2 - 2 0 0 0 - hp - str   Eschig

Rapsodie espagnole   17'
  *4 *3 *3 *4 - 4 3 3 1 - tmp+6 - 2hp, cel - str Durand;
                               Fischer, C.

Shéhérazade   12'
  soprano solo   Durand;
  *3 *3 2 2 - 4 2 3 1 - tmp+3 - 2hp, cel - Fischer, C.
  str
    Contents--Asie; La flûte enchantée; L'indifférent.

Le tombeau de Couperin   17'
  2 *2 2 2 - 2 1 0 0 - hp - str   Durand

Tzigane, violin and orchestra   10'
  *2 2 2 2 - 2 1 0 0 - 1perc - hp, cel - str Durand;
                                 Fischer, C.

La valse   15'
  *3 *3 *3 *3 - 4 3 3 1 - tmp+6 - 2hp - str Durand

Valses nobles et sentimentales   16'
  2 *3 2 2 - 4 2 3 1 - tmp+6 - 2hp, cel - str Durand

    REGER, MAX, 1873-1916

Variations and fugue on a merry theme of
  Johann Adam Hiller, op.100   39'
  2 2 2 *3 - 4 2 3 1 - tmp - hp - str   Bote

Variations and fugue on a theme of Mozart, op.132 35'
  3 2 2 2 - 4 2 0 0 - tmp - hp - str   Kalmus; Peters

RESPIGHI, OTTORINO, 1879-1936

Adagio con variazioni, violoncello and orchestra   8'
  *3 *3 2 2 - 2 0 0 0 - hp - str   Bongiovani
  This work may be out of print, but orchestral
  materials are in the Fleisher Collection.

Ancient airs and dances   Ricordi
  Based on lute music of the 16th century. Each
  set available separately.

    Set I   15'
      2 *3 0 2 - 2 1 0 0 - hp, hpsd - str

    Set II   20'
      *3 *3 2 2 - 3 2 3 0 - tmp - hp, hpsd 4-hands
      (1 hpsd player doubling on cel) - str

    Set III   16'
      str

La boutique fantasque (after Rossini)   35'
  *3 *3 2 2 - 4 3 3 1 - tmp+5 - hp, cel - str   Chester

Brazilian impressions   20'
  *3 *3 *3 2 - 4 3 2 1 - tmp+3 - hp, cel, pf - str   Ricordi

Feste romane (Roman festivals)   23'
  *3 *3 =4 *3 - 4 4 3 1 - 3 buccine or extra   Ricordi
    trumpets - tmp+9 - pf 4-hands, org,
    mandoline - str

Fontane di Roma (Fountains of Rome)   18'
  *3 *3 *3 2 - 4 3 3 1 - tmp+2 - 2hp, cel,   Ricordi
  pf, (opt org) - str

Lauda per la natività del Signore   25'
  chorus - solos SSA (or SAT)   Ricordi
  *2 *2 0 2 - 1perc - pf 4-hands

Pini di Roma (Pines of Rome)   20'
  *3 *3 *3 *3 - 4 3 4 0 - 6 buccine (2 soprano,   Ricordi
    2 tenor, 2 bass) - tmp+5 - hp, cel, pf,
    org - str
  (Buccine parts are cued in orchestral brass. 4th
  trombone part often played on tuba.)

Rossiniana   25'
  *3 *3 2 2 - 4 3 3 1 - tmp+5 - hp, cel - str   Simrock
  Freely transcribed from Rossini's "Le riens."

Il tramonto   16'
  mezzo-soprano solo   Ricordi
  string orchestra or string quartet

Trittico Botticelliano   18'
  1 1 1 1 - 1 1 0 0 - 1perc - hp, cel, pf - str   Ricordi

Gli uccelli (The birds)   20'
  *2 1 2 2 - 2 2 0 0 - hp, cel - str   Ricordi

Vetrate di chiesa   28'
  *3 *3 *3 *3 - 4 3 3 1 - tmp+4 - hp, cel,   Ricordi
    pf, org - str

    REYNOLDS, ROGER, 1934-

Graffiti   9'
  *3 *3 *3 *3 - 4 3 3 1 - tmp+7 - 2hp, pf - str   Peters

Quick are the mouths of earth   18'
  3 1 0 0 - 0 1 2 0 - 2perc - pf - 3vc   Peters

Wedge   8'
  *2 0 0 0 - 0 2 2 1 - 3perc - pf/cel - db   Peters

    REZNIČEK, EMIL NIKOLAUS VON, 1860-1945

Donna Diana: Overture   5'
  *3 2 2 2 - 4 2 0 0 - tmp+1 - (opt hp) - str   Kalmus;
                                                    Universal

    RHEINBERGER, JOSEPH, 1839-1901

Concerto, organ, no.1, op.137, F major   25'
  3hn - str   Forberg; Kalmus

Concerto, organ, no.2, op.177, G minor   22'
  brass 2 2 0 0 - tmp - str   Forberg

RIEGGER, WALLINGFORD, 1885-1961

Dance rhythms, op.58   8'
  2 2 2 2 - 2 2 2 0 - tmp+4 - hp - str   AMP

Music for orchestra, op.50   7'
  *3 *3 2 *3 - 4 3 3 1 - tmp+3 - str   AMP

RIMSKY-KORSAKOV, NIKOLAI, 1844-1908

Capriccio espagnol, op.34   15'
  *3 *2 2 2 - 4 2 3 1 - tmp+5 - hp - str Belaieff; Kalmus

Christmas eve: Suite   23'
  *3 2 +3 2 - 4 3 3 1 - tmp+4 - hp, cel - str   Belaieff;
  (optional chorus)   Kalmus

Christmas eve: Polonaise   6'
  *3 2 +3 2 - 4 3 3 1 - tmp+4 - hp - str Belaieff; Kalmus

Concerto, piano, op.30, C-sharp minor   13'
  2 2 2 2 - 2 2 3 0 - tmp - str   Belaieff; Kalmus

Concerto, trombone and band   11'
  *3 2 =5 2 - 4 4 3 1 - 2asx, tsx, bsx -   MCA
    alto clarinet, baritone horn - 3perc
  Adapted for American band by Walter Nallin.

Conte féerique (Fairytale), op.29   13'
  *3 2 2 2 - 4 2 3 1 - tmp+3 - hp - str   Belaieff
  This work may be out of print, but orchestral
  materials are in the Fleisher Collection.

Le coq d'or: Suite   26'
  *3 *3 *3 *3 - 4 3 3 1 - tmp+4 - 2hp, cel - str   Kalmus;
                                                             VAAP

Le coq d'or: Introduction and Wedding march   8'
  *3 *3 *3 *3 - 4 3 3 1 - tmp+4 - 2hp, cel -   Forberg;
    str   Kalmus

Dubinushka, op.62   4'
  (optional chorus)   Belaieff;
  *3 2 3 2 - 4 3 3 1 - tmp+4 - str   Kalmus;
  (3rd trumpet optional.)   VAAP

Fantaisie de concert, op.33, violin and orchestra   12'
  2 2 2 2 - 2 2 0 0 - tmp+1 - str   Belaieff

The maid of Pskov: Overture and three entr'actes   27'
  *3 2 2 2 - 4 2 3 1 - tmp+2 - str   Breitkopf
  Although published under this title, the
  overture is actually that of "Boyarina Vera Sheloga,"
  op.54, which is a prologue to "The maid of Pskov."
  This is a different overture from the one listed below.

The maid of Pskov: Overture   8'
  *3 *3 *3 *3 - 4 3 3 1 - tmp - str   Breitkopf
  This is the overture to the opera proper, and not
  the same work as the overture listed above.

May night: Overture   8'
  2 2 2 2 - 4 2 3 0 - tmp - str   Belaieff; Kalmus

Mlada: Suite   15'
  (optional chorus)   Belaieff;
  =4 *3 *4 *3 - 6 3 3 1 - tmp+5 - 3hp - str   Kalmus

Overture on Russian themes, op.28   12'
  *2 2 2 2 - 4 2 3 0 - tmp+1 - (opt hp) -   Belaieff;
    str   Kalmus

Russian Easter overture (Grand Paque Russe), op.36   14'
  *3 2 2 2 - 4 2 3 1 - tmp+4 - hp - str   Belaieff;
                         Kalmus

Sadko: Tableau musical   13'
  *3 2 2 2 - 4 2 3 1 - tmp+3 - hp - str   Kalmus

Scheherazade, op.35   41'
  *3 *2 2 2 - 4 2 3 1 - tmp+5 - hp - str   Belaieff;
                         Kalmus

The snow maiden (Snegourotchka): Suite   12'
  *3 *2 2 2 - 4 2 3 1 - tmp+4 - str   Breitkopf;
                 Kalmus; Universal

The snow maiden (Snegourotchka): Dance of
  the buffoons   4'
  *3 2 2 2 - 4 2 3 1 - tmp+4 - str   Kalmus

Symphoniette on Russian themes, op.31   20'
  2 2 2 2 - 4 2 3 0 - tmp - str   Belaieff; Kalmus

Symphony no.1, op.1, E-flat minor   25'
  2 2 2 2 - 4 2 3 0 - tmp - str   Breitkopf; VAAP

Symphony no.2, op.9 ("Antar")   30'
  *3 *2 2 2 - 4 2 3 1 - tmp+4 - hp - str   Breitkopf;
                            Kalmus; VAAP

Symphony no.3, op.32, C major   30'
  *3 2 2 2 - 4 2 3 1 - tmp - str   Belaieff

Tsar Saltan: Suite, op.57   19'
  *3 *3 3 *3 - 4 2 3 1 - tmp+4 - hp, cel -   Breitkopf;
    str   Kalmus
  (Contrabassoon is optional.)

Tsar Saltan: Flight of the bumblebee   3'
  2 2 2 2 - 2 0 0 0 - str   Breitkopf; Kalmus; VAAP

The tsar's bride: Overture   7'
  *3 2 2 2 - 4 2 3 1 - tmp - hp - str   Belaieff; Kalmus

    ROCHBERG, GEORGE, 1918-

Black sounds   12'
  *2 1 =2 0 - 2 2 2 1 - tmp+3 - pf/cel   Presser

Cheltenham concerto   15'
  1 1 1 1 - 1 1 1 0 - str   Presser

Night music   12'
  *3 *3 *3 *3 - 4 3 3 1 - tmp+1 - hp - str   Presser

Time-span (II)   10'
  3 *3 *3 2 - 4 3 3 1 - 2perc - cel, pf - str   MCA

    RODGERS, RICHARD, 1902-1979

Slaughter on Tenth Avenue   10'
  *2 *2 *3 2 - 4 3 3 1 - tmp+3 - hp, pf/cel -   Chappell
    str
  Arr. Robert Russell Bennett.

RODRIGO, JOAQUÍN, 1902-

Concierto de Aranjuez, guitar and orchestra   21'
  *2 *2 2 2 - 2 2 0 0 - str   UME

Concierto serenata, harp and orchestra   20'
  *2 2 2 2 - 2 2 0 0 - str   UME

Zarabanda lejana y villancico   8'
  str   Eschig

ROGERS, BERNARD, 1893-1968

The musicians of Bremen   22'
  narrator   Presser
  *1 1 1 1 - 1 1 0 0 - tmp+1 - pf - str (without va)
  (May be performed with one string player on a part.)

Once upon a time; five fairy tales for small orchestra 12'
  *2 2 2 2 - 2 2 1 0 - tmp+3 - hp -   Kalmus
    "clavi-cembalo (adapted piano)" - str

Soliloquy for flute and strings   6'
  str   Fischer, C.

Three Japanese dances   12'
  (optional mezzo-soprano)   Presser
  =3 *3 *3 *3 - 4 2 3 1 - tmp+4 - hp, cel, pf - str
  One flutist also doubles on bass flute in C, but
  both bass and alto flutes are optional.

ROREM, NED, 1923-

Design   18'
  *2 2 2 2 - 4 2 2 0 - tmp+5 - hp, cel, pf - str   Boosey

Eagles   8'
  *3 *3 =4 *3 - 4 3 3 1 - tmp+7 - hp, cel,   Boosey
    pf - str

Ideas for easy orchestra   12'
  1 1 1 1 - 2 1 1 0 - tmp+2 - hp, pf - str   Boosey

ROSSINI, GIOACCHINO, 1792-1868

In general, Rossini editions are poor and untrustworthy. The various editions differ with each other, and the scores often conflict even with the parts to which they ostensibly belong.

Il barbiere di Siviglia: Overture 8'
  *2 2 2 2 - 2 2 3 0 - tmp+1 - str   Breitkopf; Kalmus; Ricordi

La boutique fantasque
  See under: Respighi, Ottorino, 1879-1936

La Cenerentola (Cinderella): Overture 8'
  *2 2 2 2 - 2 2 1 0 - tmp+1 - str   Kalmus; Ricordi

La gazza ladra (The thieving magpie): Overture 10'
  *2 2 2 2 - 4 2 1 0 - tmp+4 - str   Kalmus; Ricordi

L'Italiana in Algeri: Overture 9'
  1 2 2 2 - 2 2 0 0 - tmp - str   Breitkopf; Kalmus; Ricordi

Les riens
  See: Respighi, Ottorino, 1879-1936
        Rossiniana

Robert Bruce: Overture 7'
  *2 2 2 2 - 4 4 3 1 - tmp+3 - str
  This work is out of print, but orchestral
  materials are in the Fleisher Collection.

La scala di seta: Overture 7'
  *1 2 2 1 - 2 0 0 0 - str   Kalmus; Ricordi

Semiramide: Overture 12'
  *2 2 2 2 - 4 2 3 0 - tmp+1 - str   Breitkopf; Kalmus; Ricordi

Serenata per piccolo complesso 8'
  fl, ob, Eh - str quartet   Kalmus

The siege of Corinth (L'assedio di Corinto): Overture 10'
  *3 2 2 2 - 4 2 4 0 - tmp+2 - str   Carisch; Kalmus; Ricordi

Il signor Bruschino: Overture   5'
  1 2 2 1 - 2 0 0 0 - str   Carisch; Kalmus; Ricordi

Sonatas   ca.12' each
  str (without va)   Kalmus
  Originally chamber music for 2vn, vc, db, but
  frequently performed by string orchestra.
  Sonatas available separately.

    No.1, G major

    No.2, A major

    No.3, C major

    No.4, B-flat major

    No.5, E-flat major

    No.6, D major

Stabat mater   57'
  chorus - solos SSTB   Kalmus; Ricordi;
  2 2 2 2 - 4 2 3 0 - tmp - str   Schirmer, G.; Schott

Tancredi: Overture   6'
  2 2 2 2 - 2 2 0 0 - tmp - str   Kalmus; Ricordi

The thieving magpie
  See his: La gazza ladra

Il Turco in Italia: Overture   9'
  2 2 2 2 - 2 2 1 0 - tmp+1 - str   Ricordi

Variations for clarinet and small orchestra   9'
  1 0 2 1 - 2 0 0 0 - str   Luck
  Other editions, from EMT, Sikorski, and Zanibon,
  list 2 oboes rather than 2 clarinets in the
  accompaniment.

Il viaggio a Reims: Overture   8'
  *2 2 2 2 - 2 2 3 0 - tmp+2 - str   Carisch;
  Ricordi edition calls for an extra flute and   Ricordi
  an extra trombone.

William Tell: Overture   12'
  *2 *2 2 2 - 4 2 3 0 - tmp+3 - str   Breitkopf;
                                          Kalmus; Ricordi

William Tell: Pas de six   6'
   *2 2 2 2 - 2 2 0 0 - str   Luck

ROUSSEL, ALBERT, 1869-1937

Bacchus et Ariane, op.43: Suite no.1   17'
   *3 *3 *3 *3 - 4 4 3 1 - tmp+4 - 2hp, cel - str   Durand

Bacchus et Ariane, op.43: Suite no.2   20'
   *3 *3 *3 *3 - 4 4 3 1 - tmp+4 - 2hp, cel - str   Durand

Concerto for small orchestra, op.34   14'
   *2 2 2 2 - 2 1 0 0 - tmp - str   Durand

Concerto, piano, op.36   17'
   *2 *2 2 2 - 2 2 0 0 - tmp+3 - str   Durand

Fanfare for a pagan rite (Fanfare pour un sacre païen)   2'
   brass 4 4 3 0 - tmp   Durand

Le festin de l'araigne (The spider's feast), op.17   16'
   *2 *2 2 2 - 2 2 0 0 - tmp+1 - hp, cel - str   Durand

Le marchand de sable qui passe... (incidental music)   16'
   1 0 1 0 - 1 0 0 0 - hp - str   Eschig

Petite suite, op.39   11'
   *2 2 2 2 - 2 2 0 0 - tmp+3 - str   Durand

Pour une fête de printemps, op.22   12'
   *3 *3 2 3 - 4 2 3 1 - tmp+2 - hp - str   Durand

Rapsodie flamande, op.56   9'
   *3 *3 *3 *3 - 4 3 3 1 - tmp+3 - hp - str   Durand

Sinfonietta, op.52   10'
   str   Durand

Suite in F, op.33   15'
   *3 *3 *3 3 - 4 4 3 1 - tmp+3 - hp, cel - str   Durand

Symphony no.2, op.23, B-flat   40'
   *3 *3 *3 *4 - 4 4 3 1 - tmp+3 - 2hp, cel - str   Durand

Symphony no.3, op.42, G minor   25'
  *3 *3 *3 *3 - 4 4 3 1 - tmp+5 - 2hp, cel - str   Durand

Symphony no.4, op.53, A major   24'
  *3 *3 *3 *3 - 4 4 3 1 - tmp+3 - hp - str   Durand

    RUBBRA, EDMUND, 1901-

Festival overture, op.62   8'
  2 2 2 2 - 4 2 3 1 - tmp+1 - str   Lengnick

Improvisation for violin and orchestra, op.89   12'
  2 *2 2 2 - 2 2 0 0 - tmp+1 - hp, cel - str   Lengnick

    RUBINSTEIN, ANTON, 1829-1894

Concerto, piano, no.3, op.45, G major   35'
  2 2 2 2 - 2 2 0 0 - tmp - str   Fischer, C.; Luck

Concerto, piano, no.4, op.70, D minor   31'
  *3 2 2 2 - 2 2 0 0 - tmp - str   Kalmus; Simrock

Melody in F, op.3, no.1 (arr. Vincent d'Indy)   5'
    violoncello solo   Kalmus
  2 2 2 2 - 2 0 0 0 - tmp - str

    RUGGLES, CARL, 1876-1968

Angels   3'
    brass 0 4 3 0   AME
    (Although scored for muted brass, this composition
    may be played by any seven instruments of equal timbre.)

Men and mountains (original version)   15'
    *2 *2 1 1 - 2 2 1 0 - 1perc - pf - 2vn, 2va,   AME
    2vc, db

Men and mountains (version for large orchestra)   15'
    *3 *3 *3 *3 - 4 3 3 1 - tmp+3 - pf - str   AME

Organum   8'
    *3 *3 =4 *3 - 4 3 3 1 - tmp+1 - pf - str   AME

Portals   6'
  str   AME

Sun-treader   15'
  *5 *5 =5 *4 - 6 5 5 1 - tenor tuba (=euphonium) -   AME
  tmp+1 - 2hp - str

SAINT-SAËNS, CAMILLE, 1835-1921

Africa, op.89   11'
  solo piano   Durand;
  2 2 2 2 - 2 2 3 0 - tmp+1 - str   Kalmus

Allegro appassionato, piano and orchestra, op.70   7'
  2 2 2 2 - 2 2 0 0 - str   Durand; Fischer, C.

Allegro appassionato, violoncello and orchestra, op.43   4'
  2 2 2 2 - 2 0 0 0 - str   Durand; Luck

Carnival of the animals   23'
  2 solo pianos   Durand;
  *1 0 1 0 - 2perc - str quintet   Luck
  Often performed with full string section.

Christmas oratorio (Oratorio de Noël), op.12   40'
  chorus - solos SAATB   Durand; Kalmus;
  str - org, hp   Schirmer, G.

Concerto, piano, no.1, op.17, D major   28'
  2 2 2 2 - 4 2 0 0 - tmp - str   Durand; Fischer, C.

Concerto, piano, no.2, op.22, G minor   23'
  2 2 2 2 - 2 2 0 0 - tmp - str   Durand; Kalmus

Concerto, piano, no.3, op.29, E-flat major   28'
  2 2 2 2 - 2 2 3 0 - tmp - str   Durand; Kalmus

Concerto, piano, no.4, op.44, C minor   25'
  2 2 2 2 - 2 2 3 0 - tmp - str   Durand; Kalmus

Concerto, piano, no.5, op.103, F major   28'
  *3 2 2 2 - 4 2 3 0 - tmp - str   Durand; Kalmus

Concerto, violin, no.1, op.20, A major   10'
  2 2 2 2 - 2 2 0 0 - tmp - str   Kalmus

Concerto, violin, no.2, op.58, C major   14'
   2 2 2 2 - 2 2 3 0 - tmp - hp - str   Durand; Kalmus

Concerto, violin, no.3, op.61, B minor   27'
  *2 2 2 2 - 2 2 3 0 - tmp - str   Durand; Kalmus

Concerto, violoncello, no.1, op.33, A minor   18'
   2 2 2 2 - 2 2 0 0 - tmp - str   Durand; Kalmus

Concerto, violoncello, no.2, op.119, D minor   16'
   2 2 2 2 - 4 2 0 0 - tmp - str   Durand; Kalmus

Coronation march, op.117   8'
  *3 2 2 *3 - 4 4 3 1 - tmp+3 - hp - str   Kalmus

Danse macabre, op.40   8'
  *3 2 2 2 - 4 2 3 1 - tmp+3 - (opt hp) - str   Durand;
                                         Kalmus

La foi
   See his: Trois tableaux symphoniques d'après "La foi"

Havanaise, op.83   11'
   solo violin   Fischer, C.;
   2 2 2 2 - 2 2 0 0 - tmp - str   Kalmus

Introduction and rondo capriccioso, op.28   10'
   solo violin   Fischer, C.;
   2 2 2 2 - 2 2 0 0 - tmp - str   Kalmus

La jeunesse d'Hercule   16'
  *3 2 2 2 - 4 5 3 1 - tmp+3 - 2hp (doubling   Durand;
    one real part) - str   Kalmus

Marche héroïque, op.34   7'
  *3 2 2 2 - 4 2 3 1 - tmp+3 - hp - str   Fischer, C.;
                                         Kalmus

Morceau de concert, harp and orchestra, op.154
   2 2 2 2 - 2 2 0 0 - tmp - str   Luck

Morceau de concert, horn and orchestra, op.94   9'
   2 2 2 2 - 0 0 3 0 - tmp - str   Durand; Kalmus

La nuit, op.114   10'
   female chorus - solo soprano   Durand
   2 2 2 2 - 4 0 0 0 - hp - str

Odelette, op.162   14'
  solo flute   Durand
  0 2 0 2 - str

Orient et occident, op.25   6'
  *3 *3 *3 *3 - 4 3 3 1 - tmp+4 - str   Durand; Luck

Phaéton, op.39   9'
  *3 2 2 *3 - 4 2 3 1 - 3tmp, 3perc - 2hp - str   Durand;
  (Contrabassoon is optional.)   Kalmus

La Princesse Jaune, op.30: Overture   6'
  2 *2 2 2 - 4 2 3 0 - tmp+1 - hp - str   Durand; Kalmus

Requiem, op.54   31'
  chorus - solos SATB   Durand
  4 *4 0 4 - 4 0 4 0 - 4hp (doubling 2 real parts) -
  org - str

Rhapsodie d'Auvergne, op.73   10'
  solo piano   Durand;
  *3 2 2 2 - 4 2 3 0 - tmp+1 - str   Kalmus

Romance, op.36   5'
  solo horn (or violoncello)   Durand;
  2 1 2 1 - str   Kalmus

Romance, op.37   6'
  solo flute (or violin)   Durand;
  0 2 2 2 - 4 2 0 0 - tmp - str   Kalmus

Le rouet d'Omphale, op.31   9'
  *3 2 2 2 - 4 2 3 0 - tmp+2˚- hp - str   Durand; Kalmus

Samson et Dalila: Bacchanale   8'
  *3 *3 *3 *3 - 4 4 3 1 - tmp+4 - hp - str   Durand; Kalmus

Septet, op.65   15'
  tp - pf - 2vn, va, vc, db   Durand

Suite algérienne, op.60   18'
  *3 2 2 2 - 4 4 3 1 - tmp+3 - str   Durand; Kalmus

Symphony no.1, op.2, E-flat major   31'
  *3 *2 *3 2 - 4 4 3 0 - bass and contrabass   Durand;
    saxhorns (=euphonium and tuba) - 2tmp,   Luck
    1perc - 4hp (doubling a single part) - str

Symphony no.2, op.55, A minor   24'
  *3 *2 2 2 - 2 2 0 0 - tmp - str   Durand; Kalmus

Symphony no.3, op.78, C minor ("Organ symphony")   37'
  *3 *3 *3 *3 - 4 3 3 1 - tmp+2 - org,   Durand;
    pf 4-hands - str   Kalmus

Tarantelle, op.6   7'
  solo flute - solo clarinet   Durand;
  *1 2 0 2 - 2 2 2 0 - tmp - str   Kalmus

Trois tableaux symphoniques d'après "La foi"   16'
  *3 *2 2 2 - 4 3 3 0 - tmp+3 - 2hp (doubling   Durand
    a single part), harm - str

       SAMMARTINI, GIOVANNI BATTISTA, 1701-1775

Concertino, G major   8'
  str, cnt   Peters
  Ed. Newell Jenkins.

Concerto in E-flat   7'
  solo string quartet   Augener
  str
  Arr. and ed. Adam Carse.

Concerto, violin (or violoncello piccolo), C major   12'
  str, cnt   Eulenburg
  Ed. Newell Jenkins.

Magnificat   20'
  chorus - solos SATB   Eulenburg;
  0 2 0 0 - 0 2 0 0 - str, cnt   Schirmer, G.

Sinfonia, J.-C. 2, C major   15'
  0 2 0 1 - 2 0 0 0 - tmp - str   Carisch
  Ed. Fausto Torrefranca.

Sinfonia, J.-C. 4, C major   7'
   2hn - str   Zanibon
   Ed. Ettore Bonelli.

Sinfonia, J.-C. 32, F major   12'
   str, cnt   Peters
   Ed. Newell Jenkins.

Sinfonia, J.-C. 39, G major   7'
   str, cnt   Peters
   Ed. Newell Jenkins.

Sinfonia, J.-C. 47, G major   9'
   2 2 0 0 - 2 0 0 0 - str, cnt   Carisch
   Ed. Fausto Torrefranca. (Flutes and oboes are optional.)

SAMMARTINI, GIUSEPPE, ca.1693-ca.1770

Concerto grosso, op.5, no.6 ("Christmas concerto")   15'
   2 solo violins   Vieweg
   str, cnt
   Ed. Karlheinz Schultz-Hauser.

SAPIEYEVSKI, JERZY, 1945-

Surtsey   15'
   str   Mercury

Summer overture   10'
   *3 3 *3 3 - 5 3 3 1 - tmp+2 - hp - str   Mercury

SARASATE, PABLO DE, 1844-1908

Carmen fantasie, op.25, on themes of Bizet   20'
   violin solo   Kalmus
   *2 2 2 2 - 4 2 3 0 - tmp+1 - hp - str

Introduction and tarantella, op.43   7'
   violin solo   Fischer, C.;
   2 2 2 2 - 2 2 0 0 - tmp+1 - str   Kalmus; Luck

Zigeunerweisen (Gypsy airs), op.20   10'
  solo violin   Fischer, C.;
  2 2 2 2 - 2 2 0 0 - tmp,(+1perc opt) - str   Kalmus;
                                                  Luck

SATIE, ERIK, 1866-1925

Les aventures de Mercure   20'
  *2 1 2 1 - 2 2 1 1 - 3perc - str   Universal

Cinq grimaces pour "Un songe d'une nuit d'été"   3'
  *3 *3 2 *3 - 2 3 3 1 - tmp+3 - str   Universal

Deux préludes posthumes et une gnossienne   9'
  2 *2 2 2 - 2 2 2 0 - hp - str   Salabert
  Orchestrated by Francis Poulenc.

Gymnopédies nos.1 and 3 (orchestrated by Debussy)   8'
  2 1 0 0 - 4 0 0 0 - 1perc - 2hp - str   Kalmus; Salabert

Gymnopédie no.2 (orchestrated by Roland-Manuel)   4'
  2 1 1 0 - 4 1 0 0 - 2perc - 2hp, cel - str   Salabert

Jack in the box (orchestrated by Milhaud)   7'
  *2 2 2 2 - 2 2 2 0 - tmp+3 - str   Universal

Parade   14'
  *3 *3 +3 2 - 2 3 3 1 - tmp+4 - hp - str   Salabert

Trois petites pièces montées   5'
  1 1 1 1 - 1 2 1 0 - 2perc - str   Eschig
  This work may be out of print, but orchestral
  materials are in the Fleisher Collection.

SCARLATTI, ALESSANDRO, 1660-1725

Christmas cantata
  solo soprano   Oxford
  str, cnt
  Ed. Edward Dent.

Concerto, G minor
  str   AMP
  Ed. Paul Glass.

Concerto grosso no.1, F minor; no.2, C minor   9', 7'
  str, cnt   Vieweg
  Ed. Walter Upmeyer.

Concerto grosso no.3, F major   8'
  2 solo violins, solo violoncello   Vieweg;
  str, cnt   Zanibon

Concerto grosso no.6, E major   9'
  2 solo violins, solo violoncello   Ricordi
  str, cnt
  Ed. Renato Fasano.

Piccola suite   10'
  str   Zanibon
  Assembled from various works by Franco
  Michele Napolitano.

Sinfonia no.1, F major   8'
  2rec - str, cnt   Bärenreiter; Schott

Sinfonia no.2, D major   7'
  1 0 0 0 - 0 1 0 0 - str, cnt   Bärenreiter
  Ed. Raymond Meylan.

Sinfonia no.4, E minor   14'
  1 1 0 0 - str, cnt   Bärenreiter
  Ed. Raymond Meylan.

Sinfonia no.5, D minor   9'
  2fl - str, cnt   Bärenreiter
  Ed. Raymond Meylan.

Sinfonia no.6, A minor   12'
  rec - str, cnt   Peters
  Ed. Rolf-Julius Koch.

Sinfonia no.8, G major   12'
  rec - str, cnt   Peters
  Ed. Rolf-Julius Koch.

Sinfonia no.10, A minor   12'
  rec - str, cnt   Peters
  Ed. Rolf-Julius Koch.

SCARLATTI, DOMENICO, 1685-1757

Five sonatas in form of a suite   10'
  str   Zanibon
  "Freely elaborated" from harpsichord sonatas
  by Ettore Bonelli.

The good-humored ladies: Suite   14'
  2 2 2 2 - 4 2 0 0 - tmp+1 - hpsd - str   Chester
  Five harpsichord sonatas arr. Vincenzo Tommasini.

Serenata (Contest of the seasons)   50'
  chorus - solos SATB   Ricordi
  1 0 0 0 - 2 2 0 0 - str, cnt
  Ed. Renato Fasano.

SCHEIN, JOHANN HERMANN, 1586-1630

Banchetto musicale: Suite no.1   9'
  str   Kahnt
  Ed. Arnold Schering.

SCHICKELE, PETER, 1935-

A zoo called Earth   15'
  taped narration (Schickele's voice, altered   Presser
    to sound like that of an extraterrestrial
    visitor)
  *2 2 2 2 - 4 3 3 1 - tmp+3 - cel - str

SCHOENBERG, ARNOLD, 1874-1951

Begleitungsmusik zu einer Lichtspielscene (Accompaniment
  to a cinematographic scene)   8'
  *1 1 2 1 - 2 2 1 0 - tmp+4 - pf - str   Peters

Chamber symphony no.1, op.9   22'
  1 *2 =3 *2 - 2 0 0 0 - 2vn, va, vc, db   Universal

Chamber symphony no.1, op.9b (orchestral version)   22'
  *3 *3 =3 *3 - 4 2 3 0 - str   Schirmer, G.;
  Orchestrated by the composer.   Universal

Chamber symphony no.2, op.38   21'
  *2 *2 2 2 - 2 2 0 0 - str   Schirmer, G.

Concerto, piano, op.42   28'
  *2 2 2 2 - 4 2 3 1 - tmp+3 - str   Belmont; Schirmer, G.

Concerto, violin, op.36   32'
  *3 3 =3 3 - 4 3 3 1 - tmp+4 - str   Schirmer, G.

Concerto, violoncello   19'
  *2 2 2 2 - 2 2 1 0 - tmp+3 - hp, cel - str Schirmer, G.
  After a harpsichord concerto by G. M. Monn (1746).

Five pieces for orchestra, op.16 (1909 version)   19'
  *4 *4 =5 *4 - 6 3 4 1 - tmp+3 - hp, cel - str   Peters
  One clarinetist also doubles on contrabass
  clarinet in A.

Five pieces for orchestra, op.16 (1949 version)   19'
  *4 *3 =4 *3 - 4 3 3 1 - tmp+3 - hp, cel - str   Peters
  A 1973 edition by Richard Hoffmann makes many
  corrections in this 1949 version.

Five pieces for orchestra, op.16 (chamber
  orchestra version)   19'
  *1 1 1 1 - 1 0 0 0 - pf, harm - 2vn, va, vc, db Peters
  Arr. Felix Greissle.

Gurre-Lieder   130'
  chorus - solos SATTB - speaker   Universal
  *8 *5 =7 *5 - 10 6 7 1 - bass tp - tmp+6 -
    4hp, cel - str
  Horns 7-10 double on Wagner tubas. Among the
  aggregate woodwind numbers above, the following
  numbers of secondary instruments are required:
  4pic, 2Eh, 2scl, 2bcl, 2cbn. A version for
  normal-size orchestra is also available.

Gurre-Lieder: Lied der Waldtaube   13'
  solo soprano   Universal
  *1 *2 =3 *2 - 2 0 0 0 - pf, harm - 2vn, va, vc, db
  Versions for the huge Gurre-Lieder orchestra, and
  for a normally large orchestra are also available.

Kol nidre, op.39   18'
   chorus - speaker   Boelke-Bomart
   *2 1 =3 1 - 2 2 2 1 - tmp+3 - str

Ode to Napoleon Bonaparte, op.41   16'
   reciter - pf - str   Belmont; Schirmer, G.

Pelléas und Mélisande, op.5   41'
   *4 *4 =5 *4 - 8 4 5 1 - tmp+4 - 2hp - str   Universal
   Version for reduced orchestra is also available.

Pierrot lunaire, op.21   40'
   fl/pic, cl/bcl, vn/va, vc, pf, Sprechstimme   Universal

Prelude (Genesis suite), op.44   6'
   wordless chorus   Belmont
   *3 *3 *3 *3 - 4 3 3 1 - tmp+3 - hp - str

Serenade, op.24   30'
   bass-baritone voice   Hansen
   cl, bcl - gtr, mandoline - vn, va, vc

Six songs, op.8   22'
   soprano solo   Universal
   *3 *3 *3 *3 - 4 3 3 1 - tmp+3 - hp - str

Suite for string orchestra   20'
   str   Schirmer, G.

A survivor from Warsaw, op.46   9'
   narrator - unison male chorus   Boelke-Bomart
   *2 2 2 2 - 4 3 3 1 - tmp+5 - hp - str
   Score revised by Jacques-Louis Monod, 1979,
   available from EAM.

Theme and variations, op.43b   14'
   *3 *3 *3 *3 - 4 3 3 1 - tmp+3 - str   Belmont;
   Originally for concert band.   Schirmer, G.

Variations for orchestra, op.31   23'
   *4 *4 =5 *4 - 4 3 4 1 - tmp+5 - hp, cel,   Universal
      mandoline - str

Verklärte Nacht, op.4   26'
   str   AMP
   Originally for string sextet. Revised version 1943.

SCHREINER, ADOLPH

The worried drummer   8'
  solo percussionist   Belwin;
  *2 2 2 2 - 2 2 1 0 - str   Kalmus;
  Luck version calls for 3 trombones.   Luck

SCHUBERT, FRANZ, 1797-1828

Alfonso and Estrella, D.732: Overture   7'
  2 2 2 2 - 2 2 3 0 - tmp - str   Breitkopf;
  Used as overture to Rosamunde incidental music. Kalmus

Claudine von Villa Bella, D.239: Overture   8'
  2 2 2 2 - 2 2 0 0 - tmp - str   Breitkopf

Des Teufels Lustschloss, D.84: Overture   9'
  2 2 2 2 - 2 2 3 0 - tmp - str   Breitkopf

Fierrabras, D.796: Overture   9'
  2 2 2 2 - 4 2 3 0 - tmp - str   Breitkopf; Kalmus

Die Freunde von Salamanka, D.326: Overture   7'
  2 2 2 2 - 2 2 0 0 - tmp - str   Breitkopf

Der häusliche Krieg, D.787: Overture   7'
  2 2 2 2 - 2 2 0 0 - tmp - str   Doblinger
  Completed by Fritz Racek.

Konzertstück, D.345, D major   8'
  solo violin   Breitkopf;
  0 2 0 0 - 0 2 0 0 - tmp - str   Kalmus

Magnificat, D.486
  chorus - solos SATB   Kalmus;
  0 2 0 2 - 0 2 0 0 - tmp - org - str   Schirmer, G.

Marche militaire, D.733 (op.51), no.1   5'
  *3 2 2 2 - 4 3 3 1 - tmp+5 - str   Luck;
  Arr. Leopold Damrosch from a work for   Schirmer, G.
  piano 4-hands.

Mass no.1, D.105, F major   43'
  chorus - solos SSATTB   Gray;
  0 2 2 2 - 2 2 3 0 - tmp - org - str   Schirmer, G.

Mass no.2, D.167, G major   26'
  chorus - solos STB   Breitkopf;
  0 2 0 2 - 0 2 0 0 - tmp - org - str   Gray;
  (Winds and tmp added by Ferdinand Schubert, and   Kalmus
  are optional. Kalmus edition calls for strings only.)

Mass no.3, D.324, B-flat major   30'
  chorus - solos SATB   Breitkopf;
  0 2 0 2 - 0 2 0 0 - tmp - org - str   Gray; Kalmus

Mass no.4, D.452, C major   25'
  chorus - solos SATB   Breitkopf;
  2ob (or 2cl) - 2tp - tmp - org - str   Kalmus;
  (Winds and timpani are optional.)   Schirmer, G.

Mass no.5, D.678, A-flat major   55'
  chorus - solos SATB   Breitkopf;
  1 2 2 2 - 2 2 3 0 - tmp - org - str   Gray; Kalmus

Mass no.6, D.950, E-flat major   61'
  chorus - solos SATTB   Breitkopf;
  0 2 2 2 - 2 2 3 0 - tmp - str   Gray; Kalmus; Peters

Octet, D.803, F major   60'
  cl, bsn, hn - 2vn, va, vc, db   Luck; Peters

Offertorium, D.963 ("Intende voci")   15'
  chorus - tenor solo   Breitkopf
  0 1 2 2 - 2 0 3 0 - str

Overture, D.8, C minor   6'
  str   Peters
  Ed. Ernst Hess.

Overture, D.8, C minor (orchestrated by
  Wolfgang Hofmann)   6'
  1 0 2 1 - 2 0 0 0 - str   Peters

Overture, D.12, D major   9'
  2 2 2 2 - 2 2 3 0 - tmp - str   Breitkopf

Overture, D.26, D major   9'
  2 2 2 2 - 2 2 3 0 - tmp - str   Breitkopf

Overture, D.470, B-flat major   7'
  0 2 0 2 - 2 2 0 0 - tmp - str   Breitkopf

Overture, D.556, D major   7'
  2 2 2 2 - 2 0 0 0 - tmp - str   Breitkopf

Overture, D.590, D major ("In the Italian style")   8'
  2 2 2 2 - 2 2 0 0 - tmp - str   Breitkopf

Overture, D.591, C major ("In the Italian style")   7'
  2 2 2 2 - 2 2 0 0 - tmp - str   Breitkopf; Kalmus

Overture, D.648, E minor   8'
  2 2 2 2 - 4 2 3 0 - tmp - str   Breitkopf

Rondo, violin and strings, D.438, A major   14'
  str   Breitkopf; Kalmus

Rosamunde, D.797   56'
  chorus - alto solo   Schirmer, G.
  2 2 2 2 - 4 2 3 0 - tmp - str
    Contents--Entr'acte I; Ballet music I; Entr'acte
  II; Romance (alto aria); Spirits' chorus;
  Entr'acte III; Pastoral music; Shepherds' chorus;
  Huntsmen's chorus; Ballet music II.

Rosamunde: Overture, D.644   10'
  2 2 2 2 - 4 2 3 0 - tmp - str   Breitkopf;
  Actually the overture to "Die Zauberharfe,"   Kalmus
  though commonly known as "Rosamunde."

Rosamunde: Ballet music   13'
  2 2 2 2 - 2 2 3 0 - tmp - str   Breitkopf;
    Contents--Ballet music I; Ballet music II   Kalmus
  (nos.2 and 9, respectively, of the incidental
  music).

Rosamunde: Entr'actes   16'
  2 2 2 2 - 2 2 3 0 - tmp - str   Breitkopf;
    Contents--Entr'acte I, B minor; Entr'acte   Kalmus
  II, D major; Entr'acte III, B-flat major (nos.1,
  3a, and 5, respectively, of the incidental music).

Salve Regina, D.106, B-flat major
  tenor solo   Breitkopf
  0 2 0 2 - 2 0 0 0 - org - str

Salve Regina, D.223, op.47, F major
  soprano solo
  0 0 2 2 - 2 0 0 0 - org - str

Salve Regina, D.676, A major   13'
  soprano solo - str   Breitkopf

Der Spiegelritter, D.11: Overture
  2 2 2 2 - 2 2 0 0 - tmp - str

Stabat mater, D.175, G minor ("The little")   6'
  chorus   Kalmus
  0 2 2 2 - 0 0 3 0 - org - str

Stabat mater, D.383, F minor
  chorus - solos STB   Breitkopf;
  2 2 0 *3 - 2 0 3 0 - str   Kalmus

Symphony no.1, D.82, D major   27'
  1 2 2 2 - 2 2 0 0 - tmp - str   Breitkopf; Kalmus

Symphony no.2, D.125, B-flat major   27'
  2 2 2 2 - 2 2 0 0 - tmp - str   Breitkopf; Kalmus

Symphony no.3, D.200, D major   23'
  2 2 2 2 - 2 2 0 0 - tmp - str   Breitkopf; Kalmus

Symphony no.4, D.417, C minor ("Tragic")   28'
  2 2 2 2 - 4 2 0 0 - tmp - str   Breitkopf; Kalmus

Symphony no.5, D.485, B-flat major   26'
  1 2 0 2 - 2 0 0 0 - str   Breitkopf; Kalmus; Peters

Symphony no.6, D.589, C major ("Little")   31'
  2 2 2 2 - 2 2 0 0 - tmp - str   Breitkopf; Kalmus

Symphony (no.7), D.729, E major   33'
  2 2 2 2 - 4 2 3 0 - tmp - str   Universal
  Completed from Schubert's sketches by
  Felix Weingartner.

Symphony no.8, D.759, B minor ("Unfinished")   23'
  2 2 2 2 - 2 2 3 0 - tmp - str   Breitkopf;
  A critical edition of the score is   Kalmus;
  published by Norton.   Peters

Symphony no.9, D.944, C major ("The great")   47'
  2 2 2 2 - 2 2 3 0 - tmp - str   Breitkopf;
  Often listed as Symphony no.7.   Kalmus

Tantum ergo, D.962   4'
  chorus - solos SATB   Peters;
  0 2 2 2 - 2 2 3 0 - tmp - str   Schirmer, G.

Der Teufel als Hydraulicus, D.4: Overture   5'
  2 0 2 2 - 2 0 0 0 - str   Breitkopf;
                      Carisch

Teufels Lustschloss
  See his: Des Teufels Lustschloss

Trauermarsch, D.859, op.55, C minor
  2 2 2 2 - 4 2 3 1 - tmp+1 - str   Luck
  Transcribed by Wilhelm Kienzl. Originally
  "Grande marche funèbre" for piano duet.

Der vierjährige Posten, D.190: Overture   8'
  2 2 2 2 - 2 2 0 0 - tmp - str   Breitkopf; Heugel

Wanderer fantasy, op.15, D.760   21'
  solo piano   Kalmus
  2 2 2 2 - 2 2 3 0 - tmp - str
  Arr. by Franz Liszt, from a work for piano.

Die Zauberharfe
  See his: Rosamunde: Overture, D.644

Die Zwillingsbrüder, D.647: Overture   5'
  2 2 2 2 - 2 2 0 0 - tmp - str   Breitkopf; Kalmus

    SCHUETZ, HEINRICH, 1585-1672
      See: Schütz, Heinrich, 1585-1672

    SCHULLER, GUNTHER, 1925-

American triptych   14'
  *3 *3 *3 *3 - 4 3 3 1 - tmp+3 - hp - str   AMP

Concertino for jazz quartet and orchestra   19'
  solo jazz quartet: vibraphone, piano,   MJQ
    percussion, string bass
  *2 2 2 2 - 2 3 2 0 - 1perc - str

Contours   23'
  *1 1 =2 1 - 1 1 1 0 - 3perc - hp - str   AMP; Schott

Five bagatelles   15'
  *3 *3 *2 *3 - 4 3 3 1 - tmp+2 - hp, pf - str   AMP

Five etudes for orchestra   14'
  *3 3 2 2 - 4 3 3 1 - tmp+3 - hp, pf - str   AMP

Journey into jazz   16'
  jazz ensemble: asx, tsx, tp, db, drums -   AMP
    narrator
  1 1 1 1 - 1 1 0 0 - 1perc - hp - str

Seven studies on themes of Paul Klee   23'
  *3 *3 *3 *3 - 4 3 3 1 - tmp+5 - hp, pf - str   Universal

Spectra   23'
  =4 *4 =4 *4 - 4 4 3 1 - tmp+4 - hp - str   AMP; Schott

SCHUMAN, WILLIAM, 1910-

American festival overture   9'
  *3 *3 *3 *3 - 4 3 3 1 - tmp+3 - str   Schirmer, G.
  (Contrabassoon is optional.)

Credendum (An article of faith)   18'
  *4 *4 =5 *4 - 6 4 3 2 - tmp+4 - pf - str   Merion

Judith   24'
  *3 *3 *3 *3 - 4 2 3 1 - tmp+2 - pf - str   Schirmer, G.
  (May be performed with woodwinds *2 *2 2 2)

New England triptych   16'
  *3 *3 =4 2 - 4 3 3 1 - tmp+3 - str   Merion

Newsreel   8'
  *3 *3 =5 *4 - 4 3 3 1 - 2asx, tsx -   Schirmer, G.
    tmp+4 - pf - str
  (Possible with: *2 1 2 1 - 2 3 3 1 - tmp+4 - str)

The orchestra song   4'
   *2 1 *2 1 - 4 3 3 1 - tmp+3 - str   Merion
   (Bass clarinet is optional; three additional
   percussionists may be used.)

A song of Orpheus   20'
   violoncello solo   Merion
   *3 *3 *3 2 - 4 0 0 0 - hp - str

Symphony no.3   29'
   *3 *3 =4 2 - 4 4 4 1 - tmp+3 - pf - str   Schirmer, G.
   (Optional additional instruments: fl, ob, cl,
   bsn, cbn, 4hn.)

Symphony no.5 (Symphony for strings)   18'
   str   Schirmer, G.

Symphony no.6   27'
   *3 *3 *3 *3 - 4 3 3 1 - tmp+2 - str   Schirmer, G.

Symphony no.7   28'
   *3 *3 *3 *3 - 4 3 3 1 - tmp+3 - pf - str   Merion
   (Optional additional instruments increase the
   size of the wind sections to: *4 *4 =5 *4 - 6 4 3 2)

Symphony no.8   31'
   *4 *3 *3 *3 - 6 4 4 1 - tmp+5 - 2hp, pf - str   Merion
   (Optional additional instruments: ob, cl, bsn.)

Undertow   25'
   *3 *3 3 3 - 4 2 3 1 - tmp+2 - pf - str   Schirmer, G.

   SCHUMANN, ROBERT, 1810-1856

Adagio and allegro, op.70   12'
   solo horn (or violoncello)   Schott
   2 1 2 2 - 2 0 0 0 - tmp - str
   Orchestrated by Blair Fairchild.

Adventlied, op.71
   chorus - solos SATB   Breitkopf;
   2 2 2 2 - 4 2 3 0 - tmp - str   Luck

Braut von Messina: Overture   9'
   *3 2 2 2 - 2 2 3 0 - tmp - str   Breitkopf; Kalmus

Concert-allegro with introduction, op.134   13'
  solo piano   Breitkopf;
  2 2 2 2 - 2 2 1 0 - tmp - str   Kalmus

Concerto, piano, op.54, A minor   31'
  2 2 2 2 - 2 2 0 0 - tmp - str   Breitkopf; Kalmus

Concerto, violin, D minor   30'
  2 2 2 2 - 2 2 0 0 - tmp - str   Schott

Concerto, violoncello, op.129, A minor   23'
  2 2 2 2 - 2 2 0 0 - tmp - str   Breitkopf; Kalmus

Concertstück, op.86, F major   21'
  4 solo horns   Breitkopf;
  *3 2 2 2 - 2 2 3 0 - tmp - str   Kalmus;
  (Orchestral horns are optional.)   KaWe; Luck

Fantasia, op.131   14'
  solo violin   Breitkopf
  2 2 2 2 - 2 2 0 0 - tmp - str

Faust: Overture   6'
  2 2 2 2 - 4 2 3 0 - tmp - str
  This work may be out of print; however, orchestral
  materials are in the Fleisher Collection.

Genoveva: Overture   10'
  2 2 2 2 - 4 2 3 0 - tmp - str   Breitkopf; Kalmus

Hermann und Dorothea: Overture   8'
  *3 2 2 2 - 2 2 0 0 - 1perc - str   Breitkopf

Introduction and allegro appassionato, op.92   15'
  solo piano   Breitkopf;
  2 2 2 2 - 2 2 0 0 - tmp - str   Kalmus

Julius Caesar, op.128: Overture   9'
  *2 2 2 2 - 4 2 3 1 - tmp - str   Breitkopf

Manfred, op.115   72'
  chorus - solos SATB   Breitkopf;
  *3 *2 2 2 - 4 3 3 1 - tmp+2 - hp - str   Fischer, C.;
                                                       Kalmus

Manfred: Overture   11'
  2 2 2 2 - 4 3 3 0 - tmp - str   Breitkopf; Kalmus

Manfred: Suite   8'
  2 *2 2 2 - 2 1 0 0 - hp - str   Durand
  This work may be out of print, but orchestral
  materials are in the Fleisher Collection.
    Contents--Entr'acte; Ranz des vaches; Apparition
  de la fée des Alpes.

Mass, op.147, C minor   50'
  chorus - solos STB   Breitkopf
  2 2 2 2 - 2 2 3 0 - tmp - (opt org) - str

Overture, scherzo, and finale   18'
  2 2 2 2 - 2 2 3 0 - tmp - str   Breitkopf;
  (Trombones are optional.)   Kalmus

Requiem, op.148, D-flat major   43'
  chorus - solos SATB   Breitkopf
  2 2 2 2 - 2 2 3 0 - tmp - str

Requiem for Mignon, op.98b   15'
  chorus - solos SSAAB   Breitkopf
  2 2 2 2 - 2 2 3 0 - tmp - (opt hp) - str

Symphony no.1, op.38, B-flat major ("Spring")   32'
  2 2 2 2 - 4 2 3 0 - tmp+1 - str   Breitkopf; Kalmus

Symphony no.2, op.61, C major   36'
  2 2 2 2 - 2 2 3 0 - tmp - str   Breitkopf; Kalmus

Symphony no.3, op.97, E-flat major ("Rhenish")   31'
  2 2 2 2 - 4 2 3 0 - tmp - str   Breitkopf; Kalmus

Symphony no.4, op.120, D minor   29'
  2 2 2 2 - 4 2 3 0 - tmp - str   Breitkopf; Kalmus

Träumerei (arr. Arthur Luck)   3'
  str   Luck
  From "Kinderscenen," op.15, no.7.

SCHÜTZ, HEINRICH, 1585-1672

Christmas oratorio (Historia der Geburt Jesu Christi)   50'
  chorus - solos STB   Bärenreiter
  2rec, bsn - 2tp, 2tbn - 2 violettas (=treble
    viols) - cnt - str
  Other editions from Breitkopf, Kalmus, and G. Schirmer
  differ somewhat in instrumentation. The Bärenreiter
  version is based on the Schütz collected edition.

Easter oratorio (Historia der Auferstehung Jesu Christi)
  chorus - solos SSAATTBB   80'
  str - hpsd, org   Bärenreiter
  Ed. Walter Simon Huber.

  SCHWARTZ, ELLIOTT, 1936-

Texture   8'
  1 1 1 1 - 1 1 1 0 - str (or str quintet)   Broude, A.

  SCRIABIN, ALEXANDER, 1872-1915

Concerto, piano, op.20, F-sharp minor   27'
  *3 2 2 2 - 4 2 3 0 - tmp - str   Belaieff; Kalmus

Le divin poème (Symphony no.3), op.43   43'
  *4 *4 *4 *4 - 8 5 3 1 - tmp+1 - 2hp -   Belaieff;
    str 16.16.12.12.8   Kalmus

The poem of ecstasy (Symphony no.4), op.54   24'
  *4 *4 *4 *4 - 8 5 3 1 - tmp+5 - 2hp, cel,   Belaieff;
    org (or harm) - str   Kalmus

Prometheus; poem of fire (Symphony no.5), op.60   25'
  solo piano - "clavier à lumières - chorus   Boosey;
  *4 *4 *4 *4 - 8 5 3 1 - tmp+6 - 2hp, org - str   Kalmus

Symphony no.1, op.26, E major   45'
  chorus - solo tenor and mezzo-soprano   Belaieff;
  *3 2 3 2 - 4 3 3 1 - tmp - hp - str   Kalmus

Symphony no.2, op.29, C minor   50'
  *3 2 3 2 - 4 3 3 1 - tmp+1 - str   Belaieff; Kalmus

SEROCKI, KAZIMIERZ, 1922-

Segmenti   7'
  *1 1 =2 1 - 1 1 1 1 - asx, cornetto piccolo (or   Moeck
  E-flat trumpet), tenor saxhorn (or another
  trombone) - tmp+3 - hp, pf, hpsd/cel, electric
  gtr, electric mandoline.
Graphic notation.

SESSIONS, ROGER, 1896-

The black maskers: Suite   22'
  =3 *3 =4 *3 - 4 4 3 1 - tmp+4 - pf, (opt org) -   Marks
  str

Concerto, violin   33'
  +3 *3 =3 *3 - 4 2 2 0 - basset horn (or   Marks
  alto clarinet) - tmp+1 - str (without vn)

Idyll of Theocritus   42'
  soprano solo   Marks
  2 *2 *2 2 - 4 2 3 1 - tmp+2 - hp, cel - str (maximum
  8.8.6.5.4)

Symphony (no.1)   23'
  *3 *3 =4 *3 - 4 4 3 1 - tmp+5 - pf - str   Marks

Symphony no.2   30'
  *3 *3 *3 2 - 4 3 3 1 - tmp+3 - pf - str   Schirmer, G.

Symphony no.3   32'
  *3 *3 =4 *3 - 4 2 3 1 - tmp+4 - hp, cel - str   Marks

Symphony no.4   24'
  *3 *3 =4 *3 - 4 3 3 1 - tmp+4 - hp, pf/cel - str   Marks

SHOSTAKOVICH, DMITRI, 1906-1975

The age of gold, op.22: Suite   19'
  *2 *2 =3 *2 - 4 3 3 1 - ssx, baritone horn -   Kalmus;
  tmp+4 - harm - str   Universal;
    Contents--Introduction; Adagio; Polka;   VAAP
  Danse.

The age of gold, op.22: Polka   2'
  *2 *2 =3 *2 - 4 3 3 1 - ssx - tmp+2 - str   Kalmus; Luck

Ballet suite no.1, op.84   20'
  *2 1 2 1 - 3 2 2 1 - tmp+3 - pf/cel - str   Kalmus;
    Contents--Valse lyrique; Dance; Romance;   VAAP
  Polka; Valse badinage; Galop.

Concerto, piano, no.1, op.35   20'
  solo trumpet as well as solo piano   Kalmus;
  str   VAAP

Concerto, piano, no.2, op.102   16'
  *3 2 2 2 - 4 0 0 0 - tmp+1 - str   MCA

Concerto, violin, op.99   36'
  *3 *3 *3 *3 - 4 0 0 1 - tmp+2 - hp, cel - str   MCA
  Designated by the composer as op.77.

Concerto, violoncello, no.1, op.107   29'
  *2 2 2 *2 - 1 0 0 0 - tmp - cel - str   MCA

Festive overture, op.96   7'
  *3 3 3 *3 - 4 3 3 1 - tmp+4 - str   Kalmus;
  (Optional extra brass 4 3 3 0.)   VAAP

The gadfly: Suite   40'
  *3 3 3 *3 - 4 3 3 1 - tmp+4 - hp, cel/pf - str   VAAP
  The clarinetists double on 3 alto saxophones.

The golden age
  See his: The age of gold

Hamlet: Film suite (1964), op.116
  *3 2 2 2 - 4 3 3 1 - tmp+5 - hp, pf/hpsd - str   Kalmus;
    Contents--Introduction; Ball at the palace;   VAAP
  The ghost; In the garden; Scene of the poisoning;
  The arrival and scene of the players; Ophelia;
  The duel and death of Hamlet.

Hamlet: Incidental music (1932), op.32   21'
  1 1 1 1 - 2 2 1 1 - tmp+3 - str   Kalmus

Memorable year 1919, op.89
  *3 3 3 *3 - 4 6 6 1 - tmp+4 - hp, cel, pf - str   MCA
  This work may be out of print.

Song of the forests, op.81   33'
  chorus, boys' chorus - tenor and bass solos   VAAP
  *3 *3 3 2 - 4 9 9 1 - tmp+4 - 2hp - str
  Six of the trumpets and six of the trombones appear
  only in the last movement, as a separate brass choir.

Symphony no.1, op.10   31'
  *3 2 2 2 - 4 3 3 1 - tmp+4 - pf - str   Kalmus

Symphony no.2, op.14 ("To the October Revolution")   20'
  chorus   Kalmus;
  *3 2 2 2 - 4 3 3 1 - tmp+4 - str   VAAP

Symphony no.3, op.20 ("May Day")   29'
  (optional chorus)   Kalmus;
  *3 2 2 2 - 4 2 3 1 - tmp+3 - str   VAAP

Symphony no.4, op.43   60'
  *6 *4 =6 *4 - 8 4 3 2 - 2tmp, 7perc -   Kalmus;
    2hp, cel - str   VAAP
  (Reduced version available.)

Symphony no.5, op.47   44'
  *3 2 +3 *3 - 4 3 3 1 - tmp+4 - 2hp (doubling   Kalmus;
    a single part), pf/cel - str   VAAP

Symphony no.6, op.53   33'
  *3 *3 =4 *3 - 4 3 3 1 - tmp+5 - hp, cel - str   VAAP

Symphony no.7, op.60 ("Leningrad")   70'
  *3 *3 =4 *3 - 8 6 6 1 - tmp+4 - 2hp, pf - str   VAAP

Symphony no.8, op.65   61'
  *4 *3 =4 *3 - 4 3 3 1 - tmp+5 - str   Breitkopf; VAAP

Symphony no.9, op.70   25'
  *3 2 2 2 - 4 2 3 1 - tmp+2 - str   Breitkopf;
                                                   Kalmus; VAAP

Symphony no.10, op.93   49'
  *3 *3 +3 *3 - 4 3 3 1 - tmp+3 - str   Kalmus; VAAP

Symphony no.11, op.103 ("The year 1905")   59'
  *3 *3 *3 *3 - 4 3 3 1 - tmp+5 - 2-4hp, cel -   Kalmus;
    str   VAAP

Symphony no.12, op.112 ("The year 1917;" or "Lenin")   40'
  *3 3 3 *3 - 4 3 3 1 - tmp+5 - str   Breitkopf;
                                             Kalmus; VAAP

Symphony no.13, op.113 ("Babi Yar")   56'
  bass solo - male chorus   MCA
  *3 *3 =3 *3 - 4 3 3 1 - tmp+4 - 2-4hp, cel, pf - str

Symphony no.14, op.135   55'
  soprano and bass solos   MCA
  2perc - cel - str (10vn, 4va, 3vc, 2db)

Symphony no.15, op.141   43'
  *3 2 2 2 - 4 2 3 1 - tmp+6 - cel - str   MCA

    SHULMAN, ALAN, 1915-

Threnody   6'
  str   Broude, A.

    SIBELIUS, JEAN, 1865-1957

The bard, op.64   6'
  2 2 *3 2 - 4 2 3 0 - tmp+1 - hp - str   Breitkopf

Canzonetta, op.62a   4'
  str   Breitkopf

Concerto, violin, op.47, D minor   32'
  2 2 2 2 - 4 2 3 0 - tmp - str   Kalmus; Lienau

Finlandia, op.26   8'
  2 2 2 2 - 4 3 3 1 - tmp+1 - str   Breitkopf; Kalmus

Humoresque I, op.87, no.1, D minor   4'
  solo violin   Hansen
  2 2 2 2 - 2 0 0 0 - tmp - str

Humoresque II, op.87, no.2, D major   3'
  solo violin   Hansen
  2hn - tmp - str

Karelia overture, op.10   9'
  *3 2 2 2 - 4 3 3 1 - tmp+3 - str   Breitkopf

Karelia suite, op.11   14'
  *3 2 2 2 - 4 3 3 1 - tmp+3 - str   Breitkopf;
  (Optional English horn.)   Kalmus

Kuolema: Valse triste   6'
  1 0 1 0 - 2 0 0 0 - tmp - str   Breitkopf; Kalmus

Legends, op.22

  1. Lemminkäinen and the maidens of Saari   16'
     *2 2 2 2 - 4 3 3 0 - tmp+2 - str   Breitkopf

  2. The swan of Tuonela   10'
     solo English horn   Breitkopf;
     0 1 *1 2 - 4 0 3 0 - tmp+1 - hp - str   Kalmus

  3. Lemminkäinen in Tuonela   17'
     2 *2 *2 2 - 4 3 3 0 - 2perc - str   Breitkopf

  4. Lemminkäinen's return   7'
     *2 2 2 2 - 4 3 3 1 - tmp+3 str   Breitkopf; Kalmus

Night ride and sunrise, op.55   16'
  *3 2 *3 *3 - 4 2 3 1 - tmp+3 - str   Lienau

The Oceanides, op.73   17'
  *3 *3 *3 *3 - 4 3 3 0 - 2tmp - 2hp - str   Breitkopf

Pan and Echo (Dance intermezzo no.3), op.53a   5'
  2 2 2 2 - 4 2 3 0 - tmp+2 - str   Kalmus; Lienau

Pelléas and Mélisande, op.46   23'
  *1 *1 2 2 - 2 0 0 0 - tmp - str   Kalmus; Lienau

Pohjola's daughter, op.49   17'
  *3 *3 *3 *3 - 4 4 3 1 - tmp - hp - str   Kalmus; Lienau

Rakastava, op.14   13'
  str - tmp/triangle   Breitkopf; Kalmus

Romance, op.42, C major   5'
  str   Breitkopf; Luck

A saga (En saga), op.9   20'
  2 2 2 2 - 4 3 3 1 - 2perc - str   Breitkopf; Kalmus

The swan of Tuonela
  See his: Legends, op.22, no.2

Symphony no.1, op.39, E minor   40'
  2 2 2 2 - 4 3 3 1 - tmp+2 - hp - str   Breitkopf; Kalmus

Symphony no.2, op.43, D major   43'
  2 2 2 2 - 4 3 3 1 - tmp - str   Breitkopf; Kalmus

Symphony no.3, op.52, C major   30'
  2 2 2 2 - 4 2 3 0 - tmp - str   Kalmus; Lienau

Symphony no.4, op.63, A minor   33'
  2 2 2 2 - 4 2 3 0 - tmp+1 - str   Breitkopf

Symphony no.5, op.82, E-flat major   30'
  2 2 2 2 - 4 3 3 0 - tmp - str   Hansen

Symphony no.6, op.104, D minor   29'
  2 2 *3 2 - 4 3 3 0 - tmp - hp - str   Hansen

Symphony no.7, op.105, C major   21'
  2 2 2 2 - 4 3 3 0 - tmp - str   Hansen

Tapiola, op.112   18'
  *3 *3 *3 *3 - 4 3 3 0 - tmp - str   Breitkopf

The tempest: Prelude   5'
  *3 2 =3 2 - 4 3 3 1 - tmp+3 - str   Hansen

The tempest: Suite no.1   20'
  *3 2 =3 2 - 4 3 3 1 - tmp+4 - hp - str   Hansen

The tempest: Suite no.2   12'
  2 2 *2 2 - 4 0 0 0 - tmp+1 - hp - str   Hansen

Valse triste
  See his: Kuolema

    SKALKOTTAS, NIKOS, 1904-1949

Five Greek dances   9'
  str   Universal
  Ed. Walter Goehr.

Ten sketches for strings   19'
  str   Universal

SKROWACZEWSKI, STANISŁAW, 1923-

Ricercari notturni   27'
  solo saxophone, doubling on soprano, alto,   EAM
  and baritone, (or solo clarinet, doubling on
  B-flat clarinet and bass clarinet)
  *3 0 0 2 - 2 2 3 1 - tmp+3 - amplified hpsd -
  str 8.8.6.6.4

SLONIMSKY, NICOLAS, 1894-

My toy balloon; variations on a Brazilian tune   6'
  *3 2 2 2 - 2 2 3 1 - tmp+6 - (opt hp),   Shawnee
  pf (doubling on opt cel) - str
Includes popping of balloons at end.

SMETANA, BEDŘICH, 1824-1884

The bartered bride: Overture   7'
  *3 2 2 2 - 4 2 3 0 - tmp - str   Breitkopf; Kalmus

The bartered bride: Three dances   11'
  *3 2 2 2 - 4 2 3 0 - tmp+3 - str   Kalmus
Arr. Hugo Riesenfeld.
  Contents--Polka; Furiant; Dance of the comedians.

Haakon Jarl   10'
  *3 2 *3 2 - 4 2 3 1 - tmp+3 - hp - str   Lengnick;
                          Simrock; Supraphon

My country (Má vlast)

  1. Vyšehrad   12'
    *3 2 2 2 - 4 2 3 1 - tmp+2 - 2hp - str   Breitkopf;
                      Kalmus; Supraphon

  2. The Moldau (Vltava)   12'
    *3 2 2 2 - 4 2 3 1 - tmp+3 - hp - str   Breitkopf;
                      Kalmus; Supraphon

  3. Šárka   9'
    *3 2 2 2 - 4 2 3 1 - tmp+2 - str   Kalmus; Supraphon

  4. From Bohemia's meadows and forests   12'
    *3 2 2 2 - 4 2 3 1 - tmp+2 - str   Breitkopf;
                      Kalmus; Supraphon

My country (Má vlast), cont.

  5. Tábor   13'
    *3 2 2 2 - 4 2 3 1 - tmp+1 - str   Kalmus; Supraphon

  6. Blaník   14'
    *3 2 2 2 - 4 2 3 1 - tmp+2 - str   Kalmus; Supraphon

Richard III   11'
    *3 2 2 2 - 4 2 3 1 - tmp+3 - hp - str   Lengnick;
                                       Supraphon

Wallenstein's camp   14'
    *3 2 2 2 - 4 4 3 1 - tmp+4 - str   Simrock; Supraphon

    SPOHR, LUDWIG, 1784-1859

Concerto, clarinet, op.26, C minor   22'
  2 2 0 2 - 2 2 0 0 - tmp - str   Bärenreiter; Kalmus;
                                Musica Rara; Peters

Concerto, violin, no.8, op.47, A minor
  ("Gesangsszene")   19'
  1 0 2 1 - 2 0 0 0 - tmp - str   Breitkopf;
                                Kalmus; Peters

Concerto, violin, no.9, op.55, D minor   27'
  2 2 2 2 - 2 2 3 0 - tmp - str   Breitkopf; Kalmus

Nonet, op.31, F major   32'
  1 1 1 1 - 1 0 0 0 - vn, va, vc, db   Peters

Octet, op.32, E major   29'
  cl, 2hn - vn, 2va, vc, db   Bärenreiter

    STAMITZ, ANTON, 1754-ca.1809

Concerto, viola, no.4, D major
  str   Breitkopf;
  Ed. Walter Lebermann.   Luck

STAMITZ, JOHANN WENZEL ANTON, 1717-1757

Concerto, flute, C major   25'
  str, cnt   Peters
  Ed. Herbert Koelbel.

Concerto, flute, D major   15'
  str (without violas)   Eulenburg; Kalmus

Concerto, oboe, C major   14'
  str, cnt   Sikorski
  Ed. H. Töttcher and H. F. Hartig.

Concerto, viola, G major   15'
  str, cnt   Peters
  Ed. Rudolf Laugg.

Sinfonia pastorale, op.4, no.2, D major   15'
  0 2 0 0 - 2 0 0 0 - str, cnt   Vieweg

Symphony, op.3, no.3, G major   12'
  str - (2hn opt)   Augener
  Ed. Adam Carse.

Three Mannheim symphonies   Möseler
  str
  Ed. Adolf Hoffmann.

    No.1, G major   11'

    No.2, A major   15'

    No.3, B-flat major   11'

STAMITZ, KARL, 1745-1801

Concerto, bassoon, F major   15'
  0 2 0 0 - 2 0 0 0 - str   Sikorski
  Ed. Johannes Wojciechowski.

Concerto, clarinet, E-flat major   18'
  2 0 0 0 - 2 0 0 0 - str   Hofmeister; Sikorski

Concerto, clarinet, no.3, B-flat major   18'
  0 2 0 0 - 2 0 0 0 - str   Peters
  Ed. Johannes Wojciechowski.

Concerto, clarinet and bassoon, B-flat major   20'
  2hn - str   Sikorski
  Ed. Johannes Wojciechowski.

Concerto, flute, G major   16'
  str   Leuckart
  Ed. Ingo Gronefeld.

Concerto, viola, op.1, D major   22'
  0 0 2 0 - 2 0 0 0 - str   Kalmus; Peters

Concerto, violoncello, no.1, G major   17'
  2 0 0 0 - 2 0 0 0 - str   Bärenreiter
  Ed. Walter Upmeyer.

Concerto, violoncello, no.2, A major   15'
  2 0 0 0 - 2 0 0 0 - str   Bärenreiter
  Ed. Walter Upmeyer.

Concerto, violoncello, no.3, C major   14'
  0 2 0 0 - 2 0 0 0 - str   Bärenreiter
  Ed. Walter Upmeyer.

Sinfonia concertante, D major   20'
  solo violin and solo viola   Kneusslin
  2hn - str

STARER, ROBERT, 1924-

Elegy for strings   3'
  str   MCA

Samson Agonistes   13'
  *3 *3 *3 *3 - 4 3 3 1 - tmp+4 - pf/cel - str   MCA

STEVENS, HALSEY, 1908-

Sinfonia breve   15'
  *2 2 2 2 - 4 2 3 1 - tmp+1 - hp, pf/cel - str   CFE

Symphonic dances   15'
  =3 *3 *3 *3 - 4 3 3 1 - tmp+3 - 2hp, pf/cel -   Peters
    str

STILL, WILLIAM GRANT, 1895-1978

Afro-American symphony   24'
  *3 *3 *4 2 - 4 3 3 1 - tmp+3 - hp, cel,   Novello
  tenor banjo - str

Darker America   13'
  2 *2 2 2 - 1 1 1 0 - 1perc - pf - str   Fischer, C.

Festive overture   10'
  *3 *3 *3 2 - 4 3 3 1 - tmp+4 - hp, cel -   Fischer, J.
  str

STOCKHAUSEN, KARLHEINZ, 1928-

Gruppen, for three orchestras   25'
  =5 *5 =5 3 - 8 6 6 1 - bsx, contrabass tbn -   Universal
  12perc - 2hp, 2cel, pf, electric gtr -
  str 14.12.10.8.6
  One clarinetist also doubles on alto saxophone.
  Three conductors are required.

Kontra-Punkte no.1   12'
  1 0 *2 1 - 0 1 1 0 - hp, pf - vn, vc   Universal

Punkte   21'
  =3 *3 =3 *3 - 3 3 2 1 - tmp+2 - 2hp,   Universal
  2pf (one doubling on cel) - str 8.8.8.6.4
  One oboist also doubles on oboe d'amore.

STRAUSS, JOHANN, JR., 1825-1899

Egyptian march   4'
  *2 2 2 2 - 4 2 3 1 - 5perc - str   Kalmus; Luck

Emperor waltzes (Kaiser-Walzer)   10'
  2 2 2 2 - 4 2 3 0 - tmp+1 - hp - str   Breitkopf;
                                                   Kalmus; Luck

Fledermaus: Overture   9'
  *2 2 2 2 - 4 2 3 0 - tmp+2 - str   Breitkopf;
                                                   Kalmus; Luck

Fledermaus: Du und du   5'
  *2 2 2 2 - 4 2 3 0 - tmp+2 - str   Breitkopf;
                                                   Kalmus; Luck

Graduation ball (arr. Antal Dorati)   48'
  2 2 2 2 - 4 2 3 0 - tmp+4 - hp - str   Belwin

Gypsy baron (Zigeunerbaron): Overture   8'
  *2 2 2 2 - 4 2 3 0 - tmp+3 - hp - str   Kalmus; Luck

Künstler Quadrille, op.201   6'
  *2 2 2 2 - 4 2 1 1 - tmp+1 - str   Luck
    Quotes amusingly from Mendelssohn (Wedding march),
Weber (Oberon and Freischütz), Paganini (Campanella),
Schubert (Wandering), and Berlioz (Rakoczy march).

Morning papers (Morgenblätter)   10'
  *2 2 2 2 - 4 2 1 1 - tmp+2 - str   Luck; Mapleson

On the beautiful blue Danube (An der schönen
  blauen Donau)   9'
  *2 2 2 2 - 4 2 1 1 - tmp+2 - hp - str   Breitkopf;
  (Optional male chorus.)   Kalmus; Luck

Perpetuum mobile, op.257   3'
  *2 2 +2 2 - 4 2 1 0 - tmp+1 - hp - str   Fischer, C.;
                                                   Kalmus; Luck

Pizzicato polka (composed with Josef Strauss)   3'
  *2 2 2 2 - 4 3 3 1 - tmp+2 - str   Luck
  Frequently performed with just strings and
two percussion.

Roses from the south (Rosen aus dem Süden)   7'
  *2 2 2 2 - 4 2 3 0 - tmp+3 - hp - str   Breitkopf;
                                                   Kalmus; Luck

Tales from the Vienna Woods (Geschichten aus
  dem Wienerwald)   11'
  *2 2 2 2 - 4 3 3 1 - tmp+2 - hp,   Breitkopf;
  (opt zither) - str   Kalmus; Luck

Thunder and lightning polka   3'
  *2 2 2 2 - 4 3 3 1 - tmp+3 - str   Kalmus; Luck

Voices of spring (Frühlingsstimmen)   6'
  *2 2 2 2 - 4 2 3 0 - tmp+1 - hp - str   Breitkopf;
                                      Kalmus; Luck

Wiener Blut   7'
  *2 2 2 2 - 4 2 3 0 - tmp+2 - str   Breitkopf;
                                        Kalmus; Luck

Wine, women and song (Wein, Weib, und Gesang)   7'
  *2 2 2 2 - 4 2 3 0 - tmp+2 - hp - str   Breitkopf;
                                        Kalmus; Luck

STRAUSS, JOHANN, SR. 1804-1849

Radetzky march   3'
  *3 2 2 2 - 4 2 3 1 - 2perc - str   Kalmus; Luck

STRAUSS, JOSEF, 1827-1870

Mein Lebenslauf ist Lieb' und Lust   7'
  *2 2 2 2 - 4 4 3 1 - tmp+1 - hp - str   Luck

Music of the spheres (Sphärenklänge)   9'
  2 2 +2 2 - 4 4 3 1 - tmp+2 - hp - str   Kalmus; Luck

Pizzicato polka
  See under: Strauss, Johann, Jr., 1825-1899

Village swallows (Dorfschwalben aus Österreich)   8'
  *2 2 +2 2 - 4 2 1 0 - tmp+3 - hp - str   Kalmus; Luck

STRAUSS, RICHARD, 1864-1949

Eine Alpensinfonie, op.64   47'
  *4 *3 =4 *4 - 20 6 6 2 - heckelphone -   Leuckart
    2tmp, 3perc - 2hp, cel, org - str
  Horns 5-8 double on Wagner tubas.
  (Possible with brass 8 4 5 2.)

Also sprach Zarathustra (Thus spake Zarathustra),
  op.30   34'
  *4 *4 =4 *4 - 6 4 3 2 - tmp+3 - 2hp, org - str   Kalmus;
                                        Peters

Aus Italien, op.16   46'
 *3 *2 2 *3 - 4 2 3 0 - tmp+4 - hp - str   Peters

Der Bürger als Edelmann (Bourgeois gentilhomme): Suite
 *2 *2 2 *2 - 2 1 1 0 - tmp+5, hp, pf -   37'
  6vn, 4va, 4vc, 2db   Leuckart

Burleske   17'
 solo piano   Kalmus
 *3 2 2 2 - 4 2 0 0 - tmp - str

Cäcilie, op.27, no.2   2'
 high voice   Luck; Mapleson;
 2 2 2 2 - 4 2 3 1 - tmp - hp -   Universal
  str 10.10.6.6.4

Concerto, horn, no.1, op.11, E-flat major   17'
 2 2 2 2 - 2 2 0 0 - tmp - str   Kalmus; Universal

Concerto, horn, no.2, E-flat major   25'
 2 2 2 2 - 2 2 0 0 - tmp - str   Boosey

Concerto, oboe, D major   23'
 2 *1 2 2 - 2 0 0 0 - str   Boosey

Death and transfiguration (Tod und Verklärung), op.24   23'
 3 *3 *3 *3 - 4 3 3 1 - tmp+1 - 2hp - str   Kalmus;
                                                 Peters

Don Juan, op.20   17'
 *3 *3 2 *3 - 4 3 3 1 - tmp+3 - hp - str   Kalmus; Peters

Don Quixote, op.35   38'
 solo violoncello, solo viola   Kalmus;
 *3 *3 =3 *4 - 6 3 3 1 - tenor tuba (euphonium) Peters
  - tmp+2 - hp - str

Duet-concertino   19'
 solo clarinet, solo bassoon   Boosey
 str - hp

Four last songs   25'
 high voice   Boosey
 *4 *3 *3 *3 - 4 3 3 1 - tmp - hp, cel - str
  Contents--Frühling; September; Beim Schlafengehen;
 Im Abendroth.

Ein Heldenleben, op.40   40'
  *4 *4 =4 *4 - 8 5 3 1 - tenor tuba -   Kalmus;
    tmp+4 - 2hp - str   Leuckart

Macbeth, op.23   18'
  *3 *3 *3 *3 - 4 3 3 1 - bass tp - tmp+2 - str   Kalmus;
                                                        Peters

Metamorphosen   26'
  23 solo strings: 10vn, 5va, 5vc, 3db   Boosey

Morgen, op.27, no.4   2'
  medium or high voice - solo violin   Luck; Mapleson;
  3hn - hp - str   Universal

Der Rosenkavalier: Suite   22'
  *3 *3 =4 *3 - 4 3 3 1 - tmp+5 - 1 or 2hp,   Boosey
    cel - str
  (May be performed with 3 clarinets, including
  bass clarinet.)

Der Rosenkavalier: Waltzes, first sequence   13'
  3 3 +3 3 - 4 3 3 1 - basset horn - tmp+5 -   Boosey
    2hp (doubling a single part) - str

Salome: Salome's dance   10'
  *4 *3 =6 *4 - 6 4 4 1 - heckelphone - 2tmp,   Boosey;
    6perc - 2hp, cel - str   Kalmus

Serenade, op.7, E-flat major   10'
  2 2 2 *3 - 4 0 0 0   Kalmus;
  (Tuba or double bass may substitute for   Universal
  contrabassoon.)

Six songs after poems by Clemens von Brentano, op.68   24'
  high voice   Boosey;
  *3 *3 *3 *3 - 4 3 3 1 - tmp+2 - 2hp - str   Fürstner
    Contents--An die Nacht; Ich wollt ein
  Sträusslein binden; Säusle, liebe Myrte; Als mir
  dein Lied erklang; Amor; Lied der Frauen.

Suite, op.4, B-flat major   25'
  2 2 2 *3 - 4 0 0 0   Leuckart
  (Tuba may be substituted for contrabassoon.)

Symphonia domestica, op.53   43'
  *4 *3 =5 *5 - 8 4 3 1 - ob d'amore, (4 opt sx: Bote;
  soprano, alto, baritone, bass) - tmp+2 -   Kalmus
  2hp - str

Symphony, op.12, F minor   45'
  2 2 2 2 - 4 2 3 1 - tmp - str   Kalmus; Universal

Symphony for winds, op.posth., E-flat major   36'
  2 2 *4 *3 - 4 0 0 0 - basset horn   Boosey

Three hymns, op.71   29'
  high voice   Boosey
  *3 *3 *4 *3 - 4 3 3 1 - tmp - 2hp, cel - str
    Contents--Hymne an die Liebe; Rückkehr in die
  Heimat; Die Liebe.

Till Eulenspiegels lustige Streiche, op.28   15'
  *4 *4 =4 *4 - 4 3 3 1 - tmp+2 - str   Kalmus;
  (Optional extra brass: 4hn, 3tp.)   Peters

Tod und Verklärung
  See his: Death and transfiguration

Wanderers Sturmlied, op.14   16'
  chorus   Kalmus;
  *3 2 2 *3 - 4 2 3 0 - tmp - str   Universal

    STRAVINSKY, IGOR, 1882-1971

Abraham and Isaac   12'
  baritone solo   Boosey
  +3 *2 *2 2 - 1 2 2 1 - str

Agon   20'
  *3 *3 *3 *3 - 4 4 3 0 - tmp+1 - hp, pf,   Boosey
    mandoline - str

Apollon Musagète   30'
  str   Boosey

Babel   7'
  male chorus - male narrator   Schott
  *3 2 *3 *3 - 4 3 3 0 - tmp - hp - str

Le baiser de la fée (The fairy's kiss)   45'
  *3 *3 *3 2 - 4 3 3 1 - tmp+1 - hp - str   Boosey

Le baiser de la fée (The fairy's kiss): Divertimento   20'
  *3 *3 *3 2 - 4 3 3 1 - tmp+1 - hp - str   Boosey

Canticum sacrum   17'
  chorus - tenor and baritone solos   Boosey
  1. *3 0 *3 - 0 3 3 0 - bass tp, contrabass tbn -
    hp, org - str (without vn or vc)

Capriccio for piano and orchestra   20'
  *3 *3 =3 2 - 4 2 3 1 - tmp - str   Boosey

Le chant du rossignol
  See his: Song of the nightingale

Chorale-variations on "Vom Himmel hoch da komm' ich her"
  chorus   18'
  2 *3 0 *3 - 0 3 3 0 - hp - str (without vn or vc) Boosey
  A "recomposition" of J. S. Bach's Canonic variations
  for organ.

Circus polka   4'
  *2 2 2 2 - 4 2 3 1 - tmp+3 - str   Schott

Concerto for piano and wind instruments   20'
  *3 *3 2 *2 - 4 4 3 1 - tmp - double basses   Boosey

Concerto, violin, D major   21'
  *3 *3 +3 *3 - 4 3 3 1 - tmp - str   Schott

Concerto in D   12'
  str   Boosey

Concerto in E-flat ("Dumbarton Oaks")   12'
  1 0 1 1 - 2 0 0 0 - 3vn, 3va, 2vc, 2db   Schott

Danses concertantes   20'
  1 1 1 1 - 2 1 1 0 - tmp - str   Schott

Ebony concerto   9'
  solo clarinet with jazz orchestra   Boosey
  2asx, 2tsx, bsx - hn, 5tp, 3tbn - pf, hp, gtr,
    db - 1perc

Eight instrumental miniatures   6'
 2 2 2 2 - 1 0 0 0 - 2vn, 2va, 2vc   Chester

The fairy's kiss
 See his: Le baiser de la fée

Le faune et la bergère   9'
 mezzo-soprano solo   Belaieff;
 *3 2 2 2 - 4 2 3 1 - tmp+2 - str Fischer, C.

Firebird (L'oiseau de feu)   44'
 *4 *4 =4 *4 - 4 3 3 1 - tmp+4 - 3hp, cel, Kalmus
  pf - str - backstage: 3tp, 4 Wagner tubas
 Of the woodwinds listed above, 2pic, 2bcl, and
 2cbn are required.

Firebird (L'oiseau de feu): Suite (1911 version) 30'
 *4 *4 =4 *4 - 4 3 3 1 - tmp+4 - 3hp, cel, Chester;
  pf - str   Kalmus
 Of the woodwinds listed above, 2pic, 2bcl, and
 2cbn are required. This work is sometimes
 identified as "First suite from Firebird."
  Contents--Introduction and Kastcheï's enchanted
 garden; Supplications of the Firebird; The princesses
 play with the golden apples; Round dance of the
 princesses; Infernal dance of all the subjects
 of Kastcheï.

Firebird (L'oiseau de feu): Suite (1919 version) 21'
 *2 *2 2 2 - 4 2 3 1 - tmp+3 - hp, pf (dbl Chester;
  on opt cel) - str   Kalmus; Schott
 Reorchestrated by the composer in 1919; sometimes
 identified as "Second suite from Firebird." Both
 score and parts of this version have numerous errors.
  Contents--Introduction; The firebird and its dance;
 The firebird's variation; The princesses' khorovod
 (Round); Infernal dance of King Kastcheï; Lullaby
 (Berceuse); Finale.

Firebird (L'oiseau de feu): Suite (1945 version) 28'
 *2 2 2 2 - 4 2 3 1 - tmp+3 - hp, pf - str MCA
 A reorchestration of the 1919 suite, with the
 insertion of five new sections (Pantomime I through
 Pantomime III, inclusive). Sometimes identified as
 "Third suite from Firebird."
  Contents--Introduction; Prelude and dance of the

firebird; Variations; Pantomime I; Pas de deux;
Pantomime II; Scherzo (Dance of the princesses);
Pantomime III; Rondo; Infernal dance; Lullaby
(Berceuse); Final hymn.

Firebird (L'oiseau de feu): Berceuse and finale   7'
   *2 2 2 2 - 4 2 3 1 - tmp+3 - hp, cel - str   Kalmus; Luck

Fireworks, op.4   5'
   *3 *2 *3 2 - 6 3 3 1 - tmp+4 - 2hp, cel - str   Kalmus;
                                                 Schott

Four etudes for orchestra   12'
   *3 *3 =4 2 - 4 3 2 1 - tmp - hp, pf - str   Boosey

Four Norwegian moods   9'
   *2 *2 2 2 - 4 2 2 1 - tmp - str   Schott

L'histoire du soldat: Suite   30'
   cl, bsn - tp, tbn - 1perc - vn, db   Chester; Kalmus

In memoriam Dylan Thomas   6'
   tenor solo   Boosey
   4tbn - str quartet

Jeu de cartes   21'
   *2 *2 2 2 - 4 2 3 1 - tmp+1 - str   Schott

Mass (1948)   17'
   chorus - solos SATTB   Boosey
   0 *3 0 2 - 0 2 3 0

Monumentum pro Gesualdo di Venosa   7'
   0 2 0 2 - 4 2 3 0 - str   Boosey

Movements for piano and orchestra   10'
   *2 *2 *2 1 - 0 2 3 0 - hp, cel - str   Boosey

Les noces   23'
   chorus - solos SATB   Chester;
   4pf - tmp, 6perc   Kalmus

Octet   15'
   1 0 1 2 - 0 2 2 0   Boosey
   Revised 1952.

Oedipus rex   50'
  male chorus - solos ATTBB - speaker   Boosey
  *3 *3 +3 *3 - 4 4 3 1 - tmp+1 - hp, pf - str

Orpheus   30'
  *3 *2 2 2 - 4 2 2 0 - tmp - hp - str   Boosey

Persephone   48'
  chorus, children's chorus - tenor solo -   Boosey
    female narrator
  *3 *3 *3 *3 - 4 3 3 1 - tmp+1 - 2hp, pf - str
  Revised 1948.

Petrouchka (original version, 1911)   33'
  *4 *4 *4 *4 - 4 4 3 1 - tmp+4 - 2hp, cel,   Kalmus
    pf - str
  A critical edition of the score of this version
  is published by Norton.

Petrouchka (1947 version)   42'
  *3 *3 *3 *3 - 4 3 3 1 - tmp+3 - hp, cel,   Boosey
    pf - str

Pribaoutki (Chansons plaisantes)   6'
  medium voice   Chester
  1 *1 1 1 - vn, va, vc, db

Pulcinella: Suite   24'
  solo string quintet (2vn, va, vc, db)   Boosey
  2 2 0 2 - 2 1 1 0 - str
  Revised 1949.

Rag-time   4'
  1 0 1 0 - 1 1 1 0 - 1perc - cimbalom -   Chester
    2vn, va, db

Requiem canticles   15'
  chorus - alto and bass solos   Boosey
  =4 0 0 2 - 4 2 3 0 - 2tmp, 2perc - hp, cel, pf - str

Le sacre du printemps (The rite of spring)   33'
  =5 *5 =5 *5 - 8 5 3 2 - 2tmp, 4perc - str   Boosey
  Horns 7-8 double on Wagner tubas; one trumpet also
  doubles on bass trumpet. Among the woodwinds, 2pic,
  2Eh, 2bcl, and 2cbn are required. Revised 1947.

Le sacre du printemps: Danse sacral   9'
  =5 *5 =5 *5 - 8 4 3 2 - bass tp - tmp+1 - str   AMP
This 1943 revision of the final portion of the
ballet is much more readily playable than the
original because of rescoring, rebarring, enharmonic
spelling, and larger metric units. Its use is
recommended in conjunction with the complete work,
despite the fact that they come from different
publishers.

Le sacre du printemps (reduced version)   33'
  =3 *3 *3 *3 - 4 3 3 1 - tmp+3 - str   Belwin
Orchestra reduction by Robert Rudolf, with the
sanction of the composer.

Scènes de ballet   16'
  *2 2 2 1 - 2 3 3 1 - tmp - pf - str   AMP

Scherzo à la russe   5'
  *3 2 2 2 - 4 3 3 1 - tmp+4 - hp, pf - str   AMP
Also available in a version for jazz orchestra.

Scherzo fantastique   16'
  =4 *3 =4 *3 - 4 3 0 0 - 1perc - 2hp, cel - str Kalmus;
                                                          Schott

A sermon, a narrative, and a prayer   17'
  chorus - alto and tenor solos - speaker   Boosey
  +2 2 *2 2 - 4 3 3 1 - 2perc - hp, pf - str

Song of the nightingale (Le chant du rossignol)   20'
  *2 *2 +2 2 - 4 3 3 1 - tmp+4 - 2hp, cel,   Boosey
    pf - str

Suite no.1 for small orchestra   6'
  *2 1 2 2 - 1 1 1 1 - 1perc - str   Chester; Kalmus

Suite no.2 for small orchestra   7'
  *2 1 2 2 - 1 1 1 1 - 2perc - pf - str Chester; Kalmus

Symphonies of wind instruments   12'
  3 *3 3 *3 - 4 3 3 1   Boosey
  Revised 1947.

Symphony no.1, E-flat major   29'
  *3 2 3 2 - 4 3 3 1 - tmp+3 - str   Forberg; Kalmus

Symphony in C   30'
  *3 2 2 2 - 4 2 3 1 - tmp - str   Schott

Symphony in three movements (1945)   22'
  *3 2 *3 *3 - 4 3 3 1 - tmp+1 - hp, pf - str   Schott

Symphony of psalms   22'
  chorus   Boosey
  *5 *5 0 *4 - 4 5 3 1 - tmp+1 - hp, 2pf -
    str (without vn or va)

Threni   35'
  chorus - solos SATTBB   Boosey
  2 *3 *3 0 - 4 0 3 1 - sarrusophone, contralto bugle
    (fluegelhorn) - tmp - hp, cel, pf - str
  One clarinetist doubles on alto clarinet.

Two songs by Paul Verlaine   5'
  baritone solo   Boosey
  2 0 2 0 - 2 0 0 0 - str
    Contents--La bonne chanson; Sagesse.

Variations (Aldous Huxley in memoriam)   6'
  +3 *3 *3 2 - 4 3 3 0 - hp, pf - str   Boosey

   SUBOTNICK, MORTON, 1933-

Play no.2   12'
  2 2 *3 2 - 3 2 2 0 - 2-track electronic tape -   MCA
    tmp+1 - str
  Graph notation.

   SUK, JOSEF, 1827-1870

Serenade, op.6   25'
  str   Kalmus; Simrock

   SULLIVAN, ARTHUR, 1842-1900

Overture in C (In memoriam)   13'
  2 2 2 2 - 4 2 3 1 - tmp+2 - org - str   Novello

The tempest: Three dances   11'
    2 2 2 2 - 2 2 3 0 - tmp+2 - str   Novello
        Contents--Masque; Banquet dance; Dance of
    nymphs and reapers.

    SUOLAHTI, HEIKKI, 1920-1936

Sinfonia piccola   25'
    *2 *2 2 2 - 4 3 3 1 - tmp+2 - hp - str   Boosey

    SUPPÉ, FRANZ VON, 1819-1895

Beautiful Galathea: Overture   7'
    *2 2 2 2 - 4 2 3 0 - tmp+2 - str   Kalmus; Luck

Boccacio: Overture
    *2 2 2 2 - 4 2 3 0 - tmp+3 - str   Kalmus

Jolly robbers: Overture   8'
    *2 2 2 2 - 4 2 3 0 - tmp+2 - gtr - str   Alkor; Mapleson

Light cavalry: Overture   8'
    *2 2 2 2 - 4 2 3 0 - 3perc - str   Kalmus; Luck

Morning, noon and night in Vienna: Overture   8'
    *2 2 2 2 - 4 2 3 0 - tmp+2 - str   Kalmus

Pique Dame: Overture   8'
    2 2 2 2 - 4 2 3 1 - tmp+4 - str   Kalmus

Poet and peasant: Overture   10'
    *2 2 2 2 - 4 2 3 1 - tmp+2 - hp - str   Kalmus

    SURINACH, CARLOS, 1915-

Drama jondo   8'
    *3 *3 *3 2 - 4 3 3 1 - tmp+3 - hp - str   AMP

Fandango   8'
    *3 *3 *3 2 - 4 3 3 1 - tmp+2 - hp - str   AMP

Feria magica   6'
    *2 2 2 2 - 4 2 3 1 - tmp+2 - hp - str   AMP

Ritmo jondo   20'
  *1 *1 1 1 - 1 1 1 0 - tmp+4 - str (minimum: AMP
  2.2.2.2.1; maximum: 5.4.4.3.2)

SZYMANOWSKI, KAROL, 1882-1937

Concerto, violin, no.1, op.35   22'
  *3 *3 =4 *3 - 4 3 3 1 - tmp+4 - 2hp, cel,   PWM;
  pf - str   Universal

Konzert-Ouverture, op.12   16'
  *3 *3 =4 *3 - 6 3 3 1 - tmp+3 - hp - str   Universal
  Composed 1905. A revised version for larger
  orchestra, 1913, is available from PWM.

TANSMAN, ALEXANDRE, 1897-

Sinfonietta   15'
  1 1 1 1 - 1 1 2 0 - tmp+2 - pf/cel - str   Universal

Toccata   8'
  *3 *3 *3 *3 - 4 4 3 1 - tmp+5 - hp, cel,   Eschig
  pf - str

Triptych   16'
  str   Eschig

Variations on a theme by Girolamo Frescobaldi   14'
  str   Eschig

TARTINI, GIUSEPPE, 1692-1770

Concerto, violin, no.57, D major   20'
  brass 2 2 0 0 - tmp - str   Zanibon
  Ed. Ettore Bonelli.

Concerto no.58, F major   12'
  0 2 0 0 - 2 0 0 0 - str   Zanibon
  Ed. Ettore Bonelli.

Concerto, violoncello, A major   12'
  str - (opt org)   Zanibon
  Originally for viola da gamba. Ed. Oreste Ravanello.

Sinfonia, D major   13'
  str   Schott
  Ed. Hans Erdmann.

Sinfonia pastorale, D major   11'
  violin solo - str, cnt   Kahnt

   TAYLOR, DEEMS, 1885-1966

Through the looking glass, op.12   32'
  *3 *3 *3 *3 - 4 3 3 1 - tmp+3 - pf - str   Colombo

   TCHAIKOVSKY, PETER ILICH, 1840-1893

Capriccio italien, op.45   15'
  *3 *3 2 2 - 4 4 3 1 - tmp+4 - hp - str   Breitkopf;
                          Kalmus;
                 Universal; VAAP

Concerto, piano, no.1, op.23, B-flat minor   32'
  2 2 2 2 - 4 2 3 0 - tmp - str   Breitkopf; Kalmus;
                            Universal

Concerto, piano, no.2, op.44, G major   34'
  2 2 2 2 - 4 2 0 0 - tmp - str   Alkor; Kalmus; Simrock

Concerto, piano, no.3, op.75, E-flat major   13'
  *3 2 2 2 - 4 2 3 1 - tmp - str   Kalmus;
                          Universal; VAAP

Concerto, violin, op.35, D major   33'
  2 2 2 2 - 4 2 0 0 - tmp - str   Breitkopf; Kalmus;
                            Universal

Coronation march   5'
  *3 *3 2 2 - 4 4 3 1 - tmp+3 - str   Kalmus

Eugen Onegin: Polonaise   4'
  2 2 2 2 - 4 2 3 0 - tmp - str   Kalmus; Simrock

Eugen Onegin: Waltzes   7'
  *3 2 2 2 - 4 2 3 0 - tmp - str   Breitkopf; Kalmus

Fantasy, piano and orchestra, op.56   28'
  3 2 2 2 - 4 2 3 0 - tmp+1 - str   Kalmus;
  The composer provides a special ending,   Universal
  in case the first movement (of two) is to
  be used separately.

Francesca da Rimini, op.32   22'
  *3 *3 2 2 - 4 4 3 1 - tmp+3 - hp - str   Kalmus;
                                                     Universal

Hamlet, op.67   18'
  *3 *3 2 2 - 4 4 3 1 - tmp+3 - str   Alkor; Kalmus;
                                            Universal; VAAP

Manfred, op.58   51'
  *3 *3 *3 3 - 4 4 3 1 - tmp+5 - 2hp - str   Kalmus;
                                               Simrock; VAAP

Marche slave, op.31   10'
  *4 2 2 2 - 4 4 3 1 - tmp+3 - str   Kalmus; Simrock

Mazeppa: Danse cosaque   5'
  *3 *3 2 2 - 4 4 3 1 - tmp+3 - str   Kalmus

Mozartiana
  See his: Suite no.4, op.61, G major

The nutcracker: Suite, op.71a   24'
  *3 *3 *3 2 - 4 2 3 1 - tmp+1 - hp,   Breitkopf;
    cel (or pf) - str   Kalmus;
    Contents--Miniature overture; March;   VAAP
  Dance of the sugar-plum fairy; Russian dance
  (Trepak); Arabian dance; Chinese dance; Dance of
  the reed flutes; Waltz of the flowers.

The nutcracker: Suite no.2
  *3 *3 *3 2 - 4 2 3 1 - tmp+1 - 2hp,   Kalmus
    cel (or pf) - str
    Contents--Scenes and divertissement from Act II;
  Pas de deux; Decorating and lighting of the
  Christmas tree; Little galop of the children and
  entrance of the parents; "Tempo di Grossvater."

Overture 1812, op.49   16'
  *3 *3 2 2 - 4 4 3 1 - tmp+5 - str   Breitkopf;
  Extra brass ad libitum.   Kalmus

Pezzo capriccioso, op.62   7'
 solo violoncello   Luck; Simrock;
 2 2 2 2 - 4 0 0 0 - tmp - str   Universal

Romeo and Juliet   19'
 *3 *3 2 2 - 4 2 3 1 - tmp+2 - hp - str Bote; Kalmus

Serenade, op.48   27'
 str   Breitkopf; Kalmus;
            Peters; VAAP

Sérénade mélancolique, op.26   7'
 solo violin   Fischer, C.;
 2 2 2 2 - 4 0 0 0 - str   Mapleson; Simrock

Sleeping Beauty: Suite, op.66a   23'
 *3 *3 2 2 - 4 4 3 1 - tmp+2 - hp - str   Kalmus;
  Contents--Introduction: La fée des lilas; VAAP
 Adagio: Pas d'action; Pas de caractère: Le
 chat botté et la chatte blanche; Panorama;
 Valse.

Souvenir d'un lieu cher, op.42
 Originally for violin and piano; arr. Glazunov for
 solo violin and orchestra.

  1. Méditation   6'
   solo violin   Fischer, C.;
   2 2 2 2 - 2 0 0 0 - hp - str   Kalmus;
   Originally planned as the slow movement Universal
   for the violin concerto.

  2. Scherzo   6'
   solo violin   Fischer, C.;
   2 2 2 2 - 2 0 0 0 - hp - str Kalmus; Universal

  3. Mélodie   4'
   solo violin   Fischer, C.;
   2 2 2 2 - 2 0 0 0 - str Kalmus; Universal

Suite no.1, op.43, D minor   35'
 *3 2 2 2 - 4 2 0 0 - tmp - str Kalmus; Simrock

Suite no.1, op.43: Marche miniature   2'
 *3 2 2 0 - 2perc - vn I and II, each divisi Kalmus

Suite no.2, op.53, C major   38'
  *3 *3 2 2 - 4 2 3 1 - tmp+3 - hp,   Kalmus;
    (4 opt accordions) - str   Simrock

Suite no.3, op.55, G major   37'
  *3 *3 2 2 - 4 2 3 1 - tmp+3 - str   Kalmus; Simrock

Suite no.4, op.61, G major ("Mozartiana")   25'
  2 2 2 2 - 4 2 0 0 - tmp+1 - hp - str   Kalmus; Universal

Swan lake: Suite, op.20   21'
  *3 2 2 2 - 4 4 3 1 - tmp+3 - hp - str   Kalmus;
    Contents--Scène; Valse; Danses des cygnes;   VAAP
  Scène; Danse hongroise (Czardas); Scène.

Symphony no.1, op.13, G minor ("Winter dreams")   39'
  *3 2 2 2 - 4 2 3 1 - tmp+2 - str   Kalmus; Universal

Symphony no.2, op.17, C minor ("Little Russian")   33'
  *3 2 2 2 - 4 2 3 1 - tmp+2 - str   Kalmus; VAAP

Symphony no.3, op.29, D major ("Polish")   44'
  *3 2 2 2 - 4 2 3 1 - tmp - str   Breitkopf; Kalmus; VAAP

Symphony no.4, op.36, F minor   42'
  *3 2 2 2 - 4 2 3 1 - tmp+3 - str   Breitkopf; Kalmus; VAAP

Symphony no.5, op.64, E minor   50'
  *3 2 2 2 - 4 2 3 1 - tmp - str   Breitkopf; Kalmus; VAAP

Symphony no.6, op.74, B minor ("Pathétique")   47'
  *3 2 2 2 - 4 2 3 1 - tmp+2 - str   Breitkopf;
                                Kalmus; VAAP

Symphony no.7, E-flat major   37'
  *3 2 2 2 - 4 2 3 1 - tmp+3 - hp - str   VAAP
  Reconstructed by S. Bogatyryev.

The tempest (fantasy-overture), op.18   18'
  *3 2 2 2 - 4 2 3 1 - tmp+2 - str   Kalmus
  This work is not to be confused with the
  composer's "L'orage (The tempest): Overture, op.76."

Valse-scherzo, op.34   12'
  solo violin   Kalmus;
  2 2 2 2 - 2 0 0 0 - str   Universal

Variations on a rococo theme, op.33   18'
  violoncello solo   Kalmus;
  2 2 2 2 - 2 0 0 0 - str   Simrock

Le voyévode, op.3: Overture   7'
  3 *3 2 2 - 4 2 3 1 - tmp+3 - str   Kalmus;
  Overture to the opera composed 1867-68.   Universal

Le voyévode, op.78 (symphonic ballad)   10'
  3 *3 *3 2 - 4 2 3 1 - tmp+1 - hp,   Belaieff;
    cel (or pf) - str   Fischer, C.;
  Composed in 1890-91 after Pushkin's   Kalmus
  translation of Mickiewicz's ballad.

TCHEREPNIN, ALEXANDER, 1899-1977

Georgiana suite, op.92   17'
  2 2 2 2 - 4 2 3 1 - tmp+5 - str   Eulenburg

Serenade, op.97   16'
  str   Eulenburg

Symphony no.2, op.77, E-flat major   25'
  *3 *3 *3 *3 - 4 3 3 1 - tmp+6 - hp, cel, pf - str   AMP

TELEMANN, GEORG PHILIPP, 1681-1767

Concert suite, F major   19'
  rec - str, cnt   Nagel
  Ed. Adolf Hoffmann.

Concerto, flute, D major   13'
  str, cnt   Eulenburg
  Ed. Felix Schroeder.

Concerto, flute, E minor   12'
  str, cnt   Kalmus

Concerto, 2 flutes, A minor   10'
  str, cnt   Nagel
  Ed. Fritz Stein.

Concerto, horn, D major   12'
  ob - str, cnt   Peters

Concerto, 2 horns, E-flat major str, cnt Ed. Max Seiffert.	16' Breitkopf
Concerto, oboe, D minor str, cnt Ed. Hermann Töttcher.	14' Sikorski
Concerto, oboe, E minor str, cnt Ed. Hermann Töttcher.	10' Sikorski
Concerto, oboe, F minor str, cnt Ed. Felix Schroeder.	10' Eulenburg
Concerto, recorder, F major str, cnt Ed. Manfred Ruetz.	13' Bärenreiter
Concerto, recorder and flute, E minor str, cnt Ed. Herbert Kölbel.	14' Bärenreiter
Concerto, trumpet, D major 2ob - str, cnt Ed. Hermann Töttcher.	15' Simrock
Concerto, viola, G major str, cnt Ed. Hellmuth Christian Wolff.	12' Bärenreiter
Concerto, violin, A minor str, cnt Ed. Hellmuth Christian Wolff.	10' Bärenreiter
Concerto, 2 violins, C major str, cnt Ed. Adolf Hoffmann.	Möseler

Das ist je gewisslich wahr
   See: Bach, Johann Sebastian, 1685-1750
            Cantata no.141

Don Quichotte   16'
  str, cnt   Kalmus;
  Ed. Gustav Lenzewski.   Vieweg

Ich weiss, dass mein Erlöser lebt
  See: Bach, Johann Sebastian, 1685-1750
      Cantata no.160

Overture in C major   13'
  str (without cnt)   Peters
  Ed. Helmut Mönkemeyer.

Overture in D major   10'
  0 2 0 1 - 2 0 0 0 - str, cnt   Bärenreiter
  Ed. Friedrich Noack.

Overture (Suite), G major
  str, cnt   Vieweg
  Ed. Gustav Lenzewski.

So du mit deinem Munde
  Published as the second movement of Cantata no.145
  by Johann Sebastian Bach.

Suite no.1, A minor   15'
  str, cnt   Kahnt
  Ed. Arnold Schering.

Suite, A minor   31'
  solo recorder   Eulenburg
  str, cnt
  Ed. Horst Buettner.

Suite, F major   17'
  2hn - str (without va), cnt   Eulenburg
  Ed. Horst Buettner.

Suite no.2, G minor   14'
  str, cnt   Kahnt
  Ed. Arnold Schering.

THOMAS, AMBROISE, 1811-1896

Mignon: Overture   8'
  *2 2 2 2 - 4 2 3 0 - tmp+3 - hp - str   Breitkopf; Kalmus

Raymond: Overture   7'
  *2 2 2 2 - 4 2 3 0 - tmp+4 - str   Heugel; Kalmus

   THOMPSON, RANDALL, 1899-

Symphony no.2 (1932)   28'
  *3 *3 3 3 - 4 3 3 1 - tmp - str   Fischer, C.

   THOMSON, VIRGIL, 1896-

Fugue and chorale on Yankee doodle   5'
  1 1 *3 1 - 2 3 2 0 - tmp+1 - str   Schirmer, G.

Louisiana story: Suite   18'
  *2 *2 *2 *2 - 4 2 3 1 - tmp+2 - hp - str   Schirmer, G.

Louisiana story: Boy fights alligator (fugue)   4'
  2 2 2 2 - 4 2 3 1 - tmp+3 - str   Schirmer, G.

Pilgrims and pioneers   10'
  1 *1 *2 1 - 4 2 0 0 - 2perc - str   Schirmer, G.

The plow that broke the plains: Suite   14'
  fl, ob (dbl opt Eh), cl, 2nd cl (dbl   Schirmer, G.
    opt asx), (opt bcl/tsx), bsn -
    brass 2 2 2 0 - tmp+2 - banjo/gtr (or pf
    or hp) - str
  (If bass clarinet and tenor saxophone are both
  lacking, a 2nd bassoon must be added.)

The river: Suite   25'
  *1 *2 *2 1 - 2 2 2 0 - tmp+2 - banjo - str   Southern

Sea piece with birds   5'
  *3 3 3 3 - 4 3 3 0 - 2perc - (opt hp) -   Schirmer, G.
    str

The Seine at night   8'
  *3 *3 *3 *3 - 4 3 3 1 - 1perc - 2hp,   Schirmer, G.
    cel - str

A solemn music, and a joyful fugue   12'
  *3 *3 *3 3 - 4 3 3 1 - tmp+4 - str   Schirmer, G.

Symphony on a hymn tune   19'
  *2 2 2 2 - 4 2 3 1 - tmp+3(or 6) - str   Southern

Wheat field at noon   6'
  *3 *3 *3 *3 - 4 3 3 0 - 3perc - hp - str   Schirmer, G.

    TIPPETT, MICHAEL, 1905-

Concerto for double string orchestra   22'
  str   Schott

Divertimento for chamber orchestra (Sellinger's round) 16'
  1 1 1 1 - 1 1 0 0 - str   Schott

The midsummer marriage: Ritual dances   28'
  (optional chorus)   Schott
  *2 2 2 2 - 4 2 3 0 - tmp+1 - hp, cel - str
  Both flutists double on piccolo.

    TOCH, ERNST, 1887-1964

Circus, an overture   6'
  *3 2 2 2 - 3 3 3 1 - 3perc - pf - str   Mills

Concerto, violoncello, op.35   25'
  *1 1 1 1 - 1 0 0 0 - tmp+1 - 2vn, va, vc, db   Schott

Pinocchio   6'
  *3 2 2 2 - 2 2 3 0 - tmp+2 - str   AMP

    TORELLI, GIUSEPPE, 1658-1709

Concerto, op.6, no.1, G major   7'
  str, cnt   Schott
  Ed. Walter Kolneder.

Concerto, trumpet, D major
  str, cnt   Musica Rara
  Ed. Edward Tarr. A different work from the following.

Concerto, trumpet, D major   10'
  str, cnt   Schott
  Ed. Heinz Zickler. A different work from the preceding.

Concerto, violin, op.8, no.8, C minor   6'
  str, cnt   Eulenburg
  Ed. Ernst Praetorius.

Concerto, violin, op.8, no.9, E minor   14'
  str, cnt   Peters; Ricordi; Suvini

Concerto, 2 violins, op.6, no.10, D minor   5'
  str, cnt   Nagel
  Ed. Hans Engel.

Concerto, 2 violins, op.8, no.1, C major   11'
  str, cnt   Ricordi; Suvini

Concerto, 2 violins, op.8, no.3, E major   7'
  str, cnt   Suvini
  Ed. Piero Santi.

Concerto, 2 violins, op.8, no.7, D minor   9'
  str, cnt   Suvini
  Ed. Piero Santi

Concerto grosso, 2 violins, op.8, no.2, A minor   8'
  str, cnt   Schott
  Ed. Bernhard Paumgartner.

Concerto grosso, 2 violins, op.8, no.5, G major   10'
  str, cnt   Ricordi
  Ed. A. Casella.

Concerto, 2 violins, op.8, no.6, G minor
  ("Christmas concerto")   7'
  str, cnt   Peters; Vieweg

Sinfonia, op.6, no.6, E minor   7'
  str, cnt   Kahnt
  Ed. Arnold Schering.

Sinfonia con tromba, D major   5'
  solo trumpet   King
  str, cnt

TURINA, JOAQUÍN, 1882-1949

Canto a Sevilla   40'
  soprano solo   UME
  *3 2 2 2 - 4 3 3 1 - tmp+2 - hp, cel - str

Danzas fantásticas   16'
  *3 *3 *3 *3 - 4 3 3 1 - tmp+3 - hp - str   UME

La procesion del Rocio   9'
  *3 *3 *3 *3 - 4 3 3 1 - tmp+4 - hp - str   Rouart
  This work may be out of print, but orchestral
  materials are in the Fleisher Collection.

Rapsodia sinfónica   9'
  solo piano - str   UME

Sinfonia sevillana   23'
  *3 *3 *3 *3 - 4 3 3 1 - tmp+2 - hp, cel - str   UME

USSACHEVSKY, VLADIMIR, 1911-

Rhapsodic variations
  See under: Luening, Otto, 1900-

VAŇHAL, JAN KŘTITEL, 1739-1813

Concerto, double bass, E-flat major   18'
  0 2 0 0 - 2 0 0 0 - str   Doblinger
  Score and parts to the same work are also available
  in D major (a result of the scordatura tradition
  among double bass soloists).

Sinfonia, G minor   14'
  0 2 0 1 - 4 0 0 0 - str   Doblinger;
  Peters edition calls for 2hn rather than 4,   Peters
  and uses the German spelling of the composer's
  name (Wanhal).

VARÈSE, EDGARD, 1883-1965

Amériques   29'
  =5 *4 =5 *5 - 8 6 4 2 - heckelphone,   Kerby
    contrabass trombone - 2tmp, 8perc -
    2hp, cel - str
  Revised edition by Chou Wen-chung.

Arcana   16'
  *5 *4 =5 *5 - 8 5 4 2 - heckelphone - tmp+6 - str   Kerby

Deserts   24'
  *2 0 =2 0 - 2 3 3 2 - tmp+4 - pf - 2-channel   Kerby
    magnetic tapes interpolated between instrumental
    sections
  (May be performed without electronic interpolations,
  in which case the duration is 14'.)

Ecuatorial   11'
  several bass voices   Kerby
  brass 0 4 4 0 - tmp+5 - pf, org, ondes martenot

Hyperprism   5'
  *1 0 +1 0 - 3 2 2 0 - 16perc   Kerby
  Revised edition in progress.

Intégrales   11'
  *2 1 +2 0 - 1 2 2 0 - contrabass tbn - 4perc   Kerby
  Revised edition by Chou Wen-chung.

Ionisation   8'
  12perc - pf   Kerby

Nocturnal   7'
  soprano solo - chorus of bass voices   Kerby
  *2 1 +2 1 - 1 2 3 0 - tmp+5 - pf - str
  Edited and completed by Chou Wen-chung.

Octandre   7'
  *1 1 +1 1 - 1 1 1 0 - db   Kerby
  Revised edition by Chou Wen-chung.

Offrandes   9'
  soprano solo   Kerby
  *2 1 1 1 - 1 1 1 0 - 8perc - hp - 2vn, va, vc, db
  (Reinforcement of the string parts authorized to
  the extent of 6.4.4.2.2 total strings.)

VAUGHAN WILLIAMS, RALPH, 1872-1958

Concerto, oboe (1944)   17'
  str   Oxford

Concerto, tuba   16'
  *2 1 2 1 - 2 2 2 0 - tmp+2 - str   Oxford

Concerto, violin, D minor ("Concerto accademico") 16'
  str   Oxford

English folksong suite   10'
  *2 1 2 1 - 2 2 2 0 - tmp+3 - str   Boosey
  Originally for band; arr. for orchestra by
  Gordon Jacob.

Fantasia on a theme by Thomas Tallis   15'
  solo string quartet - string orchestra   Curwen

Fantasia on Greensleeves   4'
  str - hp (or pf) - (1 or 2 optional flutes)   Oxford
  Arr. by Ralph Greaves from the score of
  the opera "Sir John in love."

Five variants of Dives and Lazarus   11'
  str - hp (preferably doubled)   Oxford

Flos campi   18'
  solo viola - chorus (textless)   Oxford
  *1 1 1 1 - 1 1 0 0 - 2perc - hp, cel - str

Hodie (This day)   54'
  chorus - solos STB   Oxford
  *3 *3 2 *3 - 4 3 3 1 - tmp+4 - hp, cel, pf, org - str
  (Possible with: *2 *2 2 2 - 2 2 3 1 - tmp+4 -
  cel, pf - str.)

Job; a masque for dancing   43'
  =3 *3 *3 *3 - 4 3 3 1 - asx - tmp+3 -   Oxford
    2hp, org - str
  (Possible with: *2 *2 2 2 - 4 2 3 1 - tmp+1 - hp - str.)

The lark ascending   13'
  solo violin   Oxford
  2 1 2 2 - 2 0 0 0 - 1perc - str
  (Possible with only one of each wind instrument.)

Prelude "49th parallel"   2'
  2 *2 2 2 - 4 2 3 1 - tmp+1 - hp - str   Oxford
  (Cued so that it may be played by strings and any
  other available parts.)

Serenade to music   14'
  16 solo voices (4S, 4A, 4T, 4B)   Oxford
  *2 *2 2 2 - 4 2 3 1 - tmp+1 - hp - str
  (May be performed by chorus instead of 16 solo voices,
  or by some combination of chorus and 4 or more solo
  voices.)

Symphony no.1 ("A sea symphony")   60'
  soprano and baritone solos - chorus   Galaxy
  *3 *3 =4 *3 - 4 3 3 1 - tmp+4 - 2hp, org - str
  (Playable with: *2 *2 2 2 - 4 3 3 1 - tmp+4 - hp -
  str, by means of cues and special parts for 2nd fl,
  Eh, and 2nd bsn.)

Symphony no.2, G major ("London")   37'
  *3 *3 *3 *3 - 4 4 3 1 - tmp+4 - hp - str   Galaxy
  Revised version. (Playable with winds:
  *2 *2 2 2 - 4 2 3 1.)

Symphony no.3 ("Pastoral")   35'
  solo soprano (or tenor)   Curwen
  *3 *3 *3 2 - 4 3 3 1 - tmp+2 - hp, cel - str
  (Possible without the voice, and with:
  *2 *2 2 2 - 4 2 3 1 - tmp+2 - hp - str.)

Symphony no.4, F minor   32'
  *3 *3 *3 *3 - 4 2 3 1 - tmp+2 - str   Oxford
  (Possible with woodwinds *2 *2 2 2.)

Symphony no.5, D major   35'
  2 *2 2 2 - 2 2 3 0 - tmp - str   Oxford

Symphony no.6, E minor   34'
  *3 *3 *3 *3 - 4 3 3 1 - tmp+3 - hp - str   Oxford
  Bass clarinetist doubles on tenor saxophone.

Symphony no.7 ("Antarctica")   42'
  brief female chorus and solo soprano   Oxford
  *3 *3 *3 *3 - 4 3 3 1 - tmp+4 - hp, cel, pf, org - str

Symphony no.8, D minor   27'
  *2 2 2 3 - 2 2 3 0 - tmp+5 - 2hp, cel - str   Oxford
  (2nd harp, 3rd bassoon, and 5th percussionist
  are optional.)

Symphony no.9, E minor   30'
  *3 *3 *3 *3 - 4 2 3 1 - 2asx, tsx, fluegelhorn -   Oxford
    tmp+3 - 2hp, cel - str
  (2 of the saxophones are optional; 3rd trumpet may
  substitute for fluegelhorn.)

Two hymn-tune preludes   6'
  1 1 1 1 - 1 0 0 0 - str   Oxford
  "Eventide" and "Dominus regit me."

The wasps: Overture   9'
  *2 2 2 2 - 4 2 0 0 - tmp+3 - hp - str   Curwen;
  (Possible with winds *2 1 2 1 - 2 1 0 0.)   Kalmus

The wasps: March past of the kitchen utensils   4'
  *2 2 2 2 - 2 1 0 0 - tmp+2 - str   Curwen
  (2nd oboe and 2nd bassoon are optional.)

  VERACINI, FRANCESCO MARIA, 1690-ca.1750

Aria schiavona   4'
  str, (opt cnt)   Zanibon
  Ed. Franco Margola.

Concerto, violin, D major   6'
  str, cnt   Bärenreiter
  Ed. Bernhard Paumgartner.

Concerto grande da chiesa; or della incoronazione   12'
  solo violin   Zanibon
  0 2 0 0 - 0 2 0 0 - tmp - str, cnt

Menuet et gavotte   4'
  solo violoncello - str   Kalmus; Salabert

Quattro pezzi (from Sonate accademiche)   16'
  str   Zanibon
  Originally for violin and continuo; "elaborated and
  freely interpreted" by Ettore Bonelli.

VERDI, GIUSEPPE, 1813-1901

Aida: Prelude   6'
  *3 2 2 2 - 4 2 3 1 - tmp - str   Leduc; Ricordi

Aida: Triumphal march and ballet   11'
  *3 2 2 2 - 4 4 3 1 - tmp+3 - str   Luck

La forza del destino: Overture   8'
  *2 2 2 2 - 4 2 3 1 - tmp+1 - 2hp - str   Kalmus; Ricordi

Messa da requiem   72'
  chorus - solos SATB   Kalmus; Peters;
  *3 2 2 4 - 4 8 3 1 - tmp+1 - str   Ricordi; Schirmer, G.

Nabucco: Overture   8'
  *2 2 2 2 - 4 2 3 1 - tmp+2 - str   Kalmus; Luck;
                                                              Ricordi

Stabat mater   12'
  chorus   Kalmus; Peters;
  3 2 2 4 - 4 3 4 0 - tmp+1 - hp - str   Ricordi

Te deum   15'
  double chorus - soprano solo   Kalmus; Peters;
  3 *3 *3 4 - 4 3 4 0 - tmp - str   Ricordi

La traviata: Prelude to Act I   4'
  1 1 1 2 - 4 0 0 0 - str   Bärenreiter;
                                                    Kalmus; Ricordi

La traviata: Prelude to Act III   4'
  1 1 2 2 - 1 0 0 0 - str   Kalmus; Luck; Ricordi

I vespri siciliani: Overture   9'
  *2 2 2 2 - 4 4 3 1 - tmp+2 - str   Kalmus; Ricordi

VIEUXTEMPS, HENRI, 1820-1881

Concerto, violin, no.4, op.31, D minor   27'
  2 2 2 2 - 4 2 3 0 - tmp - hp - str   Fischer, C.; Kalmus

Concerto, violin, no.5, op.37, A minor   18'
  1 2 2 2 - 2 2 0 0 - tmp - str   Bote; Fischer, C.;
                                                              Kalmus

VILLA-LOBOS, HEITOR, 1887-1959

Bachianas brasileiras no.1   18'
  8vc   AMP

Bachianas brasileiras no.2   20'
  *1 1 1 *1 - 2 0 1 0 - tsx/bsx - tmp+5 -   Ricordi
  cel, pf - str

Bachianas brasileiras no.3   25'
  solo piano   Colombo
  *3 *3 *3 *3 - 4 2 4 1 - tmp+2 - str

Bachianas brasileiras no.4   19'
  *3 *3 *3 *3 - 4 3 2 1 - tmp+3 - cel - str   Colombo

Bachianas brasileiras no.5   11'
  soprano solo - 8vc   AMP

Bachianas brasileiras no.5: Aria (Cantilena)   7'
  *2 *2 *2 2 - 2 2 2 0 - tmp+7 - cel, (opt hp,   AMP
  opt gtr) - str
Arr. John Krance.

Bachianas brasileiras no.8   20'
  *3 *3 *3 *3 - 4 4 4 1 - tmp+3 - str   Eschig

Bachianas brasileiras no.9   12'
  str   Eschig
For orchestra of voices or of strings.

Chôros no.8   20'
  2 solo pianos   Eschig
  *3 *3 *5 *3 - 4 2 4 1 - asx - tmp+4 - 2hp, cel - str

Chôros no.10 (Rasga o coração)   20'
  chorus   Eschig
  2 2 2 *3 - 3 2 2 0 - asx - tmp+3 - hp, pf - str

Ciranda das sete notas   10'
  solo bassoon - str   Southern

Concerto, guitar and small orchestra (1951)   20'
  1 1 1 1 - 1 0 1 0 - str   Eschig

Fantasia   14'
  solo B-flat saxophone (soprano or tenor)   Southern
  3hn - str

Mômoprecóce; fantaisie pour piano et orchestre   25'
  solo piano   Eschig
  *2 *2 1 *2 - 3 1 1 1 - asx - tmp+2 - str
  An elaboration for piano and orchestra of an earlier
  series of short piano pieces.

Sinfonietta no.1, B-flat major   18'
  2 2 2 2 - 2 2 2 0 - tmp - str   Southern

Sinfonietta no.2, C major   17'
  *1 *1 *1 1 - 3 2 2 1 - asx - tmp+1 -   Southern
  hp, cel - str

Suite for strings   14'
  str   Eschig

Uirapurú (The magic bird)   18'
  *3 *3 *3 *3 - 4 3 3 1 - ssx - tmp+2 - 2hp, cel,   AMP
  pf - violinophone - str

    VIOTTI, GIOVANNI BATTISTA, 1755-1824

Concerto, piano, G minor   41'
  2 2 2 2 - 2 2 0 0 - tmp - str   Ricordi

Concerto, violin, no.19, G minor   33'
  2 2 2 0 - 2 0 0 0 - str   Ricordi

Concerto, violin, no.22, A minor   27'
  1 2 2 2 - 2 2 0 0 - tmp - str   Breitkopf; Kalmus

    VITALI, TOMASO ANTONIO, ca.1665-?

Ciaccona (arr. Guido Guerrini)   18'
  violin solo - str, (opt cnt)   Zanibon
  Sometimes attributed to Giovanni Battista Vitali
  (1632-1692), father of Tomaso. Probably it is by
  neither of the Vitalis, but rather by an unknown
  composer of the period.

VIVALDI, ANTONIO, 1678-1741

Concerto, bassoon, P.46, C major | 11'
str, cnt | Ricordi
Ed. Gian Francesco Malipiero.

Concerto, bassoon, P.70, A minor | 10'
str, cnt | Ricordi

Concerto, bassoon, P.137, E minor | 10'
str, cnt | Ricordi

Concerto, bassoon, P.318, F major | 10'
str, cnt | Peters
Ed. Walter Kolneder.

Concerto, flute, op.10, no.2, P.342, G minor
("La notte") | 12'
solo flute or recorder | AMP;
bsn - str, cnt | Ricordi

Concerto, flute, op.10, no.3, P.155, D major
("Bullfinch") | 11'
ob, bsn - vn, cnt | AMP;
Also known as "Il cardellino," "Del | Peters;
gardellino," and "The goldfinch." | Ricordi

Concerto, flute, oboe and bassoon, P.261, op.44,
no.16 ("La tempesta di mare") | 8'
str, cnt | Eulenburg
Ed. Felix Schroeder. Flute part possibly
intended for recorder.

Concerto, guitar, P.209, D major | 11'
str, cnt | Peters
Ed. Dick Visser. Originally for lute.

Concerto, 2 horns, P.320, F major | 7'
str, cnt | Ricordi

Concerto, 2 horns, P.321, F major | 9'
str, cnt | Ricordi

Concerto, mandoline, P.134, C major | 7'
str, cnt | Ricordi
Ed. Gian Francesco Malipiero.

Concerto, oboe, P.41, C major 15'
   str, cnt   Ricordi

Concerto, oboe, P.259, op.8, no.9, D minor 8'
   str, cnt   Ricordi

Concerto, oboe, P.306, F major 10'
   str, cnt   Ricordi

Concerto, oboe and bassoon, P.129, op.42, no.3,
   G major 11'
   str, cnt   Eulenburg
   Ed. Felix Schroeder.

Concerto, oboe and violin, P.406, B-flat major 9'
   str, cnt   Ricordi

Concerto for orchestra, P.143, G major ("Alla rustica") 4'
   str, cnt   Peters; Ricordi

Concerto for orchestra, P.407, G minor 12'
   str, cnt   Ricordi

Concertos, piccolo
   *It is not known what instrument Vivaldi had in
   mind for these concertos. The term he used was
   "flautino," which could have been sopranino recorder
   or flageolet. The modern transverse piccolo flute
   did not yet exist.*

Concerto, piccolo, P.79, C major 11'
   str, cnt   Eulenburg; Ricordi

Concerto, piccolo, P.83, A minor 10'
   str, cnt   Ricordi
   Ed. Gian Francesco Malipiero.

Concerto, recorder, P.440, op.44, no.19, C minor 13'
   str, cnt   Eulenburg
   Ed. Felix Schroeder.

Concerto, 2 trumpets, P.75, C major 7'
   str, cnt   Ricordi

Concertos, violin, op.8, nos.1-4
   See his: The four seasons

Concerto, violin, op.8, no.5, P.415, E-flat major
("La tempesta di mare")   8'
str, cnt   Ricordi

Concerto, violin, op.8, no.6, P.7, C major
("Il piacere")   8'
str, cnt   Ricordi

Concerto, violin, op.8, no.7, P.258, D minor   7'
str, cnt   Ricordi

Concerto, violin, op.8, no.8, P.337, G minor   9'
str, cnt   Ricordi

Concerto, violin, op.8, no.10, P.338, B-flat major
("La caccia")   8'
str, cnt   Ricordi

Concerto, violin, op.8, no.11, P.153, D major   13'
str, cnt   Ricordi

Concerto, violin, op.8, no.12, P.8, C major   9'
str, cnt   Ricordi

Concerto, 2 violins, op.3, no.8, P.2, A minor   11'
str, cnt   Peters

Concerto, violin and violoncello, P.388, B-flat major   11'
str, cnt   Ricordi

Concerto, violoncello, P.24, A minor   10'
str, cnt   Luck; Ricordi

Concerto, violoncello, P.35, op.26, no.17, A minor   10'
str, cnt   Peters
Ed. Walter Kolneder.

Concerto, violoncello, P.282, op.26, no.9, D minor   12'
str, cnt   Eulenburg
Ed. Felix Schroeder.

Concerto, violoncello, P.434, C minor   11'
str, cnt   Ricordi

Concerto, 2 violoncellos, P.411, G minor   10'
str, cnt   Eulenburg; Ricordi

The four seasons, op.8, nos.1-4

    1. La primavera (Spring)   11'
       solo violin   Carisch; Eulenburg;
       str, cnt   Kalmus; Ricordi

    2. L'estate (Summer)   10'
       solo violin   Carisch; Eulenburg;
       str, cnt   Kalmus; Ricordi

    3. L'autunno (Autumn)   11'
       solo violin   Carisch; Eulenburg;
       str, cnt   Kalmus; Ricordi

    4. L'inverno (Winter)   11'
       solo violin   Carisch; Eulenburg;
       str, cnt   Kalmus; Ricordi

Gloria   31'
      chorus - solos SSA   Kalmus;
      0 1 0 0 - 0 1 0 0 - str, cnt   Peters;
      Kalmus edition by Clayton Westermann; Walton   Walton
      edition by Mason Martens. Peters edition
      lists solos SA only.

Gloria (arr. Alfredo Casella)   31'
      chorus - solos SSA   Ricordi
      0 2 0 0 - 0 2 0 0 - org - str
      Altered and romanticized. Vocal and orchestral
      parts for this version are not compatible with
      those of other editions.

Magnificat (ed. G. F. Malipiero)   15'
      chorus - solos SSAT   Ricordi
      0 2 0 0 - str, cnt
      Includes five longer virtuoso arias which may be
      substituted for portions of the original version;
      in this case, the 2 oboes are not required.

Magnificat (ed. H. C. Robbins Landon)   15'
      chorus - solos SSATB   Universal
      0 2 0 2 - 0 0 3 0 - cornetto - str, cnt
      (Winds are optional.)

Sinfonia, P.sinf.21, B minor ("Al santo sepolcro") 6'
      str (without cnt)   Ricordi

Sinfonia nos. 1 and 2   6' each
  str, cnt   Peters
  Ed. Ludwig Landshoff.

Sinfonia no.3, G major   6'
  str, cnt   Peters
  Ed. Ludwig Landshoff.

WAGENSEIL, GEORG CHRISTOPH, 1715-1777

Concerto, harpsichord, D major   16'
  str (without va)   Breitkopf

Concerto, violoncello, A major   10'
  str, cnt   Doblinger
  Ed. Enrico Mainardi and Fritz Racek.

Concerto, violoncello, C major   22'
  0 2 0 0 - 2 2 0 0 - str, (opt cnt)   Doblinger
  (Trumpets are optional.) Ed. Fritz Racek.

Sinfonia, G minor   15'
  0 2 0 1 - str, cnt   Universal
  Ed. Alison Copland.

WAGNER, RICHARD, 1813-1883

Adagio, clarinet and strings, D-flat major   4'
  str   Kalmus
  Actual composer is believed to be Heinrich
  Joseph Bärmann, 1784-1847.

A Faust overture   12'
  *3 2 2 3 - 4 2 3 1 - tmp - str   Breitkopf; Kalmus

Der fliegende Holländer: Overture   11'
  *3 *2 2 2 - 4 2 3 1 - tmp - hp - str Breitkopf; Kalmus

Götterdämmerung: Brünnhilde's immolation   18'
  soprano solo   Kalmus;
  *4 *4 *4 3 - 8 3 4 1 - bass tp - 2tmp, 3perc -   Schott
   6hp (doubling 2 real parts) - str
  Horns 5-8 double on Wagner tubas.

Götterdämmerung: Siegfried's funeral music   8'
  *4 *4 *4 3 - 4 3 4 1 - bass tp, 4 Wagner   Breitkopf;
    tubas - 2tmp, 3perc - 6hp (doubling   Kalmus;
    2 real parts) - str   Schott

Götterdämmerung: Siegfried's Rhine journey   10'
  *3 2 2 2 - 4 3 3 1 - tmp+2 - hp - str   Kalmus;
  Arr. Humperdinck. An insert (available on   Schott
  rental from Luck) restores 45 bars omitted by
  Humperdinck; it includes additional parts (not essential)
  for Eh, bcl, and 3rd bsn. Duration with insert: 13'

Grosser Festmarsch (American centennial march)   12'
  *4 3 3 *4 - 4 3 3 1 - bass tp - tmp+4 - str   Luck;
                                  Schott

Huldigungsmarsch   7'
  *3 2 *3 2 - 4 3 3 1 - tmp+4 - str   Kalmus; Schott

Kaiser-Marsch   9'
  *3 3 3 3 - 4 3 3 1 - tmp+4 - str   Luck

Lohengrin: Prelude, Act I   8'
  3 *3 *3 3 - 4 3 3 1 - tmp+1 - str   Breitkopf; Kalmus

Lohengrin: Prelude, Act III   3'
  3 3 3 3 - 4 3 3 1 - tmp+3 - str   Breitkopf; Kalmus

Lohengrin: Procession to the cathedral   4'
  (opt double male chorus and chorus of   Breitkopf;
    women and boys)   Kalmus
  3 *3 *3 3 - 4 3 3 1 - tmp - str

Die Meistersinger: Prelude   9'
  *3 2 2 2 - 4 3 3 1 - tmp+2 - hp - str   Breitkopf;
                           Kalmus; Schott

Die Meistersinger: Three excerpts from Act III   17'
  *3 2 2 2 - 4 3 3 1 - tmp+2 - hp - str   Breitkopf;
    Contents--Introduction to Act III;   Kalmus
  Dance of the apprentices; Procession of
  the Meistersingers.

Parsifal: Prelude   13'
  3 *4 3 *4 - 4 3 3 1 - tmp - str   Breitkopf; Kalmus

Parsifal: Good Friday spell (Charfreitagszauber)   11'
  3 *4 *4 *4 - 4 3 3 1 - tmp - str   Breitkopf;
                                Kalmus; Schott

Das Rheingold: Entry of the gods into Valhalla   9'
   2 2 2 2 - 4 3 3 1 - tmp+1 - hp - str   Kalmus;
   Arr. H. Zumpe.   Schott

Rienzi: Overture   12'
   *3 2 2 *3 - 4 4 3 1 - tmp+4 - str   Breitkopf; Kalmus

Rule Britannia!   10'
   *4 2 +3 *3 - 4 4 3 1 - tmp+4 - str   Kalmus
   Two of the flutists play piccolo.

Siegfried: Forest murmurs (Waldweben)   9'
   *2 2 2 2 - 4 2 3 0 - tmp+1 - str   Kalmus;
   Schott version requires tuba also. Breitkopf   Schott
   publishes a version ed. by W. Hutschenruyter,
   for larger orchestra.

Siegfried idyll   18'
   1 1 2 1 - 2 1 0 0 - str   Breitkopf;
   Although in the first performance of this   Kalmus
   work Wagner used only one string player to
   a part, he thereafter used orchestral strings.

Symphony, C major   26'
   2 2 2 *3 - 4 2 3 0 - tmp - str   Kalmus; Luck

Tannhäuser: Overture (Dresden version)   14'
   *3 2 2 2 - 4 3 3 1 - tmp+3 - str   Breitkopf; Kalmus

Tannhäuser: Overture and Venusberg music
   (Paris version)   21'
   *3 2 2 2 - 4 3 3 1 - 2tmp, 4perc - hp - str
   To play this composite concert piece it is necessary
   to have sets of parts for both the Overture and the
   Venusberg music. Play the Overture through the 16th
   bar after letter F; then cut to the 29th bar of the
   Venusberg music.

Tannhäuser: Arrival of the guests at Wartburg   8'
   3 2 2 2 - 4 3 3 1 - tmp+3 - str   Breitkopf; Kalmus

Tannhäuser: Prelude to Act III   8'
   *3 2 2 2 - 4 3 3 1 - tmp - str   Breitkopf

Tannhäuser: Venusberg music (Bacchanale)   12'
   *3 2 2 2 - 4 3 3 1 - 2tmp, 4perc - hp - str   Kalmus

Tristan und Isolde: Prelude and Liebestod   17'
  (optional soprano solo)   Breitkopf;
  *3 *3 *3 3 - 4 3 3 1 - tmp - hp - str   Kalmus

Tristan und Isolde: Nachtgesang   10'
  2 *3 *3 3 - 4 1 3 1 - tmp - hp - str   Breitkopf;
  Arr. Arthur Seidel. (Eh, bcl, 3rd bsn   Fischer, C.
  are optional.)

Tristan und Isolde: Prelude to Act III   9'
  0 *2 2 2 - 4 0 0 0 - tmp - str   Kalmus

Die Walküre: Ride of the Valkyries   5'
  *4 *4 *4 3 - 8 3 4 1 - tmp+3 - str   Luck;
  Two of the flutists play piccolo.   Schott

Die Walküre: Ride of the Valkyries (arr.
  Wouter Hutschenruyter)   5'
  *3 *3 *4 3 - 6 3 3 1 - tmp+3 - str   Breitkopf;
                                                     Fischer, C.

Die Walküre: Wotan's farewell and Magic fire music   18'
  *2 2 2 2 - 4 2 3 1 - tmp+3 - hp - str   Kalmus; Schott

Wesendonck songs
  Originally for soprano and piano.

  1. Der Engel (orchestrated by Felix Mottl)   3'
     soprano solo   Kalmus;
     2 2 2 2 - 2 0 0 0 - str   Luck

  2. Stehe still (orchestrated by Felix Mottl)   4'
     soprano solo   Kalmus;
     2 2 2 2 - 4 1 0 0 - tmp - str   Luck

  3. Im Treibhaus (orchestrated by Felix Mottl)   6'
     soprano solo   Kalmus;
     2 2 2 2 - 3 0 0 0 - str   Luck

  4. Schmerzen (orchestrated by Felix Mottl)   3'
     soprano solo   Kalmus;
     2 2 2 2 - 4 1 0 0 - str   Luck

  5. Träume (orchestrated by Wagner)   5'
     soprano solo (or violin solo; Wagner's   Kalmus;
       specification)   Luck
     0 0 2 2 - 2 0 0 0 - str

WALDTEUFEL, EMIL, 1837-1915

Les patineurs (Skaters' waltz)   8'
  *2 2 2 2 - 4 2 3 1 - tmp+2 - str   Kalmus; Luck

WALTON, WILLIAM, 1902-

Belshazzar's feast   35'
  chorus - baritone solo   Oxford
  *3 2 =3 *3 - 4 9 9 3 - asx (or Eh) - tmp+4 -
    2hp, (opt pf), org - str
  (6tp, 6tbn, and 2 of the tubas are optional.)

Concerto, viola   23'
  *2 *2 *2 2 - 4 2 3 0 - tmp - hp - str   Oxford
  Revised 1962.

Crown imperial (Coronation march)   7'
  *3 *3 *3 *3 - 4 3 3 1 - tmp+3 - hp,   Oxford
    (opt org) - str
  (Playable with winds reduced to: 2 2 2 2 - 4 2 3 0.)

Façade   43'
  reciter   Oxford
  fl/pic, cl/bcl - tp - asx - 1perc - 1 or 2vc

Façade: Suite no.1   10'
  *2 *2 2 2 - 4(or 2) 2 1 1 - tmp+3 - str   Oxford
    Contents--Polka; Valse; Swiss jodelling song;
  Tango - Pasodoblé; Tarantella, Sevillana.

Façade: Suite no.2   9'
  *2 *3 2 2 - 2 2 1 0 - asx - 1perc - str   Oxford
  (Either the saxophone or the English horn
  may be omitted.)
    Contents--Fanfare; Scotch rhapsody; Country dance;
  Noche espagnole; Popular song; Old Sir Faulk.

Hamlet and Ophelia   14'
  *2 *2 2 2 - 4 2 3 0 - tmp+2 - hp, cel - str   Oxford

Johannesburg festival overture   7'
  *3 *3 3 *3 - 4 3 3 1 - tmp+3 - hp - str   Oxford
  Reduced version by Vilem Tausky available, for:
  2 *2 2 2 - 4 2 3 (opt tuba) - tmp+1(or 2) - hp - str

Portsmouth Point   6'
  *3 *3 *3 *3 - 4 3 3 1 - tmp+4 - str   Oxford
  Reduced version by Constant Lambert available, for:
  *2 1 2 1 - 2 2 1 0 - 1 or 2perc - str.

Symphony no.1   42'
  *2 2 2 2 - 4 3 3 1 - 2tmp, 2perc - str   Oxford

Symphony no.2   27'
  *3 *3 =3 *3 - 4 3 3 1 - tmp+4 - 2hp, cel,   Oxford
    pf - str

    WANHAL, JOHANN BAPTIST, 1739-1813
      See: Vaňhal, Jan Křtitel, 1739-1813

    WAŃSKI, JAN, ca.1760-ca.1830

Symphony in D major   22'
  2 0 0 0 - 1 0 0 0 - str   PWM
  On themes from the overture to the opera "Pasterz
  nad Wisła" ("The shepherd by the Vistula").

Symphony in G major   19'
  2 0 0 0 - 1 0 0 0 - str   PWM
  On themes from the overture to the opera
  "Kmiotek" ("The peasant").

    WARD, ROBERT, 1917-

Adagio and allegro   12'
  *2 *2 2 2 - 4 3 3 1 - tmp+1 - str   Peer

Euphony for orchestra   10'
  *2 *2 2 2 - 4 2 3 1 - tmp+1 - str   Highgate

Jubilation; an overture   7'
  *3 *3 *3 *3 - 4 3 3 1 - tmp - pf - str   Highgate

WARLOCK, PETER, 1894-1930

Capriol suite   10'
  *2 2 2 2 - 2 2 3 1 - 1perc - str   Curwen
  Also available from Curwen in a version
  for string orchestra.

WEBER, BEN, 1916-1979

Dolmen   9'
  0 2 0 1 - 2 0 0 0 - str   Marks

Symphony on poems of William Blake, op.33   32'
  baritone solo   CFE
  *1 1 *2 1 - 1 0 1 0 - 1perc - hp, cel - vc

WEBER, CARL MARIA VON, 1786-1826

Abu Hassan: Overture   4'
  *2 2 2 2 - 2 2 1 0 - tmp+3 - str   Breitkopf; Kalmus

Andante and Rondo ongarese, op.35   5'
  solo bassoon or viola   Fischer, C.;
  2 2 0 2 - 2 2 0 0 - tmp - str   Luck; Peters

Aufforderung zum Tanz
  See his: Invitation to the dance

Beherrscher der Geister
  See his: Ruler of the spirits

Concertino, clarinet and orchestra, op.26, E-flat major 10'
  1 2 0 2 - 2 2 0 0 - tmp - str   Breitkopf; Kalmus

Concertino, horn and orchestra, op.45, E major   12'
  1 0 2 2 - 2 2 0 0 - tmp - str   Kalmus; KaWe

Concerto, bassoon, op.75, F major   15'
  2 2 0 2 - 2 2 0 0 - tmp - str   Breitkopf; Kalmus

Concerto, clarinet, no.1, op.73, F minor   18'
  2 2 0 2 - 3 2 0 0 - tmp - str   Breitkopf; Kalmus

Concerto, clarinet, no.2, op.74, E-flat major   20'
  2 2 0 2 - 2 2 0 0 - tmp - str   Breitkopf; Kalmus

Concerto, piano, no.1, op.11, C major   18'
  2 2 0 2 - 2 2 0 0 - tmp - str   Kalmus

Concerto, piano, no.2, op.32, E-flat major   21'
  2 0 2 2 - 2 2 0 0 - tmp - str   Kalmus

Euryanthe: Overture   8'
  2 2 2 2 - 4 2 3 0 - tmp - str   Breitkopf; Kalmus

Der Freischütz: Overture   10'
  2 2 2 2 - 4 2 3 0 - tmp - str   Breitkopf; Kalmus

Invitation to the dance (Aufforderung zum Tanz),op.65   9'
  *2 2 2 4 - 4 4 3 0 - tmp - 2hp - str   Breitkopf;
  Orchestrated by Hector Berlioz.   Kalmus

Jubel overture, op.59   8'
  *4 2 2 2 - 4 2 3 0 - tmp+3 - str   Breitkopf;
  Two of the flutists play piccolo.   Kalmus

Konzertstück, piano and orchestra, op.79, F minor   17'
  2 2 2 2 - 2 2 1 0 - tmp - str   Breitkopf; Kalmus

Oberon: Overture   9'
  2 2 2 2 - 4 2 3 0 - tmp - str   Breitkopf; Kalmus

Peter Schmoll: Overture   8'
  2 2 0 2 - 2 2 0 0 - tmp - str   Breitkopf

Polonaise brillante, piano and orchestra, op.72   8'
  2 2 2 2 - 2 2 3 0 - tmp+2 - str   Fischer, C.;
  Orchestrated by Franz Liszt.   Kalmus; Luck

Preziosa: Overture   9'
  2 2 2 2 - 2 2 0 0 - tmp+4 - str   Breitkopf; Kalmus

Ruler of the spirits (Beherrscher der
  Geister): Overture   7'
  *2 2 2 2 - 4 2 3 0 - tmp - str   Breitkopf;
  A revision of the earlier "Rübezahl overture."   Kalmus

Silvana: Overture   5'
  2 2 2 2 - 2 2 1 0 - tmp - str
  This work is out of print, but orchestral
  materials are in the Fleisher Collection.

Symphony no.1, C major   23'
  1 2 0 2 - 2 2 0 0 - tmp - str   Alkor; Kalmus

Symphony no.2, C major   17'
  1 2 0 2 - 2 2 0 0 - tmp - str   Alkor; Kalmus

   WEBERN, ANTON, 1883-1945

Das Augenlicht, op.26   7'
  chorus   Universal
  1 1 1 0 - 1 1 1 0 - asx - tmp+2 - hp, cel,
    mandoline - str (without db)

Cantata no.1, op.29   8'
  chorus - soprano solo   Universal
  1 1 *2 0 - 1 1 1 0 - tmp+2 - hp, cel,
    mandoline - str

Cantata no.2, op.31   13'
  chorus - solos SB   Universal
  *2 *2 *2 1 - 1 1 1 1 - asx - 1perc -
    hp, cel - str

Concerto, op.24   8'
  1 1 1 0 - 1 1 1 0 - pf - vn, va   Universal

Five movements, op.5   11'
  str   Universal
  Arranged by the composer from a work for
  string quartet.

Five pieces for orchestra, op.10   6'
  *1 1 =2 0 - 1 1 1 0 - 4perc - hp, cel,   Universal
    harm, gtr, mandoline - vn, va, vc, db

Geistliche Lieder, op.15   6'
  high voice   Universal
  1 0 *1 0 - 0 1 0 0 - hp - vn/va

Im Sommerwind   12'
  3 *3 *5 2 - 6 2 0 0 - tmp+2 - 2hp - str   Fischer, C.

Lieder, op.8   3'
  medium voice   Universal
  0 0 *1 0 - 1 1 0 0 - hp, cel - vn, va, vc

Lieder, op.13   6'
  soprano solo   Universal
  *1 0 *2 0 - 1 1 1 0 - 1perc - hp, cel - vn, va, vc, db

Lieder, op.14   8'
  high voice   Universal
  cl, bcl - vn, vc

Lieder, op.19   2'
  chorus   Universal
  cl, bcl - cel, gtr - vn

Passacaglia, op.1   11'
  *3 *3 *3 *3 - 4 3 3 1 - tmp+2 - hp - str   Universal

Six pieces for orchestra, op.6   12'
  *2 2 *3 *2 - 4 4 4 1 - tmp+5 - hp, cel - str   Universal
  Revised version, 1928.

Symphony, op.21   10'
  0 0 *2 0 - 2 0 0 0 - hp - str (without db)   Universal

Variations for orchestra, op.30   8'
  1 1 *2 0 - 1 1 1 1 - tmp - hp, cel - str   Universal

   WEILL, KURT, 1900-1950

Aufstieg und Fall der Stadt Mahagonny: Suite   25'
  *2 1 1 2 - 2 2 2 1 - asx, tsx/ssx - tmp+2 -   Universal
   pf, bass gtr, banjo - str
  Tuba doubles on 3rd trombone.

Kleine Dreigroschenmusik (Suite from "Threepenny
  opera")   21'
  *2 0 2 2 - 0 2 1 1 - asx, tsx (dbl opt ssx)   Universal
   - tmp+1 - pf, banjo (dbl gtr and bandoneon
   ad lib.)

Symphony no.1 (1921)   22'
  *2 1 *2 2 - 2(or 4) 1 1 0 - tmp+4 - str   Schott

Symphony no.2 (1933)   28'
  *2 2 2 2 - 2 2 2 0 - tmp - str   Heugel

    WEINBERGER, JAROMIR, 1896-1967

Schwanda the bagpiper: Polka and fugue   11'
  *3 2 2 2 - 4 3 3 1 - tmp+4 - hp, (opt org) - str   AMP
  4 additional trumpets backstage playing in unison.

Under the spreading chestnut tree (variations
  and fugue on an old English tune)   16'
  *3 2 2 2 - 4 3 3 1 - tmp+3 - hp, pf - str   AMP
  Two of the flutists play piccolo.

    WEISS, ADOLPH, 1891-1971

American life (Scherzo jazzoso)   6'
  *3 *3 *3 *3 - 4 3 3 1 - ssx, asx, tsx - tmp+4 - str
  This work is out of print, but orchestral
  materials are in the Fleisher Collection.

I segreti   12'
  *3 *3 *3 *3 - 4 4 3 1 - tmp+3 - hp, cel - str
  This work is out of print, but orchestral
  materials are in the Fleisher Collection.

    WELLESZ, EGON, 1885-1974

Suite, violin and chamber orchestra, op.38   18'
  violin solo   Universal
  1 *1 1 1 - va, vc

    WERNICK, RICHARD, 1934-

Visions of terror and wonder   28'
  solo mezzo-soprano   Presser
  =4 *4 =4 *4 - 4 3 3 1 - 2tmp, 5perc - hp, cel - str
  The above woodwinds include 2 piccolos,
  2 alto flutes, and 2 E-flat clarinets.

WIENIAWSKI, HENRI, 1835-1880

Concerto, violin, no.1, op.14, F-sharp minor   22'
  2 2 2 2 - 2 2 3 0 - tmp - str   Fischer, C.;
                                    Kalmus; PWM

Concerto, violin, no.2, op.22, D minor   19'
  2 2 2 2 - 2 2 3 0 - tmp - str   Kalmus; PWM; Schott

Legend, violin and orchestra, op.17   9'
  2 2 2 2 - 2 0 0 0 - tmp - str   Fischer, C.;
                                    Kalmus; PWM

Polonaise brillante no.1, op.4 (Polonaise de
  concert), D major   6'
  solo violin   Fischer, C.;
  2 2 2 2 - 2 2 2 0 - tmp - str   Luck; PWM

Polonaise brillante no.2, op.21, A major   7'
  solo violin   Fischer, C.;
  2 2 2 2 - 2 2 3 0 - tmp - str   Kalmus;
  Ed. Robert M. Wrobel.   PWM

Scherzo-tarantelle, op.16   6'
  solo violin   Kalmus;
  2 2 2 2 - 2 2 0 0 - tmp+2 - str   Sikorski
  Orchestrated by Paul Gilson. (Trumpets are optional.)

WILDER, ALEC, 1907-1980

Carl Sandburg suite   16'
  *2 *2 2 2 - 2 2 2 0 - tmp+1 - hp - str   AMP

Concerto, oboe   24'
  str - tmp+2   AMP

WITT, FRIEDRICH, 1770-1837

Jena symphony   23'
  1 2 0 2 - 2 2 0 0 - tmp - str   Breitkopf
  Ed. Fritz Stein. Formerly attributed to Beethoven.

Symphony in A   29'
  1 2 0 2 - 2 0 0 0 - str   Breitkopf

WOLF, HUGO, 1860-1903

Der Corregidor: Prelude and interlude 6'
*3 *3 2 2 - 4 3 3 1 - tmp+1 - str Bote

Der Corregidor: Suite (arr. Hans Gál) 16'
*3 *2 2 2 - 4 2 3 1 - tmp+3 - str Boosey
   Contents--Prelude; Fandango and march;
Spanish intermezzo; Notturno and entr'acte.

Italian serenade 8'
  solo viola Bote; Breitkopf;
  2 2 2 2 - 2 0 0 0 - str Bruckner Verlag

Penthesilea 30'
*3 *3 2 3 - 4 4 3 1 - tmp+4 - hp - str Alkor; Bote;
Breitkopf;
Bruckner Verlag

Scherzo and finale 8'
*3 2 2 2 - 4 3 3 1 - tmp+2 - str Alkor; Breitkopf

Two sacred songs from the "Spanisches Liederbuch"
  mezzo-soprano solo Boosey
  0 0 3 0 - 2 0 0 0 - 2vn, va, vc, db
  Instrumentation by Igor Stravinsky.
    Contents--Herr, was trägt der Boden hier;
Wunden trägst du.

WOLFF, CHRISTIAN, 1934-

Burdocks variable duration
  For one or more orchestras; any number Peters
of players; any instruments or sound sources
(but there are places which require specific
pitches to be played). In ten sections, not
necessarily to be played consecutively.

WOLF-FERRARI, ERMANNO, 1876-1948

Concertino, English horn, op.34 25'
  2hn - str Leuckart

Jewels of the Madonna: Intermezzo no.1   4'
  1 1 2 1 - 2 0 0 0 - pf - str   Luck;
  (Optional parts for 2 cornets and   Weinberger
  1 trombone have numerous cues to cover
  for other missing instruments.)

Jewels of the Madonna: Intermezzo no.2   3'
  1 1 2 1 - 2 2 1 0 - pf - str   Luck; Weinberger

The secret of Suzanne: Overture   4'
  *3 2 2 2 - 4 2 3 0 - tmp - hp - str   Kalmus; Weinberger

        WUORINEN, CHARLES, 1938-

Contrafactum   20'
  *3 *3 *3 *3 - 4 3 3 2 - 2tmp, 5perc - 2pf - str   Peters

Grand bamboula   6'
  str   Peters

        XENAKIS, YANNIS, 1922-

Akrata   12'
  pic, ob - scl, bcl, contrabass cl - bsn,   Boosey
    2cbn - 2hn, 3tp, 2tbn, tuba

Anaktoria   11'
  0 0 1 *1 - 1 0 0 0 - 2vn, va, vc, db   Salabert
  (Contrabassoon is optional.)

Analogique A   6'
  3vn, 3vc, 3db   Salabert

Atrees   15'
  1 0 *2 0 - 1 1 1 0 - 3perc - vn, vc   Salabert

Metastaseis B   8'
  *2 2 *1 0 - 3 2 2 0 - tmp+4 - str 12.12.8.8.6   Boosey

ST/48—1,240162   11'
  *2 2 *2 *2 - 2 2 2 0 - tmp+3 - str 8.8.6.6.4   Boosey

Syrmos   15'
  12vn, no va, 4vc, 2db   Boosey

YARDUMIAN, RICHARD, 1917-

Armenian suite   16'
  *4 *4 =4 *4 - 6 4 4 1 - tmp+5 - hp - str   Elkan-Vogel

Cantus animae et cordis   15'
  str   Elkan-Vogel

YSAŸE, EUGENE, 1858-1931

Chant d'hiver, op.15   12'
  solo violin   Enoch
  2 2 2 2 - 2 0 0 0 - tmp - str

ZIMMERMANN, BERND ALOIS, 1918-1970

Stillness and return; two sketches for orchestra   9'
  4 *4 *4 *1 - 4 2 1 0 - asx, contrabass tbn -   Schott
    5perc - hp, accordion - vn, va, 3vc, 3db

APPENDICES

APPENDIX A: CHORUS

Mixed chorus
  Large orchestra
  Medium orchestra
  Small orchestra
  String orchestra
  Without strings

Female chorus

Male chorus

Children's chorus

   Works within the larger categories are subdivided
by duration. If the duration of a work has been estimated for the purpose of these durational subdivisions, this is indicated by an asterisk (*).

   If solo voices are also required, these are given
in parentheses.

   Within each category or subdivision, works are
listed in chronological order according to the composer's birth date.

   For complete information on any of these works, refer back to the main alphabetical listing by composer.

MIXED CHORUS

Large orchestra

20' or less

Verdi: Stabat mater
Verdi: Te deum (S)
Wagner: Lohengrin--Procession to
 the cathedral
Rimsky-Korsakov: Mlada--Suite
Rachmaninoff: Three Russian songs
Ives: Holidays symphony--Thanksgiving
Schoenberg: Prelude (Genesis suite)
Ravel: Daphnis et Chloé--Suites 1, 2
Bartók: Cantata profana (TB)
Kabalevsky: Symphony no.3
Barber: Prayers of Kierkegaard (ST)

21'-30'

Delius: Sea drift (Bar)
Scriabin: Prometheus
Ives: Symphony no.4
Carpenter: Skyscrapers
Stravinsky: Symphony of psalms
Poulenc: Gloria (S)
Dallapiccola: Canti di liberazione
Husa: Apotheosis of this earth
Ligeti: Requiem (SMz)
Nono: Il canto sospeso (SAT)
Martino: Paradiso choruses (3S, 4Mz,
 3T, 2Bar)

31'-45'

Berlioz: Symphonie funèbre et
 triomphale
Gounod: Messe solennelle (STB)
Saint-Saëns: Requiem (SATB)
Janáček: Glagolitic mass (SATB)
Mahler: Das klagende Lied (SAT)
Debussy: L'enfant prodigue (STBar)
Delius: Appalachia
Scriabin: Symphony no.1 (MzT)
Rachmaninoff: The bells (STB)
Bloch: America
Prokofiev: Alexander Nevsky (Mz)
Milhaud: Les Choëphores (SSA)
Milhaud: Symphony no.3
Orff: Trionfo di Afrodite (SSTTB)
Poulenc: Stabat mater (S)
Duruflé: Requiem (Mz, Bar)
Walton: Belshazzar's feast (Bar)
Shostakovich: Song of the forests (TB)
Britten: Spring symphony (SAT)
Bernstein: Kaddish (S)

46'-60'

Berlioz: Te deum (T)
Vaughan Williams: Hodie (STB)
Vaughan Williams: Symphony no.1 (S, Bar)
Holst: First choral symphony (S)

Ravel: Daphnis et Chloé (complete)
Bloch: Sacred service (Bar)
Stravinsky: Persephone (T)

Over 60'

Berlioz: La damnation de Faust (MzTBarB)
Berlioz: Requiem (T)
Berlioz: Roméo et Juliette (ATB)
Liszt: Christus (SATB)
Verdi: Messa da requiem (SATB)
Dvořák: Requiem (SATB)
Elgar: The dream of Gerontius (ATB)
Mahler: Symphony no.2 (SA)
Mahler: Symphony no.8 (SSSAATBB)
Debussy: Le martyre de Saint Sébastien
 (SAA)
Schoenberg: Gurre-Lieder (SATTB)
Honegger: Jeanne d'Arc au bûcher
 (SSSATB)
Orff: Carmina burana (STB)
Britten: War requiem (STB)
Penderecki: Passion according to
 St. Luke (SBB)

Medium orchestra

20' or less

Hofer: Te deum
Haydn: Te deum for the Empress Maria
 Therese
Mozart: Kyrie
Beethoven: Fantasia for piano, chorus
 and orchestra (SSATTB)
Beethoven: Meeresstille und glückliche
 Fahrt
Beethoven: Ruins of Athens--March and
 chorus*
Schubert: Offertorium, D.963 (T)
Schubert: Tantum ergo (SATB)
Schumann: Requiem for Mignon (SSAAB)
Franck: Psalm 150
Bruckner: Psalm 150
Borodin: Prince Igor--Polovtsian dances;
 Polovtsian march
Brahms: Nänie
Brahms: Schicksalslied
Rimsky-Korsakov: Christmas eve--
 Polonaise
Rimsky-Korsakov: Dubinushka
Fauré: Pavane
Richard Strauss: Wanderers Sturmlied
Vaughan Williams: Serenade to music
 (optional solo voices)
Holst: Christmas day (SATB)
Ives: Lincoln the great commoner
Schoenberg: Kol nidre
Stravinsky: Canticum sacrum (TBar)
Stravinsky: Chorale-variations on "Vom
 Himmel hoch da komm' ich her"
Stravinsky: Requiem canticles (AB)
Stravinsky: A sermon, a narrative, and
 a prayer (AT)

Webern: Cantata no.2 (SB)
Villa-Lobos: Chôros no.10
Hanson: Cherubic hymn
Poulenc: Secheresses
Shostakovich: Symphony no.2
Barber: Vanessa--Under the willow tree
Bernstein: Chichester psalms
 (boy soprano or countertenor)
Hollingsworth: Stabat mater
Boulez: Le soleil des eaux (STB)

21'-30'

Mozart: Mass, K.317 (SATB)
Mendelssohn: Psalm 42 (STTBB)
Bruckner: Te deum (SATB)
Dvořák: Te deum (SB)
Rimsky-Korsakov: Christmas eve--Suite
Kodály: Psalmus hungaricus (T)
Kodály: Te deum (SATB)
Tippett: The midsummer marriage--
 Ritual dances
Shostakovich: Symphony no.3
Britten: Cantata academica (SATB)
Maxwell Davies: The shepherd's calendar
 (optional treble or soprano)

31'-45'

Haydn: Masses Hob.XXII:9 (SATB);
 Hob.XXII:11 (SATB); Hob.XXII:14 (SATB)
Mozart: Litaniae de venerabili altaris
 sacramento, K.243 (SATB)
Cherubini: Requiem, C minor
Beethoven: Cantata on the death of
 Emperor Joseph II (SSATB)
Beethoven: Christus am Ölberg (STB)
Beethoven: Mass, op.86 (SATB)
Schubert: Mass no.1 (SSATTB)
Mendelssohn: Die erste Walpurgisnacht
 (ATBB)
Mendelssohn: Symphony no.2 (version
 with final chorus) (SST)
Schumann: Requiem (SATB)
Bruckner: Mass no.1 (SATB)
Bruckner: Missa solemnis (SATB)
Fauré: Requiem (SBar)
Coleridge-Taylor: The song of
 Hiawatha--Hiawatha's wedding feast
 (T); The death of Minnehaha (SB);
 Hiawatha's departure (STB)
Kodály: Missa brevis
Stravinsky: Threni (SATTBB)
Del Tredici: Pop-pourri (SAT)

46'-60'

Haydn: Mass, Hob.XXII:13 (SATB)
Haydn: Seven last words of Christ
 (SATB)
Mozart: Mass, K.417a (427) (SSTB)
Rossini: Stabat mater (SSTB)
Schubert: Mass no.5 (SATB)
Schubert: Rosamunde (A)
Berlioz: Lelio (TTB)

Schumann: Mass (STB)
Bruckner: Mass no.3 (SATB)
Dubois: The seven last words of Christ
 (STB)
Dvořák: Mass, op.86 (SATB optional)*
Vaughan Williams: Hodie (STB)
Vaughan Williams: Symphony no.1 (SBar)

Over 60'

Monteverdi: Vespro della beata vergine
 (SSATTBB)
Handel: Alexander's feast (STB)
Handel: L'allegro, il penseroso ed il
 moderato (SATB)*
Handel: Joshua (SSATB)
Handel: Judas Maccabaeus (SSATBB)
Handel: Messiah (Mozart or Prout
 versions) (SATB)
Handel: Samson (SATBB)
Handel: Saul (2S, A, 5T, 4B)*
Handel: Solomon (SSSSATB)
Haydn: The creation (STB)
Haydn: The seasons (STB)
Beethoven: Missa solemnis (SATB)
Beethoven: Symphony no.9 (SATB)
Schubert: Mass no.6 (SATTB)
Berlioz: L'enfance du Christ (STBB)
Mendelssohn: Elijah (SSATB)
Mendelssohn: Lobgesang (SST)
Mendelssohn: St. Paul (SATBB)
Schumann: Manfred (SATB)
Franck: Rédemption (S)
Brahms: Ein deutsches Requiem (SBar)
Dvořák: Stabat mater (SATB)
Parker: Hora novissima (SATB)
Coleridge-Taylor: The song of
 Hiawatha (complete) (STB)
Honegger: Le roi David (SAT)

Duration uncertain

Schubert: Stabat mater, D.383 (STB)
Schumann: Adventlied (SATB)

Small orchestra

10' or less

Monteverdi: Laudate dominum (SSTTB)
Bach: Cantatas nos.50; 118; 141 (ATB)
Handel: Zadok the priest (SSAATBB)
Gossec: Christmas suite
Mozart: Alma dei creatoris (SAT)
Mozart: Benedictus sit deus (S)
Mozart: Te deum laudamus
Schubert: Stabat mater, D.175
Ives: General William Booth enters
 into heaven
Ives: Three harvest home chorales
Webern: Das Augenlicht
Webern: Cantata no.1 (S)
Webern: Lieder, op.19
Milhaud: Symphonies for small orch.--No.6

11'-20'

Purcell: Te deum and Jubilate (SSAATB)
Bach: Cantatas nos.2 (ATB); 14 (STB);
15 (SATB); 22 (ATB); 23 (SAT);
25 (STB); 26 (SATB); 27 (SATB);
28 (SATB); 40 (ATB); 46 (ATB);
48 (AT); 52 (S); 55 (T); 59 (SB);
61 (STB); 62 (SATB); 65 (TB);
67 (ATB); 68 (SB); 71 (SATB);
73 (STB); 77 (SATB); 79 (SAB);
81 (ATB); 83 (ATB); 84 (S); 85 (SATB);
86 (SATB); 89 (SAB); 90 (ATB);
91 (SATB); 96 (SATB); 98 (SATB);
103 (AT); 108 (ATB); 112 (SATB);
122 (SATB); 124 (SATB); 130 (SATB);
135 (ATB); 137 (SATB); 138 (SATB);
142 (ATB); 143 (STB); 144 (SAT);
145 (STB); 150 (SATB); 151 (SATB);
154 (ATB); 155 (SATB); 156 (ATB);
158 (B); 159 (ATB); 162 (SATB);
163 (SATB); 164 (SATB); 165 (SATB);
166 (ATB); 167 (SATB); 168 (SATB);
173 (SATB); 175 (ATB); 176 (SAB);
179 (STB); 181 (SATB); 183 (SATB);
185 (SATB); 188 (SATB); 190 (ATB)
191 (ST); 192 (SATB); 193 (SA)
Handel: Psalm 96 (ST)
Handel: Jubilate for the Peace
of Utrecht (AAB)
Sammartini: Magnificat (SATB)
Mozart: Dixit et magnificat (STB)
Mozart: Missa brevis, K.196b (220)
(SATB)
Mozart: Missa brevis, K.259 (SATB)
Vivaldi: Magnificat (SSATB)
Bruckner: Mass, C major*
Vaughan Williams: Flos campi
Britten: Cantata misericordium (TB)

21'-30'

Marc-Antoine Charpentier: Te deum
(SSATB)
Bach: Cantatas nos.1 (STB); 4 (optional
SATB); 5 (SATB); 6 (SATB); 7 (ATB)
8 (SATB); 9 (SATB); 10 (SATB);
12 (ATB); 13 (SATB); 16 (ATB);
17 (SATB); 18 (STB); 19 (STB);
24 (SATB); 29 (SATB); 31 (STB);
32 (SB); 33 (ATB); 34 (ATB);
37 (SATB); 38 (SATB); 39 (SAB);
42 (SATB); 43 (SATB); 44 (SATB);
45 (ATB); 47 (SB); 56 (B); 60 (ATB);
63 (SATB); 64 (SAB); 69 (SATB);
70 (SATB); 72 (SAB); 74 (SATB);
78 (SATB); 80 (SATB); 87 (ATB);
88 (SATB); 93 (SATB); 94 (SATB);
95 (STB); 99 (SATB); 100 (SATB);
101 (SATB); 102 (ATB); 104 (TB);
105 (SATB); 106 (SATB); 107 (STB);
109 (AT); 111 (SATB); 113 (SATB);
114 (SATB); 115 (SATB); 116 (SATB);
117 (ATB); 119 (SATB); 120 (SATB);
121 (SATB); 123 (ATB); 125 (ATB);
126 (ATB); 127 (STB); 128 (ATB);
129 (SAB); 131 (TB); 132 (SATB);
133 (SATB); 134 (AT); 136 (ATB);
139 (SATB); 148 (AT); 149 (SATB);
157 (TB); 161 (AT); 169 (A);
171 (SATB); 172 (SATB); 174 (ATB);
178 (ATB); 180 (SATB); 182 (ATB);
184 (SAT); 187 (SAB); 195 (SB);
198 (SATB); 211 (STB); 214 (SATB)
Bach: Magnificat (SSATB)
Bach: Masses BWV 233 (SAB); 234 (SAB);
235 (ATB); 236 (SATB)
Handel: Psalm 89 (STB)
Haydn: Mass, Hob.XXII:6 (SATB)
Mozart: Litaniae lauretanae,
K.186d (195) (SATB)
Mozart: Mass, K.257 (SATB)
Mozart: Vesperae solennes de confessor,
K.339 (SATB)
Mozart: Vesperae solennes de dominica,
K.321 (SATB)
Schubert: Masses nos.2 (STB);
3 (SATB); 4 (SATB)

31'-45'

Bach: Cantatas nos.3 (SATB); 11 (SATB);
20 (ATB); 21 (SATB); 30 (SATB);
36 (SATB); 41 (SATB); 57 (SB);
66 (ATB); 75 (SATB); 76 (SATB);
92 (SATB); 97 (SATB); 110 (SATB);
140 (STB); 146 (SATB); 147 (SATB);
177 (SAT); 186 (SATB); 194 (SATB);
197 (SAB); 205 (SATB); 206 (SATB);
207a (SATB); 213 (SATB); 215 (STB)
Handel: Dettingen Te deum (B)
Vivaldi: Gloria (SSA)
Haydn: Masses Hob.XXII:4 (SATB);
XXII:8 (SATB); XXII:10 (SATB or
SSATBB); XXII:11 (SATB); XXII:12 (SATB)
Michael Haydn: Missa pro defunctis
(SATB)
Michael Haydn: Missa Sancti Hieronymi
Mozart: Litaniae de venerabili altaris
sacramento, K.125 (SATB)
Bruckner: Requiem (SATB)
Duruflé: Requiem (Mz, Bar)
Hovhaness: Magnificat (STB)
Mennin: The Christmas story (ST)

46'-60'

Schütz: Christmas oratorio (STB)
Purcell: Ode for St. Cecilia's Day
(SAATBB)
Bach: Cantata no.201 (SATTBB)
Bach: Easter oratorio (SATB)
Handel: The choice of Hercules (SSAT)
Handel: Ode for St. Cecilia's Day (ST)
Domenico Scarlatti: Serenata (SATB)
Mozart: Requiem (SATB)
Britten: Saint Nicolas (T, 4 boys)

Over 60'

Bach: Christmas oratorio (SATB)
Bach: Mass, BWV 232, B minor (SSATB)
Bach: St. John passion (SATBB)
Bach: St. Matthew passion (SATBB)
Handel: Belshazzar (SAATTBB)
Handel: Israel in Egypt (SSATBB)
Handel: Messiah (SATB)
Handel: Passion nach Barthold Heinrich
  Brockes (6S, 4A, 3T, 5B; or SATTBB)
Haydn: Stabat mater (SATB)
Haydn: Mass, Hob.XXII:5 (SATB)

Duration uncertain

Wilhelm Friedemann Bach: Ehre sei Gott
  in der Höhe (STB)
Carl Philipp Emanuel Bach: Magnificat
  (SATB)
Michael Haydn: Veni, sancte spiritus
Mozart (attr.): Gloria from the Twelfth
  mass
Mozart: Masses K.167; K.258 (SATB);
  K.246a (262) (SATB); K.337 (SATB)
Mozart: Regina coeli, K.74d (108) (S);
  K.127 (S); K.321b (276) (SATB)
Mozart: Scande coeli limina (S)
Mozart: Veni sancte spiritus (SATB)
Mozart: Venite populi
Schubert: Magnificat (SATB)

String orchestra

15' or less

Monteverdi: Laudate dominum (SSTTB)
Buxtehude: Magnificat
Haydn: Masses Hob.XXII:1 (SS); XXII:3
Mozart: Ave verum corpus
Mozart: Inter natos mulierum
Mozart: Litaniae lauretanae K.74e (109)
  (SATB)*
Mozart: Sancta Maria
Donizetti: Ave Maria (S)

16'-30'

Vivaldi: Magnificat (SSAT or SSATB)
Bach: Cantatas nos.4 (optional SATB);
  61 (STB); 153 (ATB); 165 (SATB);
  196 (STB)
Handel: Dixit dominus (SSATB)
Haydn: Mass Hob.XXII:7 (S)
Mozart: Missa brevis K.186f (192)
  (SATB); K.186h (194) (SATB);
  K.272b (275) (SATB)
Schubert: Masses nos.2 (STB); 4 (SATB)

Over 30'

Schütz: Easter oratorio (SSAATTBB)
Saint-Saëns: Christmas oratorio (SAATB)

Duration uncertain

Buxtehude: Das neugebor'ne Kindelein
Pergolesi: Magnificat (SATB)
Mozart: Misericordias domini

Without strings

Bach: Cantata no.118
Bruckner: Mass no.2
Respighi: Lauda per la natività del
  Signore (SSA or SAT)
Stravinsky: Mass (SATTB)
Stravinsky: Les noces (SATB)
Dallapiccola: Canti di prigionia
Bernstein: Chichester psalms (reduced
  version) (boy or countertenor)

FEMALE CHORUS

Mendelssohn: Midsummernight's dream (SS)
Liszt: Dante symphony
Saint-Saëns: La nuit (S)
Mahler: Symphony no.3 (A)
Debussy: La damoiselle élue (Mz)
Debussy: Nocturnes
Busoni: Turandot--Suite
Vaughan Williams: Symphony no.7 (S)
Holst: The planets
Bartók: Three village scenes
Messiaen: Trois petites liturgies

MALE CHORUS

Cherubini: Requiem, D minor
Liszt: A Faust symphony (T)
Bruckner: Helgoland
Johann Strauss Jr.: On the beautiful
  blue Danube
Brahms: Alto rhapsody (A)
Brahms: Rinaldo (T)
Grieg: Landsighting (Bar)
Busoni: Concerto, piano, op.39
Schoenberg: A survivor from Warsaw
Stravinsky: Babel
Stravinsky: Oedipus rex (ATTBB)
Varèse: Ecuatorial
Varèse: Nocturnal (S)
Shostakovich: Symphony no.13 (B)

CHILDREN'S CHORUS

Berlioz: La damnation de Faust (MzTBarB)
Berlioz: Te deum (T)
Liszt: Dante symphony

Wagner: Lohengrin--Procession to the
 cathedral
Mahler: Symphony no.3 (A)
Mahler: Symphony no.8 (SSSAATBB)
Kodály: Psalmus hungaricus (T)
Stravinsky: Persephone (T)
Shostakovich: Song of the forests (TB)
Britten: Spring symphony (SAT)
Britten: War requiem (STB)
Bernstein: Kaddish (S)
Penderecki: Passion according to
 St. Luke (SBB)

APPENDIX B: SOLO VOICES

Soprano

Alto or Mezzo-soprano

Tenor

Baritone or Bass

Several solo voices
  2 solo voices
  3 solo voices
  4 solo voices (SATB)
  4 or more solo voices (not SATB)

Speaker (Narrator)

   Works within the larger categories are subdivided
by duration. If the duration of a work has been estimated for the purpose of these durational subdivisions, this is indicated by an asterisk (*).

   Within each category or subdivision, works are
listed in chronological order according to the composer's birth date.

   For complete information on any of these works, refer back to the main alphabetical listing by composer.

SOPRANO

10' or less

Mozart: A questo seno
Mozart: Ah se in ciel
Mozart: Alcandro, lo confesso
Mozart: Alma grande e nobil core
Mozart: Basta, vincesti
Mozart: Bella mia fiamma
Mozart: Chi sa, chi sa, qual sia*
Mozart: Ergo interest
Mozart: Ma che vi fece
Mozart: Mia speranza
Mozart: Misera, dove son
Mozart: Nehmt meinen dank
Mozart: No, no, che non sei capace
Mozart: Vado, ma dove, o dei*
Mozart: Voi avete un cor fedele
Mozart: Vorrei spiegarvi
R. Strauss: Cäcilie
R. Strauss: Morgen
Varèse: Offrandes
Varèse: Nocturnal
Webern: Geistliche Lieder, op.15
Webern: Lieder, op.13; op.14
Berg: Altenberg Lieder
Berg: Lulu--Lulu's song

11'-20'

Bach: Cantatas nos.51; 52; 84
Mozart: Ah, lo previdi
Mozart: Ch'io mi scordi di te
Mozart: Exsultate jubilate
Mozart: Popoli di Tessagua
Beethoven: Ah, perfido
Schubert: Salve regina, D.676
Wagner: Götterdämmerung--Brünnhilde's immolation
Wagner: Tristan und Isolde--Prelude and Liebestod
Schoenberg: Gurre-Lieder--Lied der Waldtaube
Glière: Concerto, coloratura soprano
Ravel: Shéhérazade
Berg: Der Wein
Berg: Wozzeck--Three excerpts
Villa-Lobos: Bachianas brasileiras no.5
Barber: Andromache's farewell
Barber: Knoxville, Summer of 1915
La Montaine: Songs of the rose of Sharon
Del Tredici: An Alice symphony--Illustrated Alice; The lobster quadrille

21'-30'

Bach: Cantatas nos.199; 202; 209
Berlioz: Cléopâtre
Wagner: Wesendonck songs
Chausson: Poème de l'amour et de la mer
Mahler: Sieben Lieder aus letzten Zeit

R. Strauss: Four last songs
R. Strauss: Six songs after poems by Clemens von Brentano
R. Strauss: Three hymns
Schoenberg: Six songs, op.8
Britten: Les illuminations
Bernstein: Jeremiah
Foss: Song of songs
Foss: Time cycle
Baker: Le chat qui pêche
Del Tredici: An Alice symphony--In Wonderland
Del Tredici: Pop-pourri
Del Tredici: Syzygy
Del Tredici: Vintage Alice

Over 30'

Bach: Cantatas nos.204; 210
Beethoven: Egmont
Mahler: Lieder aus "Des Knaben Wunderhorn"
Mahler: Symphony no.4
Vaughan Williams: Symphony no.3
Turina: Canto a Sevilla
Berg: Lulu--Suite
Sessions: Idyll of Theocritus
Del Tredici: An Alice symphony
Del Tredici: Final Alice
Del Tredici: In memory of a summer day

Duration uncertain

Alessandro Scarlatti: Christmas cantata
Schubert: Salve regina, D.223

ALTO OR MEZZO-SOPRANO

10' or less

Bach: Cantatas nos.53; 200
Mozart: Ombra felice
Wolf: Two sacred songs from the "Spanisches Liederbuch"*
Richard Strauss: Morgen
Ives: General William Booth enters into heaven
Stravinsky: Le faune et la bergère
Stravinsky: Pribaoutki
Webern: Lieder, op.8

11'-20'

Bach: Cantata no.54
Brahms: Alto rhapsody
Elgar: Sea pictures
Mahler: Lieder eines fahrenden Gesellen
Debussy: La damoiselle élue
Granados: Dante, op.21
Falla: El amor brujo--Ballet suite
Respighi: Il tramonto
Rogers: Three Japanese dances
Britten: Phaedra

Maxwell Davies: Stone litany

21'-30'

Bach: Cantatas nos.169; 170
Berlioz: Nuits d'été
Mussorgsky: Songs and dances of death
Chausson: Poème de l'amour et de la mer
Mahler: Kindertotenlieder
Mahler: Sieben Lieder aus letzten Zeit
Foss: Song of songs
Wernick: Visions of terror and wonder

Over 30'

Bach: Cantata no.35
Mahler: Lieder aus "Des Knaben
  Wunderhorn"
Boulez: Le marteau sans maître

TENOR

10' or less

Mozart: Clarice cara mia sposa*
Mozart: Con ossequio, con rispetto
Mozart: Misero, o sogno
Mozart: Per pietà, non ricercate
Mozart: Se al labbro mio non credi*
Mozart: Si mostra la sorte
Richard Strauss: Cäcilie
Richard Strauss: Morgen
Webern: Geistliche Lieder, op.15
Webern: Lieder, op.14
Stravinsky: In memoriam Dylan Thomas

11'-20'

Bach: Cantatas nos.55; 160; 189
Busoni: Rondo arlecchinesco

21'-30

Berlioz: Les nuits d'été
Chausson: Poème de l'amour et de la mer
Mahler: Sieben Lieder aus letzten Zeit
Richard Strauss: Four last songs
Richard Strauss: Six songs after poems
  by Clemens von Brentano
Richard Strauss: Three hymns
Britten: Gloriana--Symphonic suite
Britten: Les illuminations
Britten: Nocturne
Britten: Serenade for tenor, horn,
  and strings

Over 30'

Brahms: Rinaldo
Mahler: Lieder aus "Des Knaben
  Wunderhorn"
Vaughan Williams: Symphony no.3

Duration uncertain
Schubert: Salve regina, D.106

BARITONE OR BASS

10' or less

Mozart: Alcandro, lo confesso*
Mozart: Un baccio di mano*
Mozart: Così dunque
Mozart: Io ti lascio*
Mozart: Mentre ti lascio, o figlia
Mozart: Per questa bella mano
Mozart: Rivolgete a lui lo sguardo
Richard Strauss: Morgen
Ives: General William Booth enters
  into heaven
Stravinsky: Pribaoutki
Stravinsky: Two songs by Paul Verlaine
Webern: Lieder, op.8

11'-20'

Bach: Cantata no.203
Mahler: Lieder eines fahrenden Gesellen
Stravinsky: Abraham and Isaac
Prokofiev: Lieutenant Kijé--Suite

21'-30'

Bach: Cantatas nos.56; 82
Berlioz: Les nuits d'été
Mussorgsky: Songs and dances of death
Chausson: Poème de l'amour et de la mer
Mahler: Kindertotenlieder
Mahler: Sieben Lieder aus letzten Zeit
Schoenberg: Serenade, op.24

Over 30'

Bach: Cantata no.57
Mahler: Lieder aus "Des Knaben
  Wunderhorn"
Ben Weber: Symphony on poems of
  William Blake

SEVERAL SOLO VOICES

2 solo voices

Bach: Cantatas nos.32 (SB); 49 (SB);
  58 (SB); 59 (SB); 152 (SB); 157 (TB);
  212 (SB)
Pergolesi: Stabat mater (SA)
Mozart: Nun liebes Weibchen, ziehst
  mit mir (SB)
Mahler: Das Lied von der Erde (AT, or
  TBar)
Nielsen: Symphony no.3 (SBar)

Shostakovich: Symphony no.14 (SB)
Nono: Canti di vita e d'amore (ST)
Del Tredici: Pop-pourri (S, and
  optional countertenor or Mz)

3 solo voices

Monteverdi: Combattimento di Tancredi
  e Clorinda (SAT)
Bach: Cantatas nos.60 (ATB); 81 (ATB);
  83 (ATB); 87 (ATB); 89 (SAB);
  90 (ATB); 174 (ATB); 175 (ATB);
  211 (STB)
Mozart: Mandina amabile (STB)
Berlioz: Les nuits d'été (Mz,T,Bar)
Debussy: L'enfant prodigue (S,T,Bar)
Varèse: Ecuatorial (3 or more basses)

4 solo voices (SATB)

Bach: Cantatas nos.15; 42; 85; 86; 88;
  132; 151; 155; 162; 163; 164; 165;
  167; 168; 183; 185; 188
Milhaud: Symphonies for small
  orchestra--No.6

4 or more solo voices (not SATB)

Bach: Cantata no.208 (SSTB)
Mozart: Dite almeno in che mancai
  (STBB)
Vaughan Williams: Serenade to Music
  (4S, 4A, 4T, 4B)
Bernstein: Songfest (S,Mz,A,T,Bar,B)
Berio: Sinfonia (SSAATTBB)

SPEAKER (NARRATOR)

15' or less

Schoenberg: A survivor from Warsaw
Stravinsky: Babel (male narrator)
Copland: Lincoln portrait
Kubik: Gerald McBoing Boing
Kirk: An orchestra primer
Schickele: A zoo called Earth (taped
  narration)
Bamert: Circus parade

16'-30'

Schoenberg: Kol nidre
Schoenberg: Ode to Napoleon Bonaparte
Stravinsky: A sermon, a narrative,
  and a prayer
Prokofiev: Peter and the wolf
Rogers: The musicians of Bremen
Harsányi: L'histoire du petite tailleur

Poulenc: The story of Babar, the little
  elephant
Britten: Young person's guide to the
  orchestra
Pinkham: Signs of the zodiac
Laderman: Magic prison (2 narrators:
  1 male, 1 female)
Lees: The trumpet of the swan
Schuller: Journey into jazz
Mario Lombardo: Drakestail

Over 30'

Berlioz: Lelio
Schoenberg: Pierrot lunaire
Stravinsky: Oedipus rex
Stravinsky: Persephone (female narrator)
Honegger: Jeanne d'Arc au bûcher
  (4 spoken roles: 1 female, 3 male)
Honegger: Le roi David
Walton: Façade
Bernstein: Kaddish
Bamert: Once upon an orchestra

APPENDIX C: SOLO INSTRUMENTS

Piano
2 or more pianos
Harpsichord
2 or more harpsichords
Organ
Multiple diverse keyboards

Violin
2 or more violins
Viola
Violoncello
Double bass
Multiple diverse strings
  2 solo strings
  2 violins and violoncello
  Solo string quartet
  Other combinations of solo strings

Flute
2 flutes
Recorder
Piccolo
Oboe
English horn
Clarinet
Bassoon
Saxophone

Horn
2 or more horns
Trumpet
2 trumpets
Trombone
Tuba

Percussion
Harp
Guitar
Mandoline

Several diverse instruments
    2 solo instruments
    3 solo instruments
    4 or more solo instruments

Jazz soloists

Works within the larger categories are subdivided by duration. If the duration of a work has been estimated for the purpose of these durational subdivisions, this is indicated by an asterisk (*).

Within each category or subdivision, works are listed in chronological order according to the composer's birth date.

For complete information on any of these works, refer back to the main alphabetical listing by composer.

PIANO

10' or less

Mozart: Concert-rondo, K.382
Weber: Polonaise brillante
Mendelssohn: Rondo brillant
Chopin: Grande polonaise
Gottschalk: Grande tarantelle
Saint-Saëns: Allegro appassionato,
op.70
Saint-Saëns: Rhapsodie d'Auvergne
Stravinsky: Movements
Turina: Rapsodia sinfónica
Gershwin: "I got rhythm" variations
Françaix: Concertino, piano

11'-20'

Mozart: Concerto, piano, no.5
Beethoven: Fantasia for piano, chorus
and orchestra, op.80
Weber: Concerto, piano, no.1
Weber: Konzertstück, op.79
Mendelssohn: Capriccio brillant
Chopin: Concert-allegro, op.46
Chopin: Fantasy on Polish airs
Chopin: Krakowiak, op.14
Chopin: Variations on "La ci darem
la mano"
Schumann: Concert-allegro with
introduction, op.134
Schumann: Introduction and allegro
appassionato, op.92
Liszt: Concertos, piano, nos.1-2
Liszt: Concerto pathétique
Liszt: Hungarian fantasy
Liszt: Malediction
Liszt: Rhapsodie espagnole
Liszt: Totentanz
Franck: Les djinns
Franck: Symphonic variations
Saint-Saëns: Africa
Tchaikovsky: Concerto, piano, no.3
Rimsky-Korsakov: Concerto, piano, op.30
Fauré: Ballade, op.19
Fauré: Fantasy, op.111
Albéniz: Rapsodia española
Richard Strauss: Burleske
Roussel: Concerto, piano, op.36
Ravel: Concerto, piano (left hand),
D major
Bartók: Rhapsody, op.1
Stravinsky: Capriccio
Stravinsky: Concerto for piano and
wind instruments
Becker: Concerto arabesque
Martinu: Fantasia concertante
Prokofiev: Concerto, piano, no.1
Honegger: Concertino
Milhaud: Le carnaval d'Aix
Milhaud: Concertos, piano, nos.1, 3
Milhaud: Suite concertante

Benjamin: Concertino
Piston: Concertino, piano and chamber
orchestra
Hindemith: Concerto, piano, op.36, no.1
Gershwin: Rhapsody in blue
Gershwin: Second rhapsody

21'-30'

Mozart: Concertos, piano, nos.6, 8,
11-21, 23-24, 27
Beethoven: Concerto, piano, no.2
Kuhlau: Concerto, piano, op.7
Weber: Concerto, piano, no.2
Schubert: Wanderer fantasy
Mendelssohn: Concertos, piano, nos.1-2
Chopin: Concerto, piano, no.2
Litolff: Concerto symphonique no.4
Lalo: Concerto, piano
Saint-Saëns: Concertos, piano, nos.1-5
Tchaikovsky: Fantasy, op.56
Massenet: Concerto, piano
Grieg: Concerto, piano, op.16
D'Indy: Symphony on a French mountain
air
Albéniz: Concerto, piano, no.1
MacDowell: Concertos, piano, nos.1-2
Debussy: Fantasie
Busoni: Indianische Fantasie
Scriabin: Concerto, piano, op.20
Scriabin: Prometheus
Rachmaninoff: Concertos, piano, nos.1, 4
Rachmaninoff: Rhapsody on a theme
of Paganini, op.43
Schoenberg: Concerto, piano, op.42
Ravel: Concerto, piano, G major
Falla: Nights in the gardens of Spain
Dohnányi: Variations on a nursery song
Bloch: Concerto grosso no.1
Bartók: Concertos, piano, nos.1-3
Bartók: Scherzo, op.2
Villa-Lobos: Bachianas brasileiras no.3
Villa-Lobos: Mômoprecôce
Prokofiev: Concertos, piano, nos.3,
4 (left hand), 5
Hindemith: Theme and variations ("The
four temperaments")
Poulenc: Aubade
Poulenc: Concerto, piano
Poulenc: Concerto champêtre
Copland: Concerto, piano
Kabalevsky: Concerto, piano, no.3
Shostakovich: Concertos, piano, nos.1-2
Badings: Concerto, piano (1940)
Messiaen: Couleurs de la cité céleste
Messiaen: Oiseaux exotiques
Barber: Concerto, piano, op.38
Menotti: Concerto, piano
Britten: Diversions on a theme (left
hand)
Ginastera: Concerto, piano, no.1
Bernstein: The age of anxiety
La Montaine: Birds of paradise
La Montaine: Concerto, piano, op.9

Chou: Pien; chamber concerto
Hollingsworth: Concerto, piano
Martino: Concerto, piano

Over 30'

Viotti: Concerto, piano, G minor
Mozart: Concertos, piano, nos.9, 22, 25-26
Beethoven: Concertos, piano, nos.1, 3-6
Chopin: Concerto, piano, no.1
Schumann: Concerto, piano, op.54
Rubinstein: Concertos, piano, nos.3-4
Brahms: Concertos, piano, nos.1-2
Tchaikovsky: Concertos, piano, nos.1-2
Dvořák: Concerto, piano, op.33
Paderewski: Concerto, piano, op.17
Busoni: Concerto, piano, op.39
Rachmaninoff: Concertos, piano, nos.2-3
Dohnányi: Concerto, piano, no.1
Gershwin: Concerto, piano, F major
Chávez: Concerto, piano
Khachaturian: Concerto, piano
Britten: Concerto, piano, no.1

2 OR MORE PIANOS

Mozart: Concerto, 3 pianos, no.7, K.242
 (a version for 2 pianos also exists)
Mozart: Concerto, 2 pianos, no.10, K.316a (365)
Mendelssohn: Concerto, 2 pianos, E major
Saint-Saëns: Carnival of the animals
Bartók: Concerto, 2 pianos and percussion
Villa-Lobos: Chôros no.8
Poulenc: Concerto, 2 pianos, D minor
Britten: Scottish ballade

HARPSICHORD

15' or less

Bach: Concertos, harpsichord, nos.5, 7
Galuppi: Concerto, harpsichord, F major
Haydn: Concertino, harpsichord, Hob.XIV:11
Haydn: Concertos, Hob.XVIII:4; Hob.XVIII:7; Hob.XVIII:F1
Johann Christian Bach: Concerto, harpsichord, op.13, no.2
Dittersdorf: Concerto, harpsichord, B-flat major
Falla: Concerto, harpsichord, D major

Over 15'

Bach: Concertos, harpsichord, nos.1-4, 6

Carl Philipp Emanuel Bach: Concerto, harpsichord, W.23
Wagenseil: Concerto, harpsichord, D major
Haydn: Concerto, harpsichord, Hob.XVIII:11
Johann Christian Bach: Concertos, harpsichord op.7, no.5; op.13, no.4; Concerto in E-flat major
Poulenc: Concerto champêtre

2 OR MORE HARPSICHORDS

Bach: Concertos, 2 harpsichords, nos.1-3
Bach: Concertos, 3 harpsichords, nos.1-2
Bach: Concerto, 4 harpsichords, BWV 1065

ORGAN

15' or less

Handel: Concertos, organ, op.4, nos.1-6
Handel: Concertos, organ, op.7, nos.3, 5-6
Haydn: Concerto, organ, no.2, Hob.XVIII:8
Haydn: Concerto, organ, F major
Mozart: Sonatas, organ and orchestra, nos.1-17
Barber: Toccata festiva

Over 15'

Handel: Concertos, organ, op.7, nos.1-2, 4
Haydn: Concerto, organ, Hob.XVIII:1
Saint-Saëns: Symphony no.3
Rheinberger: Concertos, organ, nos.1-2
Hindemith: Concerto, organ
Poulenc: Concerto, organ, G minor
Copland: Symphony for organ and orchestra

MULTIPLE DIVERSE KEYBOARDS

Carter: Double concerto, harpsichord and piano
Messiaen: Trois petites liturgies (piano and ondes martenot)
Messiaen: Turangalîla-symphonie (piano and ondes martenot)

VIOLIN

10' or less

Torelli: Concerto, violin, op.8, no.8
Vivaldi: Concertos, violin, op.8,
 nos.5-8, 10, 12
Vivaldi: The four seasons--No.2
 (Summer)
Telemann: Concerto, violin, A minor
Veracini: Concerto, violin, D major
Mozart: Adagio, K.261
Mozart: Rondos, K.261a (269); K.373
Beethoven: Romances nos.1-2
Paganini: Moto perpetuo, op.11
Schubert: Konzertstück, D.345
Chopin: Romanze
Wagner: Wesendonck songs--No.5, Träume
Saint-Saëns: Concerto, violin, no.1
Saint-Saëns: Introduction and rondo
 capriccioso
Saint-Saëns: Romance, op.37
Wieniawski: Legend, op.17
Wieniawski: Polonaise brillante nos.1-2
Wieniawski: Scherzo-tarantelle, op.16
Bruch: Adagio appassionato, op.57
Tchaikovsky: Sérénade mélancolique
Tchaikovsky: Souvenir d'un lieu cher--
 1. Méditation; 2. Scherzo; 3. Mélodie
Dvořák: Romance, op.11
Sarasate: Introduction and tarantella
Sarasate: Zigeunerweisen, op.20
Sibelius: Humoresques I, II
Ravel: Tzigane
Milhaud: Concertino de printemps
Hindemith: Trauermusik
Cowell: Fiddler's jig

11'-20'

Torelli: Concerto, violin, op.8, no.9
Vitali: Ciaccona
Albinoni: Concerto, op.9, no.10
Vivaldi: Concerto, violin, op.8, no.11
Vivaldi: The four seasons--Nos.1
 (Spring), 3 (Autumn), 4 (Winter)
Bach: Concerto, violin, no.1
Veracini: Concerto grande da chiesa
Tartini: Concerto, violin, no.57
Tartini: Sinfonia pastorale, D major
Leclair: Concertos, violin, op.7,
 nos.4*-5
Sammartini: Concerto, violin, C major
Pergolesi: Concerto, violin, B-flat
 major
Haydn: Concerto, violin, no.2
Michael Haydn: Concerto, violin,
 A major
Mozart: Concerto, violin, no.1
Paganini: Concerto, violin, no.1 (arr.
 August Wilhelmj)
Spohr: Concerto, violin, no.8
Schubert: Rondo, D.438
Berlioz: Rêverie et caprice

Schumann: Fantasia, op.131
Vieuxtemps: Concerto, violin, no.5
Saint-Saëns: Concerto, violin, no.2
Saint-Saëns: Havanaise, op.83
Wieniawski: Concerto, violin, no.2
Tchaikovsky: Souvenir d'un lieu cher
 (complete work)
Tchaikovsky: Valse-scherzo, op.34
Rimsky-Korsakov: Fantaisie de concert
Sarasate: Carmen fantasie
Chausson: Poème, op.25
Ysaÿe: Chant d'hiver
Vaughan Williams: Concerto, violin,
 D minor
Vaughan Williams: The lark ascending
Bloch: Baal Shem
Bartók: Deux portraits
Bartók: Rhapsodies nos.1-2
Wellesz: Suite, op.38
Rubbra: Improvisation, op.89
Kabalevsky: Concerto, violin, op.48
Khrennikov: Concerto, violin

21'-30'

Bach: Concerto, violin, no.2
Haydn: Concertos, violin, nos.1, 3
Boccherini: Concerto, violin, G.486
Viotti: Concerto, violin, no.22
Mozart: Concertos, violin, nos.2-7
Paganini: Concertos, violin, nos.1-2
Spohr: Concerto, violin, no.9
Mendelssohn: Concerto, violin, op.64
Mendelssohn: Concerto, violin (posth.)
Schumann: Concerto, violin, D minor
Vieuxtemps: Concerto, violin, no.4
Lalo: Concerto, violin, op.20
Lalo: Symphonie espagnole
Saint-Saëns: Concerto, violin, no.3
Wieniawski: Concerto, violin, no.1
Bruch: Concertos, violin, nos.1-2
Bruch: Scottish fantasy
Glazunov: Concerto, violin, op.82
Bartók: Concerto, violin, no.1
Stravinsky: Concerto, violin, D major
Szymanowski: Concerto, violin, no.1
Berg: Concerto, violin
Martinu: Concerto, violin
Prokofiev: Concertos, violin, nos.1-2
Milhaud: Concerto, violin, no.2
Hindemith: Concerto, violin
Khachaturian: Concerto-rhapsody, violin
 and orchestra
Barber: Concerto, violin, op.14
Lees: Concerto, violin

Over 30'

Vivaldi: The four seasons (complete)
Viotti: Concerto, violin, no.19
Beethoven: Concerto, violin, op.61
Goldmark: Concerto, violin, op.28
Joachim: Concerto, violin, op.11
Brahms: Concerto, violin, op.77
Bruch: Concerto, violin, no.3

Bruch: Serenade, op.75
Tchaikovsky: Concerto, violin, op.35
Dvořák: Concerto, violin, op.53
Elgar: Concerto, violin, op.61
Nielsen: Concerto, violin, op.33
Sibelius: Concerto, violin, op.47
Schoenberg: Concerto, violin, op.36
Bloch: Concerto, violin
Bartók: Concerto, violin, no.2
Gruenberg: Concerto, violin, op.47
Sessions: Concerto, violin
Khachaturian: Concerto, violin
Shostakovich: Concerto, violin, op.99
Britten: Concerto, violin, no.1
Bernstein: Serenade

2 OR MORE VIOLINS

Torelli: Concertos, 2 violins,
  op.6, no.10; op.8, no.1; op.8, no.3;
  op.8, no.7
Torelli: Concerti grossi, 2 violins,
  op.8, no.2; op.8, no.5; op.8, no.6
Vivaldi: Concerto, 2 violins, op.3,
  no.8
Manfredini: Concerti grossi, op.3,
  no.10; op.3, no.12 (2 violins)
Telemann: Concerto, 2 violins, C major
Bach: Concerto, 2 violins, BWV 1043
Giuseppe Sammartini: Concerto grosso,
  op.5, no.6 (2 violins)
Locatelli: Concerto grosso, op.7,
  no.12 (4 solo violins)
Johann Christian Bach: Sinfonia
  concertante, E-flat major (2 violins)
Mozart: Concertone, 2 violins and
  orchestra, K.186e (190)
Arnold: Concerto, 2 violins and
  string orchestra, op.77

VIOLA

Telemann: Concerto, viola, G major
Handel: Concerto, viola, B minor
Johann Stamitz: Concerto, viola,
  G major
Karl Stamitz: Concerto, viola, op.1
Anton Stamitz: Concerto, viola, no.4
Weber: Andante and Rondo ongarese
Berlioz: Harold in Italy
Wolf: Italian serenade
Vaughan Williams: Flos campi
Bartók: Concerto, viola, op. posth.
Piston: Concerto, viola
Hindemith: Concert music for viola and
  large chamber orchestra, op.48
Hindemith: Concerto, viola, op.36, no.4

Hindemith: Der Schwanendreher
Hindemith: Trauermusik
Walton: Concerto, viola
Partos: Yiskor
Dello Joio: Lyric fantasies
Henze: Compases para preguntas
  ensimismadas

VIOLONCELLO

15' or less

Vivaldi: Concertos, violoncello, P.24;
  P.35; P.282; P.434
Veracini: Menuet et gavotte
Tartini: Concerto, violoncello, A major
Leo: Concerto, violoncello, D major
Wagenseil: Concerto, violoncello,
  A major
Boccherini: Concerto, violoncello, G.477
Karl Stamitz: Concertos, violoncello,
  nos.2-3
Schumann: Adagio and allegro, op.70
Rubinstein: Melody in F
Saint-Saëns: Allegro appassionato, op.43
Saint-Saëns: Romance, op.36
Bruch: Ave Maria
Bruch: Kol nidrei
Tchaikovsky: Pezzo capriccioso
Popper: Hungarian rhapsody
Popper: Tarantelle, op.33
Fauré: Elegy, op.24
Boëllmann: Symphonic variations, op.23
Glazunov: Chant du ménestrel
Respighi: Adagio con variazioni
Malipiero: Concerto, violoncello
Milhaud: Concerto, violoncello, no.1
Hindemith: Trauermusik
Penderecki: Sonata, violoncello and
  orchestra

16'-30'

Wagenseil: Concerto, violoncello, C major
Haydn: Concertos, violoncello,
  Hob.VIIb:2 (original and Gevaert
  arrangement); Hob.VIIb:5
Boccherini: Concertos, violoncello,
  G.474; G.482 (original and Grützmacher
  arrangement)
Karl Stamitz: Concerto, violoncello,
  no.1
Schumann: Concerto, violoncello, op.129
Lalo: Concerto, violoncello, D minor
Saint-Saëns: Concertos, violoncello,
  nos.1-2
Tchaikovsky: Variations on a rococo
  theme
Dvořák: Concerto, violoncello, (no.2)
Elgar: Concerto, violoncello, op.85
Herbert: Concerto, violoncello, no.2

Schoenberg: Concerto, violoncello
Bloch: Schelomo
Bloch: Voice in the wilderness
Toch: Concerto, violoncello, op.35
Milhaud: Concerto, violoncello, no.2
Khachaturian: Concerto-rhapsody,
  violoncello and orchestra
Kabalevsky: Concerto, violoncello, no.1
Shostakovich: Concerto, violoncello,
  no.1
Barber: Concerto, violoncello, op.22
William Schuman: A song of Orpheus
Henze: Ode an den Westwind

Over 30'

Dvořák: Concerto, violoncello, op.104
Richard Strauss: Don Quixote
Prokofiev: Sinfonia concertante,
  op.125
Britten: Symphony for violoncello
  and orchestra, op.68

Duration uncertain

Boismortier: Concerto, D major

DOUBLE BASS

Dittersdorf: Concerto, double bass,
  E major
Dittersdorf: Concerto, double bass,
  E-flat major
Vanhal: Concerto, double bass,
  E-flat major
Mozart: Per questo bella mano, K.612
Koussevitzky: Concerto, double bass,
  op.3 (original and Meyer-Tormin
  orchestration)
Miari: Concerto, double bass

MULTIPLE DIVERSE STRINGS

2 solo strings

Vivaldi: Concerto, violin and
  violoncello, P.388
Vivaldi: Concerto, 2 violoncellos,
  P.411
Graun: Concerto, violin and viola,
  C minor
Johann Christian Bach: Sinfonia
  concertante (violin and violoncello)
Dittersdorf: Sinfonia concertante,
  double bass and viola
Karl Stamitz: Sinfonia concertante,
  D major (violin and viola)

Mozart: Sinfonia concertante, K.320d
  (364) (violin and viola)
Brahms: Concerto, violin and violoncello,
  op.102
Richard Strauss: Don Quixote
  (violoncello and viola)

2 violins and violoncello

Corelli: Concerti grossi, op.6, nos.1-12
Alessandro Scarlatti: Concerti grossi
  nos. 3, 6
Manfredini: Concerto grosso, op.3, no.9
Handel: Concerti grossi no.7;
  op.3, no.2; op.6, nos.1-12
Benedetto Marcello: Concerti grossi,
  op.1, nos.1, 6-10
Geminiani: Concerto grosso, C major
  (after Corelli, op.5, no.3)
Locatelli: Concerto grosso, op.1, no.9
Boyce: Concerto grosso, B minor

Solo string quartet

Benedetto Marcello: Concerti grossi,
  op.1, nos.2-5
Geminiani: Concerto grosso no.12
Geminiani: Concerti grossi, op.3,
  nos.1-6
Geminiani: Concerto grosso, op.7, no.1
Locatelli: Concerto grosso, op.7, no.6
Sammartini: Concerto in E-flat
Mozart: Serenade no.6
Elgar: Introduction and allegro, op.47
Vaughan Williams: Fantasia on a theme
  by Thomas Tallis
Bloch: Concerto grosso no.2
Blacher: Orchesterfantasie, op.51
Canning: Fantasy on a hymn by Justin
  Morgan (2 solo string quartets)

Other combinations of solo strings

Bach: Brandenburg concerto no.3
  (3 violins, 3 violas, 3 violoncellos,
  plus double bass and continuo)
Bach: Brandenburg concerto no.6
  (2 violas, 2 viole da gamba,
  violoncello, double bass and continuo)
Locatelli: Concerto grosso, op.1, no.8
  (2 violins, 2 violas, violoncello soli)
Stravinsky: Pulcinella--Suite
  (2 violins, viola, violoncello,
  double bass soli)

FLUTE

Vivaldi: Concertos, flute, op.10,
  nos.2-3
Telemann: Concertos, flute,
  D major and E minor
Bach: Suite no.2, BWV 1067
Quantz: Concertos, flute, C major,
  C minor, D major, D major ("Pour
  Potsdam"), G major
Galuppi: Concertos, flute, D major,
  G major
Pergolesi: Concerto, flute, G major
Frederick II: Concertos, flute, nos.3-4
Gluck: Concerto, flute, G major
Johann Stamitz: Concertos, flute,
  C major, D major
Haydn: Concerto, flute, Hob.VIIf:D1
Grétry: Concerto, flute, C major
Boccherini: Concerto, flute, G.489
Karl Stamitz: Concerto, flute, G major
Mozart: Andante, K.285e (315)
Mozart: Concertos, flute, nos.1-2
Donizetti: Concertino, flute, C major
Saint-Saëns: Odelette, op.162
Saint-Saëns: Romance, op.37
Fauré: Fantasy, flute and chamber
  orchestra
Chaminade: Concertino, flute, op.107
Nielsen: Concerto, flute (1926)
Busoni: Divertimento, flute and
  chamber orchestra, op.52
Griffes: Poem for flute and orchestra
Ibert: Concerto, flute
Rogers: Soliloquy for flute and strings
Hanson: Serenade, op.35
Brant: Angels and devils
Kennan: Night soliloquy

2 FLUTES

Telemann: Concerto, 2 flutes, A minor
Galuppi: Concerto, 2 flutes, E minor
Haydn: Concerto, 2 flutes, Hob.VIIh:1
Cimarosa: Concerto (concertante),
  2 flutes, G major

RECORDER

Vivaldi: Concerto, flute, op.10, no.2
  (for flute or recorder)
Vivaldi: Concerto, recorder, P.440
Telemann: Concert suite, F major
Telemann: Concerto, recorder, F major
Telemann: Suite, A minor

PICCOLO

Vivaldi: Concertos, piccolo, P.79;
  P.83

OBOE

Albinoni: Concerto, op.7, no.3
Albinoni: Concerto, op.9, no.2
Vivaldi: Concertos, oboe, P.41; P.259;
  P.306
Telemann: Concertos, oboe, D minor,
  E minor, F minor
Graupner: Concerto, oboe, F major
Handel: Concertos, oboe, nos.1-3
Handel: Concerto, oboe, E-flat major
Benedetto Marcello: Concerto, oboe,
  C minor
Johann Stamitz: Concerto, oboe, C major
Haydn: Concerto, oboe, Hob.VIIg:C1
Cimarosa: Concerto, oboe, C minor
Mozart: Concerto, oboe, K.285d (314)
Donizetti: Concertino, oboe, F major
Bellini: Concerto, oboe, E-flat major
Richard Strauss: Concerto, oboe, D major
Vaughan Williams: Concerto, oboe (1944)
Martinu: Concerto, oboe
Goosens: Concerto in one movement, op.45
Wilder: Concerto, oboe
Barlow: Rhapsody for oboe

ENGLISH HORN

Donizetti: Concertino, English horn,
  G major
Sibelius: Legends--No.2, The swan of
  Tuonela
Wolf-Ferrari: Concertino, English horn,
  op.34

CLARINET

Karl Stamitz: Concerto, clarinet,
  E-flat major
Karl Stamitz: Concerto, clarinet, no.3,
  B-flat major
Mozart: Concerto, clarinet, K.622
Spohr: Concerto, clarinet, op.26
Weber: Concertino, clarinet and
  orchestra, op.26
Weber: Concertos, clarinet, nos.1-2
Rossini: Variations for clarinet and
  small orchestra

Donizetti: Concertino, clarinet,
B-flat major
Wagner: Adagio, clarinet and strings,
D-flat major
Debussy: Rhapsody, clarinet and
orchestra
Nielsen: Concerto, clarinet, op.57
Busoni: Concertino, clarinet and
chamber orchestra, op.48
Stravinsky: Ebony concerto
Copland: Concerto, clarinet
Skrowaczewski: Ricercari notturni
(soloist doubles on B-flat clarinet
and bass clarinet)

BASSOON

Vivaldi: Concertos, bassoon, P.46;
P.70; P.137; P.318
Graupner: Concerto, bassoon, G major
Boismortier: Concerto, D major
Karl Stamitz: Concerto, bassoon,
F major
Mozart: Concerto, bassoon, K.186e (191)
Mozart: Concerto, bassoon, no.2
Weber: Andante and Rondo ongarese
Weber: Concerto, bassoon, op.75
Villa-Lobos: Ciranda das sete notas

SAXOPHONE

Debussy: Rhapsody, alto saxophone and
orchestra
Glazunov: Concerto, alto saxophone,
op.109
Villa-Lobos: Fantasia (soprano or
tenor saxophone)
Ibert: Concertino da camera, alto
saxophone and orchestra
Martin: Ballade, saxophone and
orchestra (alto saxophone)
Skrowaczewski: Ricercari notturni
(soloist doubles on soprano, alto,
and baritone saxophones)

HORN

Telemann: Concerto, horn, D major
Haydn: Concertos, horn, nos.1-2
Michael Haydn: Concertino, horn,
D major
Mozart: Concertos, horn, nos.1-4
Mozart: Concert-rondo, horn and
orchestra, K.371
Weber: Concertino, horn, op.45

Schumann: Adagio and allegro, op.70
Saint-Saëns: Morceau de concert, horn
and orchestra, op.94
Saint-Saëns: Romance, op.36
Richard Strauss: Concertos, horn,
nos.1-2
Glière: Concerto, horn, op.91
Hindemith: Concerto, horn
Britten: Serenade for tenor, horn, and
strings, op.31
Hamilton: Voyage, for horn and chamber
orchestra

2 OR MORE HORNS

Vivaldi: Concertos, 2 horns, P.320;
P.321
Telemann: Concerto, 2 horns, E-flat
major
Kuhlau: Concertino, 2 horns, F minor
Schumann: Concertstück, op.86 (4 horns)

TRUMPET

Torelli: Concertos, trumpet (2
different concertos, each in D major)
Torelli: Sinfonia con tromba, D major
Purcell: Sonata for trumpet and strings
Telemann: Concerto, trumpet, D major
Fasch: Concerto, trumpet, D major
Leopold Mozart: Concerto, trumpet,
D major
Haydn: Concerto, trumpet, Hob.VIIe:1
Hummel: Concerto, trumpet, E or E-flat
Bloch: Proclamation for trumpet and
orchestra
Shostakovich: Concerto, piano, no.1
(solo trumpet as well as solo piano)
Chou: Soliloquy of a bhiksuni

2 TRUMPETS

Vivaldi: Concerto, 2 trumpets, P.75
Hamilton: Circus

TROMBONE

Rimsky-Korsakov: Concerto, trombone
and band
Bloch: Symphony for trombone and
orchestra

Milhaud: Concertino d'hiver
Hovhaness: Overture, op.76, no.1

Richard Rodney Bennett: Concerto, guitar
and chamber ensemble

TUBA

Vaughan Williams: Concerto, tuba

MANDOLINE

Vivaldi: Concerto, mandoline, P.134

PERCUSSION

Bartók: Concerto, 2 pianos and
  percussion (2 or 3 percussionists)
Milhaud: Concerto, percussion and
  small orchestra (1 percussionist)
Schreiner: The worried drummer
  (1 percussionist)
Kubik: Gerald McBoing Boing
  (1 percussionist)
Kraft: Configurations (4 percussionists)
Erb: Concerto for solo percussionist
  and orchestra
Colgrass: Déjà vu (4 percussionists)
Colgrass: Rhapsodic fantasy, for
  percussion soloist and orchestra

HARP

Handel: Concerto, harp, op.4, no.6
Dittersdorf: Concerto, harp, A major
Boieldieu: Concerto harp, C major
Saint-Saëns: Morceau de concert, harp
  and orchestra, op.154
Debussy: Danses sacrée et profane
Glière: Concerto, harp, op.74
Ravel: Introduction and allegro
Grandjany: Aria in classic style
Berezowsky: Concerto, harp, op.31
Rodrigo: Concierto serenata
Badings: Concerto, harp
Ginastera: Concerto, harp, op.25

GUITAR

Vivaldi: Concerto, guitar, P.209
Ponce: Concierto del sur
Villa-Lobos: Concerto, guitar and
  small orchestra (1951)
Castelnuovo-Tedesco: Concerto, guitar,
  op.99
Rodrigo: Concierto de Aranjuez
Berkeley: Concerto, guitar, op.88

SEVERAL DIVERSE INSTRUMENTS

2 solo instruments

Vivaldi: Concerto, oboe and bassoon,
  P.129
Vivaldi: Concerto, oboe and violin,
  P.406
Telemann: Concerto, recorder and flute,
  E minor
Bach: Concerto, violin and oboe,
  BWV 1060
Handel: Concerto grosso, op.3, no.3
  (fl, vn; or ob, vn)
Haydn: Concertos, flute and oboe,
  Hob.VIIh:2-VIIh:5
Karl Stamitz: Concerto, clarinet and
  bassoon, B-flat major
Mozart: Concerto, flute and harp,
  K.297c (299)
Saint-Saëns: Tarantelle, op.6 (fl, cl)
Richard Strauss: Duet-concertino
  (cl, bsn)
Bloch: Concertino (va, fl; or cl, fl)
Berg: Chamber concerto, op.8 (vn, pf)
Copland: Quiet city (tp, Eh; or tp, ob)

3 solo instruments

Vivaldi: Concerto, flute, oboe and
  bassoon, P.261
Bach: Brandenburg concerto no.4
  (vn, 2rec)
Bach: Brandenburg concerto no.5 (fl,
  vn, hpsd)
Bach: Concerto, flute, violin and
  harpsichord, BWV 1044
Handel: Concerto, organ, op.4, no.3
  (solo vn and vc, as well as organ)
Beethoven: Concerto, violin, violoncello
  and piano, op.56
Barber: Capricorn concerto (fl, ob, tp)
Kubik: Symphony concertante (tp, va, pf)
Del Tredici: Syzygy (hn, 2perc, plus
  solo soprano)

4 or more solo instruments

Bach: Brandenburg concerto no.1
(3ob, 2hn, vn)
Bach: Brandenburg concerto no.2
(rec, ob, tp, vn)
Haydn: Sinfonia concertante, op.84
(ob, bsn, vn, vc)
Mozart: Sinfonia concertante,
K.Anh.C 14.01 (297b) (ob, cl, hn, bsn)
Bartók: Concerto, 2 pianos and
percussion (2pf, 2 or 3perc)
Martin: Concerto, 7 winds (fl, ob, cl,
bsn, hn, tp, tbn)
Hindemith: Concerto for woodwinds,
harp, and orchestra (fl, ob, cl,
bsn, hp)
Berio: Tempi concertati (fl, vn, 2pf)
Amram: Triple concerto (woodwind
quintet: fl, ob, cl, bsn, hn; brass
quintet: 2tp, hn, tbn, tuba; jazz
quintet: asx, bsx, db, pf, drums)
Birtwistle: Nomos (fl, cl, hn, bsn)

JAZZ SOLOISTS

Howard Brubeck: Dialogues for jazz
combo and orchestra (varied soloists)
Kraft: Contextures (ssx, tp, db, drums)
Schuller: Concertino for jazz quartet
and orchestra (vibraphone, pf, perc,
db)
Schuller: Journey into jazz (asx, tsx,
tp, db, drums, plus narrator)
Amram: Triple concerto (jazz quintet:
asx, bsx, db, drums, pf; plus
woodwind quintet: fl, ob, cl, bsn, hn;
and brass quintet: 2tp, hn, tbn, tuba)
Baker: Le chat qui pêche (sx, pf, db,
drums, plus soprano voice)

APPENDIX D: ORCHESTRAL WORKS

LISTED BY INSTRUMENTATION

This appendix is intended to aid those who must program for certain combinations, or who may not exceed
certain limits of instrumentation. The categories
used in this appendix (see chart, p.356) progress gen-
erally from smaller combinations to larger, though
there is much backing and filling on the way. Any
category may include works requiring slightly less in
the way of instrumentation; conversely, if more instruments are called for than are in the heading, this
fact is indicated in parentheses.

Works calling for optional instruments are often
listed in more than one category in order to reflect
this variability.

Works in the larger categories are subdivided according to duration. If the duration of a particular
work is estimated for the purpose of these durational
subdivisions, that fact is indicated by means of an
asterisk (*).

Within each category or subdivision, works are
listed chronologically according to the composer's
birth date.

For complete information on any of these works,
refer to the main alphabetical listing by composer.

STRINGS	WOODWINDS	BRASS	PERCUSSION	OTHER	PAGE
	brass and/or percussion				357
works without strings	any	any	any	any	357
str orch					357
str orch				cnt	358
str orch			perc	hp, cel, pf, hpsd	359
individual str players	any	any	any	any	359
str	single winds and percussion			hp, cel, pf	360
str	2fl or 2rec				360
str		2-8 hn			360
str	0202	2000		cnt	360
str	2202	2000		cnt	361
str	2202	2200	tmp	cnt	362
str	2222	2200	tmp		362
str	2222	2200	3	hp, cel, pf	363
str	2222	2231	1		363
str	2222	2331	4	hp, cel, pf	364
str	2222	4000	2		365
str	2222	4200	3	hp, cel, pf	365
str	2222	4330	tmp		366
str	2222	4230	4		366
str	2222	4431	5		367
str	2222	4431	5	hp, cel, pf	367
str	8 woodwinds	4300	tmp	cnt	369
str	3222	4331	4		369
str	3222	4431	5	hp, cel, pf	370
str	3322	4431	6	2hp, cel, pf	371
str	9/10 woodwinds	4331	4		371
str	9/10 woodwinds	4431	6	hp, cel, pf	372
str	3332	4331	5	hp, cel, pf	373
str	11 woodwinds	4431	5	hp, cel, pf	374
str	3333	4331	5		374
str	3333	4431	6	2hp, cel, pf	375
str	3333	larger than previous categories			376
str	13 woodwinds	4431	7	2hp, cel, pf	376
str	4454	6641	8	3hp, cel, pf	377
str	larger than all previous categories				378
instrumentation indeterminate					378
multiple orchestras					378

BRASS AND/OR PERCUSSION

Brass only

Gabrieli: Canzona noni toni
Gabrieli: Sonata pian' e forte
Ruggles: Angels
Dukas: La péri--Fanfare

Percussion only

Varèse: Ionisation
Chávez: Toccata for percussion

Brass and percussion

Janáček: Sokal fanfare
Debussy: Le martyre de Saint
 Sébastien--Two fanfares
Roussel: Fanfare for a pagan rite
Copland: Fanfare for the common man

WORKS WITHOUT STRINGS

15' or less

Beethoven: Zapfenstreich march*
Donizetti: Sinfonia for winds
Mendelssohn: Overture for winds, op.24
Richard Strauss: Serenade, op.7
Stravinsky: Octet
Stravinsky: Symphonies of wind
 instruments
Varèse: Hyperprism
Varèse: Intégrales
Milhaud: Symphonies for small
 orchestra--No.5, Dixtuor
 d'instruments à vent
Chávez: Xochipilli
Poulenc: Suite française
Brant: Galaxy 2
Brant: Verticals ascending
Rochberg: Black sounds
Serocki: Segmenti
Xenakis: Akrata

Over 15'

Mozart: Serenades nos.10-12
Berlioz: Symphonie funèbre et
 triomphale
Gounod: Little symphony for wind
 instruments
Richard Strauss: Suite, op.4
Richard Strauss: Symphony for winds
Varèse: Deserts
Weill: Kleine Dreigroschenmusik
Kurka: The good soldier Schweik--Suite
Birtwistle: Verses for ensembles

STRING ORCHESTRA

5' or less

Pachelbel: Canon
Purcell: Canon on a ground bass
Veracini: Aria schiavona
Michael Haydn: Symphony, P.8
Chopin: Mazurka no.7 (arr.)
Schumann: Träumerei (arr.)
Grieg: Erotik
Grieg: Two melodies, op.53
Fauré: Shylock, op.57--Nocturne
Foote: Irish folk song
Elgar: Elegy, op.58
Sibelius: Canzonetta, op.62a
Sibelius: Romance, op.42
Vaughan Williams: Prelude "49th
 parallel"
Ives: Hymn
Cowell: Ballad
Dello Joio: Arietta
Starer: Elegy for strings

6'-10'

Gabrieli: Canzona (double string
 orchestra)
Monteverdi: Orfeo--Sinfonie e ritornelli
Schein: Banchetto musicale--Suite no.1
Corelli: Suite for string orchestra
Purcell: Chacony in G minor
Purcell: The fairy queen--Suites nos.1-2
Purcell: The Gordian knot untied--
 Suite no.2
A. Scarlatti: Concerto, G minor*
A. Scarlatti: Piccola suite
Vivaldi: Sinfonia, P.Sinf.21
D. Scarlatti: Five sonatas in form
 of a suite
B. Marcello: Introduction, aria
 and presto
Geminiani: Concerto grosso, op.2, no.2
Pergolesi: Concertino, E-flat major
Abel: Symphonies, op.1, nos.5-6
Boccherini: Sinfonia concertante,
 strings, G.268
Mozart: Adagio and fugue, K.546
Mozart: Divertimenti K.125b (137);
 K.125c (138)
Donizetti: Allegro in C major
Schubert: Overture, D.8
Borodin: Nocturne (arr. Malcolm Sargent)
Dvořák: Notturno, op.40
Grieg: Two elegiac melodies, op.34
Grieg: Two Norwegian airs, op.63
Puccini: I crisantemi
Roussel: Sinfonietta, op.52
Ruggles: Portals
Cadman: American suite
Prokofiev: Andante
Warlock: Capriol suite
Hindemith: Suite of French dances

Cowell: Hymn and fuguing tune no.2
Rodrigo: Zarabanda lejana y villancico
Skalkottas: Five Greek dances
Barber: Adagio for strings
Fine: Serious song
Shulman: Threnody
Ligeti: Ramifications
Amram: Autobiography for strings
Penderecki: Emanations (2 string
  orchestras)
Penderecki: To the victims of
  Hiroshima
Wuorinen: Grand bamboula

11'-15'

Purcell: The Gordian knot untied--
  Suite no.1
Fux: Overture, C major
Telemann: Overture in C major
Rameau: Suite for string orchestra
Tartini: Sinfonia, D major
Johann Stamitz: Symphony, op.3, no.3
Johann Stamitz: Three Mannheim
  symphonies--G major; A major;
  B-flat major
Mozart: Divertimento, K.125a (136)
Mozart: Eine kleine Nachtmusik
Rossini: Sonatas nos.1-6
Foote: Suite, op.63, E major
Elgar: Serenade, op.20
Arensky: Variations on a theme
  by Tchaikovsky
Nielsen: Little suite, op.1
Holst: Brook green suite
Holst: St. Paul's suite
Stravinsky: Concerto in D
Webern: Five movements, op.5
Berg: Lyric suite--Three pieces
Becker: Soundpiece no.2b
Villa-Lobos: Bachianas brasileiras
  no.9
Villa-Lobos: Suite for strings
Martin: Passacaille
Tansman: Variations on a theme
  by Girolamo Frescobaldi
Barbirolli: An Elizabethan suite
  (4hn in last movement only)
Křenek: Sinfonietta
Křenek: Symphonic elegy
Hovhaness: Psalm and fugue, op.40a
Dahl: Variations for string orchestra
  on a theme by C.P.E. Bach
Françaix: Sei preludi
Diamond: Rounds for string orchestra
Yardumian: Cantus animae et cordis
Xenakis: Syrmos
Sapieyevski: Surtsey

16'-20'

Lully: Le triomphe de l'amour--Ballet
  suite
Veracini: Quattro pezzi
Beethoven: Grosse Fuge, op.133

Grieg: Holberg suite, op.40
Schoenberg: Suite for string orchestra
Respighi: Ancient airs and dances--
  Set III
Miaskovsky: Sinfonietta, op.32, no.2
Martin: Etudes for string orchestra
Tansman: Triptych
Chávez: Symphony no.5
Tcherepnin: Serenade, op.97
Skalkottas: Ten sketches for strings
Wm. Schuman: Symphony no.5
Britten: Simple symphony, op.4
Persichetti: Symphony, op.61

21'-25'

Suk: Serenade, op.6
Brahms: Liebeslieder waltzes (arr.)
Janáček: Idyla
Herbert: Serenade, op.12
Bartók: Divertimento (1939)
Honegger: Symphony no.2 (opt trumpet)
Tippett: Concerto for double string
  orchestra
Gutche: Symphony no.5
Britten: Variations on a theme of
  Frank Bridge
Dello Joio: Meditations on Ecclesiastes

26'-30'

Mendelssohn: Sinfonie nos.8-9
Tchaikovsky: Serenade, op.48
Dvořák: Serenade, op.22
Richard Strauss: Metamorphosen
Schoenberg: Verklärte Nacht, op.4
Stravinsky: Apollon Musagète
Korngold: Symphonic serenade, op.39

Duration uncertain

Lully: Ballet music
Leclair: Sonata, D major
Gossec: Symphony, op.6, no.6
Kalinnikov: Chanson triste

STRING ORCHESTRA WITH CONTINUO

10' or less

Biber: Battalia
Pachelbel: Canon
Torelli: Concerto, op.6, no.1
Torelli: Sinfonia, op.6, no.6
Purcell: The rival sisters--Overture
A. Scarlatti: Concerti grossi nos.1-2
Albinoni: Concerti, op.5, nos.4, 7
Vivaldi: Concerto for orchestra, P.143
Vivaldi: Sinfonie nos.1-3
Handel: Alcina--Overture
Geminiani: Concerto grosso, op.2, no.3*
Veracini: Aria schiavona
Sammartini: Concertino, G major

Sammartini: Sinfonia, J.-C. 39
Galuppi: Concerti a quattro, nos.1-2
C.P.E. Bach: Symphony, W.182, no.1
Gluck: Overture, D major

Over 10'

Purcell: Abdelazar--Suite
Purcell: Dido and Aeneas--Suite
Fux: Overture, C major
Vivaldi: Concerto for orchestra, P.407
Manfredini: Christmas symphony, op.2,
  no.12*
Telemann: Don Quichotte
Telemann: Suites nos.1-2
Locatelli: Concerto grosso, op.1, no.6*
Locatelli: Trauer-Symphonie
Sammartini: Sinfonia, J.-C. 32
W.F. Bach: Sinfonia, F major
Frederick II: Symphonies nos.1*-2*
C.P.E. Bach: Symphonies, W.182, nos.2,
  3, 4, 5, 6*

Duration uncertain

Purcell: The double dealer--Suite
Telemann: Overture (Suite), G major
Gluck: Sinfonia, G major

STRING ORCHESTRA WITH HARP, PIANO, CELESTE, HARPSICHORD, AND/OR PERCUSSION

Purcell: Chacony in G minor (hpsd)
Haydn: Toy symphony, Hob.II:47
  (5 players for toys)
Mendelssohn: Sinfonia no.11 (3perc)
Johann Strauss, Jr.: Pizzicato polka
  (2perc)
Grieg: Erotik, op.43, no.5 (opt hp)
Mahler: Symphony no.5--Adagietto (hp)
Sibelius: Rakastava, op.14 (1perc)
Vaughan Williams: Fantasia on
  Greensleeves (hp or pf)
Vaughan Williams: Five variants of
  Dives and Lazarus (1 or 2hp)
Schoenberg: Ode to Napoleon Bonaparte
  (pf, reciter)
Bartók: Music for strings, percussion,
  and celeste (plus hp, pf)
Becker: Soundpiece no.1b (pf)
Martin: Petite symphonie concertante
  (hp, pf, hpsd)
Penderecki: Anaklasis (hp, cel, pf)

WORKS USING INDIVIDUAL STRING PLAYERS RATHER THAN STRING SECTIONS

Small ensemble (10 instruments or less)

Beethoven: Septet, op.20
Spohr: Nonet, op.31
Spohr: Octet, op.32
Rossini: Serenata per piccolo complesso
Schubert: Octet, D.803
Mendelssohn: Octet, strings, op.20
Saint-Saëns: Septet, op.65
Ives: The unanswered question
Ruggles: Angels (for strings)
Stravinsky: L'histoire du soldat--Suite
Varèse: Octandre
Webern: Concerto, op.24
Villa-Lobos: Bachianas brasileiras no.1
Milhaud: Symphonies for small orchestra--
  nos.1-4
Piston: Divertimento for nine
  instruments
Harsányi: L'histoire du petite tailleur
Walton: Façade
Dallapiccola: Piccola musica notturna
  (chamber orchestra version)
Britten: Sinfonietta
Kubik: Gerald McBoing Boing
Xenakis: Anaktoria
Xenakis: Analogique A
Chou: Yü ko
Feldman: Atlantis (version for 10
  players)
Stockhausen: Kontra-Punkte no.1

Medium ensemble (11-15 players)

Wagner: Siegfried idyll
Saint-Saëns: Carnival of the animals
Dvořák: Serenade, op.44
Schoenberg: Chamber symphony no.1
Schoenberg: Five pieces for orchestra,
  op.16 (chamber orchestra version)
Stravinsky: Concerto in E-flat
  ("Dumbarton Oaks")
Stravinsky: Eight instrumental
  miniatures
Stravinsky: Rag-time
Hindemith: Suite of French dances
Cowell: Sinfonietta
Copland: Appalachian spring (original
  instrumentation)
Rogers: The musicians of Bremen
Finney: Landscapes remembered
Bacewicz: Contradizione
Kubik: Divertimento I
Babbitt: Composition for twelve
  instruments
Maderna: Serenata no.2
Xenakis: Atrees
Ligeti: Ramifications (version for
  12 solo strings)
Davidovsky: Inflexions

Reynolds: Quick are the mouths of earth
Reynolds: Wedge
Schwartz: Texture

Large ensemble (over 15 players)

Ives: Chromâtimelôdtune
Ruggles: Men and mountains (original
  version)
Bartók: Music for strings, percussion
  and celeste
Webern: Five pieces for orchestra,op.10
Ibert: Divertissement
Prokofiev: Overture, op.42
Milhaud: La création du monde
Copland: Music for the theatre
Lutosławski: Venetian games
Blomdahl: Game for eight
Zimmermann: Stillness and return
Brown: Available forms 1
Feldman: Atlantis (version for
  17 players)

STRINGS
SINGLE WINDS AND PERCUSSION
HARP, CELESTE, PIANO

10' or less

Purcell: Trumpet overture*
A. Scarlatti: Sinfonia no.2 (cnt)
Franck: Eight short pieces
Grieg: Lyric pieces, op.68
Pierné: March of the lead soldiers
Vaughan Williams: Two hymn-tune
  preludes
Ives: Holidays symphony--Washington's
  Birthday (3 Jew's harps)
Ives: Symphony no.4--Fugue
Ives: Tone roads nos.1, 3
Honegger: Pastorale d'été
Benjamin: Two Jamaican pieces (3perc)
Cowell: Polyphonica for small orchestra
Poulenc: Deux marches et un interlude
Copland: Symphony no.1--Prelude (arr.)
Copland: Three Latin-American Sketches
Luening: Prelude to a hymn tune by
  William Billings
Glanville-Hicks: Gymnopédie no.1
La Montaine: A summer's day
Benson: Chants and graces (4perc)

11'-20'

A. Scarlatti: Sinfonie nos.4, 6, 8,
  10 (each with cnt)
Roussel: Le marchand de sable qui
  passe
Holst: Brook green suite
Respighi: Trittico Botticelliano
Becker: When the willow nods (2perc)
Hindemith: Tuttifäntchen--Suite (2perc)

Tippett: Divertimento for chamber
  orchestra
Finney: Landscapes remembered
Britten: Sinfonietta
Surinach: Ritmo jondo (5perc)
Kay: Scherzi musicali
Rochberg: Cheltenham concerto
Kirchner: Toccata (4perc)
Anderson: Chamber symphony (2perc)
Schwartz: Texture

Over 20'

Honegger: Le dit des jeux du monde
  (4perc)
Milhaud: Le carnaval de Londres
  (2perc, asx)
Rogers: The musicians of Bremen
  (narrator, 2perc)

STRINGS
2 FLUTES or RECORDERS

A. Scarlatti: Sinfonie nos.1, 5 (each
  with cnt)
W.F. Bach: Sinfonia, D minor
Foote: Air and gavotte
Vaughan Williams: Fantasia on
  Greensleeves (hp or pf)

STRINGS
2 (OR MORE) HORNS

Telemann: Suite, F major (cnt)
Sammartini: Sinfonia, J.-C. 4
Galuppi: Sinfonia, D major
Galuppi: Sinfonia, F major
Gluck: Sinfonia, F major
Joh. Stamitz: Symphony, op.3, no.3
Haydn: Divertimento, Hob.II:21
Mozart: Divertimenti, K.247;
  K.271h (287); K.320b (334)
Mozart: A musical joke
Mozart: Serenade no.8 (8hn)
Barbirolli: An Elizabethan suite (4 hn)

STRINGS
WINDS 0202-2000
CONTINUO

10' or less

Telemann: Overture in D major
Handel: Concerti grossi, op.3, nos.5-6
Handel: Overtures to Alcina; Alexander's
  feast; Judas Maccabaeus*; Orlando*;

Samson
Handel: Solomon--Entrance of the Queen
of Sheba
Leo: Santa Elena al Calvario--Sinfonia
Arne: Symphonies nos.1-3
Boyce: Overture--Ode for his majesty's
birthday (1769)
Boyce: Overture--Ode for the new year
(1772)
Boyce: Overture--Peleus and Thetis
Boyce: Symphonies nos.2-4, 6
Gluck: Orfeo ed Euridice--Dance of
the furies
Abel: Symphonies, op.1, nos.5-6
Haydn: Symphony A, Hob.I:107
Haydn: Symphony no.2
J.C. Bach: Symphonies op.3, no.2;
op.21, no.3
Michael Haydn: Symphony, P.26
Paisello: Sinfonia in tre tempi
Boccherini: Overture, op.43, G.521
Cimarosa: I traci amanti--Overture
Mozart: Apollo and Hyacinth--Prelude
Mozart: Bastien and Bastienne--Overture
Mozart: La finta giardiniera--Overture
Mozart: Symphony, K.196/121
Mozart: Symphonies nos.4, 5, 10
Ben Weber: Dolmen

11'-20'

Albinoni: Concerto, op.9, no.9
Handel: Concerto grosso, op.3, no.4
Handel: Overtures to Rodrigo; Saul;
Solomon; Theodora
Tartini: Concerto no.58
Sammartini: Sinfonia, J.-C. 2
Wagenseil: Sinfonia, G minor
Johann Stamitz: Sinfonia pastorale,
op.4, no.2
Haydn: Symphony B, Hob.I:108
Haydn: Symphonies nos.1, 3-5, 10-12,
14, 16-19, 23, 25, 27-29, 34-37, 40,
64
J.C. Bach: Symphonies, op.3, nos.1, 4;
op.6, nos.1, 6; op.21, no.1
Michael Haydn: Symphonies P.33; P.42
Gołąbek: Symphonies in D major, I-II
Vanhal: Sinfonia, G minor
Boccherini: Symphonies, G.506; G.511;
G.512; G.514
Mozart: Cassations nos.1-2
Mozart: Divertimento, K.167a (205)
Mozart: Symphonies nos.1, 2, 6, 11-13,
15-17

21'-30'

Bach: Suite no.1
Handel: Water music--Suite no.1
Haydn: Symphonies nos.15, 21,
22 (2Eh rather than 2ob), 26, 42-47,
49, 51, 52, 55, 57-59, 65-68
J.C. Bach: Symphony, op.9, no.2

Mozart: Divertimento, K.251
Mozart: Symphonies nos.29, 33
Amram: Shakespearian concerto

STRINGS
WINDS 2202-2000
CONTINUO

10' or less

Rameau: Platée--Suite des danses
Handel: Water music--Suite no.3
Sammartini: Sinfonia, J.-C. 47
Boyce: Symphony no.1
Gluck: Orfeo ed Euridice--Dance of the
blessed spirits
Michael Haydn: Symphony, P.29
Cimarosa: Sinfonia, D major
Mozart: Contradances, K.271c (267)
Mozart: Mitridate--Overture
Mozart: Serenade no.2, K.250a (101)
Mozart: Symphony no.24
Hindemith: Spielmusik, op.43, no.1

11'-20'

Rameau: Dardanus--Suite
Handel: Concerto grosso, op.3, no.1
Arne: Symphony no.4
Boyce: Symphonies nos.7-8
C.P.E. Bach: Symphonies, W.183, nos.1, 3
Haydn: Symphonies nos.9, 30, 80
J.C. Bach: Symphonies, op.18, nos.1,
3, 5, 6
Michael Haydn: Symphony, P.21
Gołąbek: Symphony in C major
Boccherini: Symphonies, G.503; G.512
Mozart: Symphonies nos.14, 21, 27, 37
Wański: Symphony in G major
Berkeley: Windsor variations
Musgrave: Night music

21'-30'

Haydn: Symphonies nos.6-8, 24, 62, 63,
71, 74, 76-79, 81, 83-85, 87, 89, 91
Boccherini: Symphony, G.518
Wański: Symphony in D major
Witt: Symphony in A major
Schubert: Symphony no.5

Duration uncertain

Lalande: Christmas symphony
Rameau: Les paladins--Suite no.2
Graun: Sinfonia, F major, M.95

STRINGS
WINDS 2202-2200
TIMPANI
CONTINUO

10' or less

Boyce: Overture--Ode for the new
  year (1758)
Boyce: Symphony no.5
Gluck: Iphigenie in Aulis--Overture
Gluck: Orfeo ed Euridice--Overture
Michael Haydn: Andromeda ed Perseo--
  Overture
Paisiello: La scuffiara--Overture
Cimarosa: Il maestro di cappella--
  Overture
Mozart: Lucio Silla--Overture
Mozart: Il re pastore--Overture
Mozart: Symphony, K.141a
Mozart: Symphonies nos.7, 22, 23
Weber: Peter Schmoll--Overture
Schubert: Overture, D.470

11'-20'

Rameau: Les fêtes d'Hébé--Divertissement
Handel: Water music--Suite no.2
C.P.E. Bach: Symphony, W.183, no.1
Haydn: Symphonies nos.20, 32, 37
Dittersdorf: Sinfonia, C major
Mozart: Symphonies nos.8, 9, 20, 26,
  28, 30, 34
Weber: Symphony no.2

21'-30'

Haydn: Symphonies nos.33, 38, 41, 48,
  50, 53, 56, 60, 61, 69, 70, 73, 75,
  82, 86, 88, 90, 92-98, 102
J.C. Bach: Symphony, op.18, no.4
Mozart: Serenades nos.1, 3, 5
Mozart: Symphonies nos.34, 36, 38, 41
Witt: Jena symphony
Weber: Symphony no.1

Over 30'

Handel: Water music
Haydn: Symphony no.54
Mozart: Serenades nos.4, 7, 9

Duration uncertain

Lully: Roland--Suite
Handel: Alceste--Instrumental pieces

STRINGS
WINDS 2222-2200
TIMPANI

10' or less

Purcell: The Gordian knot untied--
  Suite no.2
Purcell: The virtuous wife--Suite
Haydn: March for the Royal Society
  of Musicians
Paisiello: Nina--Overture
Paisiello: Sinfonia funebre
Cimarosa: Il matrimonio segreto--
  Overture
Mozart: Masonic funeral music
Mozart: Overture, K.Anh.C 11.05 (311a)
Mozart: Overtures to La clemenza di
  Tito; Così fan tutte; Don Giovanni;
  Idomeneo; The impresario; The marriage
  of Figaro
Beethoven: Overtures to Coriolan;
  Prometheus
Rossini: Overtures to L'italiana in
  Algeri; La scala di seta; Il signor
  Bruschino; Tancredi
Rossini: William Tell--Pas de six
Schubert: Overtures, D.8; D.556; D.590;
  D.591
Schubert: Overtures to Claudine von
  Villa Bella; Die Freunde von Salamanka;
  Der häusliche Krieg; Der Spiegelritter*;
  Der Teufel als Hydraulicus; Der
  vierjährige Posten; Die Zwillingsbrüder
Arriaga: Los esclavos felices--Overture
Mendelssohn: The Hebrides
Mendelssohn: Heimkehr aus der Fremde
Mendelssohn: Märchen von der schönen
  Melusine
Mendelssohn: Midsummer night's dream--
  Scherzo; Intermezzo; Nocturne
Verdi: La traviata--Prelude to Act III
Rimsky-Korsakov: Tsar Saltan--Flight
  of the bumble-bee
Fauré: Pavane
Elgar: Salut d'amour
Delius: Two pieces for small orchestra
Mascagni: Cavalleria rusticana--
  Intermezzo
Sibelius: Kuolema--Valse triste
Ives: The unanswered question
Bartók: Rumanian folk dances
Etler: Elegy for small orchestra

11'-20'

Purcell: The Gordian knot untied--
  Suite no.1
Purcell: The married beau--Suite
Rameau: Ballet suite (arr.)
Abel: Symphony, op.7, no.6
J.C. Bach: Symphony, op.18, no.2
Mozart: Divertimento, K.113

Mozart: Les petits riens
Mozart: Symphonies nos.3, 31, 35
Beethoven: Contradances
Beethoven: Musik zu einem Ritterballet
Schumann: Overture, scherzo and finale
Wagner: Siegfried idyll
Delibes: Le roi s'amuse--Airs de danse
Roussel: Concerto for small orchestra
Roussel: Petite suite
Kodály: Summer evening
Martinu: Toccata e due canzoni (pf)
Prokofiev: Classical symphony
Piston: Sinfonietta
Berkeley: Sinfonietta
Effinger: Little symphony no.1

21'-30'

Haydn: Symphonies nos.99, 101, 103, 104
Mozart: Symphonies nos.39-40
Beethoven: Symphonies nos.1, 8
Schubert: Symphonies nos.1-3
Arriaga: Symphony, D minor
Mendelssohn: Symphony no.4
Gounod: Symphony no.1
Sibelius: Pelléas and Mélisande
Schoenberg: Chamber symphony no.2
Poulenc: Sinfonietta (hp)

Over 30'

Beethoven: Symphonies nos.2, 4, 7
Schubert: Symphony no.6
Mendelssohn: Symphony no.1

STRINGS
WINDS 2222-2200
3 PERCUSSION
HARP, CELESTE, PIANO

10' or less

Mozart: The abduction from the
 seraglio--Overture (4perc)
Beethoven: Ruins of Athens--
 Turkish march (3bn)
Boieldieu: Caliph of Bagdad--Overture
Weber: Preziosa--Overture (5perc)
Berlioz: La damnation de Faust--Dance
 of the sylphs (3fl, 2hp)
Schumann: Manfred--Suite
Chabrier: Habanera
Humperdinck: Hansel and Gretel--
 Knusperwalzer
Debussy: Danse (4perc)
Debussy: Sarabande
Järnefelt: Praeludium
Vaughan Williams: The wasps--March
 past of the kitchen utensils
Vaughan Williams: The wasps--Overture
Ravel: Ma mère l'Oye--Prelude et
 Danse du rouet

Ravel: Pavane pour une infante défunte
Falla: El amor brujo--Ritual fire dance
Wolf-Ferrari: Jewels of the Madonna--
 Intermezzo no.1
Webern: Symphony, op.21
Becker: Two pieces for orchestra--
 Among the reeds and rushes
Ibert: Hommage à Mozart
Benjamin: Two Jamaican pieces
Cowell: Carol for orchestra
Dallapiccola: Piccola musica notturna

11'-20'

Grétry: Zémire et Azor--Ballet suite
Fauré: Masques et bergamasques
Debussy: Petite suite (4perc)
Roussel: Le festin de l'araigne
Ravel: Ma mère l'Oye--Suite (4perc)
Ravel: Le tombeau de Couperin
Falla: El amor brujo--Ballet suite (A)
Falla: Three-cornered hat--Scenes and
 dances from Part I
Respighi: Gli uccelli
Prokofiev: A summer day
Britten: Suite on English folk tunes

Over 20'

Haydn: Symphony no.100 (4perc)
Beethoven: Prometheus (ballet music)
Honegger: Symphony no.4

STRINGS
WINDS 2222-2231
1 PERCUSSION

10' or less

Gluck: Alceste--Overture
Mozart: Don Giovanni--Overture (arr.
 Busoni)
Mozart: The magic flute--Overture
Cherubini: Overtures to Démophoon;
 Faniska; The Portuguese inn
Boieldieu: La dame blanche--Overture
Paganini: Moto perpetuo (arr. Molinari)
Weber: Silvana--Overture
Schubert: Overtures D.12; D.26
Schubert: Overtures to Alfonso and
 Estrella; Des teufels Lustschloss
Bellini: Symphonies in C minor, D major
Glinka: Kamarinskaya
Mendelssohn: Athalia--War march of the
 priests
Mendelssohn: Trumpet overture
Bruckner: March in D minor
Bruckner: Three pieces for orchestra
Balakirev: Overture on three Russian
 folk songs
Mussorgsky: Scherzo
Janáček: Adagio

Stravinsky: Suite no.1 for small
 orchestra
Warlock: Capriol suite
Walton: Portsmouth Point (rev. version)
Benson: Five brief encounters

11'-20'

Schubert: Rosamunde--Ballet music;
 Entr'actes
Mendelssohn: Midsummer night's dream--
 Overture
Schumann: Overture, scherzo and finale
Bruckner: Overture, G minor
Holst: Egdon Heath
Ives: Symphony no.3
Stravinsky: Danses concertantes
Villa-Lobos: Sinfonietta no.1
Berio: Variazioni per orchestra
 da camera

21'-30'

Gluck: Don Juan--Four movements
Clementi: Symphonies nos.1, 4
Schubert: Symphony no.8
Weill: Symphony no.2
Carter: Symphony no.1

Over 30'

Clementi: Symphonies nos.2, 3
Schubert: Symphony no.9
Schumann: Symphony no.2
Milhaud: Saudades do Brazil

STRINGS
WINDS 2222-2331
4 PERCUSSION
HARP, CELESTE, PIANO

10' or less

Monteverdi: Orfeo--Overture (2hp, org)
Bach: Musical offering--Ricercare
 (arr. Webern)
Handel: Occasional oratorio--Overture
Michael Haydn: Pastorello, P.91
Weber: Abu Hassan--Overture
Rossini: Overtures to Il barbiere di
 Siviglia; La Cenerentola; Il Turco
 in Italia; Il viaggio a Reims
Lanner: Die Werber Walzer
Lortzing: Zar und Zimmermann--Overture
Glinka: Valse fantaisie
Mendelssohn: Athalia--Overture
Mendelssohn: Midsummer night's dream--
 Wedding march
Mendelssohn: St. Paul--Overture (org)
Gounod: Funeral march of a marionette
Delibes: Coppelia--Entr'acte and Waltz
Chabrier: Le roi malgré lui--Danse
 slav; Fête polonaise

German: Three dances from "Henry VIII"
Satie: Deux préludes posthumes et
 une gnossienne
Satie: Jack in the box
Satie: Trois petites pièces montées
Vaughan Williams: English folksong suite
Ives: Country band march (asx)
Ives: The gong on the hook and ladder
Schoenberg: Begleitungsmusik zu einer
 Lichtspielscene
Coleridge-Taylor: Christmas overture
Wolf-Ferrari: Jewels of the Madonna--
 Intermezzo no.2
Bartók: Dances of Transylvania
Bartók: Hungarian peasant songs
Stravinsky: Suite no.2 for small
 orchestra
Webern: Variations for orchestra, op.30
Griffes: The white peacock (2hp)
Riegger: Dance rhythms (5perc)
Villa-Lobos: Bachianas brasileiras
 no.5--Aria (8perc)
Martinu: Comedy on the bridge--Little
 suite
Hindemith: Cupid and Psyche--Overture
Jacob: The barber of Seville goes to
 the devil
Jacob: Fantasia on the Alleluia hymn
Cowell: Hymn and fuguing tunes, nos.3,
 16
Korngold: Theme and variations, op.42
Copland: John Henry
Copland: Rodeo--Corral nocturne;
 Saturday night waltz
Copland: Variations on a Shaker melody
Luening: Synthesis (electronic tape)
Walton: Façade--Suite no.1
Kabalevsky: The comedians--Galop
Barber: Die Natali--Silent night
Wm. Schuman: Newsreel (5perc)
Gould: American symphonette no.2
 (4sx, gtr)
Chou: All in the spring wind
Chou: Landscapes
Frackenpohl: Short overture
Corigliano: Elegy for orchestra

11'-20'

Gluck: Ballet suite no.2 (arr. Mottl)
Chabrier: Suite pastorale
Sullivan: The tempest--Three dances
Satie: Les aventures de Mercure
Ives: Three places in New England
 (chamber orchestra version)
Bartók: Hungarian sketches
Stravinsky: Scènes de ballet
Villa-Lobos: Bachianas brasileiras
 no.2 (sx, 6perc)
Milhaud: Aubade
Milhaud: Le boeuf sur le toit
Milhaud: Cortège funèbre
Milhaud: Suite française
Rogers: Once upon a time

Still: Darker America
V. Thomson: The plow that broke the plains--Suite
Tansman: Sinfonietta
Auric: La chambre
Kabalevsky: The comedians
Wilder: Carl Sandburg suite
Menotti: Sebastian--Suite
Britten: Matinées musicales
Diamond: Music for Shakespeare's Romeo and Juliet
Husa: Fantasies for orchestra
Xenakis: ST/48-1,240162
Rorem: Ideas for easy orchestra

Over 20'

Bach: Suite no.3
Richard Strauss: Der Bürger als Edelmann--Suite (6perc)
Vaughan Williams: Symphony no.5
Vaughan Williams: Symphony no.8 (5perc)
Prokofiev: Peter and the wolf (narrator)
V. Thomson: The river--Suite (banjo)
Poulenc: The story of Babar (narrator)
Copland: Appalachian spring--Suite (version for large orchestra)
Copland: Music for the theatre
Weill: Aufstieg und Fall der Stadt Mahagonny--Suite (2sx, bass gtr, banjo)
Weill: Symphony no.1 (5 perc)
Shostakovich: Hamlet--Incidental music (1932)
Barber: Medea, op.23 (ballet suite)
Ginastera: Variaciones concertantes
Schuller: Contours

STRINGS
WINDS 2222-4000
2 PERCUSSION

10' or less

Cherubini: Medea--Overture
Verdi: La traviata--Prelude to Act I
Wagner: Tristan und Isolde--Prelude to Act III
Bizet: Pearlfishers--Overture*
Mussorgsky: Khovantchina--Introduction (hp)
Elgar: Dream-children (hp)
Debussy: Clair de lune (arr.) (hp, cel)
Satie: Gymnopédies nos.1, 3 (2hp)

11'-20'

Haydn: Symphony no.13 (cnt)
Vanhal: Sinfonia, G minor
Mozart: Symphonies nos.18, 19, 25
Sibelius: The tempest--Suite no.2 (hp)

Over 20'

Haydn: Symphonies nos.31, 39, 72 (all with continuo)
Mozart: Divertimento, K.131
Dvořák: Legends--nos.6-10 (hp)

STRINGS
WINDS 2222-4200
3 PERCUSSION
HARP, CELESTE, PIANO

10' or less

Gluck: Iphigenie in Aulis--Overture (3tp)
Mozart: Symphony no.32
Beethoven: Egmont--Overture
Beethoven: Leonore overture no.1
Beethoven: Namensfeier overture
Beethoven: Ruins of Athens--Overture
Bizet: Petite suite from "Jeux d'enfants" (4perc)
Mahler: Symphony no.1--"Blumine" movement
Satie: Gymnopédie no.2 (2hp)
Vaughan Williams: The wasps--Overture (4perc)
Kodály: Háry János--Intermezzo (5perc)
V. Thomson: Pilgrims and pioneers

11'-20'

Lully: Ballet suite (arr. Mottl)
Handel: Royal fireworks music (arr. Harty) (3tp)
Handel: Water music suite (arr. Harty)
Domenico Scarlatti: The good-humored ladies--Suite (hpsd)
Chopin: Les sylphides (arr. Glazunov) (4perc)
Franck: Les Éolides
Fauré: Pelléas et Mélisande--Suite
Kodály: Galanta dances
Kodály: Marosszek dances (4perc)
Piston: Serenata
Ginastera: Estancia--Ballet suite (8perc)

21'-30'

Handel: The faithful shepherd--Suite
Schubert: Symphony no.4
Bizet: Symphony no.1
Tchaikovsky: Suite no.4
Dvořák: Legends--Nos.1-5
Bartók: Suite no.2 (2hp)
Prokofiev: Sinfonietta

Over 30'

Haydn: Seven last words of Christ
Beethoven: Egmont (incidental music)

Beethoven: Symphony no.3
Mendelssohn: Symphony no.3
Brahms: Serenade no.1

Bruch: Symphony no.1
Paine: Symphony no.1*
Dvořák: Symphony no.7

STRINGS
WINDS 2222-4330
TIMPANI

STRINGS
WINDS 2222-4230
4 PERCUSSION

10' or less

Cherubini: Overtures to Abenceragen;
Anacreon; Les deux journées
Beethoven: Fidelio--Overture
Weber: Overtures to Euryanthe;
Der Freischütz; Oberon; Ruler of
the spirits
Berwald: Estrella de Soria--Overture
Schubert: Fierrabras--Overture
Schubert: Overture, D.648
Schubert: Rosamunde--Overture
Berlioz: Overtures to Béatrice et
Bénédict; Les Troyens (4tp)
Glinka: A life for the tsar--Overture
Mendelssohn: Overtures to Die Hochzeit
des Camacho; Ruy Blas
Schumann: Overtures to Faust; Genoveva
Borodin: In the steppes of central Asia
Brahms: Hungarian dances nos.5-6
Paine: Oedipus tyrannus--Prelude
Tchaikovsky: Eugen Onegin--Polonaise
Rimsky-Korsakov: May night--Overture
Stravinsky: Monumentum pro Gesualdo
di Venosa

11'-20'

Beethoven: Consecration of the house
Beethoven: Leonore overtures nos.2, 3
Schumann: Manfred--Overture
Borodin: Symphony no.3
Rimsky-Korsakov: Symphoniette on
Russian themes

21'-30'

Berwald: Symphonies in C major;
E-flat major; G minor
Mendelssohn: Symphony no.2
Schumann: Symphony no.4
Dvořák: Symphonic variations
Rimsky-Korsakov: Symphony no.1
Chadwick: Symphony no.2
Sibelius: Symphonies nos.3, 5, 7
Einem: Meditations, op.18

Over 30'

Schubert: Symphony (no.7), D.729
Schumann: Symphony no.3
Bruckner: Symphony in F minor
Bruckner: Symphonies nos.0, 2, 3
Borodin: Symphony no.1

10' or less

Auber: Overtures to Le domino noir; Fra
Diavolo (5perc); Lestocq; Marco Spada
Rossini: La gazza ladra--Overture (5perc)
Donizetti: Overtures to Daughter of
the regiment; Don Pasquale
Lortzing: Zar und Zimmermann--Overture
Glinka: Summer night in Madrid (6perc)
Nicolai: The merry wives of Windsor--
Overture
Thomas: Raymond--Overture (5perc)
Flotow: Alessandro Stradella--Overture
Wagner: Siegfried--Forest murmurs
Litolff: Robespierre--Overture
Suppé: Overtures to Beautiful Galathea;
Boccaccio*; Jolly robbers (gtr);
Light cavalry; Morning, noon and night
in Vienna
Johann Strauss Jr.: Fledermaus--Du und
du
Johann Strauss Jr.: Fledermaus--
Overture
Johann Strauss Jr.: Wiener Blut
Brahms: Hungarian dances nos.2, 7, 17-21
Dvořák: Slavonic dances nos.1-16
Humperdinck: Hansel and Gretel--
Knusperwalzer
Sibelius: Pan and Echo
Milhaud: Ouverture méditerranéene
Xenakis: Metastaseis B (5perc)

Over 10'

Kuhlau: William Shakespeare--Overture
Rossini: Overtures to Semiramide;
William Tell
Schumann: Symphony no.1
Goldmark: Rustic wedding symphony
Bruch: Swedish dances--Series 1
Dvořák: Symphony no.5
Rimsky-Korsakov: Overture on Russian
themes
Janáček: Lachian dances (hp)
Sibelius: Legends--Lemminkäinen and the
maidens of Saari; Lemminkäinen in
Tuonela (both with 3tp)
Sibelius: Symphony no.4
Busoni: Rondo arlecchinesco (tenor voice)
Luening: Rhapsodic variations
(electronic tape)
Kirk: An orchestra primer (narrator)

STRINGS
WINDS 2222-4431
5 PERCUSSION

10' or less

Cherubini: Ali Baba--Overture
Hérold: Zampa--Overture
Meyerbeer: Fackeltanz no.1
Rossini: Robert Bruce--Overture
Berlioz: Le corsaire
Berlioz: Roman carnival
Schumann: Julius Caesar--Overture
Flotow: Martha--Overture
Verdi: Overtures to Nabucco;
  I vespri Siciliani
Moniuszko: The countess--Overture
Moniuszko: Halka--Mazur
Suppé: Pique dame--Overture
Johann Strauss Jr.: Egyptian march
Johann Strauss Jr.: Künstler quadrille
Johann Strauss Jr.: Morning papers
Johann Strauss Jr.: Pizzicato polka
Johann Strauss Jr.: Thunder and
  lightning polka
Delibes: Coppelia--Valse de la poupée
  and Czardas
Waldteufel: Les patineurs
Mussorgsky: Intermezzo in the classic
  style
Dvořák: Fest-Marsch
Sibelius: Finlandia
Sibelius: Legends--Lemminkäinen's
  return
Holst: A Somerset rhapsody
Stravinsky: Circus polka
Stravinsky: Four Norwegian moods
Honegger: Prélude pour "La tempête"
Milhaud: Murder of a great chief of
  state
Jacob: Fantasia on the Alleluia hymn
V. Thomson: Louisiana story--Boy fights
  alligator
Cowell: Hymn and fuguing tunes nos.3,
  16
Rubbra: Festival overture
Walton: Façade--Suite no.1
Wm. Schuman: The orchestra song
McBride: Pumpkin-eater's little fugue
Britten: Gloriana--Courtly dances
Ward: Euphony for orchestra

11'-20'

Buxtehude: Four chorale preludes (arr.)
Berlioz: Les franc-juges (2 tubas)
Berlioz: King Lear
Liszt: Festklänge
Franck: Rédemption--Morceau symphonique
Lalo: Le roi d'Ys--Overture
Bizet: Ouverture
Bruch: Swedish dances--Series 2
Massenet: Scènes pittoresques

Sullivan: Overture in C (org)
Sibelius: A saga
Hindemith: Concert music for strings
  and brass (without woodwinds)
V. Thomson: Symphony on a hymn tune
Tcherepnin: Georgiana suite (6perc)
Khachaturian: Masquerade--Suite
Lutosławski: Little suite
Kay: Fantasy variations
Kay: Serenade for orchestra
Ward: Adagio and allegro
Kirk: An orchestra primer (narrator)
Lees: The trumpet of the swan (narrator)

21'-30'

Liszt: Die Ideale
Dvořák: A hero's song
Massenet: Scènes alsaciennes
Stravinsky: Jeu de cartes
Hindemith: Mathis der Maler--Symphony
Hindemith: Nobilissima visione
Dello Joio: The triumph of Saint Joan

Over 30'

Bruckner: Symphonies nos.4-6
Brahms: Symphony no.2
Bruch: Symphony no.3
Dvořák: Symphonies nos.6, 8
Richard Strauss: Symphony, op.12
Nielsen: Symphony no.6
Sibelius: Symphony no.2
Vaughan Williams: Symphony no.4
Walton: Symphony no.1

Duration uncertain

Schubert: Trauermarsch, D.859

STRINGS
WINDS 2222-4431
5 PERCUSSION
HARP, CELESTE, PIANO

10' or less

Handel: Xerxes--Largo (arr.)
Bellini: Norma--Overture
Berlioz: Les Troyens--Trojan march (2hp)
Glinka: Jota aragonesa
Liszt: Hungarian rhapsody no.5
Thomas: Mignon--Overture
Verdi: La forza del destino--Overture
  (2hp)
Wagner: Rheingold--Entry of the gods
Wagner: Tristan und Isolde--Nachtgesang
Offenbach: La belle Hélène--Overture
Offenbach: Orpheus in the underworld--
  Overture
Offenbach: Tales of Hoffmann--Intermezzo
  and barcarolle

Suppé: Poet and peasant--Overture
Joh. Strauss Jr.: Emperor waltzes
Joh. Strauss Jr.: Gypsy Baron--Overture
Joh. Strauss Jr.: On the beautiful
 blue Danube
Joh. Strauss Jr.: Perpetuum mobile
Joh. Strauss Jr.: Roses from the south
Joh. Strauss Jr.: Voices of spring
Joh. Strauss Jr.: Wine, women and song
Josef Strauss: Mein Lebenslauf ist
 Lieb' und Lust
Josef Strauss: Music of the spheres
Josef Strauss: Village swallows
Saint-Saëns: La Princesse Jaune--
 Overture
Delibes: Coppelia--Prelude and mazurka
Bruch: Loreley--Prelude
Massenet: Hérodiade--Prelude to Act III
Humperdinck: Eine Trauung in der
 Bastille
Delius: The walk to the Paradise Garden
Vaughan Williams: Prelude "49th
 parallel"
Holst: Capriccio
Stravinsky: Firebird--Berceuse and
 Finale
Bacon: The muffin man
Walton: Crown imperial
Walton: Johannesburg festival overture
Barber: Essay no.1
Fine: Diversions for orchestra
Surinach: Feria magica
Bernstein: On the town--Three dance
 episodes
Bernstein: West side story--Overture
Bergsma: A carol on Twelfth Night
Chou: And the fallen petals
Floyd: In celebration
Hoag: An after-intermission overture

11'-20'

Berlioz: Rob Roy
Liszt: Hungarian rhapsody no.2
Wagner: Walküre--Wotan's farewell and
 magic fire music
Gade: Nachklänge von Ossian
Joh. Strauss Jr.: Tales from the
 Vienna woods
Delibes: Sylvia--Suite
Bizet: L'Arlésienne--Suites 1-2
Bizet: Carmen--Suites 1, 2
Bizet: Jolie fille de Perth--Scènes
 bohémiennes
Bizet: Patrie
Dvořák: Slavonic rhapsodies op.45,
 nos.2-3
Massenet: Le Cid--Ballet music (2hp)
Grieg: Sigurd Jorsalfar--Three
 orchestral pieces
Fauré: Dolly
Debussy: Printemps (pf 4-hands)
Coleridge-Taylor: Hiawatha--Suite
Carpenter: Sea drift

Bartók: Dance suite
Bartók: Deux portraits (2hp)
Stravinsky: Song of the nightingale (2hp)
Villa-Lobos: Sinfonietta no.2 (asx)
Ibert: Louisville concerto
Martinu: Estampes
Bliss: Things to come--Concert suite
V. Thomson: Louisiana story--Suite
Copland: Lincoln portrait (narrator)
Copland: Orchestral variations
Křenek: Eleven transparencies
Walton: Hamlet and Ophelia
Dallapiccola: Variations for orchestra
Creston: Invocation and dance
Shostakovich: Ballet suite no.1
Stevens: Sinfonia breve
Barber: Souvenirs
Hovhaness: Symphony no.15
Britten: Canadian carnival
Britten: Prince of the pagodas--Pas
 de six
Britten: Soirées musicales
Gould: Fall River legend--Ballet suite
Kay: Umbrian scene
Rorem: Design (6perc)
Benson: A Delphic serenade
Penderecki: De natura sonoris no.2
 (4tbn, 7perc, harm)
Bamert: Circus parade (narrator)

21'-30'

Delibes: Coppelia--Suite no.1
Mussorgsky: Pictures at an exhibition
 (arr. Goehr) (org)
Humperdinck: Dornröschen--Suite
Stravinsky: Firebird--Suite (1919 and
 1945 versions)
Hindemith: Sinfonietta in E
Křenek: Symphony "Pallas Athena"
Tippett: The midsummer marriage--
 Ritual dances
Carter: The minotaur--Ballet suite
Carter: Variations for orchestra
Wm. Schuman: Judith
Bernstein: Facsimile
Bernstein: Fancy free--Suite
Suolahti: Sinfonia piccola
Bassett: Variations for orchestra
Lees: Symphony no.2

Over 30'

Joh. Strauss Jr.: Graduation ball
Bizet: Roma
Dvořák: Symphony no.4
Albéniz: Iberia (arr. Surinach)
Sibelius: Symphony no.1
Vaughan Williams: Job
Vaughan Williams: Symphonies nos.2, 3
Maxwell Davies: Second fantasia on
 John Taverner's In nomine (2 tubas)

STRINGS
8 WOODWINDS (OTHER COMBINATIONS)
BRASS 4300
TIMPANI
CONTINUO

Bach: Musical offering
Bach: Suite no.4
Handel: Concerti a due cori nos.1-3
Handel: Royal fireworks music
Mozart: Divertimento, K.113

STRINGS
WINDS 3222-4331
4 PERCUSSION

10' or less

Bach: Sheep may safely graze (arr.)
Mozart: Turkish march (arr.)
Donizetti: Roberto Devereux--Overture
Johann Strauss Sr.: Radetzky march
Chopin: Polonaise, op.40, no.1 (arr.)
Schumann: Braut von Messina--Overture
Schumann: Hermann und Dorothea--
  Overture
Liszt: Hamlet
Liszt: Huldigungs-Marsch
Liszt: Hungarian march
Verdi: Aïda--Prelude
Wagner: Tannhäuser--Arrival of the
  guests at Wartburg
Wagner: Tannhäuser--Prelude, Act III
Smetana: The bartered bride--Overture
Smetana: My country--Šárka
Borodin: Petite suite--Scherzo and
  nocturne*
Borodin: Prince Igor--Overture
Brahms: Hungarian dances nos.1, 3,
  10 (arr. Brahms); nos.5-7 (arr.
  Schmeling)
Saint-Saëns: Danse macabre
Mussorgsky: The fair at Sorochinsk--
  Gopak
Mussorgsky: Khovantchina--Entr'acte
Tchaikovsky: Eugen Onegin--Waltzes
Tchaikovsky: Suite no.1--Marche
  miniature
Dvořák: Slavonic rhapsody, op.45, no.1
Chadwick: Rip van Winkle--Overture
Humperdinck: Hansel and Gretel--Prelude
Reznicek: Donna Diana--Overture
Wolf: Scherzo and finale
Mascagni: Cavalleria rusticana--Prelude
  and Siciliana*
Nielsen: Maskarade--Overture
Nielsen: Saul and David--Prelude to
  Act II
Sibelius: Karelia--Overture
Busoni: Lustspiel overture

Ives: Variations on "America"
Coleridge-Taylor: The bamboula
Coleridge-Taylor: Danse nègre
Becker: Two pieces for orchestra--
  The mountains
Toch: Pinocchio
Dahl: Quodlibet on American folk tunes
  and folk dances
Einem: Capriccio, op.2
Arnold: Tam O'Shanter overture

11'-20'

Gluck: Ballet suite no.1 (arr. Mottl)
Beethoven: German dances
Beethoven: Wellington's victory (6tp)
Liszt: Funeral triumph of Tasso
Liszt: Von der Wiege bis zum Grabe
Verdi: Aïda--Triumphal march and ballet
  (4tp)
Wagner: Tannhäuser--Overture
Smetana: The bartered bride--Three
  dances
Smetana: My country--From Bohemia's
  meadows and forests; Tábor; Blaník
Gottschalk: Symphony no.2
Brahms: Tragic overture
Tchaikovsky: The tempest
Dvořák: Husitská
Grieg: Peer Gynt--Suite no.1
Chadwick: Melpomene
Wolf: Der Corregidor--Suite
MacDowell: Suite no.1
Glazunov: Chopiniana
Nielsen: Helios overture
Sibelius: Karelia suite
Coleridge-Taylor: Petite suite de
  concert
Einem: Ballade

21'-30'

Gade: Symphony no.1
Borodin: Petite suite
Saint-Saëns: Symphony no.2
Rimsky-Korsakov: The maid of Pskov--
  Overture and three entr'actes
Rimsky-Korsakov: Symphony no.3
Nielsen: Symphony no.2
Kodály: Symphony
Stravinsky: Symphony in C
Hanson: Symphony no.4
Porter: Symphony no.2
Giannini: Symphony no.2
Shostakovich: Symphonies nos.3, 9
Arnold: Symphony no.6

Over 30'

Beethoven: Symphony no.6
Bruckner: Symphony no.1
Brahms: Serenade no.2
Tchaikovsky: Suite no.1
Tchaikovsky: Symphonies nos.1-6
Dvořák: Symphony no.2

Dukas: Symphony in C major
Nielsen: Symphony no.1
Einem: Wiener Symphonie
Arnold: Symphony no.3

STRINGS
WINDS 3222-4431
5 PERCUSSION
HARP, CELESTE, PIANO

10' or less

Purcell: Trumpet prelude (arr.)
Auber: Masaniello--Overture
Rossini: The siege of Corinth--Overture
(4tbn)
Schubert: Marche militaire (arr.) (6perc)
Adam: Si j'étais roi--Overture
Berlioz: La damnation de Faust--
Rakoczy march
Berlioz: Les Troyens--Royal hunt
and storm
Liszt: Hungarian rhapsodies
nos.3 (cimbalom), 6
Wagner: Götterdämmerung--Siegfried's
Rhine journey
Wagner: Die Meistersinger--Prelude
Lalo: Rapsodie norvégienne
Borodin: Prince Igor--Polovtsian march
Brahms: Hungarian dances nos.11-16
Ponchielli: La Gioconda--Dance of the
hours (2hp)
Saint-Saëns: Marche héroïque
Saint-Saëns: Le rouet d'Omphale
Mussorgsky: Khovantchina--Dance of the
Persian maidens
Mussorgsky: Mlada--Festive march
Massenet: Phèdre--Overture
Grieg: Peer Gynt--Prelude*
Rimsky-Korsakov: The snow maiden--
Dance of the buffoons
Rimsky-Korsakov: The tsar's bride--
Overture
Humperdinck: Hansel and Gretel--
Witch's ride
Delius: Sleigh ride
Mascagni: L'amico Fritz--Intermezzo
Glazunov: The seasons--Autumn (6perc);
Winter
Glazunov: Valse de concert, no.2
Wolf-Ferrari: The secret of Suzanne--
Overture
Cadman: Oriental rhapsody from
Omar Khayyam
Kodály: Háry János--Intermezzo
Stravinsky: Scherzo à la russe
Toch: Circus
Slonimsky: My toy balloon (7perc)
Copland: An outdoor overture
Copland: Rodeo--Buckaroo holiday;
Hoedown

Arnold: Four Cornish dances

11'-20'

Berlioz: Les Troyens--Ballet
Liszt: Battle of the Huns (org)
Liszt: Hungarian rhapsody no.4
Liszt: Mephisto waltzes nos.1, 2*
Liszt: Les préludes
Wagner: Der fliegende Holländer--
Overture
Wagner: Die Meistersinger--Three
excerpts from Act III
Wagner: Tannhäuser--Venusberg music
(6perc)
Smetana: My country--Vyšehrad (2hp);
The Moldau
Smetana: Richard III
Smetana: Wallenstein's camp
Borodin: Prince Igor--Polovtsian
dances (6perc)
Saint-Saëns: La jeunesse d'Hercule (5tp)
Saint-Saëns: Suite algérienne
Saint-Saëns: Trois tableaux
symphoniques (harm)
Balakirev: Russia (2hp)
Mussorgsky: Night on Bald Mountain
Grieg: Lyric suite
Grieg: Norwegian dances
Grieg: Peer Gynt--Suite no.2
Rimsky-Korsakov: Conte féerique
Rimsky-Korsakov: Russian Easter overture
Rimsky-Korsakov: Sadko--Tableau musical
Rimsky-Korsakov: The snow maiden--Suite
Rimsky-Korsakov: Capriccio espagnol
(6perc)
Noskowski: The steppe
Luigini: Ballet égyptien (2hp)
Humperdinck: Hansel and Gretel--
Three excerpts
Puccini: Capriccio sinfonico
Puccini: Preludio sinfonico
Ippolitov-Ivanov: Caucasian sketches
(6perc)
Glazunov: Stenka Razine
Rabaud: La procession nocturne
Rachmaninoff: Capriccio bohémien (6perc)
Rachmaninoff: The rock
Holst: The perfect fool--Ballet music
Bloch: Evocations (6perc)
Bartók: Mikrokosmos suite
Kodály: Concerto for orchestra
Kodály: Theater overture
Prokofiev: Lieutenant Kijé--Suite (tsx)
Hanson: Symphony no.5
Weinberger: Schwanda the bagpiper--
Polka and fugue (4tp backstage)
Weinberger: Under the spreading
chestnut tree
Copland: The tender land--Suite
Creston: Two choric dances
Phillips: Selections from McGuffey's
reader

Britten: Young person's guide to the
orchestra (6perc)
Ginastera: Pampeana no.3

21'-30'

Wagner: Tannhäuser--Overture and
Venusberg music (6perc)
Borodin: Symphony no.2
Tchaikovsky: Swan lake--Suite
Massenet: Suite no.1 (2hp)
Rimsky-Korsakov: Symphony no.2
MacDowell: Suite no.2 (4tbn)
Kodály: Háry János--Suite (6tp, 7perc,
cimbalom)
Kodály: Variations on a Hungarian
folksong
Stravinsky: Orpheus
Copland: Billy the Kid--Suite
Khrennikov: Symphony no.1

Over 30'

Liszt: A Faust symphony
Tchaikovsky: Symphony no.7
Grieg: Symphonic dances
Rimsky-Korsakov: Scheherazade (6perc)
Nielsen: Symphony no.5
Kalinnikov: Symphony no.2
Rachmaninoff: Symphony no.1 (6perc)
Reger: Variations and fugue on a
theme of Mozart
Shostakovich: Hamlet--Film suite*
(6perc)
Shostakovich: Symphonies nos.1,
15 (7perc)

STRINGS
WINDS 3322-4431
6 PERCUSSION
2 HARPS, CELESTE, PIANO

10' or less

Meyerbeer: Les Huguenots--Overture
Mussorgsky: The fair at Sorochinsk--
Introduction
Tchaikovsky: Coronation march
Tchaikovsky: Mazeppa--Danse cosaque
Tchaikovsky: Le voyévode--Overture
Dvořák: Carnival overture
Wolf: Der Corregidor--Prelude and
interlude
Debussy: Marche écossaise
Debussy: Prélude à l'après-midi d'un
faune
Delius: Dance rhapsody no.2
Rachmaninoff: Vocalise
Walton: Façade--Suite no.2

11'-20'

Liszt: Héroïde funèbre
Liszt: Nocturnal procession
Liszt: Orpheus
Liszt: Prometheus
Goldmark: Sakuntala--Overture
Tchaikovsky: Capriccio italien
Tchaikovsky: Hamlet
Tchaikovsky: Overture 1812
Tchaikovsky: Romeo and Juliet
Dvořák: Othello overture
Dvořák: Rhapsody, op.14
Dvořák: Watersprite
Liadov: Eight Russian folk songs
Ippolitov-Ivanov: Turkish fragments
Ravel: Valses nobles et sentimentales
(7perc)
Falla: Three-cornered hat--Three dances
Respighi: Ancient airs and dances--
Sets I and II (hpsd 4-hands)
Enesco: Rumanian rhapsodies nos.1-2
Malipiero: Sinfonia per Antigenida
Martinu: Sinfonia concertante for
2 orchestras
Milhaud: Suite provençale
Dallapiccola: Due pezzi per orchestra
Hovhaness: Variations and fugue
Husa: Two sonnets by Michelangelo (asx)
Schuller: Five etudes

Over 20'

Liszt: Hungaria
Tchaikovsky: Francesca da Rimini
Tchaikovsky: Sleeping Beauty
Tchaikovsky: Suites nos.2-3
Dvořák: Czech suite
Dvořák: Symphonies nos.1, 3, 9
Debussy: La boîte à joujoux
Kalinnikov: Symphony no.1
Falla: Three-cornered hat
Respighi: La boutique fantasque
Respighi: Rossiniana

STRINGS
9/10 WOODWINDS (OTHER COMBINATIONS)
BRASS 4331
4 PERCUSSION

10' or less

Handel: Overture, D major (arr.)
J.C. Bach: Symphony, D major (cnt)
Beethoven: King Stephen--Overture
Weber: Jubel overture
Berlioz: Waverley
Glinka: Russlan and Ludmilla--Overture
Brahms: Academic festival overture
Delibes: Coppelia--Ballade and Thême
slave varié (4tp)
Fauré: Pénélope--Prelude

Humperdinck: Königskinder--Prelude;
  Introduction to Act II
Sibelius: The tempest--Prelude
Hindemith: Neues vom Tage--Overture
  (asx)
V. Thomson: Fugue and chorale on
  Yankee Doodle
Copland: Our town
Shostakovich: The age of gold--Polka
  (ssx)
Barber: Essay no.2
Britten: Paul Bunyan--Overture
Dello Joio: Five images for orchestra

  11'-20'

Berlioz: Roméo et Juliette--Love scene
Mendelssohn: Calm sea and prosperous
  voyage
Wagner: A Faust overture
Brahms: Variations on a theme by Haydn
Dvořák: Amid nature
Dvořák: Midday witch
Dvořák: Suite, op.98b
Holst: Egdon Heath
Casella: Paganiniana
Subotnick: Play no.2 (electronic tape)

  21'-30'

Beethoven: Symphony no.5
Mendelssohn: Symphony no.5
Wagner: Symphony, C major
Elgar: Enigma variations
Stravinsky: Symphony no.1, E-flat major

  Over 30'

Brahms: Symphonies nos.1, 3, 4
Glazunov: Symphony no.4
Scriabin: Symphony no.2
Ives: Symphonies nos.1, 2

    STRINGS
    9/10 WOODWINDS
    BRASS 4431
    6 PERCUSSION
    HARP, CELESTE, PIANO

  10' or less

Monteverdi: Orfeo--Toccata and
  ritornelli (arr.)
Bach: Komm süsser Tod (arr.)(4tbn)
Weber: Invitation to the dance (2hp)
Wagner: Huldigungsmarsch
Smetana: Haakon Jarl
Borodin: Nocturne (arr. Tcherepnin)
Saint-Saëns: Coronation march
Saint-Saëns: Phaéton
Tchaikovsky: Marche slave
Rimsky-Korsakov: Christmas eve--
  Polonaise

Rimsky-Korsakov: Dubinushka
Janáček: Jealousy
Liadov: The enchanted lake
Delius: Irmelin--Prelude
Sibelius: The bard
Granados: Goyescas--Intermezzo (2hp)
Ives: Holidays symphony--The Fourth of
  July (7perc)
Stravinsky: Fireworks (6hn, 2hp)
Milhaud: Overture philharmonique
Harris: Ode to consonance (baritone
  horn)
Rodgers: Slaughter on Tenth Avenue
Barber: Die Natali--Silent night
Dahl: Quodlibet on American folk tunes
  and folk dances
Gillis: Short overture to an unwritten
  opera
Brant: Verticals ascending
Britten: Peter Grimes--Passacaglia
Berio: Nones (asx, electric gtr)
Feldman: ...Out of "Last Pieces"
  (btp, gtr, 8perc)
Previn: Overture to a comedy

  11'-20'

Berlioz: Benvenuto Cellini--Overture
  (6tp)
Liszt: Hungarian rhapsody no.1
Liszt: Tasso, lament and triumph
Wagner: Rienzi--Overture
Gounod: Faust--Ballet music
Lalo: Namouna--Ballet suite no.2 (2hp)
Balakirev: Thamar (2hp, 7perc)
Dvořák: Wood dove
Janáček: Lachian dances
Elgar: Cockaigne
Glazunov: Valse de concert, no.1
Sibelius: The tempest--Suite no.1
Granados: Tres danzas españolas
Ives: Holidays symphony--Thanksgiving
Ives: Three places in New England
  (large orchestra version)
Webern: Six pieces for orchestra, op.6
  (4tbn)
Coates: London suite
Milhaud: Symphony no.12
Robert Russell Bennett: Suite of old
  American dances
Hindemith: Concerto for orchestra
Copland: El salón México
Shostakovich: The age of gold--Suite
  (ssx, harm, baritone horn)
Britten: Peter Grimes--Four sea
  interludes
Gould: Spirituals for orchestra
Bergsma: Chameleon variations
Crumb: Echoes of time and the river
  (2pf, mandoline)
Martino: Ritorno

21'-30'

Lalo: Namouna--Ballet suite no.1 (2hp)
Dvořák: Golden spinning wheel
Rimsky-Korsakov: Christmas eve--Suite
Glazunov: Scènes de ballet
Sibelius: Symphony no.6
Vaughan Williams: Symphony no.8
Copland: The red pony
Foss: Baroque variations (gtr, org, hpsd)
Foss: Geod
Laderman: Magic prison (org, 2 narrators)

Over 30'

Berlioz: Symphonie fantastique
  (2hp, 2 tubas)
Liszt: Ce qu'on entend sur la montagne
Franck: Symphony in D minor
Saint-Saëns: Symphony no.1 (2 saxhorns)
Delibes: Coppelia
Balakirev: Symphonies nos.1-2
Chadwick: Symphonic sketches
R. Strauss: Aus Italien
Reger: Variations and fugue on a
  merry theme of Johann Adam Hiller
Hindemith: Die Harmonie der Welt--
  Symphony

STRINGS
WINDS 3332-4331
5 PERCUSSION
HARP, CELESTE, PIANO

10' or less

Couperin: La sultane--Overture and
  allegro (arr. Milhaud)
Handel: Prelude and fugue, D minor
  (arr.)
Tchaikovsky: Le voyévode, op.78
  (symphonic ballad)
Liadov: Kikimora
Puccini: Edgar--Preludio (4tp)
Ives: Holidays symphony--Decoration
  Day (6perc)
Falla: La vida breve--Interlude and
  dance (2hp)
Stravinsky: Variations
Still: Festive overture
Copland: Our town
Copland: Rodeo--Buckaroo holiday;
  Hoe-down
Khachaturian: Gayane--Sabre dance (asx);
  Three pieces (asx)
Barber: Fadograph of a yestern scene
Barber: Overture to The school for
  scandal
Barber: Vanessa--Intermezzo; Under the
  willow tree
Wm. Schuman: American festival overture
Surinach: Drama jondo

Surinach: Fandango
Rochberg: Time-span (II)
Mennin: Canto
Feldman: Structures for orchestra

11'-20'

Mussorgsky: Pictures at an exhibition
  (arr. Touschmaloff) (6perc)
Dvořák: Scherzo capriccioso
Rimsky-Korsakov: Tsar Saltan--Suite
Satie: Parade
Karłowicz: Lithuanian rhapsody
Respighi: Brazilian impressions
Respighi: Fontane di Roma (2hp)
Stravinsky: Le baiser de la fée--
  Divertimento
Gershwin: American in Paris (3sx)
Harris: Symphony no.3 (2 tubas)
Copland: Inscape
Khachaturian: Spartacus--Suite no.2;
  Suite no.3 (6perc)
Barber: Die Natali
Diamond: The world of Paul Klee
Persichetti: Night dances
Kay: Theater set for orchestra
Mennin: Concertato (Moby Dick)
Pinkham: Symphony no.2 (6perc)
Mario Lombardo: Drakestail (narrator)

21'-30'

Tchaikovsky: The nutcracker--Suite
Loeffler: A pagan poem (6tp)
Carpenter: Adventures in a perambulator
Martinu: Symphonies nos.2-3
Sessions: Symphony no.2
Gershwin: Porgy and Bess--Symphonic
  picture (2hp, 3sx, banjo)
Khachaturian: Gayane--Suite no.2;
  Suite no.3 (asx)
Khachaturian: Spartacus--Suite no.1
  (4tp, 6perc)
Mennin: Symphony no.6
Pinkham: Signs of the zodiac

Over 30'

Liszt: Dante symphony (2hp, harm,
  treble chorus)
Vaughan Williams: Symphony no.3
Rachmaninoff: Symphony no.2
Holst: The planets (female chorus,
  2hp, 6perc)
Stravinsky: Le baiser de la fée
Prokofiev: Symphony no.7
Khachaturian: Gayane--Suite no.1 (asx)

Duration uncertain

Tchaikovsky: The nutcracker--Suite no.2
  (2hp)

STRINGS
11 WOODWINDS (VARIOUS COMBINATIONS)
BRASS 4431
5 PERCUSSION
HARP, CELESTE, PIANO

10' or less

Meyerbeer: Le prophète--Coronation
 march
Berlioz: Roméo et Juliette--Queen Mab
 scherzo (2hp)
Wagner: Tristan und Isolde--Nachtgesang
Chabrier: España (2hp)
Chabrier: Joyeuse marche
Elgar: Pomp and circumstance--No.2
 (6perc)
Leoncavallo: Pagliacci--Intermezzo
Satie: Cinq grimaces pour "Un songe
 d'une nuit d'été"
Ravel: Alborada del gracioso (2hp, 7perc)
Riegger: Music for orchestra
Honegger: Mouvement symphonique no.3
 (asx)
Milhaud: Les funérailles de Phocion
Harris: Elegy for orchestra
Nelhybel: Music for orchestra

11'-20'

Berlioz: Roméo et Juliette--Romeo
 alone (8perc, 2hp)
Franck: Le chasseur maudit
Richard Strauss: Don Juan
Sibelius: Night ride and sunrise
Gilbert: Dance in the Place Congo
Roussel: Pour une fête de printemps
Ibert: Escales (2hp, 8perc)
Korngold: Schauspiel-Ouvertüre
Berkeley: Symphony no.3
Gould: Latin-American symphonette
Schuller: Five bagatelles
Erb: Symphony of overtures

Over 20'

Janáček: Taras Bulba (org)
Wolf: Penthesilea
Debussy: Nocturnes (16 women's voices)
Bloch: Trois poèmes juifs
Stravinsky: Symphony in three movements
Hanson: Symphony no.2
Chávez: Symphony no.4
Shostakovich: Symphony no.5

Duration uncertain

Meyerbeer: Le prophète--Ballet music

STRINGS
WINDS 3333-4331
5 PERCUSSION

10' or less

Wagner: Kaiser-Marsch
Wagner: Lohengrin--Prelude, Act I;
 Prelude, Act III; Procession to the
 cathedral
Saint-Saëns: Orient et occident
Mussorgsky: Boris Godunov--Polonaise (4tp)
Rimsky-Korsakov: The maid of Pskov--
 Overture
Liadov: Baba-Yaga
Elgar: Pomp and circumstance--No.5
Glière: Red poppy--Russian sailors'
 dance (6perc)
Weiss: American life (3sx)
Honegger: Pacific 231
Honegger: Rugby
Piston: Toccata (6perc)
V. Thomson: Sea piece with birds
Harris: Horn of plenty (4tp, baritone
 horn)
Harris: When Johnny comes marching
 home (euphonium)
Mossolov: Iron foundry (6perc)
Walton: Portsmouth Point
Shostakovich: Festive overture
Gutche: Holofernes overture
Wm. Schuman: American festival overture

11'-20'

Bach: Passacaglia (arr.)
Liszt: Mazeppa
Richard Strauss: Macbeth (btp)
Sibelius: Tapiola
Schoenberg: Theme and variations
Miaskovsky: Symphony no.21
Hindemith: Philharmonic concerto
Hindemith: Symphonic metamorphoses
V. Thomson: A solemn music, and a
 joyful fugue
Cowell: Synchrony
Chávez: Resonancias
Copland: Statements
Blacher: Orchester-Ornament
Blacher: Orchestra-variations on a
 theme of Paganini
Messiaen: Les offrandes oubliées

21'-30'

Schoenberg: Chamber symphony no.1
 (orchestral version)
Karłowicz: Odwieczne pieśni
Honegger: Symphonies nos.1, 5
Piston: Symphonies nos.1, 2
Hindemith: Pittsburgh symphony
R. Thompson: Symphony no.2
Kabalevsky: Symphonies nos.1, 2
Messiaen: L'ascension

Wm. Schuman: Symphony no.6
Dello Joio: Variations, chaconne,
  and finale
Blomdahl: Symphony no.3 (4tp)
Mennin: Symphony no.7

Over 30'

Nielsen: Symphonies nos.3, 4
Vaughan Williams: Symphony no.4
Miaskovsky: Symphony no.22
Stravinsky: Le sacre du printemps
  (reduced version)
Hindemith: Symphony in E-flat
Hanson: Symphony no.3
Shostakovich: Symphonies nos.10, 12(6perc)
Bamert: Once upon an orchestra
  (narrator)

STRINGS
WINDS 3333-4431
6 PERCUSSION
2 HARPS, CELESTE, PIANO

10' or less

Bach: Sheep may safely graze (arr.)
Saint-Saëns: Samson et Dalila--
  Bacchanale
Chabrier: Gwendolyn--Overture
Rimsky-Korsakov: Le coq d'or--
  Introduction and wedding march
Humperdinck: Königskinder--Introduction
  to Act III
Elgar: Pomp and circumstance--No.4
Albéniz: Catalonia
Albéniz: Navarra (arr. Arbós)
Roussel: Rapsodie flamande
Lehár: The merry widow--Overture
Ravel: Menuet antique
Turina: La procesión del Rocio
Griffes: Clouds
Prokofiev: Love of the three oranges--
  March and scherzo
Prokofiev: War and peace--Overture
Honegger: Chant de joie
V. Thomson: The Seine at night
V. Thomson: Wheat field at noon
Tansman: Toccata
Copland: Danzón cubano
Walton: Crown imperial
Walton: Johannesburg festival overture
Kabalevsky: Colas Breugnon--Overture
Carter: Holiday overture
Barber: Music for a scene from Shelley
Lutosławski: Postludium
Ward: Jubilation
Berio: Ritirata notturna di Madrid
Martirano: Contrasto

11'-20'

Wagner: Tristan und Isolde--Prelude
  and Liebestod
Rimsky-Korsakov: Tsar Saltan--Suite
D'Indy: Istar
Sibelius: Pohjola's daughter
Sibelius: The Oceanides
Roussel: Bacchus et Ariane--Suites 1-2
Roussel: Suite in F, op.33
Converse: The mystic trumpeter
Alfvén: Midsommarvaka
Holst: The perfect fool--Ballet music
Ruggles: Men and mountains (version for
  large orchestra)
Respighi: Pini di Roma (4tbn)
Bartók: Deux images
Turina: Danzas fantásticas
Webern: Passacaglia
Griffes: The pleasure dome of Kubla Khan
Villa-Lobos: Bachianas brasileiras no.4
Bliss: Introduction and allegro
Prokofiev: Love of the three oranges--
  Symphonic suite
Prokofiev: Romeo and Juliet--Suite no.3
Weiss: I segreti
Rogers: Three Japanese dances
Piston: Concerto for orchestra
Piston: The incredible flutist
Piston: Lincoln Center festival overture
Piston: Symphonies nos.7, 8
Piston: Three New England sketches
Auric: Phèdre
Poulenc: Les biches--Suite
Copland: Lincoln portrait (speaker)
Copland: Symphony no.2
Kabalevsky: Colas Breugnon--Suite
Stevens: Symphonic dances
Barber: Symphony no.1
Britten: The prince of the pagodas--
  Pas de six
Britten: Sinfonia da requiem
Lutosławski: Three postludes
Rochberg: Night music
Kirchner: Music for orchestra
Husa: Music for Prague 1968
Bassett: Echoes from an invisible world
Pinkham: Symphony no.1
Starer: Samson Agonistes
Schuller: American triptych
Musgrave: Concerto for orchestra
Augustyn Bloch: Enfiando per orchestra
Colgrass: As quiet as...
Richard Rodney Bennett: Zodiac

21'-30'

Rimsky-Korsakov: Le coq d'or--Suite
Elgar: Falstaff
Mahler: Symphony no.10--Movements I, III
Richard Strauss: Death and
  transfiguration
Richard Strauss: Der Rosenkavalier--
  Suite

Roussel: Symphonies nos.3, 4
Dohnányi: Ruralia hungarica
Respighi: Vetrate di chiesa (org)
Bloch: Voice in the wilderness
  (vc obligato)
Turina: Sinfonia sevillana
Martinu: Symphony no.5
Prokofiev: Cincerella--Suite no.3
Honegger: Symphony no.3
Milhaud: Symphonies nos.1, 2, 10, 11
Piston: Symphonies nos.4, 5, 6
Hindemith: Symphonia serena
Gerhard: Concerto for orchestra
Antheil: Symphonies nos.4, 5, 6
Walton: Symphony no.2
Jolivet: Symphony no.1
Wm. Schuman: Judith
Wm. Schuman: Symphony no.7
Wm. Schuman: Undertow
Britten: Gloriana--Symphonic suite
Fine: Symphony (1962)
Husa: Symphony no.1
Laderman: Concerto for orchestra
Schuller: Seven studies on themes
  of Paul Klee
Argento: In praise of music
Druckman: Windows
Blackwood: Symphony no.2

  31'-40'

Chausson: Symphony op.20
Busoni: Turandot--Suite
Rachmaninoff: Symphony no.3
Vaughan Williams: Symphonies nos.2, 6
Bartók: Concerto for orchestra
Taylor: Through the looking glass
Martinu: Symphony no.1
Prokofiev: Symphonies nos.2, 3
Grofé: Grand Canyon suite
Piston: Symphony no.3
Shostakovich: The gadfly--Suite

  Over 40'

Tchaikovsky: Manfred
Elgar: Symphony no.1
Bloch: America
Stravinsky: Petrouchka (1947 version)
Shostakovich: Symphony no.11
Maxwell Davies: Symphony

       STRINGS
       WOODWINDS 3333
       OTHERWISE LARGER THAN
         PREVIOUS CATEGORIES

  20' or less

Richard Strauss: Der Rosenkavalier--
  Waltzes, first sequence
Dukas: La péri

Rachmaninoff: Die Toteninsel
Glière: The red poppy--Suite
Ravel: Bolero
Ravel: La valse
Bartók: The miraculous mandarin--Suite
Stravinsky: Agon
Villa-Lobos: Bachianas brasileiras no.8
Villa-Lobos: Uirapurú
Martin: The four elements
Hanson: Merrymount--Suite
Halffter: La muerte de Carmen--Habanera
Hovhaness: Mysterious mountain
Blomdahl: Sisyphos
Ligeti: Apparitions
Reynolds: Graffiti
Wuorinen: Contrafactum
Sapieyevski: Summer overture

  21'-30'

Mussorgsky: Pictures at an exhibition
  (arr. Ravel)
Vaughan Williams: Symphony no.9
Ives: Symphony no.4
Carpenter: Skyscrapers
Prokofiev: Cinderella--Suite no.1
Prokofiev: Romeo and Juliet--Suites 1-2
Harris: Symphony no.5
Tcherepnin: Symphony no.2
Copland: Symphony no.1
Hartmann: Symphony no.6
Carter: Concerto for orchestra
Lutosławski: Concerto for orchestra
Dutilleux: Symphony no.2
Stockhausen: Punkte
Ishii: Kyō-sō

  Over 30'

Bruckner: Symphonies nos.7-9
Saint-Saëns: Symphony no.3
Mahler: Symphony no.10
Paderewski: Symphony
Vaughan Williams: Job
Rachmaninoff: Symphonic dances
Prokofiev: Buffoon--Symphonic suite
Shostakovich: Memorable year 1919*
Messiaen: Turangalîla-symphonie

       STRINGS
       13 WOODWINDS
       BRASS 4431
       7 PERCUSSION
       2 HARPS, CELESTE, PIANO

  10' or less

Bach: Toccata and fugue in D minor (arr.)
Berlioz: La damnation de Faust--
  Will-o-the-wisps
Wagner: Rule Britannia
Franck: Psyché--individual movements

Balakirev: Islamey (arr. Liapounow)
Chabrier: Bourée fantasque
Elgar: Pomp and circumstance--Nos.1, 3
Debussy: Images--Rondes des printemps
Debussy: L'isle joyeuse (arr.)
Ruggles: Organum
Griffes: Bacchanale
Ibert: Bacchanale
Barber: Commando march
Barber: Night flight
Bernstein: Candide--Overture
Bernstein: Slava (ssx, electric gtr, tape)
Rorem: Eagles (8perc)

11'-20'

Gottschalk: Night in the tropics
 (bsx, baritone horn)
Chadwick: Tam O'Shanter
Dukas: L'apprenti sorcier
Stravinsky: Four etudes for orchestra
Becker: Symphony no.3
Prokofiev: Le pas d'acier--Suite
Copland: Dance symphony (5tp)
Copland: El salón México
Creston: Dance overture
Creston: Invocation and dance
Barber: Essay no.3
Barber: Medea's meditation and dance
 of vengeance
Wm. Schuman: New England triptych
Berio: Still (2sx, electric org)
Aschaffenburg: Three dances
Jones: Let us now praise famous men

21'-30'

Franck: Psyché
Albéniz: Iberia (arr. Arbós) (tsx)
Debussy: La mer (5tp)
Richard Strauss: Der Rosenkavalier--
 Suite
Martinu: The frescos of Piero della
 Francesca
Martinu: Symphony no.6
Milhaud: Suite symphonique no.2
Still: Afro-American symphony
 (tenor banjo)
Sessions: The black maskers--Suite
Sessions: Symphonies nos.1, 4
Chávez: The daughter of Colchis
Chávez: Symphony no.3
Creston: Symphonies nos.2, 3
Barber: Symphony no.2
Wm. Schuman: Symphony no.3 (4tbn)
Bernstein: On the waterfront--
 Symphonic suite (asx)
Bernstein: West side story--Symphonic
 dances (asx)
Crumb: Variazioni for large orchestra
 (mandoline)

Over 30'

Elgar: Symphony no.2
Gustave Charpentier: Impressions
 d'Italie (asx)
Mahler: Symphony no.4 (soprano solo)
Roussel: Symphony no.2
Berg: Lulu--Suite (asx, soprano solo)
Martinu: Symphony no.4
Prokofiev: Le pas d'acier
Prokofiev: Symphonies nos.4-6
Sessions: Symphony no.3
Copland: Symphony no.3
Khachaturian: Symphony no.2
Shostakovich: Symphony no.6

STRINGS
WINDS 4454-6641
8 PERCUSSION
3 HARPS, CELESTE, PIANO

10' or less

Bach: Toccata and fugue in D minor (arr.)
Wagner: Walküre--Ride of the Valkyries
 (arr. Hutschenruyter)
Balakirev: Islamey (arr. Casella)
Debussy: Images--Gigues (ob d'amore)
Debussy: Le martyre de Saint Sébastien--
 La chambre magique
Wm. Schuman: Newsreel (3sx)
Ligeti: Atmosphères
Pinkham: Catacoustical measures
Penderecki: De natura sonoris no.1
 (2asx, harm)

11'-20'

Wagner: Grosser Festmarsch (bass tp)
Wagner: Parsifal--Good Friday spell
Wagner: Parsifal--Prelude
Henze: Symphony no.5 (2pf)
Rimsky-Korsakov: Mlada--Suite
Debussy: Images--Ibéria
Debussy: Jeux
Debussy: Le martyre de Saint Sébastien--
 Four excerpts
Delius: Brigg fair
Delius: Dance rhapsody no.1 (bass ob)
Richard Strauss: Till Eulenspiegel
Pfitzner: Palestrina--Three preludes
Schoenberg: Five pieces for orchestra
Ravel: Daphnis et Chloé--Suites 1-2 (9perc)
Ravel: Rapsodie espagnole
Stravinsky: Scherzo fantastique
Szymanowski: Konzert-Ouverture, op.12
Casella: Italia
Webern: Im Sommerwind
Berg: Three pieces for orchestra, op.6
Berg: Wozzeck--Three excerpts (soprano
 solo)
Gerhard: Epithalamion

Harris: Symphony no.7 (baritone horn)
Chávez: Symphony no.2
Copland: Connotations
Wm. Schuman: Credendum (2 tubas)
Ginastera: Panambí--Suite
Yardumian: Armenian suite
Maderna: Aura (14perc)
Martino: Mosaic (electric gtr)
Penderecki: Flourescences (2 tubas)

21'-30'

Schoenberg: Variations for orchestra
  (mandoline)
Karłowicz: Stanisław i Anna Oświecimowie
Bartók: Four orchestral pieces, op.12
Ibert: Le chevalier errant (asx, gtr)
Harris: Symphony no.9 (baritone horn)
Messiaen: Chronochromie
Wm. Schuman: Symphony no.7 (2 tubas)
Schuller: Spectra
Blackwood: Symphony no.1

Over 30'

Berlioz: Symphonie funèbre et triomphale
  (2 tubas)
Mahler: Symphonies nos.1 (7hn), 5
Delius: Appalachia (chorus)
Richard Strauss: Also sprach
  Zarathustra (2 tubas, org)
Holst: The planets
Ravel: Daphnis et Chloé (9perc)
Bartók: Suite no.1
Stravinsky: Firebird (extra brass
  backstage)
Stravinsky: Firebird--Suite (1911
  version)
Stravinsky: Petrouchka (original
  version)
Shostakovich: Symphony no.8
Wm. Schuman: Symphony no.8

Variable duration

Brown: Available forms 2 (2 tubas,
  gtr, bass tp)

INSTRUMENTATION LARGER THAN
ALL PREVIOUS CATEGORIES

20' or less

Bach: Komm, Gott, Schöpfer (arr.)
Bach: Passacaglia (arr.)
Bach: Prelude and fugue, BWV 552 (arr.)
Bach: Schmücke dich (arr.)
Wagner: Götterdämmerung--Siegfried's
  funeral music
Wagner: Walküre--Ride of the Valkyries
Richard Strauss: Salome--Salome's dance
Granados: Dante

Koechlin: Les bandar-log
Ruggles: Sun-treader
Stravinsky: Le sacre du printemps--
  Danse sacral
Varèse: Arcana
Chávez: Symphony no.1
Berio: Allelujah

21'-40'

Janáček: Sinfonietta
Richard Strauss: Ein Heldenleben
Scriabin: The poem of ecstasy
Scriabin: Prometheus
Respighi: Feste romane
Bartók: The wooden prince--Suite
Stravinsky: Le sacre du printemps
Varèse: Amériques
Prokofiev: Scythian suite
Wm. Schuman: Symphony no.3
Berio: Sinfonia
Stockhausen: Gruppen

Over 40'

Mahler: Symphonies nos.3, 6, 7, 9
Richard Strauss: Eine Alpensinfonie
Richard Strauss: Symphonia domestica
Scriabin: Le divin poème
Schoenberg: Pelleas and Melisande
Glière: Symphony no.3
Shostakovich: Symphonies nos.4, 7

INSTRUMENTATION INDETERMINATE

Cage: Atlas eclipticalis
Feldman: Intersection no.1
Feldman: Marginal intersection
Christian Wolff: Burdocks

MULTIPLE ORCHESTRAS

Gabrieli: Canzona
Handel: Concerti a due cori, nos.1-3
J.C. Bach: Symphonies op.18, nos.1, 5
Mozart: Serenade no.8
Bartók: Music for strings, percussion
  and celeste
Martin: Petite symphonie concertante
Martinu: Sinfonia concertante
Tippett: Concerto for double string
  orchestra
Brant: Verticals ascending
Dutilleux: Symphony no.2
Brown: Available forms 2
Stockhausen: Gruppen
Penderecki: Emanations
Christian Wolff: Burdocks

APPENDIX E: ORCHESTRAL WORKS

LISTED BY DURATION

Here orchestral works are grouped according to their
duration. Within each group, they are subdivided according to the composer's nationality, and within each
subdivision are listed chronologically by composer's
birthdate.

Thus, if a French baroque piece of about eight minutes duration is just what is needed to fill a certain
spot on a program, one can readily turn to a list of
possibilities.

The composer's nationality is normally taken to be
the country of origin, though there are exceptions
(Lully is, for the purpose of this appendix, French).
See also Appendix F, in which composers are listed
under more than one nationality where appropriate,

Where the duration of a particular work has been
estimated for the purpose of these groupings, that
fact is indicated by means of an asterisk (*).

For complete information on any of these works,
refer to the main alphabetical listing by composer.

5' OR LESS

American

Foote: Irish folk song
Ives: Country band march
Ives: The gong on the hook and ladder
Ives: Hymn (Largo cantabile)
Ruggles: Angels
Griffes: Bacchanale
Griffes: Clouds
Becker: Two pieces for orchestra (each piece less than 5')
V. Thomson: Fugue and Chorale on Yankee Doodle
V. Thomson: Louisiana story--Boy fights alligator (fugue)
V. Thomson: Sea piece with birds
Cowell: Ballad
Cowell: Polyphonica for small orchestra
Bacon: The muffin man
Copland: Danzón cubano
Copland: Fanfare for the common man
Copland: John Henry
Copland: from Rodeo--Corral nocturne; Saturday night waltz; Hoe-down
Copland: Symphony no.1--Prelude
Copland: Variations on a Shaker melody
Barber: Die Natali--Silent night
Barber: Vanessa--Intermezzo; Under the willow tree
Wm. Schuman: The orchestra song
McBride: Pumpkin-eater's little fugue
Dahl: Quodlibet on American folk tunes and folk dances
Gillis: Short overture to an unwritten opera
Brant: Galaxy 2
Dello Joio: Arietta
Etler: Elegy for small orchestra
Bernstein: Candide--Overture
Bernstein: Slava!
Bernstein: West side story--Overture
La Montaine: A summer's day
Chou: Yü ko
Pinkham: Catacoustical measures
Frackenpohl: Short overture
Starer: Elegy for strings
Hoag: An after-intermission overture

British

Purcell: Canon on a ground bass
Purcell: Trumpet prelude (arr.)
Boyce: Overture--Ode for the new year (1758)
Boyce: Overture--Ode for the new year (1772)
Elgar: Elegy
Elgar: Pomp and circumstance military marches, nos.1-5
Elgar: Salut d'amour
Delius: Irmelin--Prelude
Delius: Sleigh ride
Delius: Two pieces for small orchestra (each piece less than 5')
Vaughan Williams: Fantasia on Greensleeves
Vaughan Williams: Prelude "49th parallel"
Vaughan Williams: The wasps--March past of the kitchen utensils
Coleridge-Taylor: Christmas overture
Benjamin: Two Jamaican pieces
Jacob: The barber of Seville goes to the devil
Britten: Paul Bunyan--Overture

Eastern European

Chopin: Mazurka no.7 (arr.)
Chopin: Polonaise, op.40, no.1 (arr.)
Moniuszko: Halka--Mazur
Dvořák: Fest-Marsch, op.54a
Dvořák: Slavonic dances--op.46, nos.1-3, 5, 7-8; op.72, nos.1, 3-7
Dvořák: Legends, op.59 (10 pieces, each 5' or less)
Janáček: Sokal fanfare
Bartók: Dances of Transylvania
Kodály: Háry János--Intermezzo
Lutosławski: Postludium

French and Belgian

Berlioz: La damnation de Faust--Dance of the sylphs; Marche hongroise; Menuet de follets
Berlioz: Les Troyens--Trojan march
Franck: Eight short pieces (each piece less than 5')
Franck: Psyché--Psyché enlevée par les Zéphirs; Les jardins d'Eros
Delibes: Coppelia--Four petites suites, nos.1 and 4
Chabrier: Bourée fantasque (arr.)
Chabrier: Habanera
Chabrier: Joyeuse marche
Chabrier: Le roi malgré lui--Danse slav
Massenet: Hérodiade--Prelude to Act III
Fauré: Shylock--Nocturne
Debussy: Clair de lune (arr.)
Debussy: Le martyre de Saint Sébastien-- La chambre magique; Two fanfares
Pierné: March of the lead soldiers
Dukas: La péri--Fanfare
Satie: Cinq grimaces
Satie: Gymnopédies nos.1, 2, 3 (arr.; each less than 5')
Satie: Trois petites pièces montées
Roussel: Fanfare for a pagan rite
Varèse: Hyperprism
Ibert: Homage à Mozart
Milhaud: Murder of a great chief of state
Milhaud: Ouverture méditerranéene
Milhaud: Symphonies for small orchestra-- Nos.1 (4'), 2 (4'), 3 (3')

German and Austrian

Pachelbel: Canon
Bach: Komm, Gott, Schöpfer (arr.)
Bach: Komm süsser Tod (arr.)
Bach: Schmücke dich (arr.)
Bach: Sheep may safely graze (arr.)
Handel: Alcina--Overture
Handel: Alexander's feast--Overture
Handel: Solomon--Entrance of the Queen
  of Sheba
Handel: Xerxes--Largo (arr.)
Gluck: Orfeo ed Euridice--Dance of the
  furies; Overture
Gluck: Overture, D major
Haydn: March for the Royal Society of
  Musicians
Michael Haydn: Andromeda ed Perseo--
  Overture
Michael Haydn: Symphony, P.8, G major
Mozart: Apollo and Hyacinth--Prelude
Mozart: Overtures--Bastien and
  Bastienne; La clemenza di Tito;
  Così fan tutte; La finta giardiniera;
  Idomeneo; The impressario; The
  marriage of Figaro; Mitridate;
  Il re pastore
Mozart: Turkish march (arr.)
Beethoven: Contradances (12 dances,
  each less than 5')
Beethoven: German dances (12 dances,
  each less than 5')
Beethoven: Prometheus--Overture
Beethoven: Ruins of Athens--Turkish
  march
Weber: Abu Hassan--Overture
Weber: Silvana--Overture
Meyerbeer: Le prophète--Coronation
  march
Schubert: Marche militaire (arr.)
Schubert: Der Teufel als Hydraulicus--
  Overture
Schubert: Die Zwillingsbrüder--Overture
Joh. Strauss Sr.: Radetzky march
Mendelssohn: Athalia--War march of the
  priests
Mendelssohn: Midsummer night's dream--
  Scherzo; Intermezzo; Wedding march
Schumann: Träumerei (arr.)
Wagner: Lohengrin--Prelude, Act III;
  Procession to the cathedral
Wagner: Walküre--Ride of the Valkyries
Bruckner: March in D minor
Bruckner: Three pieces for orchestra
  (each piece less than 5')
Joh. Strauss Jr.: Egyptian march
Joh. Strauss Jr.: Fledermaus--Du und du
Joh. Strauss Jr.: Perpetuum mobile
Joh. Strauss Jr.: Pizzicato polka
Joh. Strauss Jr.: Thunder and lightning
  polka
Brahms: Hungarian dances (each of the
  many dances is 5' or less)
Bruch: Swedish dances (each 5' or less)

Humperdinck: Hansel and Gretel--
  Knusperwalzer; Witch's ride
Humperdinck: Königskinder--Introduction
  to Act II
Reznicek: Donna Diana--Overture

Italian

Monteverdi: Orfeo--Overture; Toccata
  and ritornelli
Albinoni: Concerto, op.5, no.4
Vivaldi: Concerto for orchestra, P.143
Veracini: Aria schiavona
Leo: Santa Elena al Calvario--Sinfonia
Galuppi: Concerto a quattro, no.2
Paisiello: Nina--Overture
Boccherini: Overture, op.43, G.521
Cimarosa: Il maestro di cappella--
  Overture
Paganini: Moto perpetuo, op.11 (arr.)
Rossini: Il signor Bruschino--Overture
Donizetti: Sinfonia for winds, G minor
Verdi: La traviata--Prelude to Act I;
  Prelude to Act III
Leoncavallo: I pagliacci--Intermezzo
Mascagni: L'amico Fritz--Intermezzo
Mascagni: Cavalleria rusticana--
  Intermezzo
Wolf-Ferrari: Jewels of the Madonna--
  Intermezzos nos.1, 2
Wolf-Ferrari: The secret of Suzanne--
  Overture

Russian

Glinka: Russlan and Ludmilla--Overture
Borodin: Prince Igor--Polovtsian march
Mussorgsky: The fair at Sorochinsk--
  Introduction; Gopak
Mussorgsky: Khovantchina--Introduction;
  Entr'acte
Mussorgsky: Scherzo, B-flat major
Tchaikovsky: Coronation march
Tchaikovsky: Eugen Onegin--Polonaise
Tchaikovsky: Mazeppa--Danse cosaque
Tchaikovsky: Suite no.1--Marche
  miniature
Rimsky-Korsakov: Dubinushka
Rimsky-Korsakov: The snow maiden--Dance
  of the buffoons
Rimsky-Korsakov: Tsar Saltan--Flight of
  the bumblebee
Liadov: Baba-Yaga
Stravinsky: Circus polka
Stravinsky: Fireworks
Stravinsky: Rag-time
Stravinsky: Scherzo à la russe
Mossolov: Iron foundry
Khachaturian: Gayane--Sabre dance
Kabalevsky: Colas Breugnon--Overture
Kabalevsky: The comedians--Galop
Shostakovich: The age of gold--Polka

Roussel: Sinfonietta
Ravel: Alborada del gracioso
Ravel: Ma mère l'Oye--Prélude et Danse
  du rouet
Ravel: Menuet antique
Ravel: Pavane pour une infante défunte
Varèse: Ionisation
Varèse: Octandre
Ibert: Bacchanale
Honegger: Chant de joie
Honegger: Mouvement symphonique no.3
Honegger: Pacific 231
Honegger: Pastorale d'été
Honegger: Prélude pour "La tempête"
Honegger: Rugby
Milhaud: Les funérailles de Phocion
Milhaud: Overture philharmonique
Milhaud: Symphonies for small
  orchestra--Nos.4, 5
Poulenc: Deux marches et un interlude

  German and Austrian

Schein: Banchetto musicale--Suite no.1
Biber: Battalia
Telemann: Overture in D major
Bach: Musical offering--Ricercare (arr.)
Bach: Toccata and fugue (arr.)
Handel: Concerto a due cori, no.2
Handel: Concerti grossi op.3, nos.5-6
Handel: Occasional oratorio--Overture
Handel: Overture, D major (arr.)
Handel: Prelude and fugue (arr.)
Handel: Samson--Overture
Handel: Water music--Suite no.3
W.F. Bach: Sinfonia, D minor
C.P.E. Bach: Symphony, W.182, no.1
Gluck: Alceste--Overture
Gluck: Iphigenie in Aulis--Overture
Gluck: Orfeo ed Euridice--Dance of the
  blessed spirits (arr.)
Abel: Symphonies, op.1, nos.5-6
Haydn: Symphony A; Symphony no.2
J.C. Bach: Symphony, op.3, no.2
J.C. Bach: Symphony, op.21, no.3
J.C. Bach: Symphony, D major
M. Haydn: Pastorello
M. Haydn: Symphonies P.26, P.29
Mozart: Adagio and fugue, K.546
Mozart: Contradances K.271c (267)
Mozart: Divertimenti, K.125b (137);
  K.125c (138)
Mozart: Masonic funeral music
Mozart: Overtures--The abduction from
  the seraglio; Don Giovanni; Lucio
  Silla; The magic flute
Mozart: Overture, K.Anh.C 11.05 (311a)
Mozart: Serenade no.2
Mozart: Symphonies K.141a; K.196/121
Mozart: Symphonies nos.4-5, 7, 10,
  22-24, 32
Beethoven: Overtures--Coriolan; Egmont;
  Fidelio; King Stephen; Leonore no.1;
  Namensfeier; Ruins of Athens

Weber: Invitation to the dance (arr.)
Weber: Overtures--Euryanthe; Der
  Freischütz; Jubel; Oberon; Peter
  Schmoll; Preziosa; Ruler of the spirits
Meyerbeer: Fackeltanz no.1
Meyerbeer: Les Huguenots--Overture
Schubert: Overtures--Alfonso and
  Estrella; Claudine von Villa Bella;
  Des Teufels Lustschloss; Fierrabras;
  Die Freunde von Salamanka; Der
  häusliche Krieg; Rosamunde; Der
  vierjährige Posten
Schubert: Overtures (independent)--
  D.8, 12, 26, 470, 556, 590, 591, 648
Lanner: Die Werber Walzer
Lortzing: Zar und Zimmermann--Overture
Mendelssohn: The Hebrides (Fingal's Cave)
Mendelssohn: Heimkehr aus der Fremde
Mendelssohn: Märchen von der schönen
  Melusine
Mendelssohn: Midsummer night's dream--
  Nocturne
Mendelssohn: Overtures--Athalia; Die
  Hochzeit des Camacho; Overture for
  winds; Ruy Blas; St. Paul; Trumpet
  overture
Nicolai: The merry wives of Windsor--
  Overture
Schumann: Overtures--Braut von Messina;
  Faust; Genoveva; Hermann und Dorothea;
  Julius Caesar
Schumann: Manfred--Suite
Flotow: Overtures--Alessandro Stradella;
  Martha
Wagner: Götterdämmerung--Siegfried's
  funeral music; Siegfried's Rhine
  journey
Wagner: Huldigungsmarsch
Wagner: Kaiser-Marsch
Wagner: Lohengrin--Prelude, Act I
Wagner: Die Meistersinger--Prelude
Wagner: Rheingold--Entry of the gods
  into Valhalla
Wagner: Rule Britannia!
Wagner: Siegfried--Forest murmurs
Wagner: Tannhäuser--Arival of the
  guests; Prelude, Act III
Wagner: Tristan und Isolde: Nachtgesang;
  Prelude to Act III
Suppé: Overtures--Beautiful Galathea;
  Boccaccio*; Jolly robbers; Light
  cavalry; Morning, noon and night in
  Vienna; Pique Dame; Poet and peasant
Bruckner: Three pieces for orchestra
Joh. Strauss Jr.: Overtures--Fledermaus;
  Gypsy baron
Joh. Strauss Jr.: Künstler Quadrille
Joh. Strauss Jr.: Waltzes--Emperor;
  Morning papers; On the beautiful blue
  Danube; Roses from the south; Voices of
  spring; Wiener Blut; Wine, women and
  song
Josef Strauss: Waltzes--Mein Lebenslauf

ist Lieb' und Lust; Music of the
spheres; Village swallows
Brahms: Academic festival overture
Bruch: Loreley--Prelude
Humperdinck: Hansel and Gretel--Prelude
Humperdinck: Königskinder--Prelude;
Introduction to Act III
Humperdinck: Eine Trauung in der
Bastille
Mahler: Symphony no.1--"Blumine"
movement
Mahler: Symphony no.5--Adagietto
Wolf: Der Corregidor--Prelude and
interlude
Wolf: Scherzo and finale
R. Strauss: Salome--Salome's dance
R. Strauss: Serenade, op.7
Schoenberg: Begleitungsmusik zu einer
Lichtspielscene
Webern: Concerto, op.24
Webern: Five pieces for orchestra, op.10
Webern: Symphony, op.21
Webern: Variations for orchestra, op.30
Toch: Circus, an overture
Toch: Pinocchio
Hindemith: Overtures--Cupid and Psyche;
Neues vom Tage
Hindemith: Spielmusik, op.43, no.1
Hindemith: Suite of French dances
Korngold: Theme and variations, op.42
Einem: Capriccio, op.2
Zimmermann: Stillness and return

Italian

G. Gabrieli: Canzona
G. Gabrieli: Canzona noni toni
G. Gabrieli: Sonata pian' e forte
Monteverdi: Orfeo--Sinfonie e ritornelli
Corelli: Suite for string orchestra (arr.)
Torelli: Concerto, op.6, no.1
Torelli: Sinfonia, op.6, no.6
A. Scarlatti: Concerto, G minor*
A. Scarlatti: Concerti grossi nos.1-2
A. Scarlatti: Piccola suite
A. Scarlatti: Sinfonie nos.1, 2, 5
Albinoni: Concerto, op.5, no.7
Vivaldi: Sinfonia, P.sinf.21, B minor
Vivaldi: Sinfonie nos.1-3
D. Scarlatti: Five sonatas in form of
a suite (arr.)
B. Marcello: Introduction, aria, and
presto
Geminiani: Concerti grossi, op.2,
nos.2, 3*
Sammartini: Concertino, G major
Sammartini: Sinfonie, J.-C. 4, J.-C.39,
J.-C.47
Galuppi: Concerto a quattro, no.1
Galuppi: Sinfonie in D major and
F major
Pergolesi: Concertino, E-flat major
Paisiello: La scuffiara--Overture
Paisiello: Sinfonia funebre

Paisiello: Sinfonia in tre tempi
Boccherini: Sinfonia concertante, G.268
Cimarosa: Il matrimonio segreto--
Overture
Cimarosa: Sinfonia, D major
Cimarosa: I traci amanti--Overture
Cherubini: Overtures--Abenceragen; Ali
Baba; Anacreon; Demophoon; Les deux
journées; Faniska; Medea; The
Portuguese Inn
Rossini: Overtures--Il barbiere di
Siviglia; La Cenerentola; La gazza
ladra; L'Italiana in Algeri; Robert
Bruce; La scala di seta; The siege of
Corinth; Tancredi; Il Turco in Italia;
Il viaggio a Reims
Rossini: Serenata per piccolo complesso
Rossini: William Tell--Pas de six
Donizetti: Allegro in C major
Donizetti: Overtures--Daughter of the
regiment; Don Pasquale; Roberto
Devereux
Bellini: Norma--Overture
Bellini: Symphonies in C minor and
D major
Verdi: Aida--Prelude
Verdi: Overtures--La forza del destino;
Nabucco; I vespri siciliani
Ponchielli: La Gioconda--Dance of the
hours
Puccini: I crisantemi
Puccini: Edgar--Preludio
Mascagni: Cavalleria rusticana--Prelude
and siciliana*
Busoni: Lustspiel overture
Dallapiccola: Piccola musica notturna
Berio: Allelujah
Berio: Nones
Berio: Ritirata notturna di Madrid

Russian

Glinka: Jota aragonesa
Glinka: Kamarinskaya
Glinka: A life for the Tsar--Overture
Glinka: Summer night in Madrid
Glinka: Valse fantaisie
Borodin: In the steppes of central Asia
Borodin: Nocturne (arr.)
Borodin: Prince Igor--Overture
Balakirev: Islamey (arr.)
Balakirev: Overture on three Russian
folk songs
Mussorgsky: Boris Godunov--Polonaise
Mussorgsky: Intermezzo in the classic
style
Mussorgsky: Khovantchina--Dance of the
Persian maidens
Mussorgsky: Mlada--Festive march
Tchaikovsky: Eugen Onegin--Waltzes
Tchaikovsky: Marche slave
Tchaikovsky: Le voyévode, op.3--
Overture
Tchaikovsky: Le voyévode, op.78

Rimsky-Korsakov: Christmas eve--
Polonaise
Rimsky-Korsakov: Le coq d'or--
Introduction and Wedding march
Rimsky-Korsakov: Overtures--The maid
of Pskov; May night; The tsar's bride
Liadov: The enchanted lake
Liadov: Kikimora
Glazunov: The seasons--Autumn; Winter
Glazunov: Valse de concert, no.2
Rachmaninoff: Vocalise
Glière: The red poppy--Russian
sailors' dance
Stravinsky: Eight instrumental
miniatures
Stravinsky: Firebird--Berceuse and
Finale
Stravinsky: Four Norwegian moods
Stravinsky: Monumentum pro Gesualdo
di Venosa
Stravinsky: Le sacre du printemps--
Danse sacral
Stravinsky: Suites nos.1-2 for small
orchestra
Stravinsky: Variations
Prokofiev: Andante
Prokofiev: Love of the three oranges--
March and scherzo
Prokofiev: Overture, op.42
Prokofiev: War and peace--Overture
Slonimsky: My toy balloon
Khachaturian: Gayane--Three pieces
Shostakovich: Festive overture

Spanish and Latin American

Arriaga: Los esclavos felices--
Overture
Albéniz: Catalonia
Falla: La vida breve--Interlude and
dance
Turina: La procesion del Rocio
Villa-Lobos: Bachianas brasileiras
no.5--Aria
Chávez: Xochipilli
Rodrigo: Zarabanda lejana y villancico
Halffter: La muerte de Carmen--Habanera
Surinach: Drama jondo
Surinach: Fandango
Surinach: Feria magica
Davidovsky: Inflexions

Other nationalities

Berwald: Estrella de Soria--Overture
Grieg: Lyric pieces, op.68
Grieg: Two elegiac melodies, op.34
Grieg: Two Norwegian airs, op.63
Nielsen: Saul and David--Prelude to
Act II
Sibelius: The bard
Sibelius: Finlandia
Sibelius: Karelia overture, op.10
Sibelius: Kuolema--Valse triste

Sibelius: Legends--Lemminkäinen's
return
Skalkottas: Five Greek dances
Xenakis: Analogique A
Xenakis: Metastaseis B

11' TO 15'

American

Foote: Suite, op.63
Chadwick: Melpomene
Ives: Holidays symphony--Thanksgiving
Ruggles: Men and mountains
Ruggles: Sun-treader
Griffes: The pleasure dome of Kubla Khan
Becker: Soundpieces nos.1b and 2b
Becker: When the willow nods
Weiss: I segreti
B. Rogers: Once upon a time
B. Rogers: Three Japanese dances
Piston: Concerto for orchestra
Piston: Lincoln Center festival overture
Piston: Serenata
Still: Darker America
Hanson: Symphony no.5 (Sinfonia sacra)
V. Thomson: The plow that broke the
plains--Suite
V. Thomson: A solemn music, and a joyful
fugue
Cowell: Sinfonietta
Cowell: Synchrony
Copland: Inscape
Copland: Lincoln portrait
Copland: Orchestral variations
Copland: El salón México
Copland: Symphony no.2
Creston: Dance overture
Creston: Invocation and dance
Creston: Two choric dances
Finney: Landscapes remembered
Stevens: Sinfonia breve
Stevens: Symphonic dances
Barber: Essay no.3
Barber: Medea's meditation and
dance of vengeance
Hovhaness: Psalm and fugue, op.40a
Hovhaness: Variations and fugue
Dahl: Variations for string orchestra
on a theme by C.P.E. Bach
Effinger: Little symphony no.1
Diamond: Rounds for string orchestra
Diamond: The world of Paul Klee
Kay: Fantasy variations
Kay: Theater set for orchestra
Kay: Umbrian scene
Ward: Adagio and allegro
Yardumian: Cantus animae et cordis
Rochberg: Black sounds
Rochberg: Cheltenham concerto
Rochberg: Night music

Kirchner: Music for orchestra
Kirchner: Toccata
Kirk: An orchestra primer
Bergsma: Chameleon variations
Mennin: Concertato (Moby Dick)
Rorem: Ideas for easy orchestra
Benson: A Delphic serenade
Starer: Samson Agonistes
Schuller: American triptych
Schuller: Five bagatelles
Schuller: Five etudes for orchestra
Feldman: Intersection no.1 for orchestra
Aschaffenburg: Three dances for
  orchestra
Anderson: Chamber symphony
Martino: Ritorno
Colgrass: As quiet as...
Subotnick: Play no.2

  British

Purcell: Suites--Abdelazar; Dido and
  Aeneas; The Gordian knot untied (no.1);
  The married beau
Arne: Symphony no.4
Boyce: Symphonies nos.7-8
Sullivan: Overture in C (In memoriam)
Sullivan: The tempest--Three dances
Elgar: Cockaigne
Elgar: Serenade, op.20
Delius: Dance rhapsody no.1
Vaughan Williams: Five variants of
  Dives and Lazarus
Holst: Brook green suite
Holst: Egdon Heath
Holst: The perfect fool--Ballet music
Holst: St. Paul's suite
Coleridge-Taylor: Petite suite de
  concert
Coates: London suite
Bliss: Introduction and allegro
Barbirolli: An Elizabethan suite
Walton: Hamlet and Ophelia
Berkeley: Sinfonietta
Berkeley: Symphony no.3
Berkeley: Windsor variations
Britten: Canadian carnival
Britten: Matinées musicales
Britten: Peter Grimes--Four sea
  interludes
Britten: The prince of the pagodas--
  Pas de six
Britten: Sinfonietta
Britten: Soirées musicales
Britten: Suite on English folk tunes

  Eastern European

Gołąbek: Symphonies in C major and
  D major (I)
Vaňhal: Sinfonia, G minor
Liszt: Funeral triumph of Tasso
Liszt: Hungarian rhapsodies nos.1, 2, 4
Liszt: Mephisto waltzes nos.1 and 2*

Liszt: Nocturnal procession
Liszt: Orpheus
Liszt: Prometheus
Liszt: Von der Wiege bis zum Grabe
Smetana: The bartered bride--Three dances
Smetana: My country--Vyšehrad; The
  Moldau; From Bohemia's meadows and
  forests; Tábor; Blaník
Smetana: Richard III
Smetana: Wallenstein's camp
Dvořák: Amid nature
Dvořák: Husitská
Dvořák: Othello overture
Dvořák: Scherzo capriccioso
Dvořák: Slavonic rhapsodies, op.45,
  nos.2-3
Bartók: Deux portraits (Two portraits)
Bartók: Hungarian sketches
Enesco: Rumanian rhapsodies nos.1-2
Kodály: Galanta dances
Kodály: Marosszek dances
Kodály: Theater overture
Weinberger: Schwanda the bagpiper--
  Polka and fugue
Tansman: Sinfonietta
Tansman: Variations on a theme by
  Girolamo Frescobaldi
Lutosławski: Little suite
Lutosławski: Venetian games
A. Bloch: Enfiando per orchestra
Penderecki: De natura sonoris no.2
Penderecki: Flourescences
Sapieyevski: Surtsey

  French and Belgian

Lully: Ballet suite (arr.)
Rameau: Ballet suite (arr.)
Rameau: Dardanus--Suite
Rameau: Suite for string orchestra
Grétry: Zémire et Azor--Ballet suite
Berlioz: Benvenuto Cellini--Overture
Berlioz: Les franc-juges
Berlioz: King Lear
Berlioz: Rob Roy
Berlioz: Roméo et Juliette--Romeo alone;
  Festivities at Capulet's
Berlioz: Les Troyens--Ballet
Franck: Le chasseur maudit
Franck: Les Éolides
Franck: Rédemption--Morceau symphonique
Lalo: Namouna--Ballet suite no.2
Lalo: Le roi d'Ys--Overture
Saint-Saëns: Septet, op.65
Delibes: Le roi s'amuse--Airs de danse
  dans le style ancien
Bizet: Carmen--Suite no.1
Bizet: Jolie fille de Perth--Scènes
  bohémiennes
Bizet: Ouverture
Bizet: Patrie
Fauré: Masques et bergamasques
Debussy: Nocturnes (omitting last mvt.)
Debussy: Petite suite (arr.)
Dukas: L'apprenti sorcier

Satie: Parade
Koechlin: Les bandar-log
Roussel: Concerto for small orchestra
Roussel: Petite suite
Roussel: Pour une fête de printemps
Roussel: Suite in F, op.33
Ravel: Bolero
Ravel: Daphnis et Chloe--Suite no.1
Ravel: La valse
Varèse: Intégrales
Ibert: Divertissement
Ibert: Louisville concerto
Milhaud: Le boeuf sur le toit
Milhaud: Cortège funèbre
Poulenc: Suite française
Messiaen: Les offrandes oubliées
Françaix: Sei preludi

German and Austrian

Fux: Overture, C major
Telemann: Overture, C major
Telemann: Suites nos.1-2
Bach: Passacaglia (arr.)
Handel: Concerti a due cori nos.1, 3
Handel: Concerti grossi, op.3, nos.1, 4
Handel: Overtures--Rodrigo; Saul;
  Solomon; Theodora
Handel: Royal fireworks music (arr.)
Handel: Water music--Suite no.2
W.F. Bach: Sinfonia, F major
Frederick II: Symphonies nos.1*-2*
C.P.E. Bach: Symphonies W.182, nos.2-5;
  no.6*
C.P.E. Bach: Symphonies W.183, nos.1, 3
Gluck: Ballet suite no.2 (arr.)
Gluck: Sinfonia, F major
Wagenseil: Sinfonia, G minor
J. Stamitz: Sinfonia pastorale
J. Stamitz: Symphony, op.3, no.3
J. Stamitz: Three Mannheim symphonies
  (each 11' to 15')
Abel: Symphony op.7, no.6
Haydn: Symphony B; Symphonies nos.1;
  4-5; 9-12; 16-19; 25; 27; 30; 37
Haydn: Toy symphony
J.C. Bach: Symphonies, op.3, nos.1,4;
  op.6, no.1*; op.18, nos.1-3, 5-6;
  op.21, no.1
M. Haydn: Symphony, P.33
Dittersdorf: Sinfonia, C major
Mozart: Cassations nos.1-2
Mozart: Divertimento, K.125a (136)
Mozart: Eine kleine Nachtmusik
Mozart: Symphonies nos.1-3; 6; 8-9;
  11-12; 14-19; 26-27; 37
Beethoven: Consecration of the house
Beethoven: Contradances (12 dances
  complete)
Beethoven: Leonore overtures nos.2-3
Beethoven: Musik zu einem Ritterballet
Kuhlau: William Shakespeare--Overture
Schubert: Rosamunde--Ballet music
Mendelssohn: Calm sea and prosperous

voyage
Mendelssohn: Midsummer night's dream--
  Overture
Schumann: Manfred--Overture
Wagner: Götterdämmerung--Siegfried's
  Rhine journey (version with insert)
Wagner: Grosser Festmarsch
Wagner: Overtures--A Faust overture;
  Der fliegende Holländer; Rienzi;
  Tannhäuser (Dresden version)
Wagner: Parsifal--Prelude; Good Friday
  spell
Wagner: Tannhäuser--Venusberg music
Bruckner: Overture, G minor
Joh. Strauss Jr.: Tales from the Vienna
  Woods
Brahms: Tragic overture
Bruch: Swedish dances--Series 1;
  Series 2
Humperdinck: Hansel and Gretel--Three
  excerpts
R. Strauss: Der Rosenkavalier--Waltzes,
  first sequence
R. Strauss: Till Eulenspiegels lustige
  Streiche
Schoenberg: Theme and variations, op.43b
Webern: Five movements, op.5
Webern: Im Sommerwind
Webern: Passacaglia, op.1
Webern: Six pieces for orchestra, op.6
Berg: Lyric suite--Three pieces
Křenek: Sinfonietta
Křenek: Symphonic elegy
Blacher: Orchester-Ornament
Einem: Ballade
Stockhausen: Kontra-Punkte no.1

Italian

A. Scarlatti: Sinfonie nos.4, 6, 8, 10
Albinoni: Concerto, op.9, no.9
Vivaldi: Concerto for orchestra, P.407
Manfredini: Christmas symphony*
D. Scarlatti: The good-humored ladies--
  Suite (arr.)
Tartini: Concerto no.58
Tartini: Sinfonia, D major
Locatelli: Concerto grosso, op.1, no.6*
Locatelli: Trauer-Symphonie
Sammartini: Sinfonie J.-C. 2; J.-C. 32
Boccherini: Symphonies, G.511, 512, 514
Rossini: Semiramide--Overture
Rossini: Sonatas (6 sonatas, each ca.12')
Rossini: William Tell--Overture
Verdi: Aida--Triumphal march and ballet
Puccini: Preludio sinfonico
Busoni: Rondo arlecchinesco
Respighi: Ancient airs and dances--Set I
Dallapiccola: Due pezzi per orchestra
Dallapiccola: Variations for orchestra
Berio: Still
Berio: Variazioni per orchestra da
  camera

Russian

Borodin: Prince Igor--Polovtsian dances
Balakirev: Russia
Mussorgsky: Night on Bald Mountain
Tchaikovsky: Capriccio italien
Rimsky-Korsakov: Capriccio espagnol
Rimsky-Korsakov: Conte féerique
Rimsky-Korsakov: Mlada--Suite
Rimsky-Korsakov: Overture on Russian
  themes
Rimsky-Korsakov: Russian Easter overture
Rimsky-Korsakov: Sadko--Tableau musical
Rimsky-Korsakov: The snow maiden--Suite
Liadov: Eight Russian folk songs
Ippolitov-Ivanov: Turkish fragments
Arensky: Variations on a theme
  by Tchaikovsky
Glazunov: Chopiniana
Glazunov: Valse de concert, no.1
Stravinsky: Concerto in D
Stravinsky: Concerto in E-flat
  (Dumbarton Oaks)
Stravinsky: Four etudes for orchestra
Stravinsky: Octet
Stravinsky: Symphonies of wind
  instruments
Prokoviev: Classical symphony
Prokofiev: Le pas d'acier--Suite
Prokofiev: A summer day
Khachaturian: Masquerade--Suite
Khachaturian: Spartacus--Suite no.3

Spanish and Latin American

Granados: Dante
Granados: Tres danzas españolas (arr.)
Falla: Three-cornered hat--Suites
  nos.1 and 2
Villa-Lobos: Bachianas brasileiras no.9
Villa-Lobos: Suite for strings
Chávez: Resonancias
Chávez: Symphonies nos.1-2
Chávez: Toccata for percussion
Ginastera: Estancia--Ballet suite
Ginastera: Panambí--Suite

Other nationalities

Gade: Nachklänge von Ossian
Grieg: Peer Gynt--Suite no.1
Grieg: Sigurd Jorsalfar--Three
  orchestral pieces
Nielsen: Helios overture
Nielsen: Little suite
Sibelius: Karelia suite, op.11
Sibelius: Rakastava
Sibelius: The tempest--Suite no.2
Alfvén: Midsommarvaka
Martin: Passacaille
Xenakis: Akrata
Xenakis: Anaktoria
Xenakis: Atrees
Xenakis: ST/48-1,240162

Xenakis: Syrmos
Bamert: Circus parade

16' TO 20'

American

Gottschalk: Night in the tropics
Gottschalk: Symphony no.2
Chadwick: Tam O'Shanter
MacDowell: Suite no.1
Gilbert: Dance in the Place Congo
Converse: The mystic trumpeter
Ives: Symphony no.3
Ives: Three places in New England
Carpenter: Sea drift
Becker: Symphony no.3
Robt. Russell Bennett: Suite of old
  American dances
Piston: The incredible flutist--Suite
Piston: Sinfonietta
Piston: Symphonies nos.7-8
Piston: Three New England sketches
Hanson: Merrymount--Suite
V. Thomson: Louisiana story--Suite
V. Thomson: Symphony on a hymn tune
Gershwin: American in Paris
Harris: Symphonies nos.3, 7
Copland: Connotations
Copland: Dance symphony
Copland: Rodeo--Four excerpts (complete)
Copland: Statements
Copland: The tender land--Suite
Luening: Rhapsodic variations
Phillips: Selections from McGuffey's
  reader
Wilder: Carl Sandburg suite
Barber: Die Natali
Barber: Souvenirs
Barber: Symphony no.1
Wm. Schuman: Credendum
Wm. Schuman: New England triptych
Wm. Schuman: Symphony no.5
Hovhaness: Mysterious mountain
Hovhaness: Symphony no.15
Gould: Fall River legend--Ballet suite
Gould: Latin-American symphonette
Gould: Spirituals for orchestra
Kubik: Divertimento I
Diamond: Music for Shakespeare's Romeo
  and Juliet
Persichetti: Night dances
Persichetti: Symphony, op.61
Kay: Scherzi musicali
Kay: Serenade for orchestra
Yardumian: Armenian suite
Kurka: The good soldier Schweik--Suite
Bassett: Echoes from an invisible world
Pinkham: Symphonies nos.1-2
Rorem: Design

Lees: The trumpet of the swan
Erb: Symphony of overtures
Crumb: Echoes of time and the river
M. Lombardo: Drakestail
Martino: Mosaic for grand orchestra
Reynolds: Quick are the mouths of earth
Jones: Let us now praise famous men
Wuorinen: Contrafactum

British

Delius: Brigg fair
Coleridge-Taylor: Hiawatha--Suite from
  the ballet music
Bliss: Things to come--Concert suite
Tippett: Divertimento for chamber
  orchestra
Britten: Simple symphony
Britten: Sinfonia da requiem
Britten: Young person's guide to the
  orchestra
Musgrave: Concerto for orchestra
Musgrave: Night music
Richard Rodney Bennett: Zodiac

Eastern European

Gołąbek: Symphony in D major (II)
Wański: Symphony in G major
Chopin: Les sylphides (arr.)
Liszt: Battle of the Huns
Liszt: Festklänge
Liszt: Héroïde funèbre
Liszt: Mazeppa
Liszt: Les prèludes
Liszt: Tasso, lament and triumph
Dvořák: Midday witch
Dvořák: Rhapsody, op.14
Dvořák: Suite, op.98b
Dvořák: Watersprite
Dvořák: Wood dove
Noskowski: The steppe
Janáček: Lachian dances
Karłowicz: Lithuanian rhapsody
Bartók: Dance suite
Bartók: Deux images
Bartók: Mikrokosmos suite (arr.)
Bartók: The miraculous mandarin--Suite
Kodály: Concerto for orchestra
Kodály: Summer evening
Szymanowski: Konzert-Ouverture, op.12
Martinu: Estampes
Martinu: Sinfonia concertante for
  two orchestras
Martinu: Toccata e due canzoni
Weinberger: Under the spreading
  chestnut tree
Tansman: Triptych
Bacewicz: Contradizione
Lutosławski: Three postludes for
  orchestra
Husa: Fantasies for orchestra
Husa: Music for Prague 1968
Husa: Two sonnets by Michelangelo

French and Belgian

Lully: Le triomphe de l'amour--Ballet suite
Rameau: Les fêtes d'Hébé--Divertissement
Berlioz: Roměo et Juliette--Love scene
Gounod: Faust--Ballet music
Gounod: Little symphony for wind
  instruments
Franck: Eight short pieces (complete)
Saint-Saëns: La jeunesse d'Hercule
Saint-Saëns: Suite algérienne
Saint-Saëns: Trois tableaux symphoniques
Delibes: Sylvia--Suite
Bizet: L'Arlésienne--Suites nos.1-2
Bizet: Carmen--Suite no.2
Chabrier: Suite pastorale
Massenet: Le Cid--Ballet music
Massenet: Scènes pittoresques
Fauré: Dolly
Fauré: Pelléas et Mélisande--Suite
Luigini: Ballet égyptien
D'Indy: Istar
Debussy: Images--Ibéria
Debussy: Jeux
Debussy: Le martyre de Saint Sébastien--
  Four excerpts
Debussy: Printemps
Dukas: La péri
Satie: Les aventures de Mercure
Roussel: Bacchus et Ariane--Suites 1, 2
Roussel: Le festin de l'araigne
Roussel: Le marchand de sable qui passe
Rabaud: La procession nocturne
Ravel: Daphnis et Chloe--Suite no.2
Ravel: Ma mère l'Oye--Suite
Ravel: Rapsodie espagnole
Ravel: Le tombeau de Couperin
Ravel: Valses nobles et sentimentales
Varèse: Arcana
Ibert: Escales
Milhaud: Aubade
Milhaud: La création du monde
Milhaud: Suite française
Milhaud: Suite provençale
Milhaud: Symphony no.12
Auric: La chambre
Auric: Phèdre
Poulenc: Les biches--Suite

German and Austrian

Buxtehude: Four chorale preludes (arr.)
Telemann: Don Quichotte
Telemann: Suite, F major
Bach: Prelude and fugue, BWV 552 (arr.)
Handel: Royal fireworks music
Handel: Water music suite (arr.)
Gluck: Ballet suite no.1 (arr.)
Haydn: Symphonies nos.3; 13-14; 20;
  23; 28-29; 32; 34-36; 40; 64; 80
J.C. Bach: Symphony, op.6, no.6
M. Haydn: Symphonies, P.21; P.42
Mozart: Divertimenti, K.113; K.167a (205)
Mozart: Les petits riens

Mozart: Serenades nos.8; 12
Mozart: Symphonies nos.13; 20-21; 25;
  28; 30-31; 34-35
Beethoven: German dances (12 dances,
  complete)
Beethoven: Grosse Fuge, op.133 (arr.)
Beethoven: Wellington's victory
Weber: Symphony no.2
Schubert: Rosamunde--Entr'actes
Schumann: Overture, scherzo and finale
Wagner: Die Meistersinger--Three
  excerpts from Act III
Wagner: Siegfried idyll
Wagner: Tristan und Isolde--Prelude
  and Liebestod
Wagner: Walküre--Wotan's farewell and
  Magic fire music
Goldmark: Sakuntala--Overture
Brahms: Variations on a theme by Haydn
Wolf: Der Corregidor--Suite (arr.)
R. Strauss: Don Juan
R. Strauss: Macbeth
Pfitzner: Palestrina--Three preludes
Schoenberg: Five pieces for orchestra
Schoenberg: Ode to Napoleon Bonaparte
Schoenberg: Suite for string orchestra
Berg: Three pieces for orchestra, op.6
Berg: Wozzeck--Three excerpts
Hindemith: Concert music for strings
  and brass, op.50
Hindemith: Concerto for orchestra
Hindemith: Philharmonic concerto
Hindemith: Symphonic metamorphoses of
  themes by Weber
Hindemith: Tuttifäntchen--Suite
Korngold: Schauspiel-Ouvertüre
Křenek: Eleven transparencies
Blacher: Orchestra-variations on a
  theme of Paganini
Henze: Symphony no.5

Italian

Veracini: Quattro pezzi (arr.)
Boccherini: Symphonies, G.503; G.506
Puccini: Capriccio sinfonico
Respighi: Ancient airs and dances--
  Sets II, III
Respighi: Brazilian impressions
Respighi: Fontane di Roma
Respighi: Pini di Roma
Respighi: Trittico Botticelliano
Respighi: Gli uccelli
Malipiero: Sinfonia per Antigenida
Casella: Italia
Casella: Paganiniana
Menotti: Sebastian--Suite
Maderna: Aura
Maderna: Serenata no.2

Russian

Borodin: Symphony no.3
Balakirev: Thamar

Mussorgsky: Pictures at an exhibition
  (Touschmaloff version)
Tchaikovsky: Hamlet
Tchaikovsky: Overture 1812
Tchaikovsky: Romeo and Juliet
Tchaikovsky: The tempest, op.18
Rimsky-Korsakov: Symphoniette on
  Russian themes
Rimsky-Korsakov: Tsar Saltan--Suite
Ippolitov-Ivanov: Caucasian sketches
Glazunov: Stenka Razine
Rachmaninoff: Capriccio bohémien
Rachmaninoff: The rock
Rachmaninoff: Die Toteninsel
Glière: The red poppy--Suite
Miaskovsky: Sinfonietta, op.32, no.2
Miaskovsky: Symphony no.21
Stravinsky: Agon
Stravinsky: Le baiser de la fée--
  Divertimento
Stravinsky: Danses concertantes
Stravinsky: Scènes de ballet
Stravinsky: Scherzo fantastique
Stravinsky: Song of the nightingale
Prokofiev: Lieutenant Kijé--Suite
Prokofiev: Love of the three oranges--
  Symphonic suite
Prokofiev: Romeo and Juliet--Suite no.3
Tcherepnin: Georgiana suite
Tcherepnin: Serenade, op.97
Khachaturian: Spartacus--Suite no.2
Kabalevsky: Colas Breugnon--Suite
Kabalevsky: The comedians
Shostakovich: The age of gold--Suite
Shostakovich: Ballet suite no.1

Spanish and Latin American

Falla: El amor brujo--Ballet suite
Turina: Danzas fantásticas
Villa-Lobos: Bachianas brasileiras
  nos.1-2; 4; 8
Villa-Lobos: Sinfoniettas nos.1-2
Villa-Lobos: Uirapurú (The magic bird)
Chávez: Symphony no.5
Surinach: Ritmo jondo
Ginastera: Pampeana no.3

Other nationalities

Grieg: Holberg suite
Grieg: Lyric suite, op.54
Grieg: Norwegian dances
Grieg: Peer Gynt--Suite no.2
Sibelius: Legends--Lemminkäinen and the
  maidens of Saari; Lemminkäinen in
  Tuonela
Sibelius: Night ride and sunrise
Sibelius: The Oceanides
Sibelius: Pohjola's daughter
Sibelius: A saga
Sibelius: Tapiola
Sibelius: The tempest--Suite no.1
Bloch: Evocations

Martin: Etudes for string orchestra
Martin: The four elements
Gerhard: Epithalamion
Skalkottas: Ten sketches for strings
Blomdahl: Sisyphos

21' TO 25'

American

Herbert: Serenade, op.12
Loeffler: A pagan poem
B. Rogers: The musicians of Bremen
Piston: Symphonies nos.4-6
Still: Afro-American symphony
Hanson: Symphonies nos.2, 4
Sessions: The black maskers--Suite
Sessions: Symphonies nos.1, 4
V. Thomson: The river--Suite
Porter: Symphony no.2
Gershwin: Porgy and Bess--Symphonic
  picture (arr.)
Harris: Symphony no.9
Antheil: Symphonies nos.5-6
Copland: Appalachian spring
Copland: Billy the Kid--Suite
Copland: Music for the theatre
Copland: The red pony
Copland: Symphony no.1
Giannini: Symphony no.2
Creston: Symphony no.2
Gutche: Symphony no.5
Carter: Concerto for orchestra
Carter: The minotaur--Ballet suite
Carter: Variations for orchestra
Barber: Medea--Ballet suite
Wm. Schuman: Judith
Wm. Schuman: Undertow
Dello Joio: Meditations on Ecclesiastes
Dello Joio: Variations, chaconne,
  and finale
Fine: Symphony (1962)
Bernstein: Facsimile
Bernstein: On the waterfront--
  Symphonic suite
Bernstein: West side story--Symphonic
  dances
Foss: Baroque variations
Bassett: Variations for orchestra
Mennin: Symphony no.6
Pinkham: Signs of the zodiac
Laderman: Concerto for orchestra
Laderman: Magic prison
Lees: Symphony no.2
Schuller: Contours
Schuller: Seven studies on themes
  of Paul Klee
Schuller: Spectra
Druckman: Windows
Crumb: Variazioni for large orchestra
Amram: Shakespearian concerto

Blackwood: Symphony no.2

British

Tippett: Concerto for double string
  orchestra
Britten: Variations on a theme of
  Frank Bridge

Eastern European

Wański: Symphony in D major
Liszt: Hungaria
Suk: Serenade, op.6
Dvořák: Czech suite
Dvořák: Golden spinning wheel
Dvořák: A hero's song
Dvořák: Symphonic variations
Janáček: Idyla
Janáček: Sinfonietta
Janáček: Taras Bulba
Karłowicz: Odwieczne pieśni (Eternal
  songs)
Karłowicz: Stanisław i Anna Oświecimowie
Dohnányi: Ruralia hungarica
Bartók: Divertimento
Bartók: Four orchestral pieces, op.12
Bartók: Suite no.2 for orchestra
Kodály: Háry János--Suite
Kodály: Variations on a Hungarian
  folksong
Martinu: The frescos of Piero della
  Francesca
Martinu: Symphonies nos.2, 6

French

Gounod: Symphony no.1
Franck: Psyché (complete)
Lalo: Namouna--Ballet suite no.1
Saint-Saëns: Carnival of the animals
Saint-Saëns: Symphony no.2
Delibes: Coppelia--Suite no.1; Four
  petites suites (Ballet suite no.2)
Massenet: Scènes alsaciennes
Massenet: Suite no.1
Debussy: La mer
Debussy: Nocturnes
Roussel: Symphonies nos.3-4
Varèse: Deserts
Honegger: Symphonies nos.1-2
Milhaud: Suite symphonique no.2
Milhaud: Symphonies nos.10-11
Poulenc: The story of Babar the little
  elephant
Jolivet: Symphony no.1

German and Austrian

Bach: Suites nos.1, 3, 4
Handel: The faithful shepherd--Suite (arr.)
Haydn: Symphonies nos.6-8; 15; 21-22;
  24; 26; 33; 38-39; 41-53; 55; 57-59;
  62-63; 65-71; 73-79; 81-85; 87-92;
  94-96

J.C. Bach: Symphony, op.9, no.2
J.C. Bach: Symphony, op.18, no.4
Mozart: Divertimento, K.251
Mozart: A musical joke
Mozart: Serenades nos.1, 3, 11
Mozart: Symphonies nos.29; 33;
  34 (version with minuet)
Beethoven: Symphony no.1
Witt: Jena symphony
Weber: Symphony no.1
Schubert: Symphonies nos.3; 8
Mendelssohn: Symphony no.2
Wagner: Tannhäuser--Overture and
  Venusberg music (Paris version)
Brahms: Liebeslieder waltzes (arr.)
Humperdinck: Dornröschen--Suite
Mahler: Symphony no.10--Movements
  I and III
R. Strauss: Death and transfiguration
R. Strauss: Der Rosenkavalier--Suite
R. Strauss: Suite, op.4
Schoenberg: Chamber symphonies nos.1-2
Schoenberg: Variations for orchestra
Hindemith: Sinfonietta in E
Hindemith: Nobilissima visione
Křenek: Symphony "Pallas Athena"
Weill: Aufstieg und Fall der Stadt
  Mahagonny--Suite
Weill: Kleine Dreigroschenmusik
Weill: Symphony no.1
Einem: Meditations
Stockhausen: Gruppen
Stockhausen: Punkte

Italian

Boccherini: Symphony, G.518
Clementi: Symphony no.1
Respighi: Feste romane
Respighi: Rossiniana

Russian

Borodin: Petite suite (arr.)
Mussorgsky: Pictures at an exhibition
  (Goehr version)
Tchaikovsky: Francesca da Rimini
Tchaikovsky: The nutcracker--Suite
Tchaikovsky: Sleeping beauty--Suite
Tchaikovsky: Suite no.4
Tchaikovsky: Swan lake--Suite
Rimsky-Korsakov: Christmas eve--Suite
Rimsky-Korsakov: Symphony no.1
Scriabin: The poem of ecstasy
Scriabin: Prometheus
Stravinsky: Firebird--Suite (1919
  version)
Stravinsky: Jeu de cartes
Stravinsky: Symphony in three movements
Prokofiev: Peter and the wolf
Prokofiev: Scythian suite
Prokofiev: Sinfonietta
Tcherepnin: Symphony no.2
Khachaturian: Spartacus--Suite no.1
Kabalevsky: Symphony no.1

Shostakovich: Hamlet--Incidental music
Shostakovich: Symphony no.9
Khrennikov: Symphony no.1

Spanish and Latin American

Arriaga: Symphony, D minor
Turina: Sinfonia sevillana
Chávez: The daughter of Colchis
Chávez: Symphony no.4
Ginastera: Variaciones concertantes

Other nationalities

Gade: Symphony no.1
Sibelius: Pelléas and Mélisande
Sibelius: Symphony no.7
Bloch: Trois poèmes juifs
Bloch: Voice in the wilderness
Martin: Petite symphonie concertante
Gerhard: Concerto for orchestra
Blomdahl: Game for eight
Blomdahl: Symphony no.3
Suolahti: Sinfonia piccola
Ishii: Kyō-Sō

26' TO 40'

American

Paine: Symphony no.1*
Chadwick: Symphonic sketches
Chadwick: Symphony no.2
MacDowell: Suite no.2 ("Indian")
Ives: Symphonies nos.2, 4
Carpenter: Adventures in a perambulator
Carpenter: Skyscrapers
Taylor: Through the looking glass
Grofé: Grand Canyon suite
Piston: Symphonies nos.1-3
Hanson: Symphony no.3
Sessions: Symphonies nos.2-3
Harris: Symphony no.5
R. Thompson: Symphony no.2
Antheil: Symphony no.4
Copland: Symphony no.3
Creston: Symphony no.3
Carter: Symphony no.1
Barber: Symphony no.2
Wm. Schuman: Symphonies nos.3; 6-8
Dello Joio: The triumph of Saint Joan
Bernstein: Fancy free--Suite
Foss: Geod
Mennin: Symphony no.7
Argento: In praise of music
Blackwood: Symphony no.1

British

Elgar: Enigma variations
Elgar: Falstaff

Delius: Appalachia
Vaughan Williams: Symphonies nos.2-6; 8-9
Walton: Symphony no.2
Tippett: The midsummer marriage-- Ritual dances
Britten: Gloriana--Symphonic suite
Arnold: Symphonies nos.3, 6
Birtwistle: Verses for ensembles
Maxwell Davies: Second fantasia on John Taverner's In nomine

Eastern European

Liszt: Ce qu'on entend sur la montagne
Liszt: Die Ideale
Dvořák: Serenades op.22; op.44
Dvořák: Symphonies nos.1; 3-9
Bartók: Concerto for orchestra
Bartók: Music for strings, percussion, and celeste
Bartók: Suite no.1
Bartók: The wooden prince--Suite
Kodály: Symphony
Martinu: Symphonies nos.1; 3-5
Harsányi: L'histoire du petite tailleur
Lutosławski: Concerto for orchestra
Husa: Symphony no.1

French

Berlioz: Symphonie funèbre et triomphale
Franck: Symphony in D minor
Saint-Saëns: Symphonies nos.1, 3
Bizet: Roma
Bizet: Symphony no.1
Chausson: Symphony, op.20
G. Charpentier: Impressions d'Italie
Debussy: La boîte à joujoux
Debussy: Images (complete)
Dukas: Symphony in C major
Roussel: Symphony no.2
Varèse: Amériques
Ibert: Le chevalier errant
Honegger: Symphonies nos.3-5
Milhaud: Le carnaval de Londres
Milhaud: Saudades do Brazil
Milhaud: Symphonies nos.1-2
Poulenc: Sinfonietta
Messiaen: L'ascension
Messiaen: Chronochromie
Dutilleux: Symphony no.2

German and Austrian

Handel: Water music--Suite no.1
Gluck: Don Juan--Four movements
Haydn: Symphonies nos.31; 54; 56; 60-61; 72; 86; 93; 97-104
Mozart: Divertimenti, K.131; K.247
Mozart: Serenades nos.4-5; 9-10
Mozart: Symphonies nos.36; 38-41
Beethoven: Egmont (incidental music)
Beethoven: Septet, op.20
Beethoven: Symphonies nos.2; 4-8

Witt: Symphony in A major
Spohr: Nonet, op.31
Spohr: Octet, op.32
Schubert: Symphonies nos.1-2; 4-6; 7 (reconstructed)
Mendelssohn: Octet, strings, op.20
Mendelssohn: Sinfonie, nos.8-9; 11
Mendelssohn: Symphonies nos.1; 3-5
Schumann: Symphonies nos.1-4
Wagner: Symphony, C major
Brahms: Serenades nos.1-2
Brahms: Symphony no.3
Bruch: Symphonies nos.1, 3
Wolf: Penthesilea
R. Strauss: Also sprach Zarathustra
R. Strauss: Der Bürger als Edelmann-- Suite
R. Strauss: Ein Heldenleben
R. Strauss: Metamorphosen
R. Strauss: Symphony for winds
Reger: Variations and fugue on a merry theme of Johann Adam Hiller
Reger: Variations and fugue on a theme of Mozart
Schoenberg: Verklärte Nacht
Berg: Lulu--Suite
Hindemith: Die Harmonie der Welt-- Symphony
Hindemith: Mathis der Maler--Symphony
Hindemith: Pittsburgh symphony
Hindemith: Symphonia serena
Hindemith: Symphony in E-flat
Korngold: Symphonic serenade, op.39
Weill: Symphony no.2
Hartmann: Symphony no.6
Einem: Wiener Symphonie, op.49

Italian

Clementi: Symphonies nos.2-4
Busoni: Turandot--Suite
Respighi: La boutique fantasque
Respighi: Vetrate di chiesa
Berio: Sinfonia

Russian

Borodin: Symphonies nos.1-2
Balakirev: Symphonies nos.1-2
Mussorgsky: Pictures at an exhibition (Ravel orchestration)
Tchaikovsky: Serenade, op.48
Tchaikovsky: Suites nos.1-3
Tchaikovsky: Symphonies nos.1-2; 7 (reconstructed)
Rimsky-Korsakov: Le coq d'or--Suite
Rimsky-Korsakov: The maid of Pskov-- Overture and three entr'actes
Rimsky-Korsakov: Symphonies nos.2-3
Glazunov: Scènes de ballet, op.52
Glazunov: Symphony no.4
Kalinnikov: Symphony no.1
Rachmaninoff: Symphonic dances, op.45
Rachmaninoff: Symphonies nos.1, 3

Miaskovsky: Symphony no.22
Stravinsky: Apollon Musagète
Stravinsky: Firebird--Suite (1911)
Stravinsky: Firebird--Suite (1945)
Stravinsky: L'histoire du soldat--Suite
Stravinsky: Orpheus
Stravinsky: Petrouchka (1911)
Stravinsky: Le sacre du printemps
Stravinsky: Symphony no.1, E-flat major
Stravinsky: Symphony in C
Prokofiev: Buffoon--Symphonic suite
Prokofiev: Cinderella--Suites nos.1, 3
Prokofiev: Le pas d'acier (complete)
Prokofiev: Romeo and Juliet--
 Suites nos.1-2
Prokofiev: Symphonies nos.2-4; 7
Khachaturian: Gayane--Suites nos.1-3
Kabalevsky: Symphony no.2
Shostakovich: The gadfly--Suite
Shostakovich: Symphonies nos.1; 3;
 6; 12

Spanish and Latin American

Albéniz: Iberia (Arbós version)
Falla: Three-cornered hat (complete)
Chávez: Symphony no.3

Other nationalities

Berwald: Symphonies in C major;
 E-flat major; and G minor
Grieg: Symphonic dances, op.64
Nielsen: Symphonies nos.1-6
Sibelius: Symphonies nos.1; 3-6

41' TO 60'

American

Ives: Symphony no.1
Ives: Holidays symphony (complete)

British

Elgar: Symphonies nos.1-2
Vaughan Williams: Job
Holst: The planets
Walton: Façade (complete)
Walton: Symphony no.1
Maxwell Davies: Symphony

Eastern European

Liszt: Dante symphony
Dvořák: Legends (complete)
Dvořák: Symphony no.2
Paderewski: Symphony

French

Berlioz: Symphonie fantastique
Ravel: Daphnis et Chloé (complete)

Honegger: Le dit des jeux du monde

German and Austrian

Bach: Musical offering
Handel: Water music (complete)
Mozart: Divertimenti, K.271h (287);
 K.320b (334)
Mozart: Serenade no.7
Beethoven: Prometheus (ballet music)
Beethoven: Symphony no.3
Schubert: Octet, D.803
Schubert: Symphony no.9
Bruckner: Symphony in F minor
Bruckner: Symphonies nos.0; 1; 3-4;
 6; 9 (unfinished)
Joh. Strauss Jr.: Graduation ball (arr.)
Goldmark: Rustic wedding symphony
Brahms: Symphonies nos.1-2; 4
Mahler: Symphonies nos.1; 4
R. Strauss: Eine Alpensinfonie
R. Strauss: Aus Italien
R. Strauss: Symphonia domestica
R. Strauss: Symphony, op.12
Schoenberg: Pelleas and Melisande

Russian

Tchaikovsky: Manfred
Tchaikovsky: Symphonies nos.3-6
Rimsky-Korsakov: Scheherazade
Kalinnikov: Symphony no.2
Scriabin: Le divin poème
Scriabin: Symphony no.2
Rachmaninoff: Symphony no.2
Stravinsky: Le baiser de la fée
 (complete)
Stravinsky: Firebird (complete)
Stravinsky: Petrouchka (1947 version)
Prokofiev: Symphonies nos.5-6
Khachaturian: Symphony no.2
Shostakovich: Symphonies nos.4-5;
 10-11; 15

Spanish

Albéniz: Iberia (Surinach version)

Other nationalities

Sibelius: Symphony no.2
Bloch: America
Bamert: Once upon an orchestra

OVER 60'

Eastern European

Liszt: A Faust symphony

French

Delibes: Coppelia (complete)
Messiaen: Turangalîla-symphonie

German and Austrian

Haydn: Seven last words of Christ
 (orchestral version)
Beethoven: Symphony no.9
Bruckner: Symphonies nos.2, 5, 7, 8
Mahler: Symphonies nos.3; 5-7; 9-10

Russian

Glière: Symphony no.3
Shostakovich: Symphonies nos.7-8

VARIABLE DURATION

American

Cage: Atlas eclipticalis
Brown: Available forms 1, 2
C. Wolff: Burdocks

APPENDIX F: COMPOSERS LISTED BY
NATIONALITY OR ETHNIC GROUP

American (United States)   Greek
Argentinian   Hungarian
Armenian   Italian
Australian   Japanese
Belgian   *Jewish
Brazilian   Mexican
British   Norwegian
Czech   Polish
Danish   Rumanian
Dutch   Russian
Finnish   Spanish
French   Swedish
German and Austrian   Swiss

It is occasionally necessary to create programs of music by a special group, such as Scandinavian composers, or Czech composers. This appendix is intended to make that task easier.

Each composer represented in this book is listed here according to nationality or ethnic group. Normally this means the country of origin, but there are exceptions. Lully, for instance, belongs to the history of French music, despite his Italian birth, and is thus present on both lists. Meyerbeer was Jewish, born in Germany, and did much of his important work in France; I have included him on all three lists.

Within each category, composers are listed chronologically according to birth date.

---

* I am grateful to Helen Rowin for undertaking the confusing task of determining which of these several hundred composers are Jewish and which are not.

AMERICAN (UNITED STATES)

Louis Moreau Gottschalk, 1829-1869
John Knowles Paine, 1839-1906
Arthur Foote, 1853-1937
George Whitefield Chadwick, 1854-1931
Victor Herbert, 1859-1924 (Irish-born)
Charles Martin Loeffler, 1861-1935
Edward MacDowell, 1861-1908
Horatio Parker, 1863-1919
Henry F. Gilbert, 1868-1928
Frederick Shepherd Converse, 1871-1940
Charles Ives, 1874-1954
John Alden Carpenter, 1876-1951
Carl Ruggles, 1876-1968
Charles Wakefield Cadman, 1881-1946
Edgard Varèse, 1883-1965 (French-born)
Charles Tomlinson Griffes, 1884-1920
Louis Gruenberg, 1884-1964
Wallingford Riegger, 1885-1961
Deems Taylor, 1885-1966
John J. Becker, 1886-1961
Ernst Toch, 1887-1964 (Viennese-born)
Adolph Weiss, 1891-1971
Ferde Grofé, 1892-1972
Bernard Rogers, 1893-1968
Robert Russell Bennett, 1894-
Walter Piston, 1894-1976
Nicolas Slonimsky, 1894- (Russian-born)
William Grant Still, 1895-1978
Howard Hanson, 1896-1981
Roger Sessions, 1896-
Virgil Thomson, 1896-
Henry Cowell, 1897-1965
Quincy Porter, 1897-1966
Ernst Bacon, 1898-
George Gershwin, 1898-1937
Roy Harris, 1898-1979
Randall Thompson, 1899-
George Antheil, 1900-1959
Nicolai Berezowsky, 1900-1953
 (Russian-born)
Aaron Copland, 1900-
Otto Luening, 1900-
Kurt Weill, 1900-1950 (German-born)
Richard Rodgers, 1902-1979
Vittorio Giannini, 1903-1966
Paul Creston, 1906-
Ross Lee Finney, 1906-
Gene Gutche, 1907- (German-born)
Burrill Phillips, 1907-
Alec Wilder, 1907-1980
Elliott Carter, 1908-
Halsey Stevens, 1908-
Samuel Barber, 1910-1981
William Schuman, 1910-
Thomas Canning, 1911-
Alan Hovhaness, 1911-
Robert McBride, 1911-
Gian Carlo Menotti, 1911-
Vladimir Ussachevsky, 1911- (born in
 Manchuria of Russian parents)

Wayne Barlow, 1912-
John Cage, 1912-
Ingolf Dahl, 1912-1970
Don Gillis, 1912-1978
Henry Brant, 1913- (Canadian-born)
Norman Dello Joio, 1913-
Alvin Etler, 1913-1973
Morton Gould, 1913-
Kent Kennan, 1913-
Cecil Effinger, 1914-
Irving Fine, 1914-1962
Gail Kubik, 1914-
David Diamond, 1915-
Vincent Persichetti, 1915-
Alan Shulman, 1915-
Milton Babbitt, 1916-
Howard Brubeck, 1916-
Ben Weber, 1916-1979
Ulysses Kay, 1917-
Robert Ward, 1917-
Richard Yardumian, 1917-
Leonard Bernstein, 1918-
George Rochberg, 1918-
Leon Kirchner, 1919-
Theron Kirk, 1919-
John La Montaine, 1920-
William Bergsma, 1921-
Robert Kurka, 1921-1957
Lukas Foss, 1922- (German-born)
Leslie Bassett, 1923-
Chou Wen-Chung, 1923- (Chinese-born)
William Kraft, 1923-
Peter Mennin, 1923-
Daniel Pinkham, 1923-
Ned Rorem, 1923-
Warren Benson, 1924-
Arthur Frackenpohl, 1924-
Stanley Hollingsworth, 1924-
Ezra Laderman, 1924-
Benjamin Lees, 1924-
Robert Starer, 1924-
Gunther Schuller, 1925-
Earle Brown, 1926-
Morton Feldman, 1926-
Carlisle Floyd, 1926-
Dominick Argento, 1927-
Walter Aschaffenburg, 1927-
Donald Erb, 1927-
Salvatore Martirano, 1927-
T. J. Anderson, 1928-
Jacob Druckman, 1928-
George Crumb, 1929-
André Previn, 1929-
David Amram, 1930-
David Baker, 1931-
Charles Kelso Hoag, 1931-
Mario Lombardo, 1931-
Donald Martino, 1931-
Michael Colgrass, 1932-
Easley Blackwood, 1933-
Morton Subotnick, 1933-
Mario Davidovsky, 1934- (born in
 Argentina)

Roger Reynolds, 1934-
Richard Wernick, 1934-
Christian Wolff, 1934-
Samuel Jones, 1935-
Peter Schickele, 1935-
Elliott Schwartz, 1936-
David Del Tredici, 1937-
John Corigliano, 1938-
Charles Wuorinen, 1938-

ARGENTINIAN

Alberto Ginastera, 1916-
Mario Davidovsky, 1934-

ARMENIAN

Aram Khachaturian, 1903-1978
Alan Hovhaness, 1911-
Richard Yardumian, 1917-

AUSTRALIAN

Peggy Glanville-Hicks, 1912-

BELGIAN

François Joseph Gossec, 1734-1829
André Grétry, 1741-1813
César Franck, 1822-1890
Eugene Ysaÿe, 1858-1931

BRAZILIAN

Heitor Villa-Lobos, 1887-1959

BRITISH

Henry Purcell, ca.1659-1695
Jeremiah Clarke, ca.1673-1707
Thomas Arne, 1710-1778
William Boyce, 1710-1779
Henry Charles Litolff, 1818-1891
Arthur Sullivan, 1842-1900
Edward Elgar, 1857-1934

Frederick Delius, 1862-1934
Edward German, 1862-1936
Ralph Vaughan Williams, 1872-1958
Gustav Holst, 1874-1934
Samuel Coleridge-Taylor, 1875-1912
Eric Coates, 1886-1957
Arthur Bliss, 1891-1975
Arthur Benjamin, 1893-1960
Eugene Goosens, 1893-1962
Peter Warlock, 1894-1930
 (pseudonym of Philip Heseltine)
Gordon Jacob, 1895-
John Barbirolli, 1899-1970
Edmund Rubbra, 1901-
William Walton, 1902-
Lennox Berkeley, 1903-
Michael Tippett, 1905-
Benjamin Britten, 1913-1976
Malcolm Arnold, 1921-
Iain Hamilton, 1922-
Thea Musgrave, 1928- (Scottish)
Harrison Birtwistle, 1934-
Peter Maxwell Davies, 1934-
Richard Rodney Bennett, 1936-

CZECH

Heinrich von Biber, 1644-1704
Johann Wenzel Anton Stamitz, 1717-1757
Franz Xaver Pokorný, 1729-1794
Jan Křtitel Vaňhal, 1739-1813
Bedřich Smetana, 1824-1884
Josef Suk, 1827-1870
Antonin Dvořák, 1841-1904
David Popper, 1843-1913
Leoš Janáček, 1854-1928
Bohuslav Martinu, 1890-1959
Jaromir Weinberger, 1896-1967
Vaclav Nelhybel, 1919-
Karel Husa, 1921-
Robert Kurka, 1921-1957 (an American
 composer of Czech descent)

DANISH

Friedrich Kuhlau, 1786-1832 (German-born)
Niels Gade, 1817-1890
Carl Nielsen, 1865-1931

DUTCH

Henk Badings, 1907-

FINNISH

Jean Sibelius, 1865-1957
Armas Järnefelt, 1869-1958
Heikki Suolahti, 1920-1936

FRENCH

Jean Baptiste Lully, 1632-1687
  (Italian-born)
Marc-Antoine Charpentier, 1634-1704
Michel-Richard de Lalande, 1657-1726
François Couperin, 1668-1733
Jean Philippe Rameau, 1683-1764
Joseph Bodin de Boismortier, 1691-1755
Jean Marie Leclair, 1697-1764
François Joseph Gossec, 1734-1829
  (Belgian-born)
André Grétry, 1741-1813 (Belgian-born)
François Boieldieu, 1775-1834
Daniel-François Auber, 1782-1871
Louis Joseph F. Hérold, 1791-1833
Giacomo Meyerbeer, 1791-1864 (German-
  born)
Adolph Adam, 1803-1856
Hector Berlioz, 1803-1869
Ambroise Thomas, 1811-1896
Charles Gounod, 1818-1893
Henry Charles Litolff, 1818-1891
  (British-born)
Jacques Offenbach, 1819-1880
Henri Vieuxtemps, 1820-1881
César Franck, 1822-1890
Edouard Lalo, 1823-1892
Camille Saint-Saëns, 1835-1921
Leo Delibes, 1836-1891
Théodore Dubois, 1837-1924
Emil Waldteufel, 1837-1915
Georges Bizet, 1838-1875
Emmanuel Chabrier, 1841-1894
Jules Massenet, 1842-1912
Gabriel Fauré, 1845-1924
Alexandre Luigini, 1850-1906
Vincent d'Indy, 1851-1931
Ernest Chausson, 1855-1899
Cecile Chaminade, 1857-1944
Gustave Charpentier, 1860-1956
Léon Boëllmann, 1862-1897
Claude Debussy, 1862-1918
Gabriel Pierné, 1863-1937
Paul Dukas, 1865-1935
Erik Satie, 1866-1925
Charles Koechlin, 1867-1950
Albert Roussel, 1869-1937
Henri Rabaud, 1873-1949
Maurice Ravel, 1875-1937
Edgard Varèse, 1883-1965
Jacques Ibert, 1890-1962
Marcel Grandjany, 1891-1975
Arthur Honegger, 1892-1955

Darius Milhaud, 1892-1974
Georges Auric, 1899-
Francis Poulenc, 1899-1963
Maurice Duruflé, 1902-
André Jolivet, 1905-1974
Olivier Messiaen, 1908-
Jean Françaix, 1912-
Henri Dutilleux, 1916-
Pierre Boulez, 1925-

GERMAN AND AUSTRIAN

Heinrich Schütz, 1585-1672
Johann Hermann Schein, 1586-1630
Andreas Hofer, 1629-1684
Dietrich Buxtehude, ca.1637-1707
Heinrich von Biber, 1644-1704 (Bohemian-
  born)
Johann Pachelbel, 1653-1706
Johann Joseph Fux, 1660-1741
Johann Kuhnau, 1660-1722
Johann Ludwig Bach, 1677-1741
Georg Philipp Telemann, 1681-1767
Christoph Graupner, 1683-1760
Johann Sebastian Bach, 1685-1750
George Frideric Handel, 1685-1759
Johann Friedrich Fasch, 1688-1758
Johann Joachim Quantz, 1697-1773
Georg Melchior Hoffmann, 18th century
Johann Gottlieb Graun, 1703-1771
Wilhelm Friedemann Bach, 1710-1784
Frederick II ("The Great"), 1712-1786
Carl Philipp Emanuel Bach, 1714-1788
Christoph Willibald Gluck, 1714-1787
Georg Christoph Wagenseil, 1715-1777
Johann Wenzel Anton Stamitz, 1717-1757
  (Bohemian-born)
Leopold Mozart, 1719-1787
Karl Friedrich Abel, 1723-1787
Franz Joseph Haydn, 1732-1809
Johann Christian Bach, 1735-1782
Michael Haydn, 1737-1806
Karl Ditters von Dittersdorf, 1739-1799
Karl Stamitz, 1745-1801
Anton Stamitz, 1754-ca.1809
Wolfgang Amadeus Mozart, 1756-1791
Ludwig van Beethoven, 1770-1827
Friedrich Witt, 1770-1837
Johann Nepomuk Hummel, 1778-1837
Ludwig Spohr, 1784-1859
Friedrich Kuhlau, 1786-1832
Carl Maria von Weber, 1786-1826
Giacomo Meyerbeer, 1791-1864
Franz Schubert, 1797-1828
Joseph Lanner, 1801-1843
Albert Lortzing, 1801-1851
Johann Strauss, Sr., 1804-1849
Felix Mendelssohn, 1809-1847
Otto Nicolai, 1810-1849
Robert Schumann, 1810-1856
Friedrich von Flotow, 1812-1883

Richard Wagner, 1813-1883
Franz von Suppé, 1819-1895
Anton Bruckner, 1824-1896
Johann Strauss, Jr., 1825-1899
Josef Strauss, 1827-1870
Karl Goldmark, 1830-1915
Joseph Joachim, 1831-1907
Johannes Brahms, 1833-1897
Max Bruch, 1838-1920
Joseph Rheinberger, 1839-1901
Engelbert Humperdinck, 1854-1921
Gustav Mahler, 1860-1911
Emil Nikolaus von Reznicek, 1860-1945
Hugo Wolf, 1860-1903
Richard Strauss, 1864-1949
Hans Pfitzner, 1869-1949
Max Reger, 1873-1916
Arnold Schoenberg, 1874-1951
Anton Webern, 1883-1945
Alban Berg, 1885-1935
Egon Wellesz, 1885-1974
Ernst Toch, 1887-1964
Paul Hindemith, 1895-1963
Carl Orff, 1895-
Erich Wolfgang Korngold, 1897-1957
Ernst Krenek, 1900-
Kurt Weill, 1900-1950
Boris Blacher, 1903-1975
Karl Amadeus Hartmann, 1905-1963
Gottfried von Einem, 1918-
Bernd Alois Zimmermann, 1918-1970
Hans Werner Henze, 1926-
Karlheinz Stockhausen, 1928-

GREEK

Nikos Skalkottas, 1904-1949
Yannis Xenakis, 1922-

HUNGARIAN

Franz Liszt, 1811-1886
Franz Lehár, 1870-1948
Ernst von Dohnányi, 1877-1960
Béla Bartók, 1881-1945
Zoltán Kodály, 1882-1967
Tibor Harsányi, 1898-1954
Ödön Partos, 1907-
Gyorgy Ligeti, 1923-

ITALIAN

Giovanni Gabrieli, 1551-1612
Claudio Monteverdi, 1567-1643

Jean Baptiste Lully, 1630-1687 (lived in
   France from age 14)
Arcangelo Corelli, 1653-1713
Giuseppe Torelli, 1658-1709
Alessandro Scarlatti, 1660-1725
Tomaso Antonio Vitali, ca.1665-?
Tomaso Albinoni, 1671-1750
Antonio Vivaldi, 1678-1741
Francesco Manfredini, ca.1680-1748
Alessandro Marcello, ca.1684-ca.1750
Domenico Scarlatti, 1685-1757
Benedetto Marcello, 1686-1739
Francesco Geminiani, 1687-1762
Francesco Maria Veracini, 1690-ca.1750
Giuseppe Tartini, 1692-1770
Giuseppe Sammartini, ca.1693-ca.1770
Leonardo Leo, 1694-1744
Pietro Locatelli, 1695-1764
Giovanni Battista Sammartini, 1701-1775
Baldassare Galuppi, 1706-1785
Giovanni Battista Pergolesi, 1710-1736
Giovanni Paisiello, 1740-1816
Luigi Boccherini, 1743-1805
Domenico Cimarosa, 1749-1801
Muzio Clementi, 1752-1832
Giovanni Battista Viotti, 1755-1824
Luigi Cherubini, 1760-1842
Niccolò Paganini, 1782-1840
Gioacchino Rossini, 1792-1868
Gaetano Donizetti, 1797-1848
Vincenzo Bellini, 1801-1835
Giuseppe Verdi, 1813-1901
Amilcare Ponchielli, 1834-1886
Ruggero Leoncavallo, 1858-1919
Giacomo Puccini, 1858-1924
Pietro Mascagni, 1863-1945
Ferruccio Busoni, 1866-1924
Ermanno Wolf-Ferrari, 1876-1948
Ottorino Respighi, 1879-1936
Gian Francesco Malipiero, 1882-1973
Alfredo Casella, 1883-1947
Mario Castelnuovo-Tedesco, 1895-1968
Luigi Dallapiccola, 1904-1975
Gian Carlo Menotti, 1911-
Bruno Maderna, 1920-1973
Luigi Nono, 1924-
Luciano Berio, 1925-
Giangiacomo Miari, 1929-

JAPANESE

Maki Ishii, 1936-

JEWISH

Giacomo Meyerbeer, 1791-1864
Felix Mendelssohn, 1809-1847

Jacques Offenbach, 1819-1880
Louis Moreau Gottschalk, 1829-1869
Anton Rubinstein, 1829-1894
Karl Goldmark, 1830-1915
Joseph Joachim, 1831-1907
Camille Saint-Saëns, 1835-1921
Henri Wieniawski, 1835-1880
Emil Waldteufel, 1837-1915
Georges Bizet, 1838-1875
Max Bruch, 1838-1920
Gustav Mahler, 1860-1911
Paul Dukas, 1865-1935
Ferruccio Busoni, 1866-1924
Serge Koussevitzky, 1874-1951
Arnold Schoenberg, 1874-1951
Reinhold Glière, 1875-1956
Maurice Ravel, 1875-1937
Ernest Bloch, 1880-1959
Louis Gruenberg, 1884-1964
Egon Wellesz, 1885-1974
Ernst Toch, 1887-1964
Darius Milhaud, 1892-1974
Arthur Benjamin, 1893-1960
Bernard Rogers, 1893-1968
Nicolas Slonimsky, 1894-
Mario Castelnuovo-Tedesco, 1895-1968
Jaromir Weinberger, 1896-1967
Erich Wolfgang Korngold, 1897-1957
Alexandre Tansman, 1897-
George Gershwin, 1898-1937
George Antheil, 1900-1959
Aaron Copland, 1900-
Kurt Weill, 1900-1950
Richard Rodgers, 1902-1979
Ödön Partos, 1907-
William Schuman, 1910-
Henry Brant, 1913-
Morton Gould, 1913-
Irving Fine, 1914-1962
David Diamond, 1915-
Alan Shulman, 1915-
Ben Weber, 1916-
Leonard Bernstein, 1918-
Leon Kirchner, 1919-
Lukas Foss, 1922-
Ezra Laderman, 1924-
Robert Starer, 1924-
Gunther Schuller, 1925-
Morton Feldman, 1926-
Jacob Druckman, 1928-
André Previn, 1929-
David Amram, 1930-
Morton Subotnick, 1933-
Mario Davidovsky, 1934-
Richard Wernick, 1934-

MEXICAN

Manuel Ponce, 1882-1948
Carlos Chávez, 1899-1978

NORWEGIAN

Edvard Grieg, 1843-1907

POLISH

Jakob Gołąbek, ca.1739-1789
Jan Wański, ca.1760-ca.1830
Frederic Chopin, 1810-1849
Stanisław Moniuszko, 1819-1872
Henri Wieniawski, 1835-1880
Sigismund Noskowski, 1846-1909
Ignace Jan Paderewski, 1860-1941
Mieczysław Karłowicz, 1876-1909
Karol Szymanowski, 1882-1937
Alexandre Tansman, 1897-
Grażyna Bacewicz, 1913-1969
Witold Lutosławski, 1913-
Kazimierz Serocki, 1922-
Stanisław Skrowaczewski, 1923-
Augustyn Bloch, 1929-
Krzysztof Penderecki, 1933-
Jerzy Sapieyevski, 1945-

RUMANIAN

Georges Enesco, 1881-1955

RUSSIAN

Mikhail Glinka, 1804-1857
Anton Rubinstein, 1829-1894
Alexander Borodin, 1833-1887
Mily Balakirev, 1837-1910
Modest Mussorgsky, 1839-1881
Peter Ilich Tchaikovsky, 1840-1893
Nikolai Rimsky-Korsakov, 1844-1908
Anatol Liadov, 1855-1914
Mikhail Ippolitov-Ivanov, 1859-1935
Anton Arensky, 1861-1906
Alexander Glazunov, 1865-1936
Vassili Kalinnikov, 1866-1901
Alexander Scriabin, 1872-1915
Sergei Rachmaninoff, 1873-1943
Serge Koussevitzky, 1874-1951
Reinhold Glière, 1875-1956
Nikolai Miaskovsky, 1881-1950
Igor Stravinsky, 1882-1971
Serge Prokofiev, 1891-1953
Nicolas Slonimsky, 1894- (came to the
   United States at age 27)
Alexander Tcherepnin, 1899-1977
Nicolai Berezowsky, 1900-1953 (lived
   mostly in the United States)

Alexander Mossolov, 1900–
Aram Khachaturian, 1903–1978
Dmitri Kabalevsky, 1904–
Dmitri Shostakovich, 1906–1975
Vladimir Ussachevsky, 1911– (lived
 mostly in the United States)
Tikhon Khrennikov, 1913–

SPANISH

Juan Crisostomo Arriaga, 1806–1826
 (Basque)
Edouard Lalo, 1823–1892 (A French
 composer of Spanish descent)
Pablo de Sarasate, 1844–1908
Isaac Albéniz, 1860–1909
Enrique Granados, 1867–1916
Manuel de Falla, 1876–1946
Joaquín Turina, 1882–1949
Roberto Gerhard, 1896–1970 (Swiss
 parentage and nationality, though
 born in Spain and prominently asso-
 ciated with Spanish music)
Joaquín Rodrigo, 1902–
Ernesto Halffter, 1905–
Carlos Surinach, 1915–

SWEDISH

Franz Berwald, 1796–1868
Hugo Alfvén, 1872–1960
Karl-Birger Blomdahl, 1916–1968

SWISS

Ernest Bloch, 1880–1959
Frank Martin, 1890–1974
Arthur Honegger, 1892–1955 (a French
 composer of Swiss descent)
Roberto Gerhard, 1896–1970
Matthias Bamert, 1942–

APPENDIX G: PUBLISHERS

ACA
American Composers Alliance
170 West 74th Street
New York   NY   10023

Alkor
Alkor-Edition
AGENTS: EAM
          Magnamusic
          Schirmer, G. (rentals only)

AME
American Music Edition
AGENT: Fischer, C.

AMP
Associated Music Publishers
866 Third Avenue
New York   NY   10022

Augener
Augener, Ltd.
AGENT: Galaxy

Bärenreiter
Bärenreiter-Verlag
AGENTS: EAM
          Magnamusic
          Schirmer, G. (rentals only)

Barry
Barry & Cia.
AGENT: Boosey

Belaieff
M.P. Belaieff
AGENT: Peters

Belmont
Belmont Music Publishers
P.O. Box 49961
Los Angeles   CA   90049

Belwin   Belwin-Mills Publishing Co.
1776 Broadway
New York   NY   10019

Billaudot   Editions Billaudot
AGENT: Presser

Birchard   C.C. Birchard
(Summy-Birchard)
1834 Ridge Avenue
Evanston   IL   60204

Boelke-Bomart   Boelke-Bomart Publications
Hillsdale   NY   12529

Bongiovani   Casa Musicale Francesco Bongiovani
AGENT: Belwin

Boosey   Boosey and Hawkes, Inc.
24 West 57th Street
New York   NY   10019

Bote   Bote & Bock
AGENT: AMP

Breitkopf   Breitkopf und Härtel
AGENT: AMP

Broude, A.   Alexander Broude, Inc.
225 West 57th Street
New York   NY   10019

Broude Bros.   Broude Brothers Ltd.
56 West 45th Street
New York   NY   10019

Bruckner Verlag   AGENT: Peters

Carisch   Carisch S.p.A.
AGENT: Boosey

CFE	Composers Facsimile Edition c/o American Composers Alliance 170 West 74th Street New York NY 10023
Chappell	Chappell & Co., Inc. AGENT: Presser
Chester	J. & W. Chester, Ltd. AGENT: Magnamusic
Choudens	AGENT: Peters
Colombo	Franco Colombo Publications AGENT: Belwin
Curwen	J. Curwen & Sons (Faber-Curwen) AGENT: Schirmer, G.
Da Capo	Da Capo Press, Inc. 227 West 17th Street New York NY 10011
Dania	Edition Dania AGENT: Peters
Dantalian	Dantalian, Inc. 11 Pembroke St. Newton MA 02158
Deutscher	Deutscher Verlag für Musik AGENT: Broude, A.
Doblinger	Ludwig Doblinger Verlag AGENT: AMP
Donemus	Donemus Foundation AGENT: Peters
Durand	Durand et Cie. AGENT: Presser

EAM

European American Music Corp.
195 Allwood Road
Clifton   NJ   07012

Elkan-Vogel

Elkan-Vogel, Inc.
AGENT: Presser

EMT

Editions Musicales Transatlantiques
AGENT: Presser

Enoch

Enoch & Cie.
AGENT: AMP

Eschig

Editions Max Eschig
AGENT: AMP

Eulenburg

Edition Eulenburg
AGENT: Peters

Faber

Faber Music, Ltd.
AGENT: Schirmer, G.

Fischer, C.

Carl Fischer, Inc.
56-62 Cooper Square
New York   NY   10003

Fischer, J.

J. Fischer & Bro.
AGENT: Belwin

Fleisher

Edwin A. Fleisher Collection
Free Library of Philadelphia
Logan Square
Philadelphia   PA   19103

Foley

Charles Foley, Inc.
AGENT: Belwin

Forberg

Robert Forberg--P. Jurgenson
AGENT: Peters

Fürstner

Adolf Fürstner Ltd.
AGENT: Boosey

Galaxy	Galaxy Music Corporation 2121 Broadway New York NY 10023
Gehrmans	Carl Gehrmans Musikförlag AGENT: Boosey
Glocken	Glocken Verlag AGENT: Broude, A.
Gray	H.W. Gray Co., Inc. AGENT: Belwin
Hamelle	Hamelle & Cie. AGENT: Presser
Hansen	Edition Wilhelm Hansen AGENT: Magnamusic
Heugel	Heugel & Cie. AGENT: Presser
Highgate	Highgate Press (Galaxy Music Corporation) 2121 Broadway New York NY 10023
Hinrichsen	Hinrichsen Edition, Ltd. AGENT: Peters
Hofmeister	Friedrich Hofmeister Verlag AGENT: Peters
Ione	Ione Press AGENT: Schirmer, E.
Jobert	Société des Editions Jobert AGENT: Presser
Kahnt	C.F. Kahnt, Musikverlag AGENT: Peters

Kalmus

Edwin F. Kalmus & Co., Inc.
Box 1007
Opa-Locka FL 33054

KaWe

Edition KaWe
AGENT: King

Kerby

E.C. Kerby
198 Davenport Road
Toronto M5R1J2 Canada

King

Robert King Music Co.
7 Canton Street
North Easton MA 02356

Kneusslin

Editions Kneusslin
AGENT: Peters

Leduc

Alphonse Leduc
AGENT: Presser

Lengnick

Alfred Lengnick & Co., Ltd.
c/o Frederick Harris Music Co., Ltd.
529 Speers Road
Oakville, Ontario L6K 2G4
Canada

Leuckart

F.E.C. Leuckart
AGENT: AMP

Lienau

Robert Lienau Musikverlag
AGENT: Peters

Luck

Luck's Music Library
15701 East Warren
Detroit MI 48224

Magnamusic

Magnamusic-Baton, Inc.
10370 Page Industrial Blvd.
St. Louis MO 63132

Malcolm	Malcolm Music Ltd. AGENT: Shawnee
Mapleson	Alfred J. Mapleson 208 North Broadway Lindenhurst, L.I. NY 11757
Marks	Edward B. Marks Music Corp. AGENT: Belwin
MCA	MCA Music AGENT: Belwin
Mercury	Mercury Music Corp. AGENT: Presser
Merion	Merion Music Inc. AGENT: Presser
Mills	Mills Music, Inc. AGENT: Belwin
MJQ	MJQ Music, Inc. 200 West 57th Street New York NY 10019
Moeck	Moeck Verlag AGENT: EAM
Möseler	Möseler Verlag AGENT: Magnamusic
Musica Rara	AGENT: Worldwide
Nagel	Nagels Verlag AGENT: Magnamusic
Norton	W.W. Norton & Company, Inc. 500 Fifth Avenue New York NY 10060

Novello	Novello & Co., Ltd. 145 Palisade Street Dobbs Ferry NY 10522
Oiseau Lyre	Editions de L'Oiseau-Lyre 2 rue des Ramparts Monte Carlo, Monaco
Oxford	Oxford University Press 200 Madison Avenue New York NY 10016
Paterson	Paterson's Publications, Ltd. AGENT: Fischer, C.
Peer	Peer International Corp. 1740 Broadway New York NY 10019
Pegasus	AGENT: Peters
Peters	C.F. Peters 373 Park Avenue South New York NY 10016
Presser	Theodore Presser Co. Bryn Mawr PA 19010
PWM	Polskie Wydawnictwo Muzyczne c/o Edward B. Marks Music Corp. 1790 Broadway New York NY 10019
Ricordi	G. Ricordi AGENT: AMP
Robbins	Robbins Music Corp. 729 Seventh Avenue New York NY 10019
Rouart	Rouart-Lerolle et Cie. AGENT: Schirmer, G.

Salabert	Editions Salabert AGENT: Schirmer, G.
Samfundet	Samfundet Til Udgivelse af Dansk Musik AGENT: Peters
Schirmer, E.	E.C. Schirmer Music Co. 112 South Street Boston MA 02111
Schirmer, G.	G. Schirmer, Inc. 866 Third Avenue New York NY 10022
Schott	B. Schott's Söhne, Mainz Schott & Co., Ltd., UK AGENT: EAM
Shawnee	Shawnee Press, Inc. Delaware Water Gap PA 18327
Sikorski	Hans Sikorski AGENT: Schirmer, G.
Simrock	N. Simrock AGENT: AMP
Sonzogno	Casa Musicale Sonzogno AGENT: Belwin
Southern	Southern Music Publishing Co., Inc. AGENT: Peer
Supraphon	Editio Supraphon AGENT: Boosey
Suvini	Edizioni Suvini-Zerboni AGENT: Boosey
Templeton	Templeton Publishing Co., Inc. AGENT: Shawnee

UME   Union Musical Española
                        AGENT: AMP

Universal   Universal-Edition
                        AGENT: EAM

VAAP   Copyright agency of the U.S.S,R.
                        AGENT: Schirmer, G.

Vieweg   Chr. Friedrich Vieweg
                        AGENT: Peters

Walton   Walton Music Corp.
                        c/o Lorenz Industries
                        501 East Third Street
                        Dayton OH 45401

Warner Bros.   Warner Bros, Music Publications, Inc.
                        14th Floor
                        75 Rockefeller Plaza
                        New York NY 10019

Weinberger   Josef Weinberger Ltd.
                        AGENT: Boosey

Weintraub   Weintraub Music Co.
                        33 West 60th Street
                        New York NY 10023

Worldwide   Worldwide Music Services
                        1966 Broadway
                        New York NY 10023

Zanibon   Edizioni G. Zanibon
                        AGENT: Peters